REVERBERATIONS
OF FAITH

REVERBERATIONS OF FAITH

A Theological Handbook
of Old Testament Themes

Walter Brueggemann

Westminster John Knox Press
LOUISVILLE • LONDON

© 2002 Walter Brueggemann

Unless otherwise indicated, scripture quotations are from the New Revised Standard Version of the Bible, copyright © 1989 by the Division of Christian Education of the National Council of the Churches of Christ in the U.S.A., and used by permission.

Scripture quotations marked NEB are taken from *The New English Bible,* © The Delegates of the Oxford University Press and The Syndics of the Cambridge University Press, 1961, 1970. Used by permission.

Excerpt from *Great Is Thy Faithfulness* by Thomas Chisholm © 1923. Renewal 1951 Hope Publishing Co., Carol Stream, IL 60188. All rights reserved. used by permission.

Book design by Sharon Adams
Cover design by Night & Day Design

First edition
Published by Westminster John Knox Press
Louisville, Kentucky

This book is printed on acid-free paper that meets the American National Standards Institute Z39.48 standard.

PRINTED IN THE UNITED STATES OF AMERICA

04 05 06 07 08 09 10 11 — 10 9 8 7 6 5 4 3

Library of Congress Cataloging-in-Publication Data

Brueggemann, Walter.
 Reverberations of faith : a theological handbook of Old Testament themes / Walter Brueggemann.
  p. cm.
 Includes bibliographical references and index.
 ISBN 0-664-22231-5 (alk. paper)
  1. Bible. O.T.—Theology. I. Title.

BS1192.5 .B785 2002
230'.0411—dc21

2002016869

For
Christina McHugh Brueggemann
Lisa Simcox Brueggemann

CONTENTS

Preface xi

Abbreviations xiii

The Ancestors 1

Angel 3

Apocalyptic Thought 5

The Ark 8

Asherah 10

Assyria 11

Atonement 13

Baal 15

Babylon 17

Blessing 18

Book of the Covenant 20

Canaanites 23

Canon 24

Chaos 28

The Chronicler 29

Circumcision 33

Community 35

Covenant 37

Creation..40

David..43

The Day of the Lord 45

Death 47

The Decalogue 50

Deuteronomic Theology...52

Divine Council 55

Education...56

Egypt 59

Election..61

Elijah..64

Ethics 66

Exile 69

Exodus..72

Ezra...75

Faith..76

The Fall...79

Fertility Religion 80

Festivals 83

Forgiveness..85

Glory...87

Hannah...89

Ḥerem 91

High Place..93

History 95

Holiness 98

Hope..100

Huldah 102

The Hymn...104

Image of God..105

Jerusalem 108

Jezebel..111

Jubilee..114

Kingship...116

The Lament...118

Land..120

Listening 123

Love 125

Messiah 127

Miracle 130

Miriam..132

Money 133

Monotheism 137

Moses..140

Neighbor...142

Persia 143

Plague..145

Prayer 147

Priestly Tradition 149

Priests 154

Promise 156

Prophets 158

Purim...162

Redemption 163

Reform of Hezekiah 164

Reform of Josiah 166

Remnant...169

Repentance 170

Resurrection 173

Retribution...174

Righteousness 177

Sabbath 180

Sacrifice 182

Salvation 184

Samaritans 186

Satan 187

Scribes 188

Sexuality 190

Sin 195

Sojourner 198

Spirit 199

Suffering 200

Suffering Servant 204

Temple 206

Thanksgiving 211

Theodicy 212

Theophany 214

Torah 217

Tradition 220

Vengeance 222

Violence 225

War 227

Widow 230

Wilderness 231

Wisdom 232

Worship 235

YHWH 238

Scripture Index 241

Name Index 253

PREFACE

This book had its inception at the suggestion of Cynthia Thompson, then on the editorial staff of Westminster John Knox. She proposed a book of one hundred topics of theological interest in the Old Testament. I took counsel with my colleagues Kathleen O'Connor and Christine Yoder, who helped me think about what to include in such an inventory, and their suggestions have helped me greatly. Kathleen O'Connor in particular helped me with the observation that such a presentation should not be simply a list of discrete entries, but should be a discussion that has some interpretive coherence—that the sum should be more than the parts. That suggestion remained much on my mind, and I have sought to reflect a focused theological center in my listing, though I am not sure that this approach will be apparent to readers. The truth is that the entries are, for the most part, greatly and deeply connected to each other. Tim Simpson served as my faithful editor and conversation partner, and my debts to him are great indeed.

The title of the book, *Reverberations of Faith,* alludes both to the title of my earlier work *Cadences of Home* (Westminster John Knox Press, 1997) and to the now famous notion of Clifford Geertz concerning "thick description." I have sought to show both how these entries keep echoing and how they are "thick" in their interpretive power. These entries are not dictionary definitions, with simple characterizations of each term. Rather I have attempted to reflect the complexities, depth, and interrelatedness of these entries, wherein one must entertain them all in order to sense fully any one of them.

Thus, I have in mind two reverberations. First, most of these entries reverberate in their main claims and intent with other entries, so that one must read across entries to sense the dynamism of the faith of ancient Israel. Second, most of these entries, even taken alone, are in the text on the lips of many voices in the Old Testament, each of which speaks in a somewhat different accent. The terms themselves are complex and always of more than one dimension. I am committed to

Professor George Lindbeck's notion of cultural-linguistic interpretation, so that one must live inside this particular mode of discourse in order to use sensibly and responsibly any one of these terms. That is, one must notice the allusions made from one term to another that at times reinforce and at times problematize. I believe, moreover, that the recovery of this complex mode of discourse is fundamental for the church in the United States in order to recover missional energy, for by and large the church in the United States has chosen to speak every language but its own.

I began this book with the goal of writing "one hundred entries," which is completely arbitrary, though I did discover in writing that one hundred is a large number indeed. Perhaps one-fourth of these entries are "big ticket items" and are obvious in any such list. Beyond that the topics become less obvious; as I accumulated numbers the entries devolved into lesser items, until some choices are simply preferences over other items, without any great principle of inclusion or exclusion. In such an extended listing, any interpreter—and certainly this one—is less familiar with some material than others and so is even more dependent in some cases on the work of other scholars. For the discerning reader, the fact that "one hundred entries" is arbitrary will be obvious in that one hundred and five entries (if I have at last counted correctly) appear here. The reason is not that some entries simply could not be omitted. The much more simple reason is that I miscounted, and having miscounted and written, I included them all.

My hope is that this study will be valuable to pastors and especially to thoughtful lay persons who want to understand more fully the Bible and its faith. My concern has not been more "data," but rather to invite the reader into the ongoing disputatious practice of interpretive language that is already operative in disputatious ways in the biblical text itself, disputatious because no term has one obvious meaning. My procedure in general has been (a) to state a more or less consensus position, though current scholarship does not always make such a finding obvious or even possible; (b) to state what is at issue in the interpretive question that pertains to the entry; and (c) to indicate how the interpretive question may matter to serious church people. In this last step, I have taken what for me are characteristic interpretive risks in suggesting a contemporary connection to the ancient text.

My closing comment here is to thank the patient people at Westminster John Knox and most especially Tempie Alexander, who completed this manuscript. After a long time of working together, this is Ms. Alexander's last work as my secretary. My debts to her are great and abiding, and I thank her with deep affection. I am pleased to dedicate this volume to my two daughters-in-law, Lisa and Christina, through whom my sons are manifestly blessed [see BLESSING].

Walter Brueggemann
Columbia Theological Seminary

ABBREVIATIONS

AB	Anchor Bible
BZAW	Beihefte zur Zeitschrift für die alttestamentliche Wissenschaft
CBQ	*Catholic Biblical Quarterly*
HBT	*Horizons in Biblical Theology*
HTR	*Harvard Theological Review*
JAOS	*Journal of the American Oriental Society*
JBL	*Journal of Biblical Literature*
JSOT	*Journal for the Study of the Old Testament*
JSOTSup	Journal for the Study of the Old Testament: Supplement Series
JSS	*Journal of Semitic Studies*
NCB	New Century Bible
NIB	*The New Interpreter's Bible*
OBT	Overtures to Biblical Theology
OTL	Old Testament Library
RB	*Revue biblique*
SBLDS	Society of Biblical Literature Dissertation Series
SBT	Studies in Biblical Theology
SVTP	Studia in Veteris Testamenti pseudepigraphica
VT	*Vetus Testamentum*
ZAW	*Zeitschrift für die alttestamentliche Wissenschaft*

The Ancestors "The ancestors" (or in more familiar patriarchal phrasing, "the fathers") are Abraham (Gen. 12–24), Isaac (Gen. 25–26), and Jacob (Gen. 25–36), together with their wives, Sarah, Rebekah, and Rachel. (Joseph, in Gen. 37–50, is not commonly included in this category, for the narrative of Joseph articulates a quite different story-world.)

Questions of the historicity of the ancestral narratives of Genesis are exceedingly problematic and, in the end, without resolution. Proponents of historical-archaeological research claim to readily locate the ancestors in the second millennium B.C.E., but such evidence is much disputed and widely regarded with skepticism. Certainly, though, these narrative characters are embedded in legendary folk memory. The capacity to go behind the narrative material itself into any recoverable facticity is at present impossible. The process of the formation of the textual tradition, moreover, is obscure; at present no scholarly consensus exists.

On the basis of the narrative material itself, one can make some distinctions among the "ancestors" and notice the particularity of each of the characters. Of the three, Isaac receives the least coverage and is least clearly delineated (Gen. 25–27). Concerning Abraham and Jacob, they are located in different geographical areas and revolve around different shrines, perhaps reflecting the identity of different communities that formed and preserved the narrative memories. Abraham is in the south, especially at the shrine at Hebron (Gen. 13:18), whereas Jacob is in the north and at the shrine in Bethel (Gen. 28:10–22). The distinct communities, north and south, preserved the narratives. Beyond that, Abraham, placed first, deals primarily with the *promises* of God and issues of faith, whereas Jacob is much more disputatious and is in ongo-

ing conflict with his brother Esau and his uncle Laban. Jacob's endless preoccupation is the *blessing* of God and the capacity of God to guarantee material well-being. In their different ways, each is engaged in a struggle to secure a future; that struggle is carried through a series of familial episodes of conflict and deception that marks this intergenerational family as notably dysfunctional.

Having said that, when questions of the theological import of the narratives are raised, overlooking the distinct narrative marking of each of the ancestors is possible, in order to see that the sum of the memory, constructed over time, regards this intergenerational family as the peculiar and decisive carrier of the promissory faith of Israel. In each generation of the ancestors, God gives and reiterates the promise that this family will be sustained until it receives "the land of promise" solemnly sworn by God to each new generation:

1. In each generation, the promise is announced whereby God commits to securing the promise for the new generation [see PROMISE]. The commitment of God has no grounding in a covenantal agreement or condition on the part of Israel; the commitment is a free, unencumbered gift of God.

2. The maintenance of the promise from one generation to the next depends, of course, upon having an heir who may receive the family trust for the future—in this patriarchal casting, an heir who is a son. The primary plot line of the narrative is endlessly complicated by the fact that in each generation, the prospective mother of the heir—Sarah (Gen. 11:30), Rebekah (Gen. 25:21), Rachel (Gen. 30:1)—is in turn barren and without prospect of a son and heir. The promise of the future is thus repeatedly in profound jeopardy.

3. The ancestors in each generation,

however, trust the power of God even in the face of such negating circumstance. The Bible comes to understand that trust in the promise as "faith," so that human trust is the appropriate response to divine promise. Specifically, Genesis 15:6—"He believed (trusted) . . . and the LORD reckoned it to him as righteousness"—becomes a leading motif for biblical theology. In his great exposition of a theology of grace, Paul quotes Genesis 15:6 as a statement of the good news of God before it is visible in Jesus Christ (Gal. 3:6). In Martin Luther's categories, Abraham is said to be "justified" (regarded as righteous or innocent) because of his trust in God's promise (= faith). Thus Genesis 15:6 became a key accent for Martin Luther in his presentation of Reformation teaching. This interface of promise and trust becomes definitional for the larger narrative of Genesis; by the end of the Genesis narrative, however, the promise of the land still awaits fruition.

4. While the Genesis narratives focus on Israel's future, the narrative regularly affirms that God makes the promise to Israel in order that Israel may be a blessing to other nations (see Gen. 12:2; 18:18; 22:18; 26:4; 28:14). The narrative of promise thus pushes Israel beyond its own well-being to keep other peoples in its horizon, plausibly the very peoples who are "under curse" in Genesis 3–11. Paul regards this push beyond Israel's own life as "the gospel beforehand" (Gal. 3:8).

This ancestral narrative occupies a unique and defining place in biblical faith in the five following ways:

1. This tradition of the ancestor, in its origin and transmission, is perhaps not connected in any close way to the Moses tradition or to the demands of Sinai. In some sense, the tradition stands apart from the characteristic accents of Israel's

covenant. To be sure, the notion of covenant is present in this narrative (see Gen. 15:18; 17:2–21). Unlike Sinai, however, the covenant here seems much more likely to be a covenant of grant whereby the sovereign ruler of the land freely (and arbitrarily) assigns land to favorite subjects (see the practice in 2 Sam. 9:9–10). Such a practice is quite in contrast to the more or less bilateral covenant of Sinai.

2. The very different tradition of the ancestors carries quite different theological freight. Prior to later editorial work that took fragmented memories and shaped them into a coherent tradition, that the God of the Promise is identified as YHWH, the God of Moses, is not clear. The "God of Promise" may perhaps be an antecedent subject of faith incorporated into Israel's traditions in the interest of inclusive theological formulation. In any case, the God of the ancestors is remembered as one who freely makes promises that are unconditional and that continue in their promissory effectiveness into the future. These promises from God to the ancestors constitute the basis for the land theology expressed in contemporary Zionism, a theology that views the contemporary land of Israel as God's deeply grounded intention for Jews for all time to come.

3. During the monarchial period of ancient Israel, prophetic voices that appeal primarily to the covenant of Sinai and its commands and its sanctions dominate the biblical materials. As a consequence, the promise to the ancestors is, in this literature, notably muted. By contrast, in the literature of the sixth century, when Israel had lost control of its land of promise and had to face deportation from that land, the antecedent memories of "promised land" again come into prominent play (Isa. 41:8; 51:2). The promises in this context function to assure landless,

displaced Jews that the old hopes about the land are still powerfully operative and reliable. The rearticulation of ancient promises for a later, sixth-century community is a prime example of the ways in which old traditions function as fresh theological resource in a new circumstance of crisis. What God long ago promised for the future may still be trusted as a sure future in a later time.

4. In the Christian tradition, reference to the ancestors also functions as a ground of hope. In the gospel of Luke, for example, Mary's revolutionary anthem of hope appeals to "Abraham and his descendants" (Luke 1:55). In the Lucan tradition, Jesus incorporates needy social rejects into the scope of the Abrahamic promise (Luke 13:16; 19:9). In Paul's "theology of grace," Abraham and Sarah are taken as models of faith who "qualify" with God precisely because they trust the promise (Rom. 4:1–25; Gal. 3:6–18; 4:21–5:1). In addition, in Hebrews 11:8–12, 17–22, the ancestors appear among the primal examples of faith.

5. In recent ecumenical theology, "Abrahamic faith" is a shared reference for the three "peoples of the book," Jews, Christians, and Muslims. For all their intractable differences, these lively theological traditions and the communities of faith that rely on them are rooted in deep, shared promises. Those promises, voiced in that ancient, shared text, stand behind all of the later developments of difference that are so inhospitable and destructive. The ancestors—especially Abraham (and Sarah)—stand as a defining point for the largest sweep of biblical faith, the widest generosity of God, and the deepest trust of Israel and its several derivative communities.

References: Buechner, Frederick, *Son of Laughter* (San Francisco: Harper, 1993); Clines, David J., *The Theme of the Pentateuch* (JSOTSup 10; Sheffield: JSOT Press, 1978); Moberly, R. W. L., *The Old Testament of the Old Testament: Patriarchal Narratives and Mosaic Yahwism* (OBT; Minneapolis: Fortress Press, 1992); Thompson, Thomas L., *The Historicity of the Patriarchal Narratives: The Quest for the Historical Abraham* (Berlin: Walter de Gruyter, 1974); Van Seters, John, *Abraham in History and Tradition* (New Haven: Yale University Press, 1975); Weinfeld, Moshe, "The Covenant of Grant in the Old Testament and in the Ancient Near East," *Journal of the American Oriental Society* 90 (1970): 184–203; Westermann, Claus, *The Promise to the Fathers: Studies on the Patriarchal Narratives* (Philadelphia: Fortress Press, 1980).

Angel In popular religion, the term "angel" conjures notions of ephemeral beings with wings, halos, and all manner of otherworldly accoutrements. In the Old Testament, "angel" for the most part means "messenger," one who carries messages from the sovereign government of YHWH in heaven to the earth, often especially to kings and persons in authority. (Angels may have other functions as well; note especially that an angel may be a military figure, thus the "hosts" of angels of whom YHWH is the "Lord of Hosts.") In the text, the angel is to be understood in the context of a polytheistic world, wherein the government of God (or gods) in heaven makes decisions that affect the future of the earth; the ruling authority dispatches the angel as a member of that government of heaven to declare the policy of heaven in the affairs of earth [see DIVINE COUNCIL]. As the Old Testament moves toward monotheism, the angels are obedient members of the heavenly court of YHWH's government, or they are seen as a function or manifestation of YHWH's own engagement in the earth. Two texts in particular—1 Kings 22:19–23 and Isaiah 6:1–8—evidence this latter function. In 1 Kings 22:19–23, the members of YHWH's government help plan divine strategy; in Isaiah 6:1–8, the seraphim fill the divine throne room with vigorous praise and adoration. (To be sure, the Old Testament also knows of lesser gods [angels] who are recalcitrant and who disobey the will of YHWH, as in Ps. 82.) The work of the angels in 1 Kings and Isaiah is to effect the rule of YHWH upon the earth. Insofar as they are independent agents, they are variously called "sons of God," the "hosts" of the "Lord of hosts," "cherubim," or "seraphim" (see Pss. 29:1; 82:1; Isa. 6:1–7). Among the more exotic, exceptional cases are the function of Satan (1 Chr. 21:1; Job 1–2) and other members of the Divine Council (1 Kgs. 22:19–23), and the giants of Genesis 6:1–4. This entire cluster of titles functions as an inventory of ways of speaking of YHWH's richly differentiated governance of the earth.

The messengers speak a word that is not their own but rather the word "of the one who sent me," YHWH. They characteristically introduce their utterances by the messenger formula—"Thus saith YHWH"—indicating, like any governmental ambassador, that the word announced is not their own but YHWH's, so should be taken with appropriate seriousness. Because the message is from YHWH, the accent is characteristically upon what is said and heard, much more than on the messenger's appearance or significance. Indeed, any attention paid to the appearance of the messenger primarily emphasizes the importance of the message to be delivered.

For the most part, angels appear in two parts of the Old Testament. They are found, first, in the earlier narratives of Genesis, where the reduction of faith to a severe monotheism is not yet in force (see Gen. 16:7–11; 21:15–21; 22:11–12; Exod.

3:2–6; 23:20–23). They also appear in the later part of the Old Testament when the monopoly of YHWH is expressed in quite varied ways (Dan. 4:13–26; 7:10; 10:7–10, 20; 12:1; Zech. 1:1–17; 6:1–8). In the later period, YHWH's work in the world is enacted without the full and direct engagement of the increasingly transcendent YHWH who leaves the work to these functionaries. Even here, however, the full development of an "angelology" occurs only after the period of the Old Testament and in the environment of emerging Judaism and the New Testament community. The fuller notion of angels perhaps results from the intrusion of newer foreign elements into the faith of Judaism and the increasing remoteness of YHWH from human, historical experience, so that mediating figures become more important in articulating YHWH's presence in and governance of the world.

In the middle period of the Old Testament (roughly the monarchial period), angels are much less prevalent, because YHWH's singular sovereignty is especially accented; YHWH is alone in majesty and splendor and has no helpers or advisors. In Isaiah 6, the seraphs serve with endless praise to enhance YHWH's majesty. Moreover, in this period, human persons as prophets became YHWH's representative voices, and they also speak a word not their own, vouched for by the messenger formula, "Thus says the Lord." In the context of high monotheism and human spokespersons, the function of angels apparently became less necessary. In the later period, however, Israelite traditions return more fully to the way of the early traditions in which the panoply of YHWH's governance required a number of agents and articulations.

In any case, angels are functionaries of YHWH's governance and appear as one more attempt in Israel to articulate the peculiar conviction that YHWH is the decisive governing authority in the earth. Israel needed many vehicles to make that connection evident, and angels were one of them. They have no autonomous significance in the Old Testament but attest to YHWH's undivided authority [see APOCALYPTIC THOUGHT, DIVINE COUNCIL, SATAN].

References: Albertz, Rainer, *A History of Israelite Religion in the Old Testament Period*, vol. 2, *From the Exile to the Maccabees* (OTL; Louisville, Ky.: Westminster John Knox Press, 1994); Jacob, Edmond, *Theology of the Old Testament* (New York: Harper and Brothers, 1958).

Apocalyptic Thought The Greek verb *apokalupto* means to "uncover," or "reveal," and the noun *apokalupsis* translates as "revelation," or "disclosure." Both terms refer to the sudden revealing of what has been hidden and concealed from view. The root term is variously used to refer to (a) apocalypse as a literary genre, (b) apocalyptic eschatology as a religious perspective, and (c) apocalypticism as a social ideology. The adjective "apocalyptic" identifies a major strand of faith that emerged late in the development of the Old Testament. That strand concerns the ways in which God's governance of the world—and of the historical process— is hidden from human discernment, but at the same time humans know this governance to be sure and certain. Moreover, what is hidden about God's governance of the present and the future is disclosed to special persons who bear witness to or give an account in writing—a revelation— of what has been hidden. In the Old Testament, Daniel is such a special revealer, and in the New Testament John of Patmos (Rev. 1:9–11) reports a like disclosure in the book often called "The Revelation to John." The process of revealing what is

hidden of God's governance led to the production of scrolls that were taken to be revelation, scrolls that in form seem coded, so that what is revealed remains hidden in a powerful way. That is, this literature is deliberately written in a mode of rhetoric accessible only to people perceived as insiders.

"Apocalyptic" refers, in scholarly usage, to (1) an identifiable list of scrolls (books) that share common features and (2) a certain kind of hope that is characteristically voiced in this literature. For the most part, the canonical literature of the two Testaments (Old and New) has excluded apocalyptic literature. Such literature, however, does persist in the Old Testament in Isaiah 24–27, the book of Daniel, and Zechariah 9–14; in the New Testament the book of Revelation is the primary representative, but see, as well, Matthew 24–25 and Mark 13. Nonetheless, most of the literature termed "apocalyptic" falls outside the two canonical lists and includes a variety of texts that are dated before and after the period of the New Testament, including Enoch, 4 Ezra, 2 Baruch, Jubilees, and texts from the Qumran community of the Dead Sea Scrolls. While not familiar to most people who study the Bible, this literature is relatively available and with attentive work can be engaged. Its importance for understanding the Bible is its illumination of the cultural-religious matrix in which the Bible was formed and first transmitted.

Scholars group together these several pieces of literature as "apocalyptic" because they share common assumptions, images, and expectations. Scholars mostly agree about the shared markings of this literature and its theological perspective. John Collins (*Apocalypse: The Morphology of a Genre*) suggests that the "master paradigm" of apocalyptic thought includes four characteristics:

1. Modes and manner of revelation whereby special knowledge is mediated to select persons through vision, scroll, or utterance.
2. The content of revelation has a temporal axis concerning past and present with particular accents upon an upheaval concerning the future.
3. The content of revelation has a spatial axis concerned with otherworldly region.
4. Instructions are given to the recipient of the revelation concerning what is to be hidden or published of the revelation.

To be sure, apocalyptic is a mode of religious literature and articulation that is deeply remote from more conventional religious practices in established, middle-class churches that take the Bible seriously. Two features of apocalyptic in particular contradict more conventional expressions of biblical faith: First, conventional faith, in its accent on the ethical, places great emphasis on the importance of human obedience and responsiveness in enacting God's will. In apocalyptic literature, by contrast, God's transcendent will is decisive and human intention or action affect it in no manner. Pushed to the extreme, this apocalyptic mode of faith issues in fatalism and passivity. Second, conventional faith believes in long-term human obedience that will bring good and also sustain and enhance the human condition. By contrast, apocalyptic asserts that a radical turn in the world is near and will be abrupt; human effort at long-term sustenance of present arrangements is thus futile and irrelevant to God's coming future. Apocalyptic literature is found useful in (and reinforces) communities that feel themselves helplessly surrounded by an alien cultural environment. Such a sense of jeopardy may take

the form of physical threat or even a deep sense of the dominant culture's negating power. The most the faithful community can do is watch and wait, be ready for and receptive to the new coming of God's reign of justice and well-being, which contrasts sharply with the present world condition of despair and failure.

Apocalyptic literature is dazzling in its categories of expectation, unfamiliar timetable, and wild imagery—the fruits of visionary faith. Those features, of course, must be taken seriously if we are to participate—as best we can—in the venturesome act of imagination that this literature offers. The otherworldly approach of apocalyptic literature should not mask its function, however, as a vehicle for and carrier of serious, resolved faith. The faith articulated in this genre is the conviction that while the world seems to be out of control, in truth God is the sovereign ruler who totally governs the world process; therefore, adherents to this God may trust and wait and hope in complete confidence of a good, God-given outcome that will occur soon. The defining conviction is the reliable rule of God in and through and over a world seemingly out of control.

The peculiar disclosure of this hidden rule, moreover, is characteristically given through a special seer who communicates the mystery of what God will soon do to an elect community of insiders who are thereby reassured and permitted to wait, under discipline, with hope. The large, transcendent claim for God's rule is made concretely pertinent for the community that waits knowingly and obediently. This special community is thus peculiarly linked in privileged ways to the coming rule of God.

This body of literature with its unique religious conviction generally appears in a more or less specific context. In the Old Testament, apocalyptic appeared first in the literature in the sixth or fifth century, likely emerging from prophetic traditions. The prophets of ancient Israel had affirmed that God's rule would come within the historical process of the rise and fall of the nations. As that international process became less and less attentive to the hopes of Israel, however, that hope extended beyond the historical process to a larger world vision of the end of the old world and the beginning of a new world. One can see, for example, that in Jeremiah 51:59–64 the text anticipates the historical end of Babylon; but in the late text of Jeremiah 25:8–29, the coming judgment and emergency has moved beyond the history of the empire to a cosmic judgment on all peoples. (Beyond that, in Rev. 17–18, Babylon has become a cipher in apocalyptic imagery for every power that resists the rule of God.)

Why this move of hope beyond history occurred with such force and imagination in Judaism is not clear, but a number of explanations are possible. Perhaps Persian dualism provided categories for a radical statement of God's good intention in overcoming the evil of the present age. Another possibility is that the Hellenistic period provided such an intellectually contained order of reality that hope-filled Judaism had to break beyond such intellectual containment and did so in daring and imaginative ways. In any case, the deepest, most elemental hope of Jewishness for the rule of God clearly needed a vigorous and venturesome voice in a cultural context of hopelessness, disappointment, and despair, where the world itself seemed without hope and on its way to extinction. Such imagery might occur among and appeal precisely to people who sense their own profound powerlessness and who are weary of a world in which no more possibility is open to them. In such a circumstance, relentless faith that will not surrender to despair turns from the potential of the world that has come to be null and void to the God of all creation who can move decisively against and triumph over a failed, recalcitrant world.

In the context of the New Testament period, clearly such a horizon of hope characterized the Qumran (Dead Sea) community. That community had withdrawn from the hopeless circumstance of Jerusalem in order to await God's new rule, which was to be discontinuous from the present, failed way of the world. The stunning proclamation of Jesus emerged in the same climate of despair and hope. The radicality of Jesus' initial proclamation of a new governance (see Mark 1:14–15) issued in an invitation to watch and wait (Mark 13:23, 37), and eventually in the doxology:

> "The kingdom of the world has become
> the kingdom of our Lord
> and of his Messiah,
> and he will reign forever and ever."
> (Rev. 11:15)

That doxology matches the ultimate prayer of the early church:

> Amen. Come, Lord Jesus!
> (Rev. 22:20)

Some parts of the early church had a deep sense of apocalyptic emergency, believing that the new governance set in motion by "the Messiah" would come to full fruition with the return of the Messiah. This sense is reflected, for example, in Mark 13 and the book of Revelation. At the same time, other parts of the early church (in Luke-Acts) were clearly in culture for the long haul. Thus in the New Testament, apocalyptic literature is one dimension of a rich theological pluralism.

The earnestness of that deep hope is in the wonder of the Easter resurrection, a sign and firstfruit of the coming new age.

Apocalyptic faith appears in a radical kind of trust that is articulated in an extreme rhetoric. On the one hand, the church, over its long years and as it has become an established institution of culture in the West, has been busy dismissing such faith and rhetoric as an embarrassment and as a formula for destabilization that the institutional church could not tolerate. On the other hand, even with such characteristic institutional censorship, apocalyptic expectation does break out here and there in ways that cannot be stopped—among those who are powerless, who expect nothing more from the present world, and who for that reason look beyond the present world to the God whom they trust in spite of their current condition. This radical hope among the powerless appears absurd to people who still trust in the world, but such hope is indeed the work of people who have no other ground for hope. Apocalyptic rhetoric as a result, because of its intense radicality that borders on fantasy (as in much of the current Hollywood articulation of end-time portrayal), is immensely open to world denying and escapism or otherworldly expectation and hope. In engaging this strand of biblical faith, recognizing both its extremeness and openness to distortion and its immense resolve to hope only in God is crucial.

In the present circumstance of the church in the West, as the end of the known world of modernity becomes increasingly evident, apocalyptic may be an important theological resource that has been long neglected in a stable, self-satisfied church. But responsible appeal to apocalyptic faith is not easy. On the one hand, its use invites excessive attention to its rhetoric, to the neglect of its theological claim. On the other hand, its rhetoric invites, in bad faith, religious hucksters to appeal to a cataclysmic future while exploiting and denying real hope. Serious appeal to this theological tradition may be a deep assurance that cuts underneath anxiety about what is ending and invites to a God-based buoyancy while the world is under threat. People who framed, voiced, and practiced this faith were not engaged in escape, denial, or manipulation, but they were seriously focused on the world in which they lived—permitting the God they did not doubt but in whom they trusted deeply and without reservation to completely recharacterize reality. The future poses a problem for every historical faith, and the problem is more acute in times of broad, deep cultural distress. Apocalyptic turns the future as a problem productive of deep anxiety into an arena for praise and obedience of the God who will surely prevail.

References: Charlesworth, J. H., ed., *The Old Testament Pseudepigrapha of the New Testament* (Cambridge: Cambridge University Press, 1985); Collins, John J., *The Apocalyptic Imagination: An Introduction to the Jewish Matrix of Christianity* (New York: Crossroad, 1987); Collins, John J., ed., *Apocalypse: The Morphology of a Genre. Semeia* 14 (1979); Hanson, Paul D., *The Dawn of Apocalyptic: The Historical and Sociological Roots of Jewish Apocalyptic Eschatology* (Philadelphia: Fortress Press, 1975); Koch, Klaus, *The Rediscovery of Apocalyptic* (SBT, Second Series 22; London: SCM Press, 1972); Nickelsburg, George W. E., *Jewish Literature Between the Bible and the Mishnah* (Philadelphia: Fortress Press, 1981); Stone, M. E., *Scriptures, Sects, and Visions* (Philadelphia: Fortress, 1980); VanderKam, James C., *An Introduction to Early Judaism* (Grand Rapids: Eerdmans, 2001); Vermes, G., *The Dead Sea Scrolls: Qumran in Perspective* (Philadelphia: Fortress, 1981).

The Ark   The ark, some kind of box container, was one of the central symbols of

YHWH's presence in ancient Israel. While Exodus 25:10–16 offers a detailed, though perhaps late, characterization of how the ark was remembered and conceptualized, nowhere are we provided with a clear statement of its purpose or intent. At best, from ad hoc references, we can identify three quite distinct functions of the ark that overlap but reflect different interpretive agendas in different circumstances.

1. The ark was remembered in Israel as a central symbol from ancient tribal times. The container signified the unity and coherence among the tribes in loyalty to YHWH, while also articulating YHWH's palpable, committed presence to Israel in its risky travels. Specifically the ark was the vehicle through which YHWH attended to Israel in its military endeavors, so that YHWH could be understood and trusted as leader and assurance in Israel's wars, the "Lord of Hosts" (= armies). This function is evident in what is likely a quite old narrative concerning a poetic slogan in Israel that relied upon YHWH's presence, protection, and leadership:

> Whenever the ark set out, Moses would say,
> "Arise, O LORD, let your enemies be
> scattered,
> and your foes flee before you."
> And whenever it came to rest, he would say,
> "Return, O LORD of the thousand
> thousands of Israel."
> (Num. 10:35–36)

See also Numbers 14:14 and 1 Samuel 4:3; in the latter report, after the Philistines rout them, the Israelites bring the ark to battle as an extra resource. In this battle report, the ark was of no avail. In that narrative, YHWH's attachment to the ark is clearly filled with irascible freedom and uncontrollable power. The ark thus does not guarantee Israel's victory, nor can the Philistines hold the ark captive.

2. Second and perhaps derivatively, the ark is understood as a sign of YHWH's liturgic presence in Israel. For the most part this sign is reassuring to Israel, although no guarantees accompany it. In the end, the very temple that houses the ark is destroyed, and Israel learns of YHWH's absence. Perhaps Israel understood the ark as the throne on which the invisible YHWH sat; more likely it was understood as the "footstool" for the footrest of the regal YHWH (see 1 Chr. 28:2; Ps. 99:5). (Notice that the "calf" is likely to be understood in parallel fashion as the northern competitor to what became the southern ark and ideological claim of Jerusalem [1 Kgs. 12:25–33]. The ark, like the calf, is understood as a symbol of YHWH's presence assuring life and well-being.) Acknowledged in this way, the ark can function in religious processions and festivals, whereby YHWH is placed at the head of the parade (1 Sam. 6:10–7:2; 2 Sam. 6:1–19; 1 Kgs. 8:1–8; Ps. 132:8–10, 13–14, and likely 24:7–10 with its reference to the "King of glory"). Beyond these processions, the liturgic report of 1 Kings 8:12–13 indicates that as the procession ends and the ark is put in place in the Jerusalem temple, it signifies that YHWH has now taken up permanent residence in the temple as a patron to the Davidic monarchy. In this way the prior articulation of the dynamism of YHWH is now transposed into a sign of abiding presence with the assurance, protection, and legitimacy that such presence entails.

3. A third understanding of the ark is offered in the traditions of Deuteronomy, whereby the ark is understood simply as the container for the two tablets of the decalogue that Moses received at Mt. Sinai (Deut. 10:1–5; 1 Kgs. 8:9). Such a characterization of the ark reflects a much larger interpretive contestation, whereby this tradition intends to deny the high

sacerdotal claim of real presence found in other traditions, in order to insist that what Israel knows of YHWH is in the Sinai commands; the access that Israel has to YHWH, moreover, takes the form of covenantal obedience. The ark thus becomes, in the contestation of traditions, one more arena in which interpretive dispute and pluralism are evident. The ark is permitted no simple interpretation and is a carrier of several theological claims, each of which attends to YHWH's presence but in profoundly different modes.

Unlike the Torah, the ark proved not to be a durable vehicle for Israel's faith. The last mention of the ark is in Jeremiah 3:15–18, where it is recognized as a cultic sign of presence that will be lost in the upheaval of 587 when the temple is destroyed. By the second century B.C.E., Jewish legends reported that Jeremiah had hidden the ark in order to keep it from Nebuchadnezzar and the Babylonians (see 2 Mac. 2:4–8; 2 Bar. 6). The ark is important theologically as evidence not only of the richness of interpretive activity but also of the great difficulty in Israel of speaking faithfully about YHWH's presence, which is permeated with freedom beyond every vehicle of assurance and guarantee.

References: Brueggemann, Walter, *(I)chabod toward Home* (Grand Rapids: Eerdmans, 2002); Haron, Menahem, *Temples and Temple Service in Ancient Israel: An Inquiry into Biblical Cult Phenomena and the Historical Setting of the Priestly School* (Winona Lake, Ind.: Eisenbrauns, 1985); Miller, Patrick D., *The Religion of Ancient Israel* (Louisville, Ky.: Westminster John Knox Press, 2000); Miller, Patrick D., Jr., and J. J. M. Roberts, *The Hand of the Lord: A Reassessment of the "Ark Narrative" of I Samuel* (Baltimore: Johns Hopkins University Press, 1977); Rad, Gerhard von, "The Tent and the Ark," in *The Problem of the Hexateuch and Other Essays* (New York: McGraw-Hill, 1966), 103–214; Seow, Choon Leong, *Myth, Drama, and the Politics of David's Dance* (Atlanta: Scholars Press, 1989); Vaux, Roland de, *Ancient Israel: Its Life and Institutions* (New York: McGraw-Hill, 1961).

Asherah The topic of Asherah occurs only occasionally and marginally in the Old Testament but has much occupied scholars who study the character of Israelite religion. Asherah is known as a goddess attested in Semitic religion, especially prominent in the texts of Ugarit as part of a complex community of gods and goddesses. (The term "Astarte" may be related, but the connection is not clear.)

In the Old Testament, the term "Asherah" turns up a number of times, but its meaning is far from clear and scholars dispute it. The Canaanite goddess may have also been known in some forms of Israelite religion (see 1 Kgs. 15:13; 18:19), a notion strengthened by the discovery of an inscription in a southern caravan stop from perhaps the ninth century that speaks of YHWH "and his Asherah." This citation may suggest that YHWH was known in some circles to have had a female consort, as did the other High Gods in Ancient Near Eastern practice.

In the Old Testament the term often refers to a sacred object, perhaps a "sacred pole" (2 Kgs. 21:3; 23:4). The early versions of the text, which rendered the Hebrew into Greek and Latin, understood the term as a tree or a grove of trees, likely suggesting a dimension of fertility. While some Old Testament texts condemn Asherah as a cult object as a threat to Yahwism (Deut. 16:21), the "pole"—whatever its significance and function for Israel—was not clearly inimical to Yahwism. Moreover the relation between the goddess attested elsewhere and the "pole" variously assessed in Israel is also uncertain. That such a cult object was present in ancient Israel is evident, but its status and significance are less than clear and perhaps less than stable.

The argument is complex, the data is not clear, and scholars do not agree about the meaning of the available, scant data. To the extent that Israel knew about or paid attention to such a goddess and to the extent that the sacred pole alluded in a direct way to the goddess (even if by condemnation), two learnings emerge. First, the actual religious practice of ancient Israel was intensely varied and contested. The Old Testament as we have it is unmistakably a highly partisan, one-sided presentation of ancient practice; the framers of this canon in their Yahwistic advocacy took care to exclude from the textual tradition what they regarded as untrue or harmful [see MONOTHEISM]; furthermore, the framers intended their self-conscious interpretive construal to be normative for the community. Indeed in the practice of the church, the normative tradition given us in the canon does prevail and is broadly accepted as reliable as a guide for faith and life. In reading that normative construal, however, one may usefully notice the ways in which that normativeness proceeds by an intentional process of inclusion and exclusion that over time the communities of the book have accepted as correct and faithful judgments.

Second, insofar as Asherah is a goddess, attention to her (even by condemnation) likely indicates the incorporation of the character and functions of feminine divinity into the faith of Israel and perhaps into the character of YHWH. The classical tradition of monotheism has no doubt excluded, as much as possible, hints of the feminine in the character of God. The presence of Asherah in the Old Testament (or repressed hints of that presence) may indicate an awareness that a feminine dimension of the divine is absorbed into the character of YHWH. In any case, Asherah's appearance precludes any simplistic, one-dimensional characterization of YHWH, who must be understood, according to the text, as emerging in a complex and contested religious environment.

References: Albertz, Rainer, *A History of Israelite Religion in the Old Testament Period*, vol. 1, *From the Beginnings to the End of the Monarchy* (OTL; Louisville, Ky.: Westminster John Knox Press, 1994); Day, John, "Asherah in the Hebrew Bible and Northwest Semitic Literature," *JBL* 105 (1986): 385–408; Hadley, Judith, *The Cult of Asherah in Ancient Israel and Judah: Evidence for a Hebrew Goddess* (Cambridge: Cambridge University Press, 2000); Miller, Patrick D., *The Religion of Ancient Israel* (Louisville, Ky.: Westminster John Knox Press, 2000).

Assyria   Assyria was a state with imperial achievements, located in northern Mesopotamia (present-day Iraq). It endured over many centuries and hovered in threatening ways like an ominous "Colossus of the North"over the history of Israel. Assyria's long, complex history is sporadically well documented in its own records, showing the nation with a ruthless character capable of brutal domination befitting a superpower. For our purposes, considering the history of the state over the centuries is not necessary; we need only note the points at which Assyria's interests overlapped with those of the kingdoms of Israel and Judah.

In the middle of the ninth century, Ahab, king in Samaria, was part of a coalition of small states—along with the Syrian state of Damascus—engaged in a conflict with Shalmaneser III, Assyrian king. This conflict is known from the stele that the Assyrians erected claiming victory, although in fact the outcome seems more likely to have been a stalemate.

Israel's more intense and more important engagement with Assyria took place in the eighth century B.C.E., during and after the final days of the northern kingdom of Israel. After a period of malaise, the Assyrian potential for international domination was revived through the leadership of Tiglath-pileser III, also called Pul (745–727). Tiglath-pileser mobilized Assyrian military power and began expansion to the west, toward the Mediterranean Sea, inevitably colliding with the interests of the two Israelite states. During the years from 734 to 732, North Israel again joined a coalition to resist Assyrian power, but in the end Israel was helpless before the imperial onslaught. Under the leadership of Sargon II (721–705), the Assyrian armies conquered the northern capital of Samaria in 721, terminated the state of Israel, and deported leading citizens away from Samaria into other parts of the empire (see 2 Kgs. 17:5–23). As a consequence, Israel as an independent political state disappeared from the political scene of the Near East.

The conquest and termination of the northern state was matched by the attack on Judah by Sennacherib (705–681) and the siege of Jerusalem (705–701), from which the city was "miraculously" delivered. The Assyrian empire reached its zenith with an incursion into Egypt in 663; after a brief fifty years, the empire was spent. Its capital city of Nineveh fell as the Assyrian state was terminated in 612. The book of Nahum addresses that event.

To consider the ways in which Israel's theological reflection redescribed these matters with reference to YHWH, we must pay attention to two clusters of texts, in 2 Kings and Isaiah. In 2 Kings the Assyrians figure largely in the narrative account of the demise of the northern state and the threat to Jerusalem. Already in

the time of Menahem, king in Samaria (745–737), Israel became a client state of Tiglath-pileser and purchased independence with tribute money (2 Kgs. 15:17–22). In 722, Shalmaneser V (727–722) received tribute money from Hoshea, the last king of Israel, but to no avail (2 Kgs. 17:3–4). The northern kingdom fell to Assyrian assault, a crisis understood in the narrative as the judgment of YHWH (2 Kgs. 17:5–6, 7–18).

The southern kingdom of Judah was of course not immune to this same threat, and in 2 Kings 16, Ahaz, king in Judah, is reported as submitting to Tiglath-pileser:

> "I am your servant and your son. Come up, and rescue me from the hand of the king of Aram and from the hand of the king of Israel, who are attacking me." (2 Kgs. 16:7)

This formulation, according to Judah's covenantal self-understanding, is the sort of oath of fidelity a Judean king can make only to YHWH. Thus, Ahaz's political commitment is understood theologically as violating the first commandment of Sinai (Exod. 20:3). The Assyrian preoccupation with Judah and Jerusalem finally played out in the remarkable events reported in 2 Kings 18–20, with a parallel version in Isaiah 36–39. In the period 705–701, Sennacherib had laid siege to Jerusalem. In due course, however, the Assyrian armies returned home without a victory. The people of Israel understood the rescue of Jerusalem as a mighty victory for YHWH that went far toward establishing Jerusalem as an inviolable city (2 Kgs. 19:32–34, 35–37).

The second cluster of relevant texts is in the book of Isaiah, which is endlessly concerned with Jerusalem and offers three important textual occasions concerning Assyrian status vis-à-vis Israel.

1. In Ahaz's initial confrontation with

the power of Assyria and the more immediate threat of Syrian power, the prophet Isaiah presents the crisis to the Judean king as a crisis of faith (Isa. 7:9). That is, in the face of the imperial threat, the prophet urges that trust in YHWH should be the basis for defense policy. In that context, Isaiah seems to work out the meaning of faith.

2. In Sennacherib's siege of Jerusalem in the time of King Hezekiah, the prophet boldly attests to the king the adequacy of YHWH who, in the end, will prevail even over the ominous threat of Assyria (Isa. 37:22–29).

3. In a text much later than the eighth-century prophet himself, the Isaiah tradition envisions a coming time when Israel will have peace with Assyria and Assyrians will be among YHWH's chosen peoples (Isa. 19:23–25).

In the prophetic tradition Assyria is understood as an occasion for affirming the sovereignty of YHWH, even in the face of a brutalizing superpower. Assyria is variously an instrument for YHWH's purposes (Isa. 10:5), the enemy of YHWH (Isa. 37:22–29), and eventually the protected, beloved subject of YHWH (Isa. 19:23–25). In prophetic construal the arena of *Realpolitik* is radically transposed into a matrix where the vitality and sovereignty of YHWH are decisive. In such a world, Assyrian power, a metaphor for all autonomous power, is at best penultimate. Even where not explicitly mentioned, Assyria lurks in the background as an instrument of YHWH's threat, as in Amos 7:10–17.

A third quite different text concerning Assyria is the story of Jonah. This narrative, presumably quite late, is not interested in Assyria but uses the capital city of Nineveh to help Israel reflect on the character of YHWH and the nature of obedient, inclusive faith.

References: Clements, Ronald, *Isaiah and the Deliverance of Jerusalem* (JSOTSup 13; Sheffield: JSOT Press, 1980); Oppenheim, A. L., *History of Assyria* (Chicago: University of Chicago Press, 1923); Saggs, H. W. F., *The Might That Was Assyria* (London: Sidgwick & Jackson, 1984); Seitz, Christopher R., *Zion's Final Destiny: The Development of the Book of Isaiah: A Reassessment of Isaiah 36–39* (Minneapolis: Fortress Press, 1991).

Atonement The term "atonement" is usually loaded with theological significance. "Atonement" derives from "at one," to be "at one with another," "to agree," "to be reconciled," and is the word most used to translate the Hebrew term *kpr*, which means to "cover over." In the Old Testament the term is used especially in priestly materials to speak of the salutary effect of offerings of purgation and purification that "cover over" sin and pollution and their consequences, so that Israel (who sins and pollutes) and YHWH (whom sin and pollution offends) may be reconciled to each other and "at one." These priestly texts take sin and pollution with profound seriousness; therefore, "covering" as a remedy for sin and condition of rehabilitation is approached seriously and is enacted carefully according to detailed instruction.

The focus of priestly rituals of atonement occurs on the Day of Atonement (Yom Kippur), which is given detailed attention in scripture only in Leviticus 16. The procedures prescribed there for the high priest (Aaron) are twofold. First comes the act of purgation whereby the priest places upon "the live goat" all the iniquities of Israel, which are then carried outside the camp by the goat, so that the holy place is freed of pollution. Second, an offering of "purification" is made, whereby the group is purified of its sin so that it may be forgiven (v. 9). The twin acts of purification and purgation complete a process whereby Israel is freed of its sin and the holy place is made habitable for God. The action restores right relations with God and allows the resumption of life under blessing.

As is characteristic in priestly directions, the officiant is told what to do, but the text here, as almost everywhere, tells only what is to be done [see PRIESTLY TRADITION]. This interpretive tradition places the priests at the center of the process of reconciliation, so that the priestly monopoly not only provides Israel with important religious assurance, but also at the same time creates a center of enormous political power. We are given, for example, no explanation for the process of "scapegoating" nor why the blood of the goat is important to the process. We can only conclude that in this act sin and pollution are seen to be a palpable, almost material threat that only something that is also powerful and equally material in its force can counter. Thus the blood may function to nullify the power of pollution or to seal over its threat, a threat almost as palpable as the contamination of nuclear fallout that must be contained. Even though the priestly manual seeks to order the priestly actions, Leviticus 16 does not seek to rationalize or explain, because the act confronts the primitive, palpable force of pollution and proposes and authorizes an equally primitive solution. Very old and elemental practices lie behind this priestly prescription.

We should not, however, denigrate the ritual proposal because it strikes a modern person as primitive, for we have learned, even in contemporary communities of therapy, that guilt, estrangement, and alienation have a primordial force to them that does not lend itself to rational resolution. The act of atonement thus lives very deep in Israel's sacramental awareness. Even where there is later only text and not practice (without tabernacle or temple), the imagery of the Day of Atonement is readily understood in terms of actual pollution. Such physical pollution prevents communion with God and the God-given restoration that defies human rationality. Significantly, the drama of Yom Kippur continues its transformative force in modern Judaism, which is well removed from the actual temple practices. Indeed, that, in a world of technological rationality, Judaism has preserved and continues to embrace this most hidden and transformative of rituals is sobering. Perhaps the most remarkable reality of this ritual and its continuing power is the fact that what was a cultic enactment is now a textual residue so that the ritual is remembered rather than reenacted. Even so, the remembered festival is of immense force for the community of Judaism, which each time is reconciled to YHWH at the deepest levels of existence.

From that defining sacramental act of Judaism, we may note two derivative phenomena. In its attempt to understand Jesus, the early church, in the New Testament, appealed to the tradition of Yom Kippur and asserted that Jesus had displaced older Jewish practices of atonement; Jesus has now accomplished atonement "once for all" (Hebrews 10:10). In the Christian appropriation of the practice of atonement, no more rational sense is made of the matter than in the older tradition. In Christian testimony, as in Jewish perspective, the sacramental claim goes well beyond any theological explanation. Both Judaism and Christianity hold to a practice that makes a new beginning possible, unburdened and with free access to God's own life.

Finally, in a variety of theories and practices of psychotherapy, contemporary concern for well-being seeks in the best ways it can to mediate the kind of at-one-ment that is so much more elemental and inscrutable than the rationality-based theories of a technological society can tolerate. As a consequence, an immense gap exists between many contemporary practices of reconciliation and these deep sacramental claims offered in the tradition. That gap warrants continued attention. The issue of atonement in Jewish and, derivatively, Christian tradition attests that sin is real and dangerous and that, in the end, communion with God is the offer and hope of purgation and purification.

References: Knohl, Israel, *The Sanctuary of Silence: The Priestly Torah and the Holiness School* (Minneapolis: Fortress Press, 1995); Milgrom, Jacob, *Leviticus 1–16: A New Translation with Introduction and Commentary* (AB3; New York: Doubleday, 1991); Miller, Patrick D., *The Religion of Ancient Israel* (Louisville, Ky.: Westminster John Knox Press, 2000).

■ ■ ■

Baal   Baal is the best known and most prominent god in the Canaanite pantheon of deities. While Baal was known only polemically in the Old Testament, the 1929 discovery of the Ugaritic tablets made available many documents that reflected the conventional liturgic practices and theological-mythological claims of Canaanite religion. These documents are important because they permit us to glimpse this prominent Canaanite deity through the eyes of his adherents and not only through Israelite polemic.

Baal is presented variously in these texts as a storm god, a fertility god who provides rain, and a warrior god who in regular agricultural cycles defeats the powers of death and makes possible a new cycle of agricultural productivity. This collage of images presents a quite virile god who guarantees the fertility of the earth and who is therefore its rightful lord and owner. The several documents concerning Canaanite religion reflect a well-developed set of narrative accounts of this god who was, in a Canaanite liturgical environment, regarded as the giver of life.

Because of these attributes, Baal emerges in the Old Testament as the primary rival to YHWH and on occasion as a threat to YHWH's claims. From the intense monotheistic perspective of the Old Testament, particularly in the traditions related to Deuteronomy, Baal worship is an intense danger and seduction that Israel's reform movements vigorously and even violently purged. The competition between Baal and YHWH for Israel's loyalty was most acutely expressed during the Omride dynasty in northern Israel (876–842), and especially during the reign of Ahab and Jezebel. The contest at Mt. Carmel was thus a dramatic effort to establish the superiority of YHWH and the humiliation of Baal (1 Kgs. 18). The propensity in Israel for compromise with Baalism, however, is reported as perennial, and so recurring reform efforts sought to purge Baal worship from Israel (see Judg. 6:25–32; 2 Kgs. 10; 23:4–5).

In the mid-twentieth century, Old Testament scholarship emphasized the acute difference between YHWH and Baal. Whereas Baal was understood as a generative force within the natural processes, YHWH was by contrast understood as (a) a creator God who stood outside the natural processes and presided over them with demanding ethical requirements, and (b) the God whose preferred zone of activity was in history rather than nature. This dominant interpretive perspective, preoccupied with contrast, shared the view of those Old Testament texts that regarded syncretism—the melding together of different theological visions—as a deep threat to the faith of Israel. That is, scholarship sided with the most extreme texts in hostility to Baalism. The sustained polemic against "religion" on the part of Karl Barth—a polemic contextually informed by the struggle of Christians against the "Blood and Soil" religious ideology of National Socialism in Germany—gave specific impetus to this scholarly inclination. This interpretive stance assumed a defining parallel between the threat of Baal to the faith of ancient Israel and the threat of National Socialism as a religious ideology to the faith of the church in Europe.

While the radical "either/or" option of YHWH or Baal has a strong basis in the texts noted above, the interpretive climate has changed in more recent decades to show that YHWH, in Old Testament articulation, is in fact a lot like Baal and shares many of the same functions: YHWH also is a storm God (as in Ps. 29), a mighty warrior against the powers of death (as in Exod. 15), and a fructifier of the earth (Hos. 2:14–23) who gives rain and causes agriculture to flourish as the earth yields the blessings of life and well-being, and who orders the rhythms of nature to assure viable life for all creatures (Gen. 1:1–2:25; 8:22; Pss. 104:27–28; 145:15–16; Isa. 55:12).

The relation of YHWH (the one true God of Israel) to Baal is thus complex and subject to more than one interpretation. The different readings are in part under the influence of different texts; also, though, the different readings arise in different interpretive contexts where the faith of Israel is variously understood to be under threat and in need of purgation, or where that faith can be open to impingement by other influences that may modify

it. Insofar as YHWH is understood as a "virile" God, YHWH will rival Baal, who is characterized by virility in the extreme. As YHWH is also recognized as a "fertility God" who with a blessing causes crops to grow (an insight more appreciated in a feminist hermeneutic), the polemic against "fertility" religion can be measurably softened. Carried to its extreme, this more conciliatory view is able to recognize YHWH as a fertility God who exercises the very functions as creator that Canaanite religion had assigned to Baal. The articulation of the divine power and character of YHWH is thus given different nuance in different texts read differently in different contexts. The articulation of YHWH happened not in a vacuum but always in a context of other gods from whom Israel often borrowed and against whom Israel often polemicized.

In Isaiah 62:4, by the way, the land is called "married" (NRSV), and in Hebrew "Beulah land." "Beulah" is a feminine passive participial form of the term "baal," meaning "made fruitful." In context, the land is clearly "made fruitful" by YHWH, who exercises a fertility function elsewhere often assigned to Baal. YHWH the creator would intend all the earth to be "Beulah land"!

References: Albertz, Rainer, *A History of Israelite Religion in the Old Testament Period,* vol. 1, *From the Beginnings to the End of the Monarchy* (OTL; Louisville, Ky.: Westminster John Knox Press, 1994); Cross, Frank Moore, *Canaanite Myth and Hebrew Epic: Essays in the History of the Religion of Israel* (Cambridge: Harvard University Press, 1973), sect. III; Habel, Norman C., *Yahweh versus Baal: A Conflict of Religious Culture* (New York: Bookman Associates, 1964); Harrelson, Walter, *From Fertility Cult to Worship: A Reassessment for the Modern Church of the Worship of Ancient Israel* (Garden City, N.Y.: Doubleday, 1969); Smith, Mark S., *The Early History of God: Yahweh and Other Deities in Ancient Israel*

(San Francisco: Harper and Row, 1990); Westermann, Claus, *What Does the Old Testament Say About God?* (Atlanta: John Knox Press, 1979), chap. 3.

Babylon   Babylon was an ancient and formidable culture (located in what is now Iraq) that periodically dominated the politics and trade of the Near East. Its culture was immensely advanced in science and learning, and Israel doubtlessly borrowed and appropriated much from Babylonian wisdom, law, and cult.

The decisive point of contact between the long-standing political, cultural force of Babylon and the Old Testament is a brief one in the sixth century. As the Assyrian empire waned at the end of the seventh century, a subordinated Babylon was finally able to assert its independence and establish its own ruling house in what is now called a "neo-Babylonian" form. In 625 Nabopolassar asserted independence from a waning Assyria, and in 605 his son, Nebuchadnezzar, assumed power. Nebuchadnezzar was a formidable leader and in the Old Testament is portrayed as larger than life. Nebuchadnezzar died in 562 and soon thereafter, in 539, the power of Babylon was ended and the empire displaced by the rising Persians under Cyrus.

Like the Assyrians before him, Nebuchadnezzar had territorial ambitions to the west and south and inevitably interfered in the now enfeebled government of Judah. After the death of King Josiah in 609 (2 Kgs. 23:29–30), Judah for all practical purposes had lost its independence; the Davidic dynasty remained on the throne only at the behest of external power, at varying times Egypt or Babylon. In the end, Babylon invaded Judah and in 598 deported King Jehoiachin, grandson of Josiah, to Babylon where he is reported to have survived Nebuchadnezzar, at least until 561 (2 Kgs. 24:13–17; 25:27–30). The army of Babylon came again to a recalcitrant colonial state in Jerusalem in 587 and effectively ended the state of Judah and deported a second king, Zedekiah (2 Kgs. 25:7). Finally, Nebuchadnezzar came yet a third time to Jerusalem and enacted yet a third deportation (Jer. 52:28–30). Thus Nebuchadnezzar is credited with having effectively terminated in three waves the officially ordered life of Israel and transposed the covenantal community into a displaced, deported, defeated remnant with few hopes, deep losses, and treasured memories.

Nebuchadnezzar was likely acting in a rather standard imperial manner toward a recalcitrant colony. In Israel, however, that standard imperial practice was construed theologically with reference to YHWH. Seen in that light, the destruction and deportation caused by Nebuchadnezzar, which can be readily understood in terms of the normal ambition of empire, is made into the defining, paradigmatic theological experience of all subsequent Judaism. Israel is incapable of understanding the policies of Nebuchadnezzar apart from the reality of YHWH; for that reason the disaster of destruction and deportation is given a twofold theological interpretation.

First, because the Deuteronomic-prophetic traditions understood the disaster as deserved punishment from YHWH, Nebuchadnezzar had clearly not acted autonomously but at the behest of YHWH. In that light, Nebuchadnezzar is an incidental figure in YHWH's administration. For that reason in Jeremiah 25:9 and 27:6, YHWH calls Nebuchadnezzar "my servant"; and in Isaiah 47:6, the assertion appears that YHWH, in anger, made "my people" available for the brutality of Nebuchadnezzar.

But a second interpretive claim follows quickly. Nebuchadnezzar went beyond the mandate of YHWH and showed no mercy toward Jerusalem (Isa. 47:6–7), acting autonomously and eventually in opposition to the will of YHWH. Consequently a broad strand of interpretation in the text portrays Nebuchadnezzar (and Babylon) as an autonomous force that is not only violent toward Israel but violently opposed to YHWH, who will eventually judge and terminate Babylon. Thus the book of Jeremiah, in which Nebuchadnezzar is regarded as "my servant," reverses direction and ends with an extended poetic assault on the arrogance of Babylon who dared act against YHWH's people (Jer. 50–51) and with an anticipatory narrative concerning the soon-to-come fall of Babylon (51:64; see Isa. 13–14). The tradition traces the "development" of Nebuchadnezzar from a willing instrument and obedient servant of YHWH to a recalcitrant, autonomous agent who refused YHWH's intention.

In that latter role, Nebuchadnezzar—and Babylon—take on a remarkably generative role in the imagination of Israel, and become a metaphor for arrogant, autonomous power that does evil in the world in opposition to YHWH's will. Genesis 1 is, among other claims, plausibly an assertion of the power and authority of YHWH against Babylonian gods, and certainly Genesis 11:1–9 reflects the arrogance of Babylonian self-sufficiency. This emergence of the metaphorical force of Babylon and Nebuchadnezzar is quite astonishing, because neither Assyria before nor Persia after Babylon ever took on such symbolic force for the continuing interpretive work of Judaism.

That metaphorical force is particularly evident in Daniel 2–4. In chapter 4, Nebuchadnezzar is portrayed as an autonomous power who is driven insane and restored to sanity and power only when he submits, in doxology, to the ultimate rule of YHWH (Dan. 4:34–37). In critical interpretation this usage of Nebuchadnezzar is taken to refer to Antiochus IV, the Syrian ruler who oppressed the Jews in the second century B.C.E. Thus the metaphor loses its historical locus and illuminates other concrete political realities. In parallel fashion, Revelation 18, with direct allusion to Old Testament cadences, speaks of the coming destruction of Babylon, which here is to be understood as the Roman Empire that opposed the emerging church.

Out of these biblical references, "Babylon" becomes a metaphorical way of speaking of every power that thwarts God's intention. Martin Luther famously critiqued the Roman Church with his phrase, "The Babylonian Captivity of the Church." In recent time, Wheaton and Shank (1988) have used the same imagery to portray the "global" reach of the United States into Central America as a Babylonian force. The metaphor "Babylon" is a prime example of the way in which biblical texts become generative of interpretive imagination that ranges well beyond the text and its initial field of reference in redescribing the reality of the world.

References: Bellis, Alice Ogden, *The Structure and Composition of Jeremiah 50:2–51:58* (Lewiston: Edwin Mellen Press, 1995); Hill, John, *Friend or Foe? The Figure of Babylon in the Book of Jeremiah MT* (Leiden: Brill, 1999); Saggs, H. W. F., *The Greatness That Was Babylon* (London: 1988); Smith, Daniel L., *The Religion of the Landless: The Social Context of the Babylonian Exile* (Indianapolis: Meyer Stone, 1989); Wheaton, Philip, and Duane Shank, *Empire and Word: Prophetic Parallels between the Exile Experience and Central America's Crisis* (Washington: EPICA Task Force, 1988).

Blessing   A blessing is an act—by speech or gesture—whereby one party transmits power for life to another party.

This act of transmission, which occurs in a world of intense interpersonal relationships, is not explainable in any positivistic terms. Viewed "primitively," the transmission is somehow quasi-magical, the expression of a wish that is efficacious. Viewed theologically, the transmission takes on the quality of the sacramental, so that more happens than can be explained.

The most characteristic dimension of the power for life that is transmitted in blessing concerns prosperity, wealth, health, and fertility. That is, blessing is characteristically related to generativity and productivity that assures well-being of a quite material kind and that has durability into succeeding generations. Blessing is thus an intentional, deliberate act that proposes to enhance the receiver's life in its material dimension. For that reason, blessing concerns natural processes that belong to the orbit of creation theology, wherein God's good and fruitful world is celebrated.

God, then, is the primal speaker and giver of blessing. Already in Genesis 1:22, 28, God has uttered (decreed) well-being for the earth and its inhabitants. As a result of God's utterance, the world as God's creation teems with abundance and fruitfulness. This large claim made for God's world is given concreteness and specificity in Psalm 128:3–4, for example, which celebrates the birth of children in the family. In many lesser, more specific contexts, God's offer of life and well-being is enacted through blessing.

While God's power for life is given directly in God's utterance, human agents who are seen to be bearers of God's power for life can also mediate a blessing. We may note two such cases. In the first case, in a series of texts that dominate the ancestral narrative of Genesis (Gen. 12:3; 18:18; 22:18; 26:4; 28:14), the nations of the earth are said to be blessed in and through the existence of Israel. The declaration to Abraham in Genesis 12:3 places "curse" alongside "blessing," although that link is not developed in the subsequent narrative. (That link is developed, however, in Deuteronomy 28 and Leviticus 26, where all that is said positively about blessing has its negative counterpart and force in curse.) The ultimate case of Israel's power to bless is in the pathos-filled petition of pharaoh who petitions Moses for Israel's blessing upon Egypt (Exod. 12:32).

In the second case, God's power for life is evidently mediated through priests who are known to be the special bearers of God's power for life. This pervasive function of priests is best known in the familiar priestly blessing of Numbers 6:24–26:

> The LORD bless you and keep you;
> the LORD make his face to shine upon
>   you, and be gracious to you;
> the LORD lift up his countenance upon
>   you, and give you peace.

In this utterance, the priest does more than "wish" peace, but rather by utterance, generates, assures, and bestows it. In many Christian circles, that same priestly blessing is a standard pastoral benediction whereby priest or pastor is understood to be enacting the office of the ancient priesthood. In the original characterization and in contemporary replications, the priestly utterance and bestowal of blessing is not just a polite wish or a good idea but an act of power through the pastor or priest who through a designated office mediates God's power for life.

The priestly function, moreover, is evident in the formal recitals of blessings (matched by recitals of curses) in Leviticus 26:3–13 and Deuteronomy 28:1–14, which are highly stylized and constitute a part of an ordered liturgy. The characteristic worship service is thus understood, in a covenantal transaction, as a place and occasion of blessing.

As Israel and priests in particular are agents who may mediate YHWH's power for life, so other human beings are also carriers of that power for life, and they can transmit that power to others to whom they are related. The most spectacular case is Isaac in Genesis 27, but such transmission is also evident in Genesis 48:8–20 (see also Gen. 47:7). In the narrative of Genesis 27, the patriarchal figure is loaded with the power for life, which is then given to sons and grandsons. That the power for life, carried and given by such human agents, is intimately linked to God is not always clear, but in a more intentional theological way, all such power for life is eventually referred back to the creator God.

Most interesting are the many instances in which the human agent (sometimes a lone speaker, sometimes the community of faith) blesses YHWH (Pss. 16:7; 34:1; 63:4; 103:1, 2, 20, 21, 22; 104:1, 35; 115:18; 134:1; 145:1, 21). If we understand "bless" as a bestowal of the power for life, that the process should be reversed so that blessing is moved from human persons toward God seems odd, if not problematic. No doubt such language became routinized and familiar, so that it came to mean "thanks, praise," and for some, that the language should mean more than that is unthinkable. Behind the familiar language, however, is a religious sense that on occasion YHWH is also diminished and receives new energy from the community that worships. Such rhetoric alludes to the vulnerability and fragility of God, who is enhanced by human agents who may give back something of the power of life to God. Such a transposition, undoubtedly present in the rhetoric of the text, may lead to a reconsideration of the significance of praise in worship

and may provide a glimpse of the God in whom Christians claim to see weakness on the cross on Good Friday.

In any case, in a world of technological control and cause-and-effect reasoning, that the power for life is given in other ways—interpersonally, sacramentally, hiddenly—is worth pondering. Life is seen in this transmission to be more than food and the body more than clothing (see Matt. 6:25). Food and clothing can be secured more directly, but life is given in a manner of generosity that defies all familiar explanations. In its text, Israel knows what is to be said about the gift of life; knowing, still, Israel cannot or will not say it in clear, explanatory terms, because the power of life is not a commodity to be explained or controlled . . . only uttered and given.

References: Mitchell, C. W., *The Meaning of BRK "to Bless" in the Old Testament* (SBLDS 95; Atlanta: Scholars Press, 1987); Westermann, Claus, *Blessing in the Bible and the Life of the Church* (OBT; Philadelphia: Fortress Press, 1978).

Book of the Covenant "Book of the Covenant" is the phrase used by scholars to designate the collection of commandments in Exod. 21:1–23:33. Its intentionality is indicated by the introductory formula of 21:1. The text receives its name from a reference in Exod. 24:7 to a "book of the covenant." Connecting 24:7 and its nomenclature to the formulation in 21:1–23:33 is convenient, even if the connection is only intended in the belated development of the tradition.

This collection is commonly thought to date from an early period in Israel's life; the grouping is surely the earliest of any of the collections of law now featured in the Torah. Part of the collection seems to have arisen from and been designed for a small, face-to-face agricultural community in which concern can exist for the cow or the sheep of a neighbor (Exod. 22:10–13). Other parts of the collection, however, offer a very different perspective, one that can hardly be assigned to village life.

This collection is of interest because it evidences some of the earliest and defining concerns of Israel's social formation, which the creation of a collection of case laws addressed. On the one hand, one can see some of the earliest impetus toward neighborly—humanitarian—concerns. That the very first statute limits bond-slavery and related indebtedness is surely significant. This remarkable provision was evidently intended to undermine the entire debt economy and eventuated in the "year of remission," as formulated in Deuteronomy 15:1–18. Note also the remarkable commitment to justice for the socially vulnerable—resident alien, widow, orphan—in Exodus 22:21–27, with the direct sanction of YHWH [see SOJOURNER, WIDOW]. In Exodus 23:6–9, moreover, the demand for equitable justice became a cornerstone for the entire social construction of ancient Israel (see Deut. 16:18–20).

On the other hand, the collection also reflects a tradition of harsh communitarianism that is singularly concerned to protect the community—that is, to submit individual entitlement to the perceived well-being of the whole. Exodus 21:15–17 contains a small series of commands that are sweepingly apodictic (not framed as case law) and that point without qualification to capital punishment (see also 22:18–20). In Exodus 21:22–25, moreover, the most complete statement of the law of retaliation (*lex talionis*) given anywhere in the Bible scripture is articulated. Perhaps the eye-for-an-eye formula means to say "not more than an eye for an eye," as is often suggested; in any case, the penalty is uncompromising and without qualification. In Exodus 21:26–27, some eyes and

some teeth are even more valuable and better protected than others. The implication is that after the general principle of retaliation is stated, more specific adjudication is still necessary. The inclusion of vv. 26–27 suggests that the legal question is more complicated than conventional, hard-nosed "law and order" might suggest.

The unmistakable tension between covenantal-humanitarian provisions and absolute harshness pervades the ongoing legal horizon of ancient Israel and is perhaps inescapable in any sustained legal tradition. (One can observe the same tension in current U.S. debates about capital punishment as the question variously concerns the relative deserts of the perpetrator and the victim, as well as the legitimate interests of the community.)

Alongside these two perspectives, which express the extreme options for social formation and maintenance, this law collection also includes a number of case rulings that are more or less commonsense adjudications about how neighbors are to get along and settle disputes when interests clearly conflict (Exod. 21:18–21, 28–36; 22:1–7). The collection focuses, at the end, on Sabbath rules for the rest of the land (23:10–11) and rest for the community (23:12–13), as well as a provision for periodic festivals that became the beginning of a liturgical calendar designed to enhance the self-conscious identity of the community (23:14–17; see Deut. 16:1–17) [see FESTIVALS]. The collection concludes with three absolute provisions for the public conduct of Israel in order to acknowledge Israel's difference from its cultural-religious environment in Canaan.

The collection began most probably as an independent corpus that arose as an accumulation of court precedents and ethical teachings in something like a village environment. Theological awareness is operative in the corpus, but the accent is upon pragmatic requirements and limitations for organizing a small political economy for the well-being of all of its members. The practical ordering necessary for such a community imposed firm limits on the conduct of its members. The ordering that arises from specific cases is reinforced by appeal to the authorizing will of YHWH, as in Exodus 22:23–24, 27. The mention of YHWH, however, is not as strong as might be expected, because actual reference to YHWH is sparse indeed. Likely we are to understand that the corpus grows out of social practice that was not, in the first instant, troubled by or interested in theological rationale.

While the collection was likely freestanding and arose within a particular community of practice, the present location of the text within scripture is important. Scholars have noticed that Exodus 19–24 constitutes a special section of scripture in which the primary transactions of Mt. Sinai take place; Exodus 19–24 is thus dubbed by scholars "The Sinai Pericope." This unit of text is bounded by chapter 19, which initiates the transaction of YHWH and Israel at Sinai, and by chapter 24, the enactment of the covenant—the sealing of the covenant (vv. 3–8) that then makes possible a direct encounter with YHWH on Mt. Sinai (vv. 9–18). Chapters 19 and 24 provide the context for the "book of the covenant" in the final form of the text. Or, to reverse the statement, the "book of the covenant" has now been inserted into the "covenant pericope," so that this early collection of commandments is placed just next to the Decalogue of Exod. 20:1–17 [see THE DECALOGUE].

Terming the collection the "book of the covenant" means that it is taken as the first body of law that moves the general principles of the Decalogue toward the specifics of lived reality. In its present form, the "book of the covenant" may be understood as the earliest exposition in ancient Israel of the Ten Commandments, a means whereby general Torah principles come down to cases [see TORAH]. The "book of the covenant" does not in fact relate directly to the Decalogue, but in its present form it serves that purpose and shows how the covenant of Sinai is to be implemented in the actuality of a lived human neighborhood.

This resituation of an independent legal corpus to serve a canonical purpose is a powerful example of how the reinterpretive process worked in ancient Israel and continues to work in the Bible.

The "book of the covenant" is not to be considered in isolation, but rather as an important contribution to the dynamism of Torah interpretation. The "book of the covenant" lives close to the Decalogue; at the same time a great deal of study indicates that the "book of the covenant" provided the thematics for the development of the legal corpus of Deuteronomy 12–25, which is later, more fully developed, and much more influential in biblical interpretation. Thus the "book of the covenant" is a component in an enormously complex process of biblical law.

Worth noting is the suggestion of Erhard Gerstenberger that the "book of the covenant" became the impetus for the reform of Hezekiah (2 Chr. 29–31), just as Deuteronomy became the impetus for the reform of Josiah (Deut. 22–23) [see REFORM OF HEZEKIAH, REFORM OF JOSIAH]. This novel and speculative hypothesis is an interesting illustration of the way in which older tradition in the Old Testament may continue to exercise important impact upon the development of always newer tradition.

References: Albertz, Rainer, *A History of Israelite Religion in the Old Testament Period*, vol. 1, *From the Beginnings to the End of the Monarchy* (OTL; Louisville, Ky.: Westminster John Knox Press, 1994), 180–86; Crüsemann, Frank, *The Torah: Theology and Social History of Old Testament Law* (Edinburgh: T. & T. Clark, 1996), 109–200; Hanson, Paul D., "The Theological Significance of Contradiction within the Book of the Covenant," *Canon and Authority: Essays in Old Testament Religion and Theology*, ed. George W. Coats and Burke O. Long (Philadelphia: Fortress Press, 1977), 110–31; Knight, Douglas A., "Village Law and the Book of the Covenant," in *"A Wise and Discerning Mind": Essays in Honor of Burke O. Long*, ed. Saul Olyan and Robert C. Culley (Providence, R.I.: Brown Judaic Studies, 2000); Marshall, J. W., *Israel and the Book of the Covenant* (Atlanta: Scholars Press, 1993); Patrick, Dale, *Old Testament Law* (Atlanta: John Knox Press, 1985), chap. 4; Sprinkle, J. M., *"The Book of the Covenant": A Literary Approach* (JSOTSup 174; Sheffield: Sheffield Academic Press, 1994).

■ ■ ■

Canaanites The term "Canaanite" refers to the population that already occupied the territory that Israel came to regard as the land that YHWH promised to them. The Canaanites were thus competitors for a contested land and culturally and religiously regarded as a threatening, unacceptable "other" to Israel.

The term "Canaan" refers to territory, so that the primary use of "Canaan" in the Old Testament addresses the land, the specific territory that became "the Holy Land" in conventional Christian piety (for example, Gen. 11:31; 12:5; 13:12; 16:3). The Canaanites most likely did not form an ethnically distinct group, although the inhabitants of the land, as distinct from the Philistines, were surely Semites. Most scholars believe that in every aspect of racial, ethnic, linguistic, and cultural development, the Canaanites and early Israelites were indistinguishable.

The term "Canaanite" in the Old Testament is ideological, mostly referring to two matters wherein the general population is unlike Israel. First, from a religious standpoint, an elaborate and developed narrative of the gods of Canaan must have functioned liturgically with reference to agricultural seasons of planting and reaping and the dormancy of the off-season. This mythological material is known from the tablets of ancient Ugarit; its narrative features a series of gods and goddesses, including El, the High God, and Baal, the young, assertive god [see DIVINE COUNCIL]. While Old Testament faith seems to have had no quarrel with El and may have understood YHWH as an articulation of El, the defining god of Canaanite religion from Israel's perspective is Baal (notice the juxtaposition of YHWH and *Elohim* [= El?] in the Genesis narratives). Israel's text is immensely hostile to Baal and all that he signifies theologically as a challenge and alternative to YHWH (see, above all, 1 Kgs. 18:17–40).

Second, the sociopolitical, economic organization of the land of Canaan was a feudal system of city-states presided over by city-kings, a privileged elite who lived off the surplus produce of the agricultural peasants who were menial and exploited members of the economy. A number of scholars suggest that the term "Canaanite" refers to the privileged managers and beneficiaries of a feudal economic system, and that Israel's opposition to "the Canaanites," is opposition to the exploitative system that controlled the land and to those who managed and benefitted from that control. In this hypothesis, the early "tribes" of Israel are constituted by the peasants who refused exploitative subordination to the Canaanite city-kings. The antithesis of "Canaanite-Israelite" would thus concern the class distinction of exploited producers and elitist consumers. The conclusion follows that neither "Canaanite" nor "Israelite" is an ethnic term, but both are to some extent ideological and refer to economic location, though in each case the economic location was religiously marked and legitimated.

The religious enterprise termed "Canaanite religion" and the power arrangements of the "Canaanite political economy" can be distinguished from each other. In fact, however, the two are of a piece, and "Baal" comes to represent and embody what is most unbearable for "Israelite" peasants in the economic arrangements. Conversely Yahwism is to be understood as a theological commitment, but one immediately and intimately linked to a theory of political economy that moves away from abusive stratification in the direction of a covenantal communitarianism.

The best approach, then, is to understand "Canaan" and "Canaanites" as ideological references to a total system of social reality to which the movement of Yahwism was profoundly opposed. In reading particular texts about the Canaanites, incidental and anecdotal data about them likely is best understood in terms of a clash of systems that touches every facet of life, from the religious to the economic and political. The Yahwistic movement of Israel is also best understood as a revolutionary challenge to the conventional ordering of society, so that YHWH gives warrant to the sociopolitical, economic upheaval embodied in Israel as a sustained challenge to the status quo—a challenge that is enacted, according to Israel's memory, in violent ways. The purgation of Baal, for example, in 2 Kings 10 is not to be taken as a thinly religious act, but as an act that intends to challenge and displace a total public system of production and distribution by attacking its principal symbolism.

Scholars agree that the biblical rendering of the "Canaanites" is an ideological rendering that is far removed from the historical. In the conquest narrative of the book of Joshua and in the polemics of the book of Deuteronomy, the Canaanites are thus portrayed as the other in the most destructive terms possible.

This presentation of the Canaanites, moreover, is available in contemporary polemics whereby Israel's ideological abhorrence of the Canaanites is readily redeployed upon the Palestinians, who constitute the contemporary challenge to Israelite claims as both Jews and Christians typically understand them.

References: Ahlstrom, Gosta W., *The History of Ancient Palestine* (Minneapolis: Fortress Press, 1993); Freedman, David Noel, and David Frank Graf, eds., *Palestine in Transition: The Emergence of Ancient Israel* (The Social World of Biblical Antiquity Series 2; Sheffield: Almond Press, 1983); Gottwald, Norman K., *The Politics of Ancient Israel* (Library of Ancient Israel; Louisville, Ky.: Westminster John Knox Press, 2001); idem, *The Tribes of Yahweh: A Sociology of the Religion of Liberated Israel, 1250–1050 B.C.* (Maryknoll, N.Y.: Orbis Books, 1979); Lemche, N. P., *The Canaanites and Their Land* (JSOTSup 110; Sheffield: Sheffield Academic Press, 1991); Levenson, Jon D., "Is There a Counterpart in the Hebrew Bible to New Testament Antisemitism?" *Journal of Ecumenical Studies* 22 (1985): 242–60; Thompson, Thomas L., *The Bible in History: How Writers Create a Past* (New York: Basic Books, 1999); Whitelam, Keith W., *The Invention of Ancient Israel: The Silencing of Palestinian History* (London: Routledge, 1996).

Canon   The term "canon" refers to the set of normative books (scrolls) that have come to constitute scripture for a believing community and that are regarded as normative for the life, faith, and ethics of the faith community. (Lately the term "canon" has also come to refer to the normative list of literature constituting the Western literary-cultural tradition, thus "The Western Canon.")

A great deal of scholarly energy has been invested in understanding the historical processes by which the canon of the Hebrew Bible was constituted. The Hebrew Bible is conventionally divided into three parts—the Torah, "the prophetic canon," and "the Writings"—each of which arrived at scriptural authority at a different time and with a varying degree of authority for the community. First, consensus holds that the Torah (the first five books of the Hebrew Bible = Pentateuch) arrived at normative status at the earliest time, perhaps linked to the movement of Ezra in the fifth century B.C.E. This corpus is the most authoritative scripture text for Judaism, a tradition linked to the authority of Moses.

The second part of the canon, the "prophetic canon," was apparently in place by 180 B.C.E. (see Ben Sirach, a wisdom book from the second century, also called Ecclesiasticus), and is constituted, in Jewish parlance, by four "former prophets" (Joshua, Judges, Samuel, Kings) and four "latter prophets" (Isaiah, Jeremiah, Ezekiel, and the Twelve Minor Prophets, the latter represented in a single scroll). Of particular interest is that in Jewish categories, the books of Joshua, Judges, Samuel, and Kings are reckoned as "prophetic," and not as "historical," as Christians conventionally understand them.

The third part of the canon is "the Writings," a more or less miscellaneous collection that includes Psalms, Job, Proverbs, the Five Scrolls (Megilloth: Ruth, Song of Solomon, Ecclesiastes, Lamentations, Esther)—the latter used in Judaism for particular festival occasions—plus Daniel (not reckoned in the Hebrew order as a "prophet"), 1 and 2 Chronicles, Ezra, and Nehemiah. (John Barton has proposed that instead of a three-part canon we should understand the Hebrew Bible in only two parts—"Torah" and everything else that is reckoned as "Prophets.")

The conventional approach is that the third canon, and consequently the entire canon in its three parts, was in place by and verified in the Council of Jabneh (Jamnia) in 90 C.E. Such a claim, however, is endlessly obscure and disputed. Such a moment of decision about the canon is reflected in later Jewish sources, but current scholarship has concluded that it never in fact occurred. That the "list" of "authorized books" emerged in ways hidden from us over a long period of time is certain; until very late, moreover, as attested in the Dead Sea Scrolls, the list was around the edges not stable, even though its core claims were fixed very early. Even the text of several books of the canon were quite fluid until comparatively recently. Thus the Dead Sea Scrolls gave clear evidence that much textual variation was possible as late as the New Testament period. While we may trace in rough ways the "official" moments of canonization, in fact the process of accepting literature as normative is one of test and use in the actual practice of the community, after which may come formal recognition and verification. In any case, near the time of the turn to the Christian era, Judaism had a relatively fixed list of normative books. The matter of textual stability should not be overstated, however, nor must one imagine that in the formative period of the canon even only "one text" existed. Various competing groups in Judaism held to different canons, and special notice should be taken of the Samaritans, a Jewish sect that accepted only the Torah as canon.

The three canons of Torah, Prophets, and Writings are in Hebrew called *Torah, Nebiim,* and *Kethubim.* Taking the first letter of each—*T-N-K*—and creating the term *Tanak* presents a neutral way of referring to the complete canonical list.

An alternative version of Jewish canon arose in the Greek-speaking Judaism of Alexandria, which produced an alternative list of books. This Greek "Old Testament" is called the Septuagint ("Seventy" = LXX) because of a legendary tale that seventy-two translators worked separately and independently on the translation into Greek, and when completed, all seventy-two translations agreed to the finest detail, thus attesting to the inspiration and reliability of the translation as a normative text. Of the LXX and its use, we may make four observations:

1. The LXX was not determined in its scope by what came to be the settled list of the normative Hebrew text. More inclusive than the Hebrew list, the Septuagint includes materials such as Tobit, Judith, and 1–4 Maccabees. The scope of the LXX, moreover, remained open and unstable for a very long time.

2. The order of books in the LXX is different from that of the normative Hebrew list, apparently the result of an attempt to arrange books in something like "historical sequence." A quite noticeable difference is that the "five scrolls" (Ruth, Song of Solomon, Lamentations, Ecclesiastes, Esther), grouped together as festival scrolls in the Hebrew rendering, are distributed amidst other books in the LXX in what can be viewed as an attempt at historical placement.

3. Christian appropriation of the Jewish Bible as scripture of the church followed the ordering of the LXX and not the Hebrew Bible—that is, more or less a historical ordering. Note especially that the LXX places the prophets at the end of the canon, concluding with Malachi. This ordering accented Messianic expectation, an approach that the early church readily assumed.

4. Protestantism, following Luther, retained the more restrictive list of the Hebrew canon, even while following the Greek ordering of books. In his own interpretive work, however, Luther famously rejected the legitimacy of even the New Testament books of James and Revelation. Roman Catholicism, more consistent, accepted both the Greek ordering of books and the more comprehensive list. In the days of deep dispute between Roman Catholicism and Reformation traditions, the extent of the canon was a ground for interpretive dispute; scriptural foundations were found for theological claims in the larger canon of Roman Catholicism that were not present in the more restrictive usage of the Reformation churches. Both parties to the dispute could thus argue from a different canon that a particular belief or practice was or was not scripturally based.

More recently, theological shape and intent of the canon have received great attention. The canon, in this perspective, is not simply an authorized list (which it is), but also a theological statement on its own. Most important in this regard is the work of Brevard Childs, who argued in 1979 that each book of the Old Testament has been deliberately placed in order to make a normative theological statement. More recently, in 1993, Childs has moved his understanding of canon closer to authorized church reading to propose that a "canonical reading" of the text is to be done in conformity to the church's "Rule of Faith." In making this argument, Childs returns to the difficult, disputatious sixteenth-century question of the relation of scripture to tradition, appearing to give the upper hand to tradition in the church's capacity to read scripture rightly. James Sanders offers a more dynamic understanding of the canonical process, urging that it features an interpretive propensity toward the claim of the one true God, but that claim is not a flat, one-dimensional imposition of that view. Rather the issue of monotheism must be seen in relation to a text that is rich and complex, and which admits of no simple or single canonical reading. In any case, the newer discussion of canon assures that theological intentionality in the formation of normative literature is of immense importance, so that canonicity is not simply a historical question.

Perhaps in response to a heavy focus on the theological intentionality of the canonizing process—which is, of course not theologically disinterested—a more critical perspective on canonization is also currently underway. This perspective focuses on the fact that the canonizing process is essentially a political process, whereby those who controlled the process imposed their hegemonic interpretation upon the faith community and effectively excluded and silenced other interpretive voices to which they objected. Certainly, exclusion from canon was an effective and durable mode of silencing contrary opinion. This perspective on canon of course lives in deep tension with interpreters who place themselves inside canonical perspective and view the process of canon as a valid fence for true teaching to the exclusion of false teaching.

Separating the claim of true interpretation from political imposition is impossible, and a judgment on the matter reflects, inescapably and characteristically, the interpreter's social location and horizon. In any case, canon is a means whereby "true teaching" is articulated and boundaries are set to preclude "false teaching." The canon, in its final form, thus sets the limit and establishes the perspective within which ongoing, valid theological interpretation take place.

The actual extent of the literature, however, allows for wide latitude and does not necessarily require the conclusions urged by the closest readings of what is termed "canonical reading." Even inside the canon, room exists for dispute among readings, and simply making the claim of "canonical" does not of itself demonstrate the case. Garrett Green, moreover, has nicely articulated a notion of "canonical imagination" whereby ongoing constructive theological work is undertaken with imaginative openness, but within the parameters indicated by the normative literature. While "canon" settles some questions, its authority and claim open a field for continued dispute in interpretive practice within the community of faith.

References: Abraham, William J., *Canon and Criterion in Christian Theology: From the Fathers to Feminism* (Oxford: Clarendon Press, 1998); Alter, Robert, *Canon and Creativity: Modern Writing and the Authority of Scripture* (New Haven, Conn.: Yale University Press, 2000); Barton, John, *Oracles of God: Perceptions of Ancient Prophecy in Israel after the Exile* (Oxford: Oxford University Press, 1986); Bloom, Harold, *The Western Canon: The Books and School of the Ages* (New York: Harcourt Brace, 1994); Brueggemann, Walter, *The Creative Word: Canon as a Model for Biblical Education* (Philadelphia: Fortress Press, 1982); Childs, Brevard S., *Biblical Theology of the Old and New Testaments: Theological Reflection on the Christian Bible* (Minneapolis: Fortress Press, 1993); idem, *Introduction to the Old Testament as Scripture* (Philadelphia: Fortress Press, 1979); Green, Garrett, *Imagining God: Theology and the Religious Imagination* (San Francisco: Harper & Row, 1989); Leiman, S., *The Canonization of Hebrew Scripture: The Talmudic and Midrashic Evidence* (Hamden,

28   Chaos

Conn.: Academy of Arts & Sciences, 1991);
Saebo, Magne, *On the Way to the Canon: Creative Tradition History in the Old Testament* (JSOTSup 191; Sheffield: Sheffield Academic Press, 1998); Sanders, James A., "Adaptable for Life: The Nature and Function of Canon," in *Magnalia Dei: The Mighty Acts of God: Essays on the Bible and Archaeology in Memory of G. Ernest Wright*, ed. Frank Moore Cross et al. (Garden City, N.Y.: Doubleday, 1976), 531–60; idem, "The Exile and Canon Formation," in *Exile: Old Testament, Jewish, and Christian Connections*, ed. James M. Scott (Supplements to the Journal for the Study of Judaism 56; Leiden: Brill, 1997), 37–61; idem, *Torah and Canon* (Philadelphia: Fortress Press, 1972); Wisse, Ruth R., *The Modern Jewish Canon* (New York: Free Press, 2000).

Chaos In much of the Old Testament, YHWH as creator is fully sovereign and in control of all reality; creation is consequently a well-ordered, stable environment for life and well-being. Against that portrayal of reality, however, numerous texts witness to the power of chaos, a force and reality that are loose in the world, opposed to the rule of YHWH, and therefore life-threatening. Chaos is to be understood not simply as a situation of disorder but as an active agency that is engaged in challenging the rule of YHWH, undermining the possibility for life, and so seeking to negate the prospect for well-being in the world. In articulating such a force of negation, Israel doubtlessly drew upon the religious traditions and mythological formulations that long predated its own theology. Theological honesty and seriousness caused Israel to make use of such earlier traditions.

The most important phrasing for this active negating power is *tôhûwabôhû*, perhaps an onomatopoeic phrase that itself means "to sound the sounds of confusion,"and familiarly translated in the KJV as "formless and void" (Gen. 1:2 [see CRE-ATION]). As a consequence creation, as celebrated in Genesis 1, was not "out of

nothing" (= *ex nihilo*), but instead dealt with the sovereign ordering of the formless stuff that was already there and that resisted YHWH's ordering. The notion of creation out of nothing is a common claim in Christian teaching, but no clear textual evidence of such a notion occurs until 2 Maccabees 7:28, a very late text. The Old Testament itself has no interest in the origin of such formless stuff but begins in the recognition that the stuff was there, is always there, and is always being tamed and ordered by YHWH the creator, whose work is ordering. The capacity of Israel to imagine and articulate such a primordial dualism (that is, active hostility to the rule of YHWH) partly depends upon the antecedent mythological sources; but that capacity likely also reflects the lived reality of Israel: that in its lived experience resides a negating power of death that is immensely powerful and that seeks to distort God-given life. The other familiar text where this power is recognized as a force is in Psalm 46:2–3, in which Israel expresses complete confidence in YHWH's capacity to withstand that pervasive threat. While the power of chaos is stated most often in public and cosmic terms, in the Psalms of individual lament, the speaker often speaks as though in the grip of a power that would kill (see Pss. 18:4; 55:4).

Two important factors in the notion of chaos emerge in some parts of the Old Testament. First, the cosmic, primordial force of chaos is sometimes treated historically and said to be present in nameable historical form. In Psalm 87:4, for example, Egypt is mentioned in parallel terms with Assyria, but under the name "Rahab," the evil sea monster. The reference is historical but by using the mythic name, Egypt (and Pharaoh) are reckoned to be a force for chaos in the world. And of course, in the narrative of Exodus 7–11, Pharaoh is a force that destabilizes the "natural" world of the creation. In Jeremiah 4–6, moreover, the poetic allusion is likely to Babylon, but Babylon is assigned the attributes of chaos. The exile of the sixth century, more generally, was an acute historical experience of disorder for which the rhetoric of cosmic chaos was credible. Thus in Isaiah 51:9–10 an imperative prayer is addressed to YHWH who had defeated chaos and who now must face Babylon. In Isaiah 54:9, exile is likened to the flood, a great exhibit of the force of chaos.

Second, while chaos is sometimes understood as an active force that challenges YHWH, in other texts YHWH is the one who rules chaos and who can mobilize chaos as a tool for governance (see Ps. 77:19; Isa. 5:26–29; Ezek. 38:19–20). In the flood narrative of Genesis 6–9 and in the song of Exodus 15, the chaotic waters clearly function at the behest of YHWH, in order to enact YHWH's will. In Genesis 9:8–17 (see also Isa. 54:9–10), YHWH'S promise of fidelity assures Israel in the face of the threat of chaos. Psalm 104:24–27, moreover, exhibits chaos (the evil sea monster) as YHWH's plaything. The parade example for this motif is Jeremiah 4:23–26, in which the poetry details the step-by-step undoing of creation and the return of chaos, but at the behest of YHWH according to YHWH's anger.

A serious theological recognition of chaos in biblical faith opens the Bible beyond the conventional, simplistic preoccupation with sin and guilt that so pervades our society. Such a recognition suggests that the large theological issue to be considered in our culture is not some small moralistic question, but the largest issue of the ordering of life in the world that can readily be seen to be at risk. This motif of biblical faith has been neglected in much recent interpretation. Its recovery is important, for theological interpreta-tion in the West must now deal with the collapse of the "old order" that is widely experienced morally, economically, and politically as chaos. Biblical faith is an immense resource both for acknowledging the present reality of chaos in God's world and for the evangelical assurance that God governs chaos (as in Ps. 104:24–26).

Beyond the scope of the Old Testament, we find in ancient Jewish texts regarding the origin of chaos and its future power in the world much speculation that frequently takes apocalyptic form. In the Old Testament itself, however, Israel largely resisted such speculation and stayed with the theological claims of the two realities of chaos and God's governance. In the long run, God's governance will prevail. In many short runs, Israel knows about the palpable power of chaos as a present reality not yet brought under God's control. Christians should not too glibly imagine that the New Testament settles such questions, for the texts about chaos in the Old Testament live close to the continued lived reality of disorder in the world. To be sure, Israel lives in hope, but that hope is not romantic denial about the negations of life that continue to stalk the earth.

References: Barth, Karl, *Church Dogmatics* III/3 (Edinburgh: T. & T. Clark, 1960), 289–368; Childs, Brevard S., "The Enemy from the North and the Chaos Tradition," *JBL* 78 (1959): 187–98; Fishbane, Michael, "Jer. 4:23–26 and Job 3:1–13: A Recovered Use of the Creation Pattern, " *VT* 21 (1971): 151–67; Levenson, Jon D., *Creation and the Persistence of Evil: The Jewish Drama of Divine Omnipotence* (San Francisco: Harper, 1985).

The Chronicler The term "Chronicler" refers to the person, persons, or tradition of interpretation that produced the books of 1 and 2 Chronicles. Scholars had long thought that the work of the Chronicler included the texts of Ezra and Nehemiah, but opinion now regards those texts as distinct from Chronicles and from a different hand. The Chronicler, known only in 1 and 2 Chronicles, rewrote and reinterpreted the historical memory of Israel in the Persian period, in the fifth or perhaps fourth century B.C.E. The writer's intent was to let ancient memory of Israel memory connect to and inform the practice and understanding of Judaism in the Persian period, after leading Jews had returned from exile in Babylon and reconstituted a viable community of worship together with a limited form of self-governance.

The Chronicler doubtlessly used and transformed older source materials. Specifically the Chronicler relied upon and appropriated the work of the Deuteronomist [see DEUTERONOMIC THEOLOGY]. His use of that material, however, went through a process of extensive editing by means of which the material was transposed into a quite new statement. Because the work uses and echoes the Deuteronomists, the common assumption held that the Deuteronomic history itself is more reliable than is the Chronicler, and, in fact, that the Chronicler offers something of a religious fantasy that played fast and loose with "historical facts" [see HISTORY]. De Vries terms the portrayal of the Chronicler "ideal Israel." For this and other reasons, the Chronicler has been studied little in the long history of scholarship. (One other likely reason is that this tradition is largely preoccupied with cultic, liturgical matters, a subject of little interest to the Protestants who have dominated scholarship and whom questions of "history" have mesmerized.) A text that is viewed as playing fast and loose with history is of little

interest to scholars focused on historical questions.

More recently, however, increasing numbers of scholars think that the Chronicler was not simply a poor, unreliable, second-rate version of the Deuteronomist, but rather that the Chronicler also used sources not available to the Deuteronomist. As a result, the Chronicler is now considered to be a more reliable historical source than previously thought. (That shift in opinion also entails the recognition that the Deuteronomist is also not "good history," but is, in its commitment to an interpretive *Tendenz*, as tilted in its historical rendition as is the Chronicler.) The Chronicler may now be viewed as something of a reliable historical source, though great care must be taken in how specific data are handled and how they are to be adjudicated.

The Chronicler is of special interest as a study in the endless process of Judaism whereby old memories, traditions, and texts are endlessly reformulated in a "culture of interpretation," in order to connect tradition to the current circumstance of the interpreting community. From an "objective" point of view—that is, from the notion of Enlightenment rationality—such a process is highly suspect. But when interpretation is viewed as a dynamic process of serious faith practiced with uncommon theological imagination, these much neglected texts become both an important resource for understanding the faith of Judaism and an invitation to engage in the interpretive process that is inescapable in this "religion of the book."

The most interesting and important matter for appreciating the Chronicler's interpretive achievement is to notice the defining features of the text. (Fortunately we have the Deuteronomist for contrast, but our entry into the Chronicler should not be with any privileging of the Deuteronomist, as has been customary.) Among the defining features of the Chronicler are the following six:

1. The Chronicler begins with a long genealogy that goes all the way back to Adam (1 Chr. 1:1) and moves through a long series of names to a final paragraph on Saul, his son Jonathan, and his grandson Meribaal (1 Chr. 9:35–44). While this text contains interesting data that has been used to recover the history and pedigree of the priestly houses mentioned, we should not miss the large purview of the entire unit. The genealogy (not unlike Luke 3:23–38) makes a grand connection between the specificities of history and the cosmic drama of creation, so that the specifically remembered names in Israel link directly to the history of the world.

2. Other than the sparse note of 9:35–44, Saul receives only one chapter of attention (1 Chr. 10), and that only to report his death. The verdict of 10:13–14 serves to condemn Saul and to remove him from the scene, and so to open the way for David. This writer deftly omits from the narrative the long, troubled encounter between Saul and David given in the narratives of 1 Samuel. For this "historian," the story to be told is only the story of David; Saul is scarcely even an inconvenience in proceeding to the main character.

3. David occupies all of 1 Chronicles 11–29, which culminates in Solomon's coronation. Everything is focused on David. This David, however, is not the ambiguous character of the books of Samuel, but a single-minded leader who is preoccupied with building the temple and making provision for its right and faithful conduct. (The memory of Uriah and Bathsheba, a defining narrative in the books of Samuel, receives here no attention at all.)

Thus 1 and 2 Chronicles likely give the David that was needed and readily imag-

ined in the Persian period when the small community of Jerusalem had no serious political prospect and was transformed by necessity into a community of worship. In that environment, the maintenance and well-being of the community depended upon right worship. While surely vigorous and able functionaries were available to guide proper worship (commonly thought to be choral guilds with considerable power, such as the Levites, and the sons of Asaph and of Korah, groups that are mentioned in the superscriptions of the Psalms; see Pss. 76; 77; 78; 84; 85), David is the one who authorizes the community for this crucial work.

At the culmination of the David report, the king engages in a great act of liturgy, a prayer of gratitude whereby he cedes all credit for his success to the generosity of YHWH:

> Blessed are you, O LORD, the God of our ancestor Israel, forever and ever. Yours, O LORD, are the greatness, the power, the glory, the victory, and the majesty; for all that is in the heavens and on the earth is yours; yours is the kingdom, O LORD, and you are exalted as head above all. Riches and honor come from you, and you rule over all. In your hand are power and might; and it is in your hand to make great and to give strength to all. And now, our God, we give thanks to you and praise your glorious name. (1 Chr. 29:10–13)

David's submissive piety culminates in his "decreasing" as YHWH "increases":

> But who am I, and what is my people, that we should be able to make this freewill offering? For all things come from you, and of your own have we given you. (v. 14)

This concluding statement has become a familiar and treasured offertory statement in much of the church, signifying that the true ground of life in faith is in gratitude enacted as stewardship. The David who speaks here is uncompromised by the cunning self-serving of which he is seen capable in the books of Samuel.

4. Not surprisingly, Solomon, the temple builder, receives extended coverage, though not as much as his father who organized the entire project of the temple (2 Chr. 1–9).

5. The royal history of Jerusalem from the death of Solomon (922) to the fall of Jerusalem (587) is narrated through the recital of the Davidic line (2 Chr. 10–36). Unlike the Deuteronomist, the Chronicler has no real interest in the northern monarchy. The northern kings are mentioned only incidentally as they bear upon the Southern history (as in 13:2–20; 16:1–6; and 18:1–34). The Chronicler does not bother with a sequenced recital of the northern kings who are of no significance for the reading of the past. Two northern prophets—Micaiah (18:8–27) and Elijah (21:12–15)—are mentioned, but their function in the narrative is greatly reduced from what we know in the narrative in Kings. The story line moves singularly toward its denouement in the destruction of Jerusalem (36:17–21), the spectacular reforms of Hezekiah (29–31) and Josiah (34–35) notwithstanding.

6. Of exceptional interest is the ending of the work of the Chronicler (2 Chr. 36:22–23). The Chronicler does not include the enigmatic ending of the Deuteronomist (2 Kgs. 25:27–30; see Jer. 52:31–34), but looks with certainty beyond that historical notation to the invitation of the Persian regime. The final paragraph of the Chronicler may be its signature articulation; the most important matter for the Chronicler is the readiness of Cyrus the Persian to have Jews, long since deported to Babylon, return home (see also Ezra 1–2). The decree of Cyrus opens the way for the return, the recovery of Jerusalem, and what was to become the reconstitution of Judaism. Cyrus has now authorized the return. In this telling who will respond and go up is not yet known:

Whoever is among you of all his people, may the Lord his God be with him! Let him go up. (2 Chr. 36:23)

Perhaps the Chronicler withholds data about the return. Perhaps the Chronicler wants us to recognize that the return was no widespread phenomenon, but depended upon the immense courage of elite leaders who would try again. In any case, the final paragraph is an unambiguous statement of hope and possibility deeply fixed on Judaism's new beginnings.

This ending is all the more spectacular when we notice that in the Hebrew canon, 2 Chronicles comes last in the list of books [see CANON]. As a result these verses are the final verses of the Hebrew Bible. The last thing to be said is that Jews can come home! For a Christian reader, this claim needs to be fully appreciated, even today, given the Jewish diaspora and the state of Israel. Beyond that, we may ponder how differently the canon ends if we contrast this Jewish ending with the ending of the Christian Bible in Malachi 4:5–6.

Two texts in Chronicles—1 Chronicles 4:9–10 and 2 Chronicles 7:14—currently receive attention in North American popular religion. The prayer of Jabez, 1 Chronicles 4:9–10, is much used and celebrated as an easy formula for material success. Second Chronicles 7:14 is used to make moralistic urgings of the narrowest kind in the service of nationalism. Both contemporary appropriations suggest (a) that the Chronicler is vulnerable to interpretive distortion because so little of the report is understood, and (b) current understanding and use of the Bible in popular U.S. religion is shamelessly ideological and embarrassingly jingoistic in the interest of materialism and nationalism of the most uncritical kind.

The Chronicler is an exercise in theological imagination. History is taken seriously, but history can be told in more than one way. The way taken here is to let the story-life of fidelity and infidelity touch down in a particular moment. The story line of scripture characteristically touches down specifically, each time different, each time with the specificity linked to the abiding reality of this God of creation, who gives words even to Gentiles like Cyrus.

References: Braun, R. L., "Solomon, the Chosen Temple Builder: The Significance of I Chronicles 22, 28, 29 for the Theology of the Chronicler," *JBL* 95 (1976): 581–90; idem, "Solomonic Apologetic in Chronicles," *JBL* 92 (1973): 502–14; Brettler, Marc Zvi, *The Creation of History in Ancient Israel* (London: Routledge, 1998); De Vries, Simon J., *1 and 2 Chronicles* (The Forms of the Old Testament Literature XI; Grand Rapids: Eerdmans, 1989); Japhet, S., *I and II Chronicles: A Commentary* (OTL; Louisville, Ky.: Westminster John Knox Press, 1993); Jones, Gwilym H., *1 and 2 Chronicles* (Old Testament Guides; Sheffield: Sheffield Academic Press, 1993); Myers, Jacob M., "The Kerygma of the Chronicler: History and Theology in the Service of Religion," *Interpretation* 20 (1966): 259–73; Newsome, J. D., "Toward a new Understanding of the Chronicler and His Purposes," *JBL* 94 (1975): 201–17; Rad, Gerhard von, *Old Testament Theology I* (San Francisco: Harper & Brothers, 1962), 347–54; idem, "The Levitical Sermons in I and II Chronicles," in *The Problem of the Hexateuch and Other Essays* (New York: McGraw-Hill, 1966), 267–80; Throntveit, M. A., *When Kings Speak: Royal Speech and Royal Prayer in Chronicles* (Chico, Calif.: Scholars Press, 1987); Williamson, Hugh G., *Israel in the Books of Chronicles* (Cambridge: Cambridge University Press, 1977); idem, *1 and 2 Chronicles* (NCB; Grand Rapids: Eerdmans, 1982).

Circumcision   The origin and early religious significance of circumcision elude us, though the practice clearly predates and had a farther reach than ancient Israel. Joshua 5:2–9 offers a narrative account of Israelite circumcision as the tribes entered the new land of promise. (I can only mention Exod. 4:24–26, which comments on circumcision, because the meaning of the text completely escapes current scholarship.) Clearly Genesis 17, a priestly text dated to the exile, is most important for a theological understanding of circumcision. In this text, circumcision is understood as a sign of the covenant, signifying that one is a party to YHWH's promises and requirements. We cannot overstate the importance of the function of a "sign" as understood in the priestly tradition, for the sign in some important sacramental way participates in the matter that it signs. (In the priestly tradition see, as well, the significance of the Sabbath [Gen. 2:1–4a] and the rainbow [Gen. 9:12].) Because the priestly text is commonly dated to the sixth-century exile, circumcision likely became a definitive sign of Jewishness only in the exile, a social circumstance when exilic Jews needed to distinguish themselves from the nations around them and when maintaining Jewish identity required great discipline and intentionality.

Circumcision thus became a distinguishing mark of Israel. The people of YHWH were thus set apart from the "uncircumcised," who were then treated with contempt as socially and theologically disqualified by the "circumcised"— the approved of YHWH. Principal among the uncircumcised are the Philistines who constitute in the Old Testament the paradigmatically dismissed "other" against whom Israel forged its own social identity (Judg. 14:3; 15:18; 1 Sam. 14:6; 17:26, 36; 31:4). More broadly, the same criterion is used for "otherness" that stands under a death sentence (Ezek. 28:10; 31:18; 32:19–32).

Of particular interest is Jeremiah 9:25–26, a text that contrasts circumcised Israel and a list of uncircumcised peoples. That contrast, however, takes a surprising turn and is a polemic not against the uncircumcised but against Israel who is "circumcised only in the foreskin" but "uncircumcised in heart." Thus the text makes a distinction between circumcision as a fleshly mark and circumcision as a serious theological identity. This move from the literal to the metaphorical opens the way for a broader use of circumcision as a metaphor:

circumcision of the heart (Lev. 26:41; Deut. 10:16; 30:6; Jer. 4:4)

circumcision of the ears (Jer. 6:10)

circumcision of the lips (Exod. 6:12, 30)

These texts use the notion of circumcision metaphorically to refer to organs (other than the penis) that are to function freshly in obedient responsiveness to the demands of YHWH's covenant. The usage suggests a means of making the organ more sensitive and responsive, so that circumcision is now removed from fleshly literalness to theological commitment.

Beyond the Old Testament, two important developments may be noted. First, in the Hellenistic world, circumcision was a sign of Jewishness that among some young Jewish males was an embarrassment; circumcision identified them as Jewish in the gymnasium and they wished not to be seen as odd when contrasted with the natural state of uncircumcision among men. Jews in Hellenistic context, as 1 Maccabees 1:15 reports, could restore the foreskin and so remove the mark of Jewish distinctiveness and awkwardness. Such a restoration of the foreskin, while a physical matter, also implied embarrassment about Jewish theological identity.

Second, Paul contrasted trust in the God of the Gospel with external acts of "the law" as a way of polemicizing against Judaism as an "external" religion. In the interest of this polemic, Paul dismisses circumcision as an irrelevant external mark (Rom. 2:25–29; Gal. 5:3, 6; 6:15; 1 Cor. 7:19). While his argument, in dispute with the Jews, seeks to cast the spiritual reality of Christian faith as superior to the crude physical mark of Judaism, in fact Paul is doing no more than reiterating the critical claims already articulated in Jeremiah 9:25–26 to which he apparently alludes in Galatians 5:6:

For in Christ Jesus neither circumcision nor uncircumcision counts for anything; the only thing that counts is faith working through love.

To Paul, as in Jeremiah 9:25–26, the external sign of covenant is without theological significance unless it matches and bespeaks a serious, intentional theological–covenantal passion.

The polemic against Jewish circumcision, however, need give Christians no aid or comfort, even though the long history of Christian anti-Semitism traded upon just such polemics. For the parallel to such external circumcision without theological commitment has been unmistakable in the Christian practice of baptism throughout the long history of Euro-American Christendom. For the most part, baptism has become an empty sign and does not function in any important way as a serious offer of an alternative identity in faith. Indeed the polemic against Christendom and its baptism, in the Mennonite tradition from as early as the sixteenth century, exposed baptism within Christendom as largely an empty sign. Christian practice thus shares with Judaism the perennial task of recovering its initiatory rite as a serious theological sign. To be sure, circumcision pertains only to male members of the Jewish community, but *mutatis mutandis*, the issue of serious theological identity is parallel among Jews and Christians.

References: Eilberg-Schwartz, Howard, *The Savage in Judaism: An Anthropology of Israelite Religion and Ancient Judaism* (Bloomington: Indiana University Press, 1990); Fox, Michael V., "The Sign of the Covenant: Circumcision in Light of the Priestly *'oth* Etiologies," *RB* 81 (1974): 557–96; Hays, Richard B., *Echoes of Scripture in the Letters of Paul* (New Haven, Conn.: Yale University Press, 1989), 34–83; Jobling, David, *1 Samuel* (Brit Olam; Studies in Hebrew Narrative and Poetry; Collegeville, Minn.: The Liturgical Press, 1998), 199–211; Neusner, Jacob, *The Enchantments of Judaism: Rites of Transformation from Birth through Death* (New York: Basic Books, 1987), 43–52.

Community   The theological constant of Israel's sense of community in the Old Testament is Israel's self-understanding as a people convened and given life by YHWH, summoned to live in faithful obedience and glad praise, and responsive to YHWH. In the broadest sense, covenant is an articulation of that defining relationship. Given that theological constant, however, Israel is, at the same time, a people who lived in history and was subject to all the vagaries of the historical process. The matter of community thus came to be interpreted and enacted in a rich variety of ways, given the dynamism of historical circumstance. A conventional approach is to treat the community of Israel in three successive circumstances.

First, prestate Israel, the period from Moses to David (immense problems of historicity notwithstanding), was organized in a tribal, segmented way. Each tribal or clan unit operated with a great deal of autonomy, sometimes in cooperation with other tribes, sometimes in tension or conflict with other tribes. The economy was agrarian and the social vision was at least communitarian if not egalitarian. Early Israel, defined by its commitment to Torah (which included identity-giving cultic practices) was no ethnic community (see Exod. 19–24; Josh. 24:1–28), but rather "a mixed crowd," drawn into the Yahwistic covenant from a variety of populations (see Exod. 12:38). The term "Hebrew," which connotes this mixed population, likely is a sociological term referring to people who lived precariously at the margins of society. This community consisted of diverse peoples drawn into a religious covenant, roughly sharing a precarious socioeconomic status and pledged to a radical social ethic congruent with that marginal social status. Late readers need not romanticize this community; the narrative of the book of Judges, for example, suggests enormous social stress within the community, even to the point of barbaric violence. Israel was never a "pure" community but always one impinged upon and responsive to the concrete requirements of life in the world.

Second, the monarchial period stretched from David (1000) to the destruction of Jerusalem in 587. Again the historical questions for the period are complicated. Israel's self-presentation, in any case, presents the founding of the monarchy as constituting an immense shift in Israel's life and self-understanding that in turn radically reformulated the community. Solomon's reign (962–922) was remembered in Israel as a time of expansive wealth. This change brought with it a new stratification of society, a division of labor, a rise of surplus wealth at the expense of the peasants, and the formation of a privileged urban elite who maximized their own political and economic advantage. Relationships became formal and complex, evoking, with time, large measures of social resentment. That social resentment is apparent in the narrative of the tax revolt of Jeroboam (1 Kgs. 12:1–19).

This new, grand self-presentation of wealth and privilege, reinforced by an elitist management of wisdom, required a different sort of religious legitimation. The Jerusalem temple, designed as the ideological legitimator of the regime, functioned by appropriating the great ancient Near Eastern myths of creation that understood the king as the human designee who embodied God-given social order. That such an appropriation of external accoutrements would inescapably bring with it various "foreign" influences that led to the transformation of religious traditions was viewed by those with long memories as a dangerous development (see 1 Kgs. 11:1–8).

Alongside the new royal characterization of Israelite community, however, subcommunities rooted in the older, prestate tradition continued to exist. The most radical of these was the Rechabites (see 2 Kgs. 10:15–17; Jer. 35:1–11); the most significant were the subcommunities that maintained and were represented by the prophets of the ninth, eighth, and seventh centuries and their communities of support. These prophets were not isolated individuals. They were advocates of an older social vision that continued to champion covenantal commitments and who therefore mounted a sustained critique of the monarchial alternative.

Third, with the failure of the monarchy at the hands of Babylon (viewed in the Old Testament as the judgment of YHWH upon Israel for failed covenant), the community of Israel now was required to live without the visible support of either the political power of kingship or the ideological force of the temple. A particular focus of that community without conventional supports was the development of a textual tradition of written scrolls that eventuated in canon. The pivotal mentions of authoritative scroll in Joshua 24:26; 2 Kings 22:8–13; Jeremiah 36; and Nehemiah 8:1–8 make clear that the authoritative scroll became a defining resource for the community that was without other resources. In that circumstance Israel reengaged more intensely what appear to be the older, prestate traditions. The movement of reform and restoration that clustered around Ezra reorganized what became Judaism around an intense commitment to Torah with its radical ethic and its separatist implications. Judaism became a religious community of practice and discipline that was now required to live without large political claim or hope. This community likely became a client community of the Persian Empire, continuing to cherish and practice its old, deep, radical alternative vision of life with YHWH.

This community had to live amidst all of the characteristic troubles and tribulations of life in a variety of socioeconomic, political relationships. At the same time, the longevity of its survival and the passion of its uncompromised vision may dazzle us. The tribulations that beset the community were recurrent:

Local power in tension with external power

Egalitarian and stratified social organizations

The purity of the community in tension with the unity of the community

Maintaining the community required no doubt a mix of visionary passion and prudent management, a mixture that would produce endless tensions and require endless negotiations. By the end of the Old Testament period, the community at Qumran was termed *'ahad,* "the one," the one unity of faith. That unity, however, was neither easily achieved nor easily maintained in stability, because its members were real people in the real world. (With the necessary accommodations, one can see that such tensions, settlements, and disequilibriums are present in the contemporary church with roughly the same issues and roughly the same energy.) The trick of community is to hold together real differences of interest in the midst of treasuring a passionate commitment to belong faithfully to one another.

References: Albertz, Rainer, *A History of Israelite Religion in the Old Testament Period I, II* (OTL; Louisville, Ky.: Westminster John Knox Press, 1994); Gottwald, Norman K., *The Politics of Ancient Israel* (Louisville, Ky.: Westminster John Knox Press, 2001); idem, *The Tribes of Yahweh: A Sociology of the Religion of Liberated Israel, 1250–1050 B.C.* (Maryknoll, N.Y.: Orbis Books, 1979); Hanson, Paul D., *The People Called: The Growth of Community in the Bible* (San Francisco: Harper and Row, 1986); Neusner, Jacob, *From Politics to Piety: The Emergence of Pharisaic Judaism* (Englewood Cliffs, N.J.: Prentice-Hall, 1973); Sanders, James A., *Canon and Community: A Guide to Canonical Criticism* (Philadelphia: Fortress Press, 1984); Weinberg, Joel, *The Citizen-Temple Community* (JSOTSup 151; Sheffield: JSOT Press, 1992); Wilson, Robert R., *Prophecy and Society in Ancient Israel* (Philadelphia: Fortress Press, 1980).

Covenant The covenant that God makes with Israel is perhaps the central and defining theological affirmation of the Old Testament. The covenant is at the same time a theological idea, a liturgic practice, and a durable public institution in Israel. In its largest sweep, the covenant affirms that the God of all creation has made an abiding commitment of fidelity to this chosen people, Israel. This commitment, moreover, is not grounded in anything other than God's own resolve to be in the relationship. Because of that abiding commitment of fidelity, Israel is marked for all time as the people of YHWH, and YHWH is marked for all time as the God of Israel (Jer. 11:4; 24:7; 30:22; 31:33; 32:38; Ezek. 11:20; 14:11). This bilateral commitment (enacted at Mt. Sinai, Exod. 19–24) asserts that the Bible is fundamentally about a God who is related (not at all a God in isolated splendor). This relatedness evokes in the Old Testament both what is interesting and generative and what is troublesome about faith. Unilateral commitments of covenant made by YHWH to Abraham (Gen. 15:7–21), Noah (Gen. 9:8–17), and David (2 Sam. 7:1–16) complement this covenant. While the bilateral covenant is primary, both modes are essential to Israel's sense of covenantal fidelity.

The center of covenanting (as an immediate liturgical act of mutual promises and commitments) lies in the Sinai traditions of Exodus 19–24 and more expansively in Exodus 19:1–Numbers 10:10. Indeed, the most authoritative traditions in the Old Testament are aimed toward and centered in this remembered meeting at Sinai. While the act of making and renewing covenant as a periodic liturgical act has a number of characteristic features, we can identify three in particular:

1. God announces directly to Israel the defining *commands and conditions* of the

covenant, which are familiar to us as the "Ten Commandments" (Exod. 20:1–17). The commands are absolute and seek to bring every part of Israel's life under YHWH's governance and into conformity with YHWH's will and purpose. These commandments stake out the ground for Israel's relationship with YHWH and pertain particularly to the community of faith.

2. Israel swears an *oath of fidelity* and is for all time bound in obedience to these terms of the relationship (Exod. 24:3, 7).

3. *Sanctions* make clear that obedience to these commands is the necessary condition of life and well-being (Lev. 26 and Deut. 28). Where the commands are violated, a curse will make life miserable and unbearable for the community. The harshness of the curses indicates that obedience is a life-or-death matter as the Sinai covenant is shaped in rigorously conditional terms.

This founding covenant, which the tradition places at Sinai, was no doubt shaped for periodic reiteration and reenactment in a variety of liturgical settings. Israel presumably took care to renew the covenant so that, in each new generation, the children of the covenant renewed vows, accepted commands, and submitted to its sanctions, for this commitment to YHWH defined Israel in each succeeding generation. While renewed in each generation, the Sinai covenant was the burden borne by the great prophets of Israel (Hosea, Amos, Jeremiah); as the Bible now stands, Israel so profoundly violated the covenant that it was terminated. That judgment—that disobedience brings disaster from God—is a characteristic way in which the Old Testament understands the destruction of Jerusalem in 587 and the ensuing exile. Because it is harshly conditional, the covenant serves to interpret Israel's life and to keep the

vagaries of lived experience within the matrix of this relationship.

While God's relation with Israel is decisive for the Old Testament, two other aspects of covenant also figure prominently. First, the covenant pertains particularly to Israel, so in Genesis 9:8–17 the covenant after the flood is made with "all flesh"—that is, with all nations and with nonhuman creation. This covenant, moreover, is unconditional its unilateral guarantee for the future well-being of the world. The God who commits to Israel is the God who commits to the well-being of creation. This remarkable affirmation becomes an important resource for ecological concerns and for an ethic of the care of the earth.

Second, just as this God makes the covenant of creation larger in scope than the covenant with Israel, so this same God makes covenant in a smaller scope, especially with pivotal persons in Israel's memory. Specifically, the tradition asserts that, at the outset, God makes a covenant with Abraham, the father of Israel's faith, thereby guaranteeing to Israel for all time the land of promise that is one ingredient in God's fidelity (Gen. 15:7–21). The promise to Abraham, remembered through the generations, comes to fruition in the promise made to David and to David's family for all time to come. God's particular, quite personal commitment to Abraham-David, moreover, is unconditional, a free, unqualified promise (2 Sam. 7:1–16; Ps. 89:1–17, though in Ps. 132:11–12 the promise to David's family is conditioned by obedience). These individual promissory covenants are likely to be understood in the completed tradition as subsets of Sinai, so that the unconditional promises serve the larger command-based commitment of Sinai. In any case, the evidence points to a rich interpretive field around the questions of conditional and unconditional, bilateral and unilateral, as texts can be identified for each.

The several covenants at Sinai and with Abraham and David were placed in profound jeopardy by the events around 587 in which Israel discerned that God had abandoned it, given up on the covenant, and abrogated God's promised fidelity. This crisis, however, proved to be Israel's most generative theological moment, for something fresh and imaginative now needed to be said about God's covenant commitments to Israel and about Israel's reliance upon and response to YHWH. Israel did not, in sum, entertain the thought of terminating the covenant, and so needed to find other ways to affirm it. Three such responses to the crisis continue to be crucial theological resources:

1. Israel spoke of YHWH's "everlasting covenant" that could not be broken or ultimately violated by disobedience (Gen. 9:16; 17:7–19; Isa. 55:3; 61:8; Ezek. 37:26). This affirmation is that YHWH's love for Israel is unilateral, does not depend upon Israel's obedience, and therefore can be relied upon in every circumstance, including that of exile. Most remarkably, these statements are characteristically made in texts judged to be from the exile. That is, Israel's deepest affirmation of God's trustworthiness is made in the midst of Israel's greatest tribulation.

2. Israel could not, even with its great confidence in YHWH, deny the profound experience of loss, displacement, and absence that could only result from YHWH's abandonment. For that reason Israel acknowledged momentary abandonment by YHWH in exile, insisting still that the absence *is* just momentary and does not signify termination of the covenant. Thus Isaiah 54:7–8 can assert that God is absent "for a brief moment"; but that moment is promptly overcome by "great compassion" and "everlasting

love" that reflect "steadfast love" and "my covenant of peace" (v. 10). That absence of YHWH from the life of Israel, while powerful, is not termination but eclipse.

3. More radically, exilic Israel can entertain the thought that the covenant is broken beyond repair because of Israel's disobedience. Yet that broken relationship will be a relationship renewed (Jer. 31:31–34), precisely because YHWH wills to continue the connection to Israel. This new covenant, moreover, is a renewed covenant with Israel, and not, as much Christian interpretation has proposed, a rejection of Israel and an embrace of Christians.

As a crucial theological datum in Israel that cannot be reduced to a single uniform formulation, the covenant is as rich and plural as is any lively relationship. It still lives as Israel, in its deep trust, adjudicated YHWH's harsh demands and deep commitments. The covenant poses for Israel the difficult issue of fidelity from God and toward God. Israel knows that fidelity on God's part is freely given, but is never cheap and never mocked.

In the Christian tradition, Jesus is the bearer of the new covenant (Heb. 8:8–13) that is made palpable in the Eucharist (1 Cor. 11:25). In Matthew 26:26–29, moreover, Jesus himself speaks the covenant formula concerning his significance for his disciples. As a liturgical datum, the covenant subsequently became, through the tradition of John Calvin, a defining theological principle and subsequently a grounding for a theory of the democratic ordering of public power.

References: Anderson, Bernhard W., *Contours of Old Testament Theology* (Minneapolis: Fortress Press, 1999); Hillers, Delbert R., *Covenant: The History of a Biblical Idea* (Baltimore: Johns Hopkins Press, 1969); Lohfink, Norbert, *The Covenant Never Revoked: Biblical Reflections on Christian-Jewish Dialogue* (New York: Paulist

Press, 1991); McCarthy, Dennis J., *Old Testament Covenant: A Survey of Current Opinions* (Oxford: Blackwell, 1972); McKenzie, Steven L., *Covenant* (St. Louis: Chalice Press, 2000); Nicholson, Ernest W., *God and His People: Covenant and Theology in the Old Testament* (Oxford: Clarendon Press, 1986); Rendtorff, Rolf, *The Covenant Formula* (Edinburgh: T. & T. Clark, 1998).

Creation Conviction about the meaning of creation is a central Old Testament teaching that affirms a peculiar relation between God and the world. "Creation," the identification of God as "creator," and the verb "create" together attest that (a) God and the world are completely unlike and incommensurate in their character and grounding, but (b) they are intensely and definitively linked together in a relationship of fidelity.

The Old Testament used older ancient Near Eastern traditions about creation that the great founding myths of old societies had expressed. Israel did not just take over these antecedent traditions, however; they were drastically revised in order to serve and accommodate Israel's own confession of faith.

Whereas the older materials tended to portray creation as an arbitrary show of power by quixotic gods, Israel cast creation in terms of covenantal relationships. In the faith of ancient Israel, the relation of God and world is not arbitrary, but one in which God's generative power to create a fruitful, life-sustaining system is exercised as an act of fidelity that evokes glad, ready obedience in response. The interaction of God's fidelity and the world's obedience assures that the world as God's creation will be well ordered in life-giving, life-enhancing ways. On the one hand, God will not act arbitrarily; on the other hand, the world is not autonomous, going its own way, but must live and func-

tion according to the ordered intention of the creator. These texts clearly are not and do not intend to be scientific descriptions of how the world came into being. Rather, they are doxological, theological assertions of who the creator is and what creation is in response to the creator God.

Genesis 1–2 begins with a great, panoramic vision of creation. Moreover, Genesis 1:1–2:4a and Genesis 2:4b–25 constitute two quite distinct narrative accounts of creation that are cast in different styles and that perform quite different narrative functions. The first of these passages, 1:1–2:4a, is a majestic liturgical poem, a vigorous doxology as an act of worship at the beginning of Israel's canonical text. Its cadences of grandeur enunciate the main claims of Israel's creation faith. The text is likely a world-making liturgy that invites the congregation to respond in regular litany, "It is good . . . very good."

The liturgy of God's majestic governance of the world in vv. 1–2 attests that God did not make the world out of nothing (*ex nihilo*), but rather ordered pre-existing chaos through a series of "separations" of light from dark and land from waters [see CHAOS]. (No clear statement is made that God created the world "out of nothing" until 2 Macc. 7:28, a very late text.) This liturgy asserts that God willed a productive, coherent system of food production; that God designated human persons (male and female) to oversee the generative system; and that God blessed the whole to be an arena of abundant life. In a dramatic climax, the repeated affirmation of goodness is intensified in 1:31, "very good." Moreover, this account of "goodness" culminates in the celebration of Sabbath (2:1–4a), signifying both a world free of anxiety and a Jewish community that regularly enacts, by its Sabbath, the ordered, reliable, life-giving character of the world as gift of God. Unlike its Babylonian counterpart and antecedent, the *Enuma Elish,* Israel's doxology asserts that every aspect of the cosmos is derivative from, dependent upon, and obligated to the rule of the creator God.

The second creation narrative, in Genesis 2:4b–25, is a more intimate account that is interested more particularly in the role and place of humankind in creation. The second narrative affirms that humankind is part of the earth—made from dust—that humankind is caretaker for the whole, and most especially that profound limits are set on human conduct with reference to the "tree of knowledge of good and evil."

This narrative delineates the defining contrast between God and humankind. Humankind is more akin to the rest of creation than to God, and any attempt to break that defining gap between God and humankind will end in death. Unlike the first Genesis account, which ends in the serenity of Sabbath, this narrative culminates in chapter 3, in a profound tale of alienation (perhaps extended in chap. 4 into the next generation). The two narratives together attest to the grandeur and precariousness of creation, to the well-ordered generativity of the world willed by God, and to the extreme vulnerability of that order, which can readily be put at risk.

The flood narrative of Genesis 6–9 follows closely after the creation texts. In the flood narrative, the God-willed power of chaotic waters overwhelms the earth. The flood narrative exhibits (a) YHWH's complex relationship to creation and (b) the endless vulnerability of the world. As liturgy and narrative, these materials express their religious claims in quite conventional and unexceptional form, as acts of communal imagination that frame both

the Bible to come and the story of Israel that the Bible tells. For all of the conventionality of form, however, the substantive claims made here are astonishing in power and insight, characterizing this God-world relation as a dynamic interaction that refuses both the arbitrary sovereignty of God and the autonomy of the world, locating both creator and creation in a context of dynamic, interactive fidelity.

Taking these opening chapters of Genesis as the primary Old Testament teaching on creation would, however, be a serious mistake. Certainly as important, even if unnoticed, are the doxological materials in the Psalms and in Isaiah 40–55.

Creation faith is offered in a variety of Psalms:

Psalm 8 celebrates the centrality of human agents in creation.

Psalm 33 celebrates the generative power of God's utterance.

Psalm 29 portrays God's massive power in a storm.

Psalm 96 dramatizes and anticipates God's welcome rule over the sea, mountains, fields, and trees, all governed in equity and justice.

Psalm 104 sketches the coherence of all of creation as a reliable and generous food chain that supports and maintains all creatures.

These hymns voice Israel's exuberant confidence in and gratitude for the life-friendly world that God has ordered as human habitat.

The second cluster of creation doxologies, in Isaiah 40–55, also attests to the grandeur of God's governance (Isa.

40:12–31; 41:17–20; 45:18–19; 48:12–19). Unlike the Psalms, these poems are situated in a larger context that reflects a concrete historical crisis. In its original utterance Isaiah 40–55 was addressed to Jewish exiles who were subjected to imperial Babylonian power. The creation hymns are poetic assertions that the power of the God of Israel—who is creator of heaven and earth—is stronger than the Babylonian gods and will prevail. As a consequence, the Babylonian gods are defeated. Israel is thus liberated to reengage its life of covenantal freedom with its own God. This particular usage suggests that "creation faith" is not an innocuous religious sensibility, but a declaration of truth that makes a decisive difference in the public life of the world. The claim of creation pertains concretely to the reality of a world as a viable place for life, in which distortion, abuse, exploitation, and oppression are ultimately untenable and will be overthrown.

In both Psalms and Isaiah, that creation faith is expressed in lyrical poetry as exuberant doxology is important. This expression is not a truth claim given in exacting, reasoned discourse, but instead operates as a faith commitment that is more elemental and unrestrained; the poetry of Psalms and Isaiah signifies not an objective picture of the world, but a readiness to enact faithful obedience appropriate to the God who is praised.

For all its exuberance about the creator, Israel is under no illusion about the world as creation. Israel knows that the world is provisional—existing, producing, and prospering only by the generosity of God. Recalcitrance and resistance to God's will, therefore, places the world in jeopardy. For that reason, Jeremiah 4:23–26 can envision the ending and termination of the world in a sequence that negatively inverts the sequence of Genesis 1. That undoing of the world in rejecting rage has as its counterpart the vision of new creation in Isaiah 65:17–25. The God who ordered the world, and who in exhausted impatience may end a world, can in power and grace create yet a new world that more fully responds to God's intention.

This sweeping cluster of traditions cannot be reduced to a single formulation. Rather the tradition attests to a lively, generative, demanding, hope-filled, and dynamic interaction of God and world. From that central conviction, three current issues relate to our theme.

1. Current debates about "creation and evolution" variously appeal to these texts. Mobilizing creation texts in such a controversy is clearly misguided, though, for creation faith is a lyrical, doxological response of gratitude that is not committed to or allied with a scientific explanation of the world's origin. Creation faith is not about origins, but it is about the ongoing dynamic of fidelity that characterizes the world in its life with God. This faith must be understood as a theological response that is not to be distorted into a scientific explanation. The so-called "creation-evolution" debate is a powerful modern distraction from the harsh reality of creation faith that systemic human disobedience can damage and finally dismantle the world that YHWH generously willed.

2. Only belatedly has humankind paid attention to biblical claims that pertain to the current crisis in environmental ecology. When the question of the environment is raised with clarity, however, the assertion of creation faith—in its own prescientific idiom—is alert to the risks and vulnerability of the creation. The world belongs to and is ordered by God. Any attempt to live in or use the world apart from that ordering is inescapably destruc-

tive, both to human agents and to the nonhuman creaturely environment. This theme proves immensely important in emerging biblical study.

3. Current science, in the disciplines of physics, astronomy, and cosmology, has come to a consensus view that in due course our universe will either burn up or freeze over, either way ending in humankind's death. In the face of what at present is an assured scientific judgment, creation faith is immediately pertinent, for that faith has always warned against any ultimate confidence in the world. The Bible has always confessed that creation is provisional and limited. Certainly biblical faith casts its confidence and its gratitude not toward creation but toward the creator, who may in good time and in good ways evoke yet new creations that teem with abundance and joy. Only misplaced attachment to the world makes deeply problematic a scientific judgment about the end. Creation faith deeply distinguishes between the world as provisional habitat and ultimate ground for creaturely well-being rooted only in the creator.

References: Anderson, Bernhard W., *Creation Versus Chaos: The Reinterpretation of Mythical Symbolism in the Bible* (Philadelphia: Fortress Press 1987); idem, *From Creation to New Creation: Old Testament Perspectives* (OBT; Minneapolis: Fortress Press, 1994); Brueggemann, Walter, "The Loss and Recovery of Creation in Old Testament Theology," *Theology Today* 53 (1996): 177–90; Gilkey, Langdon, *Maker of Heaven and Earth: The Christian Doctrine of Creation in the Light of Modern Knowledge* (Lanham, Md.: University Press of America, 1985); Hiebert, Theodore, *The Yahwist's Landscape: Nature and Religion in Early Israel* (Oxford: Oxford University Press, 1996); Polkinghorne, John, and Michael Welker, eds., *The End of the World and the Ends of God: Science and Theology on Eschatology* (Harrisburg, Pa.: Trinity Press International, 2000); Stuhlmueller, Carroll, *Creative Redemption in Deutero-Isaiah* (Analecta

Biblica 43; Rome: Biblical Institute Press, 1970); Wybrow, Cameron, *The Bible, Baconianism, and Mastery over Nature: The Old Testament and Its Modern Misreading* (American University Studies Series VII, Theology and Religion 112; New York: Peter Lang, 1991).

■ ■ ■

David   In a book of theological themes such as this, mentioning personalities may seem a bit odd. I do so, however, with four men from the tradition—Moses, David, Elijah, and Ezra—because in each case that individual person embodies a crucial theological claim of the Old Testament.

Historical issues related to David are deeply problematic. The minimalist view of the historicity of ancient Israel casts doubt on the historical existence of David; archaeologists point to a ninth-century inscription that is the earliest nonbiblical evidence for David, but the inscription itself is judged problematic. Thus we are left (yet again) with the character of David as remembered and portrayed in the biblical tradition: a Judean "nobody" who by wile, bravery, and the protection of YHWH became the king of the kingdoms of Israel and Judah and established a rule in Jerusalem that his son Solomon would enhance even more in time to come. More sober critical judgment suggests that David was a tribal chieftain who, in terms of developed political practice, fell far short of kingship.

For our purposes, we may note four claims that tradition makes for David:

1. Astonishingly, David is portrayed as a ruthless, ambitious power player, warts and all. The so-called succession narrative of 2 Samuel 9–20 focuses on the pivotal event of his seizure of Bathsheba and murder of Uriah. By Nathan's prophetic

critique, the memory of Israel marks that event as the defining reality of monarchial Israel (2 Sam. 11–12). Israel, moreover, remembered that event in its subsequent historiography (1 Kgs. 15:5; see Matt. 1:6). First Chronicles 11–29, a later literature that serves a very different purpose, offers a less candid presentation of David, without the sordid elements. In this later text, David is largely transposed into a liturgic leader and is portrayed in a less ambiguous, more idealistic way.

2. In the midst of that seemingly candid initial presentation of David, the defining text for theological reflection is 2 Samuel 7:1–16, in which YHWH, through the same Nathan, makes an unconditional promise of kingship to David and to his sons who are to come after him (see the same promise reiterated in Pss. 89; 132). This promise gives ideological legitimacy to David's dynasty of remarkable durability (twenty kings in four hundred years!). Beyond that political reality, that unconditional promise became the driving force of royal expectation in Israel, which was eventually transposed into messianic expectations. Given the historical failure of the Davidic monarchy, Israel came to expect a true and perfect Davidic king in time to come whom YHWH would give and who would enact Israel's best hopes and YHWH's best promises.

3. Alongside the narratives, David—as person and as office—comes to occupy a prominent place in the Psalms. Special attention may be given to the ten royal psalms (Pss. 2; 18; 20; 21; 45; 72; 89; 101; 110; 144). These psalms disregard any "warts" that historical kings may have had and deal with the office of the king as the carrier of YHWH's future. (Scholars now accept, moreover, that these royal psalms are deliberately placed in the sequence of Psalms in order to give structure and form to the entire Psalter.) The royal psalms, particularly Psalms 2 and 110, are quoted prominently in the New Testament when the early church accents the royal office of Jesus. In addition, a number of psalms are given superscriptions that connect the psalm to a particular episode in David's life that is reported in the narrative tradition. (The most familiar case is Ps. 51, which by superscription is connected to David's guilt over the Uriah-Bathsheba incident.) Critical scholarship regards these superscriptions not as historical reports but as clues concerning how the Psalter is to be interpreted canonically. The presence of the king, specifically David, in the Psalter indicates David's domination of the liturgical imagination of Judaism well into the Second Temple period.

4. The later parts of the Old Testament include a number of prophetic oracles that anticipate the coming of the new David, the messianic figure, a human king who will establish the rule YHWH has intended on the earth. (The most obvious of these passages is Zech. 9:9–10.) The New Testament interpretation of Jesus applied these texts to illuminate Jesus as "the true David" who would establish a new governance of freedom, peace, justice, and mercy.

On all counts, in Israel's liturgical imagination, David is unmistakably the promise carrier of Israel concerning the good future that YHWH surely will give. The unconditional promise made in 2 Samuel 7 persists in spite of all the vagaries and defeats of history and provides the basis of messianic expectation. Jews wait for a messiah who will surely come. Christians, after Easter and the ascension of Jesus, wait for the return of the Messiah. Jews and Christians together believe that a human agent designated by God will come in peace to renovate the public historical process toward wellbeing. This new anticipated role is the one for which Christians pray when they say, "Your kingdom come . . . on earth as it is in heaven" (Matt. 6:10). David is the quintessential ground of biblical hope that tenaciously trusts in a good God-given future in the face of all data to the contrary. David functions quite specifically as hope against circumstance, as hope expressed in the "though . . . though . . . though . . . yet" of Habakkuk 3:17–18.

References: Beron, A., and J. Naveh, "The Tell Don Inscription: A New Fragment," *Israel Exploration Journal* 45 (1995): 1–18; Brueggemann, Walter, *David's Truth in Israel's Imagination and Memory* (Philadelphia: Fortress Press, 1985); Childs, Brevard S., "Psalm Titles and Midrashic Exegesis," *JSS* 16/2 (1971): 137–50; Flanagan, James W., *David's Social Drama: A Hologram of Israel's Early Iron Age* (The Social World of Biblical Antiquity Series 7; Sheffield: Almond Press, 1988); Gunn, David M., *The Story of King David* (JSOTSup 6; Sheffield: University of Sheffield, 1978); Halpern, Baruch, *David's Secret Demons: Messiah, Murderer, Traitor, King* (Grand Rapids: Eerdmans, 2001); Jobling, David, *1 Samuel* (Berit Olam; Collegeville: Liturgical Press, 1998); Kraus, Hans-Joachim, *Theology of the Psalms* (Minneapolis: Augsburg, 1986), chap. 4; McKenzie, Steven L., *King David: A Biography* (New York: Oxford University Press, 2000); McNutt, Paula, *Reconstructing the Society of Ancient Israel* (Louisville, Ky.: Westminster John Knox Press, 1999); Polzin, Robert, *David and the Deuteronomist: A Literary Study of the Deuteronomic History, Part 3: 2 Samuel* (Bloomington: University of Indiana Press, 1993); Simpson, Timothy F., "Paradigm Shift Happens: Intertextuality and a Reading of 2 Samuel 16:5–14," *Proceedings of the Eastern Great Lakes and Midwest Biblical Societies* 17 (1997): 55–70; Steussy, Marti J., *David: Biblical Portraits of Power* (Columbia: University of South Carolina Press, 1999).

The Day of the Lord   The phrase "the Day of the Lord" is a technical term in Israel's vocabulary of hope that antici-pates a moment when an act of power and self-assertion will fully and decisively establish YHWH's rule. As an act of vigorous expectation on the part of Israel, the phrase (a) looks boldly to an actual, concrete, this-worldly occurrence; (b) regards the coming assertion of YHWH's rule as utterly reliable and beyond question; and (c) refuses to speculate about any time or schedule for such a coming rule [see HOPE]. Thus the phrase is a subset of Israel's deep and abiding hope and its reliance upon YHWH's rule in the world to establish justice and well-being, which without YHWH would remain forever remote and beyond fruition.

This confidently expected hope, in the rhetoric of Israel, may variously concern the harsh judgment of YHWH, who defeats all rivals, or YHWH's victorious, glorious establishment of good governance.

"The day" may indeed be a day of judgment—against Israel. The best known text about this stance is Amos 5:18–20:

> Alas for you who desire the day of the
>   LORD!
>   Why do you want the day of the LORD?
> It is darkness, not light; . . .
> Is not the day of the LORD darkness, not
>   light,
>   and gloom with no brightness in it?

Evidently convinced of their own privileged status with YHWH, Israelites anticipated that YHWH's coming rule would favor them. The burden of the prophet is to assert that "the day" will be against Israel when Israel has been grossly disobedient (see Isa. 2:12–22; Joel 2:1–2; Mic. 2:1–4). Conversely and more often, the harsh judgment of "the day" will be against other nations (in a way that may derivatively benefit Israel), because the other nations have not acknowledged and conformed to the rule of YHWH (see Isa. 24:21; Jer. 46:10; Zech. 14:12–14).

In one of the clearest, most eloquent announcements of "the day" of judgment, the referent is not fully identified:

> The great day of the LORD is near,
>   near and hastening fast;
> the sound of the day of the LORD is bitter,
>   the warrior cries aloud there.
> That day will be a day of wrath,
>   a day of distress and anguish,
> a day of ruin and devastation,
>   a day of darkness and gloom,
> a day of clouds and thick darkness,
>   a day of trumpet blast and battle cry
> against the fortified cities
>   and against the lofty battlements.
>   (Zeph. 1:14–16)

By themselves, these verses might refer to any people, any foreign nation. In context, however, the subject of the poetry is clearly Judah and Jerusalem. Israel and the nations thus stand together before the fierce coming of YHWH's rule. These same verses from Zephaniah, in a different context, could conceivably be addressed to a foreign nation.

In other utterances, "the day" can be, positively, a day of rescue, deliverance, and well-being, such as when Jerusalem will be glorified in the eyes of the nations (Isa. 11:10; see Amos 9:11–15). The same rhetoric can anticipate well-being, healing, and blessing for the nations as well (as in Isa. 19:23–25).

Negatively or positively, as judgment or as deliverance, for Israel or for the nations—all of these possibilities are brought to fruition on "the day." The subject of "the day" is none of them but only YHWH: YHWH's sovereign authority and YHWH's resolve to act in decisive, transformative ways. The source for such a way of speaking and imagining is not

known. That this language derives from military rhetoric is certainly possible; many usages reflect such a context. The day is a time of military activity when YHWH is determining defeats and victories. For example, in Isaiah 9:4, the "day of Midian" remembers defeat of the Midianites, which, in this context, becomes a pretext for YHWH's coming military victories through a Davidic leader.

Other scholars urge, however, that "the day" is a great liturgical event when in public worship the new rule of YHWH is acknowledged and celebrated, and perhaps established in the liturgical process. Such festivals would not have been unlike the great liturgic Christian pageants of Christmas and Easter when the Church celebrates the new reality of rescue in Christ.

Choosing between these several explanatory hypotheses is neither necessary nor possible, for undoubtedly rhetorical usage that became standard in Israel appropriated various sources in order to speak in a fresh way about YHWH's coming rule, upon which Israel had staked everything.

When we speak and think in conventional religious cadences, this claim for "the day" may sound routine and conventional. We should, however, notice in this rhetoric a claim that is always "strange and new": Israel's sustained assertion that the public life of the world is fully answerable to the personal rule of this God. Such a claim deabsolutizes our human pretensions, all the claims of self-assured superpowers, all of the blind trust in "might" that "makes right," all the notions of a manageable moral calculus that orders and controls the world.

Against all such claims that are deprivileged in Israel's theological rhetoric, Klaus Koch has rightly spoken of a "metahistory" or a "suprahistory"—the rule of YHWH that turns the public processes of power into shapes and in directions beyond the will of all the "rulers of this age." Israel's way of speaking in such theological confidence is one of expectation of the coming of God's rule. In light of such Israelite expectation, we are able to sense Jesus' deep and radical claim that "the kingdom of God has come near" (Mark 1:15). In Christian affirmation a primal claim was that all the "days" that Israel anticipated are now at hand in Jesus. Israel's hope and the claim of the early church are not linked automatically. We are able to see, however, how the New Testament interpreters boldly took up these expectations of Israel and claimed them for Jesus. (See positively 1 Cor. 1:8; Phil. 1:10; and negatively Matt. 10:15; Rom. 2:5; 1 John 4:17; Rev. 6:17.)

References: Cerny, Ladislav, *The Day of Yahweh and Some Relevant Problems* (V Praze, Nákl: Filosofické fakulty Univ. Karlovy, 1948); Koch, Klaus, *The Prophets,* vol. 1, *The Assyrian Period* (Philadelphia: Fortress Press, 1983); Rad, Gerhard von, "The Origin of the Concept of the Day of Yahweh," *JSS* 4 (1959): 97–108.

Death   For ancient Israel death was both an undeniable and undenied reality and a profound mystery that evoked a variety of interpretations. The commonsense perspective (which must have comprehended much of the experience of Israel) was that death is an inescapable, "natural" reality of life, a termination that belongs to all lived reality.

In order to understand this reality from a theological perspective, one must understand the basic sense of human personhood assumed in Israel (and in the ancient Near East generally). The human person consists in flesh (*basar*) or "dust" (*'aphar*)—the stuff of the earth—that becomes enlivened and given vitality only when God's breath (wind, spirit; *ruah*) breathes upon the flesh. The flesh itself can have no vitality but remains dormant and passive until God breathes upon it (see Gen. 2:7). When breathed upon, the human organism is evoked: a *nephesh,* a living human being, a term we conventionally and not quite correctly translate "soul." The term "soul" is only appropriate if understood as a whole organism and not part of a dualism (see Ps. 103:1–2).

This notion of human physiology is commonsense, because anyone could see that when the breath departs, the organism dies. The breath, moreover, is always a gift upon which human life is dependent—a gift for it cannot be "held" or possessed. Human life thus depends daily, moment by moment, upon the life-giving generosity and attentiveness of the creator God, apart from whom life is not possible.

This characterization of human life is important because it contradicts completely the popular religious notion of an immortal soul that lives on in death and is the autonomous property of the self, apart from God. Theologically, Israel understands that human life is derived from and directed toward the God who gives life. In this Old Testament understanding, the self has no permanent properties of its own but is marked by ultimate and complete dependence. In the normal course of life, Israel observed and affirmed, at best after "seventy years, or perhaps eighty" (Ps. 90:10), full of days, the breath departs and the person dies. The person may be said to be "gathered to his people" (Gen. 49:33) or to "descend into Sheol" (cf. Ps. 139:8), a gray, undifferentiated place in the center of the earth. Thus the Old Testament knows about a good death in which the normal human life span is not interrupted and in which life is well governed and submitted to the rule of God (see Gen. 25:7–11;

49:29–33). In neither phrasing is such a fate marked by any punishment or threat. The place of the dead is simply a place of non-being that stretches limitlessly into the future where the dead person may be remembered, but no future, so to speak, is there. Characteristically the Old Testament views death as closure, beyond which the text makers have no access. To be sure, Israel thought otherwise and traces of that popular religous influence are clear in the text (see 1 Sam. 28:3–25; Isa. 8:17–22).

Given this assumed and uncritical physiology, we may mention two important awarenesses:

1. "Life" and "death" are not simply absolute final states of a person, but are the extremes of a spectrum of strength and weakness. When one is weakened in any way—by sickness or hunger or social isolation—one may said to be "dying." Conversely, when one is strengthened—by healing or food or social affirmation—one is "given life" or "restored to life."

2. When the dead sleep with their fathers or abide in Sheol, that death may be to perpetuity. Hope for new life for an individual person, such as it is in the Old Testament, depends completely upon the will and initiative of the creator God who may give breath to the dead and so "raise to new life." The dead have within themselves no power for new life but instead depend upon divine intervention; they have so little power that they cannot praise God, the first act of vitality (see Pss. 30:9; 88:10–12; Isa. 38:16–19). One can see in Ezekiel 37:1–14 this way of thinking utilized in a metaphor for hopeless Israel in exile. Only at the edges of the Old Testament—in Isaiah 25:6–9 and 26:19, and Daniel 12:2—is the prospect of resurrection to new life voiced. This understanding of human personality leads to Paul's formulation of "spiritual bodies" because Paul, Jew that he is, could not imagine new life

given by God other than in a bodily form (1 Cor. 15:42–49). In the creed, moreover, the church asserts the promise of "the resurrection of the body" that appeals to the same understanding of the human person.

The above commonsense perception of life and death governs much Old Testament thinking on the subject. A more extreme rhetoric is expressed, however, in which "death" is not a normal termination of a well-lived life, but an unwelcome or premature disruption of a life not yet fully lived. First, in an articulation of the ferocious enactment of YHWH's governance, the Old Testament entertains the thought that YHWH will punish with death the recalcitrants who violate the commandments, those who bring upon themselves the curses that serve as negative sanctions for covenant. The covenant curses of Deuteronomy 28 and Leviticus 26 thus prescribe famine, war, pestilence, and drought as creator-enacted sanctions to punish and destroy the disobedient. God's violent behavior here can be rationalized as appropriate to maintenance of a governing order; nonetheless YHWH's severe intervention causes the life-giving God to act to kill. With rhetorical harshness, prophetic judgments declare God's intent toward Israel.The language of such divine threats is sweeping and extreme and is not on the same practical immediate level as the commonsense reality of death discussed above. This rhetoric about death as divine punishment nonetheless brings to Israel's horizon the conviction that death comes upon those who fall outside covenant and who consequently receive harsh punishment from the God of life, who gives life only on the terms of divine governance. Because the Old Testament thinks communally about human reality, YHWH's harsh judgment of death may come not only upon individual persons, but upon the entire community or state (see Ezek. 37:1–14).

Another version of this claim is found in the Wisdom literature, wherein foolishness leads to death—that is, the diminution and termination of life (see Prov. 8:35–36). A sapiential expression of this theme does not allude to YHWH's direct, distinct intervention; rather, the threat arises in the process of living and choosing itself. The divine sanctions are not, for that reason, any less clear, inescapable, or ominous. Wisdom in Proverbs attests to an ordered creation that cannot be violated without the ultimate cost of life.

Second, Israel's extreme rhetoric entertains the notion that within creation exists a force against life that opposes YHWH and YHWH's will for life. The god Mot, taken from older Canaanite myths, seeks to undermine and destroy human life. *Môt* is the Hebrew word for "death," so that this god is called Death. This great enemy of YHWH is often noted in the Psalms:

The cords of death encompassed me;
    the torrents of perdition assailed me;
the cords of Sheol entangled me;
    the snares of death confronted me.
                              (Ps. 18:4–5)

. . . to deliver their soul from death.
    and to keep them alive in famine.
                              (Ps. 33:19)

Like sheep they are appointed for Sheol;
    Death shall be their shepherd;
straight to the grave they descend,
    and their form shall waste away. . . .
                              (Ps. 49:14)

Let death come on them;
    let them go down alive to Sheol. . . .
                              (Ps. 55:15)

For you have delivered my soul from
        death,
    and my feet from falling. . . .
                              (Ps. 56:13)

Death is sometimes portrayed in the Old Testament as a vigorous, aggressive power before whom the human speaker is impotent and helpless (see Eccl. 12:1–8). In such cases Israel's prayers are designed to mobilize YHWH on behalf of the speaker against the power of death, for that YHWH is stronger than the power of Death is not doubted. In Hosea 13:14 (quoted in 1 Cor. 15:54–55), the redeemed of YHWH gloat over Death and taunt its failed power when YHWH has triumphed.

To be sure, the Old Testament includes some interesting psychological questions related to death. For our purposes, those issues are transposed into issues of faith. Finally Israel entrusts its life to YHWH, the God of life, confident that the powers of death cannot undo the well-being given in YHWH's fidelity. The Old Testament is for the most part quite reluctant to speculate about life beyond death. When it does speak about such matters, however, the subject is YHWH's reliability, power, and fidelity in the face of every threat. Paul is thus completely faithful to his Jewish tradition when he celebrates God's adequacy in the face of such threats:

For I am convinced that neither death, nor life, nor angels, nor rulers, nor things present, nor things to come, nor powers, nor height, nor depth, nor anything else in all creation, will be able to separate us from the love of God in Christ Jesus our Lord. (Rom. 8:38)

We do not live to ourselves, and we do not die to ourselves. If we live, we live to the Lord, and if we die, we die to the Lord; so then, whether we live or whether we die, we are the Lord's. (Rom. 14:7–8)

Neither the individual nor the community has resources to cope with or make sense of death. All that counts and all that matters is life entrusted to the God of life who

> keeps the dead,
>
> is finally reliable and not angry, and who
>
> defeats the powers of death.

The sole, adequate antidote to the reality of death is the greater reality of YHWH. Israel's confident response to the mystery of death is the greater mystery of the God of life whose power and fidelity are durable and reliable. For good reason, Israel's needy complaint against the threat of death characteristically ends in glad, exuberant praise to the God of life.

References: Bailey, Lloyd R., Sr., *Biblical Perspectives on Death* (OBT; Philadelphia: Fortress Press, 1979); Johnson, Aubrey R., *The Vitality of the Individual in the Thought of Ancient Israel* (Cardiff: University of Wales Press, 1949); Levenson, Jon D., *Creation and the Persistence of Evil: The Jewish Drama of Divine Omnipotence* (Princeton: Princeton University Press, 1994); Lindström, Fredrik, *Suffering and Sin: Interpretations of Illness in the Individual Complaint Psalms* (Stockholm: Almqvist & Wiksell International, 1994); Martin-Achard, Robert, *From Death to Life: A Study of the Development of the Doctrine of the Resurrection in the Old Testament* (Edinburgh: Oliver and Boyd, 1960); Pedersen, Johannes, *Israel: Its Life and Culture*, vols. 1 and 2 (London: Oxford University Press, 1954).

The Decalogue   The Ten Commandments constitute the bottom line and reference point for all Old Testament thinking about ethics (Exod. 20:1–17). The fact that the Ten Commandments are situated in the covenant-making process of Mt. Sinai (Exod. 19–24) indicates that they are to be understood not as positivistic law, but as stipulations for the covenant Israel now has with YHWH. That is,

YHWH has pledged to be the guardian and protector of Israel, and under these terms that relationship of mutual fidelity can flourish.

A plausible assumption would be that the list of ten commands has a long and complex history; determining when the list of ten may have become stable is impossible. More important, however, is the singular place that these ten commands occupy in the canonical form of the text. They are presented as YHWH's own utterance to Israel on the mountain in the context of a theophany (Exod. 19:16–25), after which Israel, in fear, asks Moses to be a mediator (Exod. 20:18–21). This passage is, thus, YHWH's only direct utterance to Israel. Moreover, the commands (with the exception of Exod. 20:8–11, 12) are in the apodictic form, "Thou shalt not." They are absolute and without qualification and do not even entertain the prospect of punishment for disobedience. They are completely nonnegotiable as they are given to Israel.

Given the introductory formula of verse 2 with reference to the Exodus, the commands are to be understood in the context of Israel's emancipation from Egypt and purport to offer the guidelines for an alternative community that is completely contrasted to that of pharaoh. They preclude idolatry (and commodity fetishism) and guard the well-being of the neighbor against exploitation; as a consequence, they sanction and envision a communitarian ethic that is tilted in an egalitarian direction (see the dissent of Clines). As these commands provide for a covenantal, neighborly ethic, they also provide a barrier against the social chaos that ensues from unbridled acquisitiveness grounded in self-securing.

The Ten Commandments generated and continue to generate a radical social imagination that seeks to bring every aspect of life—personal and public— under the governance of this covenant-making God who enacts liberation and who has ordered heaven and earth for generative well-being.

1. That the Ten Commandments are reiterated in Deuteronomy 5:6–21 is of immense importance. The slightly varied form noticeably shifts the motivation for the Sabbath command (Deut. 5:12–15) from the fabric of creation (as in Exod. 20:11) to the economic matters of social equity and rest. The difference indicates the elasticity of the commands and their openness to variation in interpretation. Several scholars suggest, moreover, that the laws of Deuteronomy 12–25 are organized sequentially around the list of ten, so that Deuteronomy may be regarded as an early exposition of the Decalogue. That is, the Ten Commandments is not a flat list, but is the normative material out of which Israel continued to do its radical, intense ethical reflection in the context of ongoing covenant.

2. In Hosea 4:2 and Jeremiah 7:9, the prophets obviously appeal to and are informed by the list of ten commands. We may suppose that as it was readily available to these prophets, the Decalogue in general was an important component in the dynamism of Israel's covenantal reflection.

3. The Decalogue is clearly an ongoing point of reference in Judaism. Thus Jesus, in good rabbinic fashion, alludes to the Decalogue as a reference for his demanding teaching; in his statement of "old/ new" in Matthew 5:21–37, he exhibits the way in which the ten commands contribute to and require continuing interpretation (see Matt. 19:16–30).

4. In a variety of ways and sometimes with great contentiousness, the Ten Commandments have functioned as a defining point in shaping the ethical assumptions of Western culture. The continual reference of the normative theological traditions of the church, the ethical radicality of continuing Judaism, and the civic assumptions of Western culture concerning the core of holiness and the guarantees of human life and human worth all attest to the generative force of the commandments. The commands stand negatively as a resistance against every totalitarianism that would replicate pharaoh and positively as a radical invitation to reorganize public life around the mystery of God that deabsolutizes human control and fosters neighborly entitlement. Unfortunately many interpretations have removed the commands from a proper covenantal context, and as a result they are then understood as rules without reference to relationship, which Sinai never intended. A sorry example of this distorted understanding is evident in current attempts to retain or restore the Decalogue to the walls of U.S. courtrooms.

References: Brueggemann, Walter, *Theology of the Old Testament: Testimony, Dispute, Advocacy* (Minneapolis: Fortress Press, 1997), 181–201; Childs, Brevard S., *Old Testament Theology in a Canonical Context* (Philadelphia: Fortress Press, 1985), 63–83; Clines, David J. A., "The Ten Commandments, Reading from Left to Right," in *Interested Parties: The Ideology of Writers and Readers of the Hebrew Bible* (JSOTSup 205; Sheffield: Sheffield Academic Press, 1995), 26–45; Crüsemann, Frank, *The Torah: Theology and Social History of Old Testament Law* (Edinburgh: T. & T. Clark, 1996); Harrelson, Walter, *The Ten Commandments and Human Rights* (OBT; Philadelphia: Fortress Press, 1980); Miller, Patrick D., "The Human Sabbath: A Study in Deuteronomic Theology," *The Princeton Seminary Bulletin* 6/2 (1985): 81–97; Nielsen, Eduard, *The Ten Commandments in New Perspective* (SBT 7, Second Series; Chicago: Allenson, 1968); Olson, Dennis T., *Deuteronomy and the Death of Moses: A Theological Reading* (OBT; Minneapolis: Fortress Press, 1994); Phillips,

Anthony, *Ancient Israel's Criminal Law: A New Approach to the Decalogue* (Oxford: Blackwell, 1970); Pleins, J. David, *The Social Visions of the Hebrew Bible: A Theological Introduction* (Louisville, Ky.: Westminster John Knox Press, 2001).

Deuteronomic Theology   Scholars commonly use the phrase "Deuteronomic theology," which recurs in interpretive books about the Old Testament. During the period of intense historical critical study of the Old Testament in the eighteenth and nineteenth centuries (mostly German Protestant researchers), scholars were able to identify and isolate different literary-theological sources in the text. In those days these sources were regarded as distinct "documents" that had been subsequently edited together, although today we might prefer to call them "voices" in the text rather than "documents." The precise dating and location of these sources is much in dispute, but the concept that different "voices" have a say in the text seems beyond challenge.

Among these different voices (= interpretive traditions), perhaps the most important and most easily recognizable is an ongoing, powerful interpretive tradition that scholars term "Deuteronomic theology." This particular theological advocacy seems rooted in and informed by the book of Deuteronomy; as we shall see, though, this lively interpretive tradition continues well beyond the book of Deuteronomy itself.

The book of Deuteronomy presents itself as a series of addresses by Moses "[b]eyond the Jordan in the land of Moab," some distance removed in space and time from Sinai (Deut. 1:5). Critical judgment about the book (and the "Deuteronomic movement" that is represented in the book) suggests that the literature that eventually became the book of Deuteronomy was formulated in the eighth and seventh centuries B.C.E., perhaps under the influence of treaty documents from the Assyrians of that period. Scholars think that some version of the book of Deuteronomy was presumably found in the temple in 2 Kings 22, which in turn became the impetus for a major religious reform by King Josiah, thus "the Deuteronomic reform" [see HULDAH; REFORM OF JOSIAH].

One cannot overstate the importance of the book of Deuteronomy for understanding Old Testament theology. The book of Deuteronomy presents the categories of covenant as normative for Israel's faith, perhaps introducing into Israel the normative, fully developed notion of covenant, developing the inchoate categories of the traditions of Sinai and Moses. We may identify three dimensions of the theology of the book of Deuteronomy:

1. The structure of the book of Deuteronomy seems to reflect a conscious covenantal pattern:

The proclamation of YHWH's saving deeds (Deut. 1–11)

The articulation of YHWH's covenantal commands (Deut. 12–25)

The making of mutual vows of covenantal fidelity (Deut. 26:16–19)

The recital of sanctions of blessing and curse (Deut. 28)

Through this sequence (which may have been liturgically performed), YHWH and Israel are bound to each other in solemn oaths of fidelity and, in Israel's case, in an oath of obedience.

2. The sequence of commandment-oath-sanction places obedience to Torah at the center of faith, so that, in a schematic way, obedient Israel receives blessing and

disobedient Israel receives curse—or more broadly and generically, "good people prosper and evil people suffer." This defining formulation is expressed in Deuteronomy 30:15–20 and eventually became a primary way in which Israel understood and interpreted the destruction of Jerusalem in 587, as a covenant curse evoked by covenantal disobedience. While the tradition developed in order to refine and nuance the formulation and to acknowledge difficulties with it, the core claim of this covenantal formulation is tightly linked behavior and consequence yielding a morally coherent world, presided over by a sovereign God who exercises complete hegemony over the historical process. That broad theory of moral coherence is worked out through the detail of a variety of specific texts.

3. Over time, the interpretive practice of this ongoing theological tradition evidences a remarkable consistency, not only of theological horizon and ethical perspective, but in the recurrence of a certain rhetorical pattern and linguistic usage. Certain patterns (as in Deut. 13:4, for example) are thus easily transferred from one usage to another, and they are so consistent that they are readily recognizable when they appear elsewhere.

While the tradition of Deuteronomy no doubt draws on older memories and traditions, the process of finding the scroll in 2 Kings 22 and responding to it in obedience was very important in attaching Israel to a scroll tradition that became canon and eventuated in Judaism as a religion of the book.

On the basis of the readily identified theology and rhetorical pattern in the book of Deuteronomy, Martin Noth in 1943 offered what became a master hypothesis. Noth proposed that the extended corpus of literature that runs from Joshua through Judges and Samuel to Kings constitutes a "Deuteronomic" theology of history—that is, the refraction of the story of Israel from its entry into the land (Josh. 1–4) to the exile and the loss of the land in 2 Kings 25 through the theological conviction of the book of Deuteronomy. These biblical books that we too easily term "history," Noth argued, are in fact an interpretation of history that used many old sources but, by rereading the sources and memories through the lens of Deuteronomy, made much diverse material into a coherent interpretation of the story of Israel and Judah. Thus the overarching pattern is to consider the characteristic practice of Torah disobedience in Israel by its kings and to view the culminating curse of the destruction of Jerusalem and the loss of land as the divine response to a long history of disobedience. From this perspective, Noth was able to conclude that this long history is retold in this way to explain the destruction of 587 as a punishment enacted by the God of Deuteronomy. Thus, the material is not at all historical reportage but rather quite self-conscious interpretation that is fundamentally informed by the book of Deuteronomy as "Introduction."

The defining features of this interpretive tradition include the following four:

1. In the book of Judges, a recurring fourfold formula dominates the narrative and is commonly taken to reflect Deuteronomic understandings of YHWH's governance of history: (a) disobedience, (b) judgment through an enemy people, (c) a cry for help addressed to YHWH, and (d) the gift of a savior-judge by YHWH (as in 3:7–11; 10:6–16; see Deut. 11:8–32).

2. The characteristically negative judgment against kings (as in 1 Kgs. 14:9–14; 15:3, 11–15), made especially acute with reference to Solomon (1 Kgs. 11:1–8), is a Deuteronomic verdict that kings had

largely failed to obey Torah and so brought down on their realms deserved covenant curses (see Deut. 17:14–20).

3. The peculiar promise that YHWH makes to David in 2 Samuel 7:1–16 constitutes an important qualification in the simple disobedience-curse formula. YHWH's special, seemingly unconditional commitment to David's dynasty requires a modification of the simpler formula. Interpretation must allow for it on the grounds that this disobedient dynasty of David lasted much longer than it had reason to expect. The David promise is an important modification in Deuteronomic theory and a defining theological datum for Israel's faith.

4. The good King Josiah represents an important exception to the recurring negative judgment about kings (Hezekiah being the other important exception). As a consequence, Josiah emerges as something of a model for the Deuteronomist as a genuine covenant keeper (see 2 Kgs. 23:25).

Along with the book of Deuteronomy and the Deuteronomic history, we may also consider the book of Jeremiah in its final form. The book of Jeremiah consists of a collection of poems that reflect on the anger and pathos of YHWH as Judah moves willfully toward its own destruction. That poetry, however, has been edited and organized according to a series of prose passages that impose a certain interpretation on the poetry and that surely reflect the same assumptions and cadences that are elsewhere regarded as Deuteronomic. The Deuteronomic edition of Jeremiah is likely a belated reflection on the destruction of Jerusalem to which the poetry bears witness, in order to equip the generations of the subsequent exilic community to recover its identity as a people of obedience to the Torah.

In the book of Jeremiah three particular points illuminate the Deuteronomic connection. First, the presence of the scribes Baruch (Jer. 36, 45) and Seriah (51:59–64) suggests, as Weinfeld opines, that the Deuteronomic edition of the book reflects a development of a scribal influence that was to shape emerging Judaism.

Second, King Jehoiachim's destruction of the scroll of Jeremiah and the rewriting of the scroll in Jeremiah 36 suggest a negative parallel to the finding of the scroll in 2 Kings 22, so that Josiah and his son Jehoiachim are both models for "good king, bad king" but also for ally and adversary of the Deuteronomic movement. The reference to the scroll in chapter 36 supports the thought that the Deuteronomic movement is a development of a "scroll consciousness" that already reflects, in an inchoate way, what became the notion of canon and the people of the book.

Third, the powerful presence of the family of Shaphan as a patron to the prophet Jeremiah and as a pro-Babylonian adversary to the royal policy in Jerusalem may help locate the ongoing tradition of Deuteronomy in the politics of Jerusalem (Jer. 36:10–12; 2 Kgs. 22:3–14; apparently a different Shaphan is mentioned in Jer. 26:24; 39:14; 40:5–11; 41:2; 43:6). That is, the covenantal theology of this tradition is not mere "religion," but a sociopolitical advocacy deeply rooted in covenantal tradition and resistant to the self-indulgent, self-destructive propensity of the royal house in Jerusalem. As the earlier Deuteronomic movement developed toward scribalism, some of the same interpretive accents reappear and function in the later interpretive history of 1 and 2 Chronicles and in the remarkable achievement of Ezra in reconstituting Judaism as a religion of Torah (see Neh. 8). Thus the imaginative, generative, interpretive impetus of

Deuteronomic tradition stands as a mediating force between the old memories of Moses and the later scribal work of funding Judaism.

This theological tradition of covenantalism continued with vitality into the New Testament (where Deuteronomy is one of the most quoted Old Testament texts) and into the covenantal aspects of Western political theory. Among other assertions, this tradition insists that human conduct (as obedience or disobedience) is a decisive determinant in the shape of a public future. Torah-keeping matters to the prospects for public life!

References: Campbell, Anthony F., and Mark A. O'Brien, *Unfolding the Deuteronomic History: Origins, Upgrades, Present Text* (Minneapolis: Fortress Press, 2000); McCarthy, Dennis J., "2 Samuel 7 and the Structure of the Deuteronomic History," *JBL* 84 (1965): 131–38; Nicholson, E. W., *Preaching to the Exiles: A Study of the Prose Tradition in the Book of Jeremiah* (Oxford: Blackwell, 1970); Noth, Martin, *The Deuteronomistic History* (JSOTSup 15; Sheffield: JSOT Press, 1981); Olson, Dennis T., *Deuteronomy and the Death of Moses: A Theological Reading* (OBT; Minneapolis: Fortress Press, 1994); Polzin, Robert, *Moses and the Deuteronomist: A Literary Study of the Deuteronomic History,* Part One: *Deuteronomy Joshua Judges* (New York: Seabury, 1980); Rad, Gerhard von, *Old Testament Theology I* New York: Harper & Brothers, 1962), 69–77, 219–30, 334–47; Stulman, Louis, *Order Amid Chaos: Jeremiah as Symbolic Tapestry* (The Biblical Seminar 57; Sheffield: Sheffield Academic Press, 1998); Weinfeld, Moshe, *Deuteronomy and the Deuteronomic School* (Oxford: Clarendon Press, 1972); Wolff, Hans Walter, "The Kerygma of the Deuteronomic Historical Work," in *The Vitality of Old Testament Traditions,* ed. Walter Brueggemann and Hans Walter Wolff (Atlanta: John Knox Press, 1975), 83–100.

Divine Council   The theological articulation of the Old Testament eventually reached an expression of monotheism: there is one God. But this expression of faith only coalesced later in the religious history of ancient Israel. The faith of Israel, moreover, emerged in a cultural world of polytheism: the conviction and practice that many gods exist, each with a different function and identity, and with varying commitments to different peoples. Israel's theological rhetoric had to be negotiated and adjudicated between this cultural environment of polytheism and a late theological passion for monotheism. That negotiation left a clear residue of polytheism in Israel's rhetoric, even though the Old Testament makes primal claims for monotheism.

The principal mode of negotiating the issues of polytheism and monotheism was by means of what scholars have come to call the "divine council," a mythic, poetic affirmation of many gods—sons of gods, angels, and other holy beings—who are alive and active, and who congregate in heaven and in concert make the ultimate decisions for the world. In the Canaanite rendition from which Israel borrowed, El is the High God who presides over the assembly of the gods, but El is old and remote. The young god Baal has energy and vitality, and he takes initiatives. The Israelite version of this imagery organizes the gods into an ordered community over which YHWH, the God of Israel, presides with full and unquestioned sovereignty. This YHWH is, like El, the presiding God, but like Baal has energy and vitality. YHWH combines features of various gods distinguished in Canaanite lore. The poetic settlement of the question of the gods also allows for many gods and affirms YHWH's singular sovereignty in heaven and over the earth.

The notion of "divine council" is most clearly and dramatically attested in the narrative of 1 Kings 22:19–23, which reports that the prophet had a vision—a religious discernment beyond the ordinary, a sense of the reality of God that the narrative itself takes seriously. Micaiah's vision is of "the host of heaven" in a meeting presided over by "the LORD" (YHWH), planning to subvert the rule of King Ahab of Israel "so that he may go up and fall at Ramoth-gilead" (v. 20). The portrayal is indeed primitive, for it presents the gods scheming on how to cause the death of the king. Granted its primitiveness, the imagery of divine assembly articulates a world in which the governance of the gods has a real and decisive effect on public, human affairs.

This imagery helps to explain the odd divine plural that is expressed, for example, in Genesis 1:26, 3:22, and 11:7, and Job 1–2, where the gods are making policy decisions about how to manage human affairs. The prophets, moreover, operate with a notion that the divine council authorizes and dispatches them to announce the verdict of heaven upon the affairs of earth—thus the authorizing formula "Thus says the Lord." Such a rubric helps to illuminate the divine plural in Isaiah 6:8 and the notion of being in and from the "divine council" in Jeremiah 23:15–22 and Amos 3:7.

The doxological tradition of Israel imagined that the lesser gods engage in worship of YHWH, the presiding God, and thus we find "sons of gods" ("heavenly beings") in Psalm 29:1 and "angels . . . mighty ones . . . hosts" in Psalm 103:20–21. These texts imagine harmony between YHWH and the lesser gods; but Psalm 82, where God sits in the "divine council," pictures YHWH as the one who judges and condemns lesser gods for failing to practice justice for widows and orphans, to which the High God is committed. Perhaps, then, the "assembly," under the rule of YHWH, could be harmonious or in disputatious conflict. An extreme disputatiousness would produce what is called, in postbiblical development, "fallen angels," heavenly beings that refuse the rule of YHWH.

Tracing any direct connection between this archaic imagery and the much later development of the Christian doctrine of the Trinity is not possible. The notion of "divine assembly" offers a societal divinity nonetheless, a notion that has resurfaced in the understanding of the Christian doctrine of the Trinity in the work of Jürgen Moltmann and Leonardo Boff. Both cases powerfully undermine the reductionist notion of a divine person as an isolated monolith. In both cases, the governing God is a God whose power is decisively marked by relatedness.

References: Boff, Leonardo, *Trinity and Society* (Maryknoll, N.Y.: Orbis Books, 1988); Clines, David J. A., "The Image of God in Man," *Tyndale Bulletin* 19 (1968): 53–103; Miller, Patrick D., "Cosmology and World Order in the Old Testament: The Divine Council as Cosmic-Political Symbol, *HBT* 9 (1987): 53–78; idem, *The Religion of Ancient Israel* (Louisville, Ky.: Westminster John Knox Press, 2000), 25–28; Moltmann, Jürgen, *The Trinity and the Kingdom: The Doctrine of God* (San Francisco: Harper and Row, 1981); Mullen, E. Theodore, *The Assembly of the Gods: The Divine Council in Canaanite and Early Hebrew Literature* (Cambridge: Harvard University Press, 1980).

■ ■ ■

Education   Like every community that seeks to sustain itself from generation to generation, early Israel enacted informal education of its young through a process of socialization into the lore and moral vision of the community. Two important elements in that socialization process were carried on particularly in the family, though perhaps in larger family units such as the clan or tribe.

1. Children were inducted into the narrative lore of the family; Israel regarded the transmission of such a narrative account of its past as immensely important. (An older influential scholarly hypothesis proposed that stylized creedal recitals were the taproot of such narrative lore.) This importance is indicated in a series of instructions advising the adult community to be prepared to answer the questions of children who inquire about the meaning of common ritual activity:

> "And when your children ask you, 'What do you mean by this observance?' you shall say, 'It is the passover sacrifice to the LORD, for he passed over the houses of the Israelites in Egypt, when he struck down the Egyptians but spared our houses.'" (Exod. 12:26–27; see Exod. 13: 8–10, 14–15; Deut 6:20–25; Josh. 4:21–24)

Indeed, the prescribed common cultic activities almost seem designed to evoke such questions from the child. The response of the adult community to the children is to be a narration of the fundamental memories of YHWH's key interventions and transformations in Israel's past. The goal of the transmission of such memories is to make YHWH narratively present and credible in the community into the next generation.

The urgency of this matter is evident in Psalm 78, which regards the future hope and obedience of Israel as dependent upon such narrative testimony:

> He established a decree in Jacob,
>   and appointed a law in Israel,
> which he commanded our ancestors
>   to teach to their children;
> that the next generation might know them,
>   the children yet unborn,
> and rise up and tell them to their children,
> so that they should set their hope in God,
> and not forget the works of God,
>   but keep his commandments.
>   (Ps. 78:4–7)

While some narrative socialization occurs in worship, narrative nurture also took place in other venues, such as at the village well:

> Tell of it, you who ride on white donkeys,
>   you who sit on rich carpets
>   and you who walk by the way.
> To the sound of musicians at the watering places,
>   there they repeat the triumphs of the LORD,
>   the triumphs of his peasantry in Israel.
>   (Judg. 5:10–11)

In that venue as well the subject is the "triumphs" of YHWH in which past generations of Israel had an active part. The three verbs of verse 10 that inform the initial imperative "tell"—ride, sit, walk—indicate that such narrative nurture was to be consistently undertaken in every circumstance. This triad of verbs, moreover, parallels the instruction of Deuteronomy 6:7, which again admonishes to tell all the time:

> Recite them to your children and talk about them when you are at home and when you are away, when you lie down and when you rise.

2. A second element of the socialization process also undertaken in the family was sapiential reflection on lived experience as written in the book of Proverbs, many sayings of which arise in the context of family and clan. This instruction is much more practical, designed to help the young reflect critically upon what they have seen and know firsthand. The

lessons seek to consider the hidden but firm connections between certain acts and certain consequences, and to ponder both the intractable givens of lived reality that cannot be safely violated and the zones of freedom that require moral discernment and choice. While concrete and practical, the instruction also rests on the assumption that lived reality is an ordered moral coherence governed and presided over by the creator God. In an understated way, this instruction also thus helps to situate the life of the young in a Yahwistic world; the result is that the process of socialization through practical reflection, as through narrative lore, is intensely and intentionally theological.

As the society of Israel was reformulated as a state, new modes of education emerged that came from neighboring societies. The more informal worship practices of a simple agrarian society now had as a parallel the great liturgies enacted in the temple. These liturgies apparently reenacted the great myths of creation that were known elsewhere in the Near East. Specifically the Jerusalem temple reenacted something like an Enthronement Festival, wherein YHWH was rearticulated regularly not only as governor and savior of Israel's life but as the creator of heaven and earth (see Pss. 93, 96–99). What's more, the liturgy was also instruction, providing the means and the occasions whereby the world could be reimagined in Yahwistic formulation.

The early socialization processes of family, clan, and tribe were, so far as we know, completely informal. As Israel became a more complex state society, perhaps formal schools emerged, but the evidence concerning this development is greatly in dispute. On the one hand, clear evidence for such schools in Israel is found as late as Ben Sirach in the Hel-

lenistic period. On the other hand, however, scribes handled the necessary "paperwork" for the monarchy. While it cannot be demonstrated, some formal education must have existed in the monarchial period through which the sons of the urban elite became equipped for the management of public, royal power. These scribes certainly had to be able to read and write; beyond that they had to be instructed in the practice of state power and hopefully in the arts of discernment so essential to the responsible practice of power.

The more formal emergence of a scribal class that exercised immense social power was originally a state function. With the end of the monarchy and the reformation of Judaism, however, scribes came to be the learned power class that enjoyed power without being accountable to a sponsoring or supervising monarchy. The scribes surely were the learned group who managed the formal educational processes and who developed the sapiential literature that we have, not only in the centrist articulation of Proverbs in both its empirical and speculative modes, but also in the disputatious considerations of truth and reality reflected in the books of Job and Ecclesiastes. The literature that probes the hidden ordering of reality is as close to scientific knowledge as the Old Testament comes.

As we trace the development of education from informal socialization in the family and simple liturgy to the more formal institutions of the state, and as we consider the emergent forms of education in prestate, state, and poststate circumstances in Israel, education was evidently a pervasive and crucial process for Israel that took a variety of forms, depending on circumstance and available resources. These several forms surely existed side by side, and each worked in its own way. All of these forms of instruction, education, socialization, and nurture had an immediate practical agenda concerning the well-being of the community as well as the management of life processes that had a deeply hidden theological dimension. Along with such practical concerns, all of these modes of teaching and learning broadly assumed a Yahwistic world order.

Religious education was not a separate, discrete enterprise. Rather an entire vision of life was nurtured, valued, and critiqued with reference to the God who inhabited the most ancient lore and the most splendid liturgies. As a consequence, all such education had within it, either explicit or implied, a covenantal assumption that well-being required coming to terms with the ordered reality that remained partly enigmatic and partly discernable, an ordered reality given by YHWH and not open to excessive human invention. While in agreement on this elemental conviction, this pluriform education was, in each case, filtered through and shaped by perceptions and engagements that were immediately and intensely in the service of vested interest, each case of which conserve, but some of which dispute—all of which want to know, but must along the way "trust and obey."

References: Blenkinsopp, Joseph, *Sage, Priest, and Prophet: Religious and Intellectual Leadership in Ancient Israel* (Library of Ancient Israel; Louisville, Ky.: Westminster John Knox Press, 1995); idem, *Wisdom and Law in the Old Testament: The Ordering of Life in Israel and Early Judaism* (Oxford: Oxford University Press, 1995); Brown, William P., *Character in Crisis: A Fresh Approach to the Wisdom Literature of the Old Testament* (Grand Rapids: Eerdmans, 1996); Crenshaw, James L., *Education in Ancient Israel: Across the Deadening Silence* (New York: Doubleday, 1998); Fishbane, Michael, *Text and Texture: Close Readings of Selected Biblical Texts* (New York: Schocken, 1979), 79–83; Lemaire, Andre, "The Sage in School and Temple," in *The Sage in Israel and the Ancient Near East,* ed. John G. Gammie and Leo G. Perdue (Winona Lake, Ind.: Eisenbrauns, 1990), 165–181; Perdue, Leo G. et al., *Families in Ancient Israel* (Louisville, Ky.: Westminster John Knox Press, 1997).

Egypt   As a very ancient culture, already ancient in the time of the Old Testament, Egypt sat intransigent as the southern anchor of the Fertile Crescent. The nation characteristically functioned as a counterpoint politically and militarily to the rising and falling dominant powers to the north. For that reason, Egypt regularly sought to claim the in-between territory of Syria-Palestine as a buffer against its northern rivals. As a consequence, conquering the land of Israel was always a goal of Egypt's, and from time to time they succeeded. Egypt's intrusion on Israel in the Old Testament period is especially evident in the incursion of Shishak (1 Kgs. 14:25) and in the later monarchial period of Israel when Egypt functioned as a foil to the rising power of Babylon (see 2 Kgs. 23:28–29).

In the imaginative construal of Egypt in the Old Testament, Egypt as a political-military reality clearly takes on important symbolic, metaphorical power well beyond anything that can be established historically. We may identify five important points at which Egypt figures in Israel's self-presentation.

1. In the Joseph narrative (Gen. 37–50), Egypt is the breadbasket of that part of the world to which others came in the midst of famine (see Gen. 12:10–20). As a land of abundance, however, Egypt was already portrayed in Genesis 47:13–26 as a monopolizing power that deprived peasants of their land and livelihood. Even the affirmation of Egypt as "breadbasket"

serves as a harbinger of the Exodus narrative to come. We already know in Genesis 47 how some ended in slavery.

2. The primary reference to Egypt in the Old Testament concerns the Exodus narrative, which portrays Egypt as a place of bondage from which YHWH has emancipated Israel. Egyptian power is portrayed as completely antagonistic to the will of YHWH, so that the struggle between Pharaoh and YHWH in Exodus 7–12 is a struggle to determine the true sovereign of Egypt. The victory of YHWH claimed in Israel's songs and narratives is a decisive reference point for Old Testament faith. Negatively, the ultimate curse in the long curse recital of Deuteronomy 28 concerns Egypt:

> The LORD will bring you back in ships to Egypt, by a route that I promised you would never see again; and there you shall offer yourselves for sale to your enemies as male and female slaves, but there will be no buyer. (Deut. 28:68)

This curse seems to be enacted in the narrative of Jeremiah 43–44, which tells of a dramatic return to Egypt, thus nullifying the entire history of emancipation (see Deut. 17:16).

3. In the narrative of Solomon (1 Kgs. 3–11), the text is at pains to connect Solomon to Pharaoh by way of marriage (1 Kgs. 3:1; 7:8; 9:24; 11:1). These references, scattered throughout the narrative, may indicate an important political alliance between Solomon and Egypt. If, however, we allow the text to have an ironic dimension, the narrative likely intends the reader to notice that Solomon, in his success and opulence, began to govern like Pharaoh in ruthless, exploitative ways. Thus the narrative serves to establish Solomon's guilt by association, for his rule largely disregarded the covenantal restraints and possibilities so central in Israel's self-understanding.

4. Perhaps connected to the memory of Solomon, Egyptian traditions clearly influence Israelite wisdom. The text of Proverbs 22:17–23:12 is demonstrably dependent on the Egyptian "Instruction of Amenenope," suggesting a common element of shared culture.

5. In the later oracles against the nations, Egypt figures prominently (Isa. 19; Jer. 46; Ezek. 29–30, 32). These references may occur because in a later period Egypt endlessly meddled in Israel's affairs. More likely Egypt has become, from the outset of Israel's memory, a defining image of hostility to YHWH's governance. Thus in Ezekiel 29:3, Egypt is quoted as making an immense claim for autonomy, the very autonomy that in Genesis 47 permitted Pharaoh to be a monopolizer and in the Exodus narrative permitted oppressive policy. In Psalm 87:4, the same negative judgment on Egypt is intensified when the poet names Egypt "Rahab," the evil sea monster who in chaos opposes the rule of YHWH (see Isa. 30:7). As a symbol of resistance to YHWH, that Ezekiel offers laments for a failed Egypt that cannot survive in resistance to YHWH (Ezek. 30–32) is not surprising. Even recalcitrant "Egypt" becomes a way of affirming YHWH's sovereignty.

Two remarkable texts that suggest the ultimate hope of Israel that eventually even Egypt does not lie beyond the sphere of YHWH's sovereignty. Isaiah 19:23–25 anticipates that Egypt will become "my people." In Ezekiel 32:31, as Davis has shown, Pharaoh will in the end repent and submit to YHWH. These notices are important for the extremity of Israel's hope in YHWH's good sovereignty. For the most part, however, Israel sees Egypt as threat and seduction, to which the only alternative is YHWH's liberating, covenanted rule.

The durable power of the imagery of Egypt is evident in the New Testament in Matthew's reference to Egypt as the place from which Jesus and his parents were taken (Matt. 2:19–23).

References: Ash, Paul S., *David, Solomon, and Egypt: A Reassessment* (JSOTSup 292: Sheffield: Sheffield Academic Press, 1999); Brueggemann, Walter, "Pharaoh as Vassal: A Study of a Political Metaphor," *CBQ* 57 (1995): 27–51; Davis, Ellen, "'And Pharaoh Will Change His Mind . . .' (Ezekiel 32:31): Dismantling Mythical Discourse," in *Theological Exegesis: Essays in Honor of B. S. Childs,* ed. Christopher R. Seitz and Kathryn Green-McCreight (Grand Rapids: Eerdmans, 1998), 224–39; Fretheim, Terence E., "The Plagues as Ecological Signs of Historical Disaster," *JBL* 110 (1991): 385–96; Friedman, Richard E., "From Egypt to Egypt: Dtr1 and Dtr2," in *Traditions in Transformation: Turning Points in Biblical Faith,* ed. Baruch Halpern and Jon D. Levenson (Winona Lake, Ind.: Eisenbrauns, 1981), 167–92; Grimal, N., *A History of Ancient Egypt* (Oxford: Blackwell, 1992); Redford, Donald B., *Egypt, Canaan, and Israel* (Princeton: Princeton University Press, 1992).

Election   "Election" is a traditional way of expressing the conviction that YHWH has "chosen" Israel to be YHWH's special people in the world and has singularly committed YHWH's own future to Israel's well-being. This conviction, expressed especially by the verb "choose" (*bḥr*), is the pervasive, governing premise of faith in the Old Testament. The premise asserts that YHWH is the God who has made such a decision and is irrevocably linked to Israel, and that Israel's life and future are inalienably connected to YHWH's character and purpose.

Several Old Testament traditions express this conviction. Of Abraham, the Scriptures state, "I have chosen him" (Gen. 18:19). In the Exodus tradition, Israel is YHWH's "firstborn son" (Exod. 4:22). At Sinai Israel is to be "my treasured possession out of all the peoples" (Exod. 19:5). In an older poem, Israel is YHWH's "own portion . . . allotted share . . . the apple of his eye" (Deut. 32:9–10). In the tradition of Deuteronomy, the conviction of chosenness is made most clear and decisive:

> For you are a people holy to the LORD your God; the LORD your God has chosen you out of all the peoples on earth to be his people, his treasured possession.
> It was not because you were more numerous than any other people that the LORD set his heart on you and chose you—for you were the fewest of all peoples. It was because the LORD loved you and kept the oath that he swore to your ancestors, that the LORD has brought you out with a mighty hand, and redeemed you from the house of slavery, from the hand of Pharaoh king of Egypt.
> (Deut. 7:6–8; see 9:4–7; 14:2)

> Although heaven and the heaven of heavens belong to the LORD your God, the earth with all that is in it, yet the LORD set his heart in love on your ancestors alone and chose you, their descendants after them, out of all the peoples, as it is today.
> (Deut. 10:14–15)

Israel's special status as YHWH's chosen people evidently carries with it a deep, nonnegotiable requirement to live in obedience to YHWH by adhering to the Torah. YHWH chose Israel as YHWH's own treasured people from all the peoples of the earth in order that Israel should conform to YHWH's will. Thus the wonder of election is intimately connected to the reality of Torah commandments. The God who loves Israel is the God who will be sovereign in Israel's life, and the eighth- and seventh-century prophets thereby regularly speak of that special status being the ground for punishment because of disobedience:

You only have I known
  of all the families of the earth;
therefore I will punish you
  for all your iniquities.

(Amos 3:2)

A case can be made that the disaster of the sixth century—the destruction of Jerusalem and the deportation—is a massive rejection of Israel as YHWH's chosen people, although the traditions themselves disagree about the depth of that rejection. In any case, the salvation oracles of exilic Isaiah reconfirm that Israel is YHWH's chosen people, a status that endures the deep disruption:

But you, Israel, my servant,
  Jacob, whom I have *chosen*,
  the offspring of Abraham, my friend;
you whom I took from the ends of the
    earth,
  and called from its farthest corners,
saying to you, "You are my servant,
  I have chosen you and not cast you
    off";
do not fear, for I am with you,
  do not be afraid, for I am your God.

(Isa. 41:8–10, emphasis added)

But now hear, O Jacob my servant,
  Israel whom I have *chosen*!
Thus says the Lord who made you,
  who formed you in the womb and will
    help you:
Do not fear, O Jacob my servant,
  Jeshurun whom I have *chosen*.

(Isa. 44:1–2, emphasis added; see 43:1;
Ezek. 20:5)

In these utterances, even the unbearable loss of exile is contained within the conviction of enduring chosenness.

The tradition also is able to affirm that YHWH—as a choosing God, in less celebrated fashion—also makes other, subordinate choices, including priests of particular orders (Deut. 18:5; Ps. 105:26) and specific individuals, as in the case of Jeremiah (1:5) and Isaiah 49:5, where the "servant" is likely Israel personified. Most interesting is the claim in Psalm 78 that YHWH is committed to the Jerusalem establishment, including the temple (on which see 2 Chr. 7:16) and dynasty:

He rejected the tent of Joseph,
  he did not choose the tribe of Ephraim;
but he *chose* the tribe of Judah,
  Mount Zion, which he loves. . . .
He *chose* his servant David,
  and took him from the sheepfolds;
from tending the nursing ewes he brought
    him
  to be the shepherd of his people Jacob,
  of Israel, his inheritance.

(Ps. 78:67–71, emphasis added)

Thus the conviction of chosenness can become quite particular and, evidently, readily lent itself to ideological use, for this text exhibits a claim not only for Jerusalem but against a rival claim for the North and particularly against the sanctuary at Shiloh (v. 60).

This defining conviction of the Old Testament lives in tension with an awareness, also present in the text, that the God of Israel is the creator of heaven and earth, and therefore the God of many peoples. In traditional usage, the function of the "Noah covenant" is to articulate this universal claim for YHWH (Gen. 9:8–17). The text of the Old Testament is put together to affirm at the same time both the wide expanse of YHWH's governance and YHWH's particular commitment to Israel, although different texts tilt the tension in different ways. In Genesis 12:1–3, YHWH's promise to Abraham provides that through Abraham all peoples will be blessed, so that even in this act of intimate commitment the others are in view. In Amos 9:7, for example, the poet entertains the thought that YHWH does "exoduses" for many peoples—including Israel's enemies—alongside Israel's exodus. In Isaiah 42:6–7 and 49:6, Israel is to be "a light to the nations." Isaiah 19:23–25, moreover, can envision a coming time when YHWH will have a plurality of chosen peoples and Israel will have no monopoly on that status. The text hints many times that this God has other peoples with their own stories of chosenness.

The claim for chosenness is doubtlessly an affront to "universal reason" that eschews all particularity and finds it abhorrent to think that God takes sides in the world. This so-called "scandal of particularity"—that YHWH would "elect Israel"—is familiarly celebrated in the light verse of Ogden Nash: "How odd of God / to choose the Jews." Chosenness is unmistakably a defining oddity of the text. Failure to recognize the defining quality of that claim for the text, moreover, is a measure of how deeply misunderstood the Old Testament text can be. Indeed, one can make the case that the long, brutal history of anti-Semitism in Western culture is the venomous attempt to eradicate that claim of particularity upon which the Bible stands or falls. But after all such attempts, the claim stands that YHWH has engaged the world in this particular way and is not—never intended to be—a neutral, nonpartisan, uncommitted God. Choosing Israel is a premise for which no explanation is offered; this act is of this God, who need provide no explanation (see Exod. 33:19).

Three derivative points about election can be instructive here:

1. The "scandal of particularity," whereby YHWH has chosen Israel, continues to haunt Christian faith, as is evidenced in Paul's difficult reasoning in Romans 9–11. The Christian claim for "Jesus as Messiah," moreover, is a parallel, albeit derivative, claim upon which Christian faith stands or falls—that the creator of heaven and earth came fully present in this one man. Thus Judaism and Christianity share this "scandalous claim" about the creator of heaven and earth.

2. The liberation theology of Roman Catholics in Central America has enunciated a new notion of election under the rubric of "God's preferential option for the poor," a phrase which asserts that God has chosen the poor as God's special people. This claim is rooted in a reading of the Bible which believes that Israel at the outset was not an ethnic community, but that God gathered the poor people of the land and formed them into the community of Israel. That claim for election has been in tension with the Jewish claim of election, which has some ethnic dimensions to it. The claim of liberation theology can likely be sustained in a credible way, but only as derived from the primal Jewish claim to chosenness.

3. A peculiar claim such as chosenness is open to shameless and perhaps destructive ideological manipulation. In the text itself, such chosenness became a warrant in the book of Joshua for the extermination of other peoples (Josh. 12:7–24). In the long history of the church—and perhaps in the contemporary state of Israel—the notion of chosenness has served and may continue to function as self-justification for actions incongruent with the God who chooses.

In the subsequent development of Christian theology, especially in the tradition of John Calvin, the notion of "the elect" was hardened and perhaps unfortunately reified into teaching about predestination and double predestination. These formulations are attempts to root assurance of salvation in the inscrutable will of God. Such a formulation, however, lies well beyond the scope of this investigation and turns the notion of YHWH's choosing in ways not intended or envisioned in the text. A less triumphalist view among Christians of election as "God's chosen people" may be emerging in newer discernment about the mission of the church in the twenty-first century.

References: Bellis, Alice Ogden, and Joel S. Kaminsky, eds., *Jews, Christians, and the Theology of the Hebrew Scriptures* (Atlanta: Society of Biblical Literature, 2000); Brueggemann, Walter, "'Exodus' in the Plural (Amos 9:7)," in *Many Voices, One God: Being Faithful in a Pluralistic World: In Honor of Shirley Guthrie*, ed. Walter Brueggemann and George W. Stroup (Louisville, Ky.: Westminster John Knox Press, 1998), 15–34; idem, "A Shattered Transcendence? Exile and Restoration," in *Biblical Theology Problems and Perspectives: In Honor of J. Christiaan Beker*, ed. Steven J. Kraftchick et al. (Nashville: Abingdon Press, 1995), 169–82; Levenson, Jon D., *The Hebrew Bible, the Old Testament, and Historical Criticism* (Louisville, Ky.: Westminster/John Knox Press, 1993), 127–59; Miller, Patrick D., "God's Other Stories: On the Margins of Deuteronomic Theology," in *Israelite Religion and Biblical Theology: Collected Essays* (JSOTSup 267; Sheffield: Sheffield Academic Press, 2000), 593–602; Rowley, H. H., *The Biblical Doctrine of Election* (London: Lutterworth Press, 1950); Van Buren, Paul, *Discerning the Way: A Theology of the Jewish-Christian Reality* (New York: Seabury Press, 1980).

Elijah   In a book of theological themes such as this, mentioning personalities may seem a bit odd. I do so, however, with four men from the tradition—Moses, David, Elijah, and Ezra—because in each case that individual person embodies a crucial theological claim of the Old Testament.

Elijah appears only briefly in the narrative of the Old Testament, in materials that are commonly regarded as "legends"— that is, narratives without the kind of good "historical evidence" that scholars require of a text in order for it to have critical weight. As with Moses and David, we are limited to the presentation of Elijah given in the biblical text itself.

Elijah is presented as the quintessential prophet in the wake of Moses, perhaps referred to as "a prophet like you" anticipated in Deuteronomy 18:17, clearly linked to and patterned after Moses:

1. Elijah is invested with remarkable powers to enact transformative miracles that through his life bespeak the lively presence of YHWH (1 Kgs. 17:8–16, 17–24).

2. Elijah is presented as the great champion of YHWH and of religious Yahwism in its life-or-death struggle with Baalism (1 Kgs. 18). The so-called "contest" at Mt. Carmel is a defining moment in the religious history of Israel when Baalism, championed by the dynasty of Omri in North Israel, was regarded as the sharp antithesis of Yahwism and as a primal threat to YHWH's rule. Elijah, in prophetic fierceness, is portrayed as YHWH's fearless champion who establishes the singular claim of YHWH against entrenched religious, political power.

3. The fierce and deeply religious contrast of YHWH versus Baal is matched, according to narrative presentation, by an equally fierce conflict between competing economic theories of land and property, which are linked to religious claims. In 1 Kings 21, Elijah, on behalf of Naboth, is spokesperson for an old tribal theory of inheritance that precludes the royal notion of land as a tradable commodity. By connecting the religious contest of 1 Kings 18 to the economic conflict of chapter 21, the text makes clear that religious loyalty and economic-political practices

are intimately linked to each other. The outcome of the Naboth confrontation is that Elijah pronounces a massive prophetic threat against the dynasty of Ahab (1 Kgs. 21:20–24), a prophetic threat that awaited fulfillment until 2 Kings 9:30–37. The connection between oracle and narrative fulfillment functions to attest that the prophetic word of Elijah is indeed powerful and effective in the historical process.

4. In 2 Kings 2:9–12, Elijah is bodily taken up into heaven in the presence of eyewitnesses. That he "ascended" attests that he did not die but continues to live. (The only other such case in the Old Testament concerns Enoch, of whom the text tersely reports, "God took him" [Gen. 5:24]. This report became immensely generative in Jewish mysticism and resulted in an extended speculative literature on Enoch.) The narrative exhibits no interest in this remarkable account of ascent. The important point for the developing tradition is, instead, the claim that Elijah still lives. His departure means in turn that he has the capacity to reappear in Israel's future in unthinkable ways, to "come again" with power into the future. The narrative of 2 Kings no doubt understands Elisha, disciple of Elijah, as a carrier of the same inscrutable power that Elijah exhibited. The evidence of Elijah's durable power is the fact that in the Christian Old Testament (unlike the Hebrew Bible of Judaism), the literature is arranged so that Elijah is present in a promissory way in the very last verses of Malachi:

Lo, I will send you the prophet Elijah before the great and terrible day of the LORD comes. He will turn the hearts of parents to their children and the hearts of children to their parents, so that I will not come and strike the land with a curse. (Mal. 4:5–6)

In this ending of the Christian Old Testament, the canon seems to terminate with Elijah ready and poised to leap dramatically and prophetically into the future. Indeed, he does! Out of the notion of his ascent has emerged an extended literature outside the canon that served speculation about the future. (The literature emerged from Enoch for the same reason.)

In one such leap into the future, Elijah appears prominently and in important ways in the New Testament. His importance is thus as a principal vehicle whereby the core prophetic faith of Israel is carried into the New Testament. He is more than a historical possibility, but a device for futuring, as his prophetic perspective continues to operate into the future. For good reason, the early church in the New Testament found his futuring resonant with what they discerned of Jesus:

Elijah is intimately connected to John the Baptist as a forerunner (Matt. 11:14; 17:11–12; Mark 9:11–13; Luke 9:8, 19).

Some people confuse Jesus himself with Elijah (Matt. 16:14; Mark 8:28; John 1:21–25).

Elijah appears with Moses to Jesus at the mountain, perhaps the pair embodying "the law and the prophets" (Matt. 17:3; Mark 9:4–5; Luke 9:30–33).

Jesus on the cross is thought to appeal to Elijah (Matt. 27:47–49; Mark 15:35–36).

In addition, Luke 1:17 alludes to Malachi 4:5–6. More broadly, Luke 4:25–26, Romans 11:2–4, and James 5:17 all recall the life and ministry of Elijah as a way to understand the present reality of Christian life. Elijah is thus the primary character in the Old Testament who continues to have presence and vitality in the New Testament, linking the two Testaments and the two interpretive communities together.

Christians clearly have no monopoly on Elijah's future. Among Jews a chair is left empty at Passover, in anticipation of the return of Elijah into the reality of Jewish life and faith, a harbinger of the messianic age.

References: Brueggemann, Walter, *Testimony to Otherwise* (St. Louis: Chalice Press, 2001); Culley, Robert C., *Studies in the Structure of Hebrew Narrative* (Philadelphia: Fortress Press, 1976); Napier, Davie, *Word of God, Word of Earth* (Philadelphia: United Church Press, 1976).

Ethics The Old Testament is of course a literature that is concerned with ethics, but its ethical dimension is immensely complex and is often abused by attempts to reduce it to a manageable simplicity. The Old Testament is an attempt to redescribe the world with reference to YHWH, who is the creator of heaven and earth and who is the covenant partner of Israel. As concerns ethics, the Old Testament attempts to reconstrue responsible human conduct in terms of YHWH's will and purpose. The redescription of the world and reconstrual of human conduct, however, are not done in any systematic fashion. Rather only bits and pieces of narrative, song, poem, and law are present, which can be connected and construed in a variety of ways. Moreover, the discernment of YHWH's will and purpose is filtered through concrete historical circumstance and social interest. Thus, from the outset we are forewarned against any attempt to regard the Old Testament as a clear and unambiguous ethical guide or as a casebook on ethical behavior.

We may consider ethics in the Old Testament through several predominant constructs:

1. The Old Testament reflects a *covenantal ethic.* That is, Israel is bound to YHWH, who as sovereign ruler is the one whom Israel must obey. The key issue in ethics then is YHWH's character and intention, so that obedience is to bring human life into harmony with YHWH. Consequently from a theological perspective no autonomous rules or positivistic laws exist, but only the will of the Lord of the covenant to whom Israel seeks to respond responsibly. The practice of ethics is an effort at fidelity to this defining relationship.

2. In the Old Testament, the will of the Lord of the covenant is given in the *commands of Sinai,* which are organized into two unequal parts: the Decalogue and the rest of the Torah. The first part, the Decalogue, is the Ten Commandments of Exodus 20:1–17. [See THE DECALOGUE.] In the awesome theophanic context of Sinai, YHWH issued directly to Israel ten commands that form the foundation of all biblical ethics. The commands concern (a) the honor due to YHWH in order to avoid the distortion of idolatry and (b) neighbor practices that honor the life of the neighbor and so make a neighborly society possible.

In a theological sense, the remaining Torah instruction may be said to derive from and interpret the ten commands of Sinai. The purpose of the ongoing interpretive traditions from the core teaching of Sinai is to ensure that YHWH's sovereign purpose extends to every phase of Israel's life in every circumstance, so that Israel can live life in joyous response to YHWH, who has made Israel's life possible.

The interpretive traditions concern attentiveness to the love of God (the practice of holiness) and the love of neighbor (the practice of justice). While this extended interpretive material, rooted in Sinai and expressed in Exodus-Leviticus-Numbers-Deuteronomy, is richly varied and attentively detailed, we may usefully attend to two extreme extrapolations from Sinai. Concerning the interpretive trajectory of the love of God, the text arrives at the Day of Atonement, which is the extreme expression of Israel's yearning for communion with the Holy God; in that festival Israel is made eligible for such communion by way of atonement (Lev. 16). In parallel fashion, the extreme expression of love of neighbor is articulated in the festival of Jubilee, which enacts the unqualified entitlement of even vulnerable neighbors (Lev. 25). These two festivals suggest a radically alternative vision of reality resulting from the radical character of the commanding God.

3. By and large, *the prophetic tradition of the eighth- and seventh-century prophets* is an ethical articulation that purports to be rooted in the covenant traditions of Torah. While the several prophets may have a variety of origins and social locations, in canonical form these poetic traditions concern (a) YHWH's covenantal commands, (b) Israel's persistent and systemic violation of those commands, and (c) the inescapable sanctions that Israel's disobedience evokes. Out of this concern has emerged a vision of justice, for the most part negatively voiced, that envisions public policy rooted in trust of YHWH and expressed as distributive justice toward the vulnerable and resourceless.

4. Alongside the Sinai tradition that in canonical form funds the prophetic traditions are *the creation traditions* that are voiced in the familiar creation narratives but also in Israel's doxologies. In these traditions, creation is understood as a network of creaturely relationships arranged to form a coherent, ethical whole by the power and goodness of the creator. YHWH wills that creation be a generative organism that produces life and well-being in extravagant measure. The creation as YHWH's abundant gift, however, is not devoid of ethical form, for the God of Sinai would not create a morally indifferent world. The creation traditions carry both their own sense of the ethical "givenness" that is nonnegotiable in creation and the ethical curbs that are intrinsic to the processes of creation. In the two creation stories, human creatures are thus given positive mandates (Gen. 1:28; 2:15) and a prohibition that precludes autonomy (Gen. 2:17), the violation of which carries the seeds of death.

In articulating the creation as a moral coherence, Israel's doxological traditions do not appeal specifically to covenantal matters. Nonetheless, the creation itself issues mandates of obedience that must be honored, all of which are designed to curb the destructive autonomy of creation or any of its creatures. This design is evidenced in the conclusions of the two great hymns of creation that celebrate the generosity of creation but end with a severe notice:

> Let sinners be consumed from the earth,
>   and let the wicked be no more.
>   (Ps. 104:34)

> The LORD watches over all who love him,
>   but all the wicked he will destroy.
>   (Ps. 145:20)

The content of "the wicked" is not specified and no doubt refers to the content of the Sinai commands. On its own terms, however, the "wickedness" warned against concerns violating the requirements intrinsic to creation itself, requirements only of late noticed through the environmental crisis.

This notion of intrinsic requirements of creation has led scholars, in the wake of Barthian resistance, to postulate a "natural theology," that is, that creatureliness itself knows something of God's intent that must not be violated. Barton has observed that the oracles against the nations in Amos 1–2, for example, savagely condemn the unethical practice of the nations who know nothing of Sinai but who, in their creatureliness, are expected to know and honor the limits of brutality and violence.

5. The traditions of covenant and creation are fully of a piece. They are nicely brought together in the *Psalter of Israel*, which embodies a kind of ecumenical gathering of Israel's several distinct traditions into a unified affirmation of glad response to YHWH's extravagance in creation and YHWH's solidarity in covenant. These traditions are brought together in the singing of Israel, as two examples can show:

(a) In Psalm 19, verses 7–10 celebrate the Torah commandments and affirm that obedience to Torah is a source of life and well-being. In verses 1–6, however, the wonder of creation is celebrated. In the completed Psalm the creation is the matrix in which the specificity of the Torah is situated, so that the two together lead to an affirmation that obedience to Torah is the way in which Israel receives the gift of life from the creator.

(b) In Psalm 24 Israel affirms that the world belongs to YHWH (vv. 1–2) and that the king of glory, creator of heaven and earth, is in the midst of Israel (vv. 7–10). Between these two great doxological utterances, Israel ponders and embraces the quite specific requirements of covenantal neighborliness (vv. 3–6). The readiness to act responsibly is not "rule based"; instead, out of these several traditions emerges a quite clear characteri-

zation of what an obedient, generative, joyous life looks like when lived in response to YHWH's generosity and fidelity.

6. The ethical traditions rooted in creation are given detailed and sustained articulation in *the wisdom teaching of the book of Proverbs*, which includes reference to "wisdom" and "foolishness," terms not much used elsewhere. Scholars now generally concur that wisdom teaching is essentially a close pondering of creation in order to determine the kinds of behaviors that enhance or diminish life. Thus "wisdom" is action that is congruent with the ordered way of creation and that therefore enhances life; conversely, "foolishness" is action that contradicts YHWH's will for creation and that therefore diminishes life and ultimately brings death. What's more, ethical reflection in sapiential moves opened Israel to the wide horizon of international ethics, for wisdom reflection is shared across many cultures. Openness to this mode of reflection is set alongside the more rigorous in-house traditions of Sinai and brings to Israel a worldly perspective in a very broad scope.

7. One other script of ethics is of particular interest. The *book of Deuteronomy*, and especially the commands of chapters 12–25, is related to Sinai, but they are not given at Sinai. They are uttered later, "in the land of Moab" (1:5). As a radical restatement of the ethics of Sinai for a later time, place, and circumstance, the book of Deuteronomy is thus an example, within scripture, of the dynamic processes whereby the requirements of YHWH are endlessly under review, open to interpretation, and extrapolated in quite fresh directions. The book of Deuteronomy is unmistakable evidence that the ethics of the Old Testament is not a closed, fixed, flat, settled code of conduct; rather, Old Testament ethics is an ongoing interpre-

tive tradition undertaken to determine how, in any particular context, to make glad response to the generosity of the creator and to the expectations of the God of Sinai. The broad lines of ethical guidance are clearly taken to be congruent with YHWH's character; the concreteness and specificity of ethical conduct, however, is to be worked out in context.

No easy or direct way is available to use the Bible in ethical reflection. We can readily identify two great temptations in this regard. The first temptation is to take in simplistic fashion particular phrasing from the biblical text and transpose it into a flat, absolute rule, without recognizing that every such textual utterance is context specific. Such simplistic moralizing tends to elevate particulars into absolutes, all the while missing the main point of glad, responsible gratitude. The second temptation, an easy one given Christian stereotypes of Old Testament "law," is to think that the Christian gospel supersedes or makes obsolete the specific requirements of "Old Testament law." Of course, such a dismissive attitude is simply a convenience to avoid the hard work of ethical responsibility.

A third alternative exists to simplistic legalism and dismissive antilegalism: critical interpretive reflection. Responsible engagement with the ethical force of the Old Testament is not done *de novo* or in a vacuum. Long interpretive traditions of ethical teaching in both Judaism and Christianity form the context for undertaking continued ethical reflection. This approach is not to deny that the ethical traditions themselves may practice distortion, as in the extreme patriarchy of some forms of Judaism or in the collusion with slavery in some forms of Christianity. On balance, however, the depth and longevity of the interpretive traditions provide ballast and wisdom for contemporary obedience. The God of Israel has a long history with this people that seeks to be obedient. When the current generation—Jewish and Christian—assumes that task, the long process of interpretation steps up to the present. The urgency of our own reflection is not diminished, but our ethical reflection is set deep in communities of obedience and gratitude.

References: Barton, John, *Amos's Oracles Against the Nations: A Study of Amos 1:3–2:5* (Cambridge: Cambridge University Press, 1980); idem, "Understanding Old Testament Ethics," *JSOT* 9 (1979): 44–64; Birch, Bruce C., *Let Justice Roll Down: The Old Testament, Ethics, and Christian Life* (Louisville, Ky.: Westminster/John Knox Press, 1991); Childs, Brevard S., *Biblical Theology of the Old and New Testaments: Theological Reflection on the Christian Bible* (Minneapolis: Fortress Press, 1993), 658–716; Crüsemann, Frank, *The Torah: Theology and Social History of Old Testament Law* (Edinburgh: T. & T. Clark, 1996); Fohrer, Georg, "The Righteous Man in Job 31," in *Essays in Old Testament Ethics,* ed. James L. Crenshaw and John T. Willis (New York: KTAV Publishing House, 1974), 1–22; Janzen, Waldemar, *Old Testament Ethics: A Pragmatic Approach* (Louisville, Ky.: Westminster John Knox Press, 1994); Muilenburg, James, *The Way of Israel: Biblical Faith and Ethics* (New York: Harper & Brothers, 1961); Petersen, David, *The Roles of Israel's Prophets* (Sheffield: JSOT Press, 1981); Pleins, J. David, *The Social Visions of the Hebrew Bible* (Louisville, Ky.: Westminster John Knox Press, 2001); Rad, Gerhard von, *Wisdom in Israel* (Nashville: Abingdon Press, 1972).

Exile   The process of deporting and displacing conquered and subjugated peoples was not a rarity in the ancient Near East. Dominating imperial forces seem regularly to have relocated leading citizens of a conquered community into alien political environments while leaving in residence "lesser" peoples who were unlikely to resist or rebel against domination. Exile is understood as a consequence of imperial policy designed to establish new political and economic order in a subjugated realm.

The Assyrian empire in the eighth and seventh centuries B.C.E. clearly practiced such a policy through which individuals and families were harshly displaced for reasons of state (see Isa. 36:17). Specifically, 2 Kings 17 reports on such a deportation in 722 when Assyrian armies conquered the northern kingdom of Israel and its capital Samaria, incorporating that territory into Assyria's own imperial administration. The text describes in some detail the fact that the territory "Samaria" was not only depopulated, but also repopulated by a new population from elsewhere. Consider, though, that this highly polemical report is given from a southern perspective, and thus is likely to be quite hyperbolic, running well beyond the event's reality.

For the Bible, however, the northern exile in 722 is but a harbinger of the southern exile from Judah and Jerusalem a century later at the hands of the Babylonian empire. Because of the restlessness and instability of the Davidic dynasty in its last decade, the relationship of the state of Judah to Babylon was also unstable. As a consequence, the Babylonians deported the leading citizens of Jerusalem in three waves (Jer. 52:28–30), settling them far from home in Babylon (see Ps. 137). One cannot overstate the defining importance of this destruction and deportation for the history of Judah and, much more, for the faith of Israel.

Quite practically and concretely, the three deportations and the decisive destruction of Jerusalem in 587 meant the total loss of a known world of public institutions. The temple was razed, the city walls were dismantled, and the Davidic monarchy came to an ignoble end. The destruction meant the termination of Judah's political identity (except for a brief period during the Maccabean movement), until the United Nations formed the modern state of Israel in 1948. The public, political loss in this crisis is immense.

Beyond that, however, in Old Testament reflection that event of destruction and deportation needs to be understood theologically—with reference to YHWH's will and purpose. As the exile is normatively interpreted in the Old Testament, two central themes are articulated. First, the crisis is a sign of God's abandonment of Jerusalem and rejection of Israel, and an ensuing absence of YHWH to God's people. Second, that abandonment, rejection, and absence is, for the most part, understood as YHWH's savage (merited?) judgment upon a recalcitrant community, just as the prophets had for so long warned [see DEUTERONOMIC THEOLOGY, RETRIBUTION]. The deportees had to "sing the Lord's song in a foreign land," learn forms of faith that would survive without visible props, and live faithfully in the absence. Thus the exile, taken theologically, is presented in the Old Testament as the death of everything that gave identity to the life of Israel.

Along with the sense of loss (expressed in the book of Lamentations) and the acknowledgment of guilt (lined out in 1 and 2 Kings), the most remarkable fact about "exile" is that the season of dislocation came to be for Israel a primary time of theological generativity. From the bottom of loss and guilt arose in Israel a series of new, imaginative poetic voices (Isa. 40–55; Jer. 30–31; Ezek. 33–48) who took the loss with deep seriousness but who shrewdly reinterpreted old faith traditions to turn exilic Israel in hope toward the future (see, for example, Isa. 43:16–21; Jer. 31:31–34;

Ezek. 37:1–14). Through this interpretation, exilic Israel is portrayed as a buoyant community of hope that believed and trusted that the God who willed Israel's deportation is the God who will faithfully enact Israel's restoration to the safety and well-being of its own proper place in Jerusalem and Judah.

The return home and the end of exile were keenly anticipated; implementation of these hopes is less than clear. Hints emerge of an initial return to Jerusalem in 537 immediately after the edict of the Persians authorizing such a return (see Ezra 1:2–11), fifty years after the destruction. More decisive is the return and the modest rebuilding that Haggai and Zechariah voice in 520. Further, in the middle of the next century, a movement led by Ezra and Nehemiah decisively shaped the restoration and emerging Judaism.

Homecoming, however, has never been fully accomplished, so that Judaism is marked perennially as a scattered, displaced community, marked as a "diaspora." The incompleteness of restoration makes exile a deeply felt image even in contemporary Judaism. Out of this matrix arose the seemingly insoluble issues of the management and deployment of the territory of the "holy land" and the singularly intractable issue of the "peace of Jerusalem." The power of the image of exile is deeply linked to concrete historical reality; at the same time, however, exile is a theological symbol that has developed in powerful and demanding ways far beyond the historicity of that time. For this reason, in liturgical imagination, the memory and reality of exile affects every adherent to Judaism.

Two contemporary, derivative uses of the term "exile" are relevant to this discussion. First, the disestablishment of the church in the United States, as a consequence of secularism and pluralism, causes the church to be in some sense displaced and so an "exiled" community— that is, a community of faith living a peculiar identity in an indifferent or hostile environment. Second, while the term for us is rooted historically and theologically in the destruction of Jerusalem and the deportation of Jews, "exile" retains some of that intensity as we notice the huge and growing number of exiles— displaced persons, marginated persons, refugees—in the contemporary world, the result of barbaric political-military action and less directly of indifferent economic practices that readily render some as hopeless outsiders. In light of September 11, 2001, the public response of anger, bewilderment, rage, and a deep sense of common loss resonates with the ancient sense of exile. The imagery related to exile is obviously enormously fruitful for interpretive imagination. Such extrapolations, however, can never be sundered from the specific Jewish matrix of destruction and deportation. In the exile, Israel found it possible to affirm that YHWH is a God who gathers exiles home:

> Thus says the Lord GOD,
>> who gathers the outcasts of Israel,
> I will gather others to them
>> besides those already gathered.
>> (Isa. 56:8)

References: Ackroyd, Peter R., *Exile and Restoration: A Study of Hebrew Thought of the Sixth Century* B.C. (OTL; Philadelphia: Westminster Press, 1968); Bayer, Charles, *The Babylonian Captivity of the Mainline Church* (St. Louis: Chalice Press, 1996); Brueggemann, Walter, *Cadences of Home: Preaching among Exiles* (Louisville, Ky.: Westminster John Knox Press, 1997); Klein, Ralph W., *Israel in Exile: A Theological Interpretation* (OBT; Philadelphia: Fortress Press, 1979); Neusner, Jacob, *Israel in Exile: A Too-Comfortable Exile?* (Boston: Beacon Press, 1985); Scott, James M., *Exile: Old Testament, Jewish and Christian Conceptions* (Leiden: Brill,

1997); Smith, Daniel L., *The Religion of the Land-less: The Social Context of the Babylonian Exile* (Indianapolis: Meyer Stone, 1989).

Exodus The exodus is remembered in Israelite literature and liturgy as the initiating, defining event in biblical faith. A great deal of energy has been expended trying to situate and verify the event historically, but almost no compelling evidence for its historicity exists. Rather the exodus is a memory that has been kept alive and central in Israel's life through a traditioning process that does not depend on historical verification. The most that can be said is that the memory situates this event in the life work of Moses, which is traditionally located in the thirteenth century B.C.E.

As a remembered tradition, however, the exodus is of immense importance, as evidenced by its crucial role in the core narrative of the Passover. Exodus 1–15 is the narrative account of the event that begins with Israel's cry of oppression in Exodus 2:23–25 and ends with Israel's song of emancipation in Exodus 15:1–18, 21. The move from the cry of oppression to the song of emancipation is accomplished, according to the narrative recital, by a series of intrusive acts by YHWH—humanly initiated by Moses and Aaron—that intimidate, instruct, and eventually defeat Pharaoh. YHWH's exhibition of immense sovereign power over Pharaoh and YHWH's intense commitment to Israel accomplish this radical turn in the narrative that permits Israel to begin its vulnerable historical existence.

The narrative, in the formation of the Bible, becomes an engine for Israel's continuing interpretive imagination. The root event itself is of course remembered; at the same time, however, the remembered event becomes paradigmatic for

Israel, so that other occurrences in its life and tradition are presented as replications of the exodus event. These replications include

the departure of Abraham from Ur (Gen. 15:7),

the crossing of the Jordan River into the land of promise (Josh. 4:23–24),

the defeat of the Philistines (1 Sam. 4:8; 6:6), and

the emancipation of Israel from exile in Babylon (Isa. 43:16–21).

We may particularly notice two other remarkable uses. In Amos 9:7, the prophet seeks to overcome the arrogant confidence of Israel in its special relation with the God of the exodus by asserting that this same God enacts exoduses for other peoples, most especially Israel's characteristic enemies, the Philistines and the Syrians. Also, in Jeremiah 21:5, the familiar language of the exodus is used to assert YHWH's fierce hostility against Israel and a will to destroy it, thus producing an "anti-exodus."

The exodus memory of course continues to sustain Jewish imagination, including the wondrous events related to the founding of the modern state of Israel, a connection made famous by Leon Uris in *Exodus*. That same memory of emancipation was taken up in rich ways in the New Testament, so that it became paradigmatic in early church reflection:

Matthew 2:15 (quoting Hos. 11:1) presents the departure of Jesus' family from the sanctuary of Egypt as an exodus.

Luke 9:31 uses the term "exodus" ("departure") in Greek to refer to the dramatic events in Jesus' life in his final days in Jerusalem.

In 1 Corinthians 5:7, Paul refers to Christ as "our paschal lamb," or as other translations have it, "our passover."

The series of Jesus' transformative miracles, summarized in Luke 7:22, evoke a collage of exodus-like transformations that Jesus wrought, enacting the power of the exodus God.

Easter and the defeat of death can plausibly be understood as a parallel to the defeat of Pharaoh. The Easter tradition, moreover, occupies a central role of importance for Christians, as does the exodus for Jews.

The privileged place that the narrative of Exodus occupies in Jewish and Christian traditions means that it articulates a number of core convictions of biblical theology:

1. The exodus asserts *the sovereign capacity* of YHWH over all rivals. Pharaoh, whoever he was "historically," functions metaphorically as the failed challenger and competitor to YHWH. Pharaoh characteristically defies YHWH, and so he is defeated and finally destroyed. Pharaoh was understood in the Egyptian ideology of his day as a "god," and he was able to rule in an unfettered way in a manner akin to the ruler of the last remaining superpower. (A pondering of Pharaoh by citizens of the United States, the last remaining superpower, might cause us to pause in a moment of self-recognition. Pharaoh's remarkable arrogance in the narrative is perhaps matched by current U.S. arrogance as voiced, for example, by Francis Fukuyama.) YHWH's will and rule cannot ultimately be resisted, according to this narrative.

2. YHWH's sovereign capacity emerges in the narrative as a will for *the redemption of the public process of history*. From this narrative comes primary material for the church's confession of God as redeemer, the one who gives (back) to Israel a livable life in the world. The exodus event, as much as any tradition, assures that biblical faith and the God of the Bible are linked definitively to the public process of history. Negatively this narrative assures that biblical faith cannot be reduced either to a private act of well-being or to a religious "idea."

3. This claim of redemption in the public process of history derivatively characterizes YHWH as *a liberating God*, the one who takes sides with the oppressed against every oppressive power. The Exodus narrative has thus become the taproot for what has become, in the late twentieth century, liberation theology, the conviction that God's work is to liberate the oppressed.

4. Fretheim has made clear, at the same time, that the interpretive propensity to see redemption-liberation as central to the Exodus narrative is matched by a recognition that, in the narrative, YHWH is *the (creator God)* who can mobilize the powers of creation (in plagues such as gnats and hail) to defeat Pharaoh, who is the power of chaos working against the creator God's life ordering will.

5. The mobilizing of God's sovereign will as creator and redeemer serves fundamentally in the narrative to establish, assert, and celebrate *YHWH's sovereignty*. YHWH will "gain glory" (Exod. 14:4, 17).

6. That exhibit of sovereignty, however, entails *a commitment to Israel*, so that Israel is shown in the narrative to be the singular recipient of YHWH's power as creator and redeemer. The narrative thus asserts

Israel's distinctive role as YHWH's people who are soon en route to Sinai for the making of covenant and the receiving of Torah. Without in any way diminishing that peculiar claim for Israel, the tradition has been inescapably extrapolated from Israel to include other oppressed peoples as the recipient of YHWH's gracious rescue, finally issuing in the conviction of "God's preferential option for the poor." The quite particular claim of Israel has become the material for great interpretive freedom, to see this same God at work in many other venues of oppression (see Amos 9:7).

7. The exodus narrative characterizes YHWH as creator and redeemer and characterizes Israel in parallel as the definitive recipient of YHWH's concern. At the same time, this narrative more broadly *characterizes public history*—the reality of social, economic, and political power in imperial perspective—as the arena of YHWH's sovereignty and thereby as the enterprise in which YHWH's emancipatory purposes are coming to pass. This peculiar discernment of public history, as Walzer has seen, has made the Exodus narrative the defining text for revolutionary political theory, even as it reaches into the contemporary world.

8. The exodus event is singularly YHWH's work. At the same time, *Moses as a human character* is indispensable to the story, so that the exodus is an attestation to the cruciality of the human will for freedom. The narrative makes clear that Moses and Aaron, while powerless slaves, do become "actors in their own history," which leads to their emancipation.

The ongoing power and authority of the exodus tradition indicates that communities of faith—and derivatively others outside those communities—continue to find in this memory and tradition ground for hope and for historical possibility that even the most oppressive totalitarianism cannot finally deny. As Pharaoh is a harbinger for all such oppressors, so the narrative makes clear that Pharaoh in the end is always defeated. This narrative and its immense generativity represent the most compelling mode the Bible has through which to enunciate the decisive conviction that the world and the reality of God are deeply intertwined, so that the well-being of the world is a gift of God's glory.

References: Anderson, Bernhard W., "Exodus Topology in Second Isaiah," in *Israel's Prophetic Heritage: Essays in Honor of James Muilenburg*, ed. Bernhard W. Anderson and Walter Harrelson (New York: Harper & Brothers, 1962), 177–95; Brueggemann, Walter, "The Book of Exodus: Introduction, Commentary, and Reflections," in *NIB* (Nashville: Abingdon Press, 1994), 675–981; idem, "The Exodus Narrative as Israel's Articulation of Faith Development," in *Hope within History* (Atlanta: John Knox Press, 1987), 7–26; idem, "'Exodus' in the Plural (Amos 9:7)," in *Many Voices, One God: Being Faithful in a Pluralistic World*, ed. Walter Brueggemann and George W. Stroup (Louisville, Ky.: Westminster John Knox Press, 1998), 15–34; Buber, Martin, *Moses: The Revelation and the Covenant* (Atlantic Highlands, N.J.: Humanities Press International, 1988); Dozeman, Thomas B., *God at War: Power in the Exodus Tradition* (Oxford: Oxford University Press, 1996); Fretheim, Terence E., "The Plagues as Ecological Signs of Historical Disaster," *JBL* 110 (1991): 385–96; Fukuyama, Francis, *The End of History and the Last Man* (New York: Free Press, 1992); Gowan, Donald E., *Theology in Exodus: Biblical Theology in the Form of a Commentary* (Louisville, Ky.: Westminster John Knox Press, 1994); Iersel, Bas von, and Alton Weiler, *Exodus: A Lasting Paradigm* (Concilium; Edinburgh: T. & T. Clark, 1987); Levenson, Jon D., "Exodus and Liberation," in idem, *The Hebrew Bible, the Old Testament, and Historical Criticism* (Louisville, Ky.: Westminster/John Knox Press, 1993); Pixley, Jorge W., *On Exodus: A Liberation Perspective* (Maryknoll, N.Y.: Orbis Books, 1983); Plastaras,

James, *The God of the Exodus* (Milwaukee: Bruce Publishing Company, 1966); Walzer, Michael, *Exodus and Revolution* (New York: Basic Books, 1985).

Ezra In a book of theological themes such as this, mentioning personalities may seem a bit odd. I do so, however, with four men from the tradition—Moses, David, Elijah, and Ezra—because in each case that individual person embodies a crucial theological claim of the Old Testament.

In the mid-fifth century, Ezra the scribe paired with Nehemiah, a civil servant, to rebuild Jerusalem and restore the faith of Israel that had never fully recovered from the destruction of 587. Christian scholarship has largely disregarded Ezra until recently, no doubt because of the usual Christian caricature of postexilic Judaism in general and of Ezra's movement in particular. In Judaism itself, however, Ezra is reckoned as the most important person in the Jewish tradition after Moses and is recognized as the founder of Judaism as revivified after the exile.

Three matters are important to note about Ezra for our purposes.

1. Ezra established (or recovered) the centrality of the Torah as the defining reference point, as it has subsequently become, for all of Judaism. He instituted rigorous and extensive reforms of every aspect of Jewish life in conformity to the Torah (Ezra 6:19–22; 9:1–4; see Neh. 10–13). More dramatically, in Nehemiah 8, Ezra presided over a convocation commonly regarded as the founding event of Judaism (the postexilic Jewish faith that is in every way to be distinguished from the faith of "early Israel"). In that event, we are told that Ezra the scribe, with his associates,

helped the people to understand the law, while the people remained in their places.

So they read from the book, from the law of God, with interpretation. They gave them sense, so that the people understood the reading. (Neh. 8:7–8)

That is, Ezra and his associates interpreted the old Torah teaching for their current context, not unlike the work of Moses in Deuteronomy (see Deut. 1:5). Like Moses, Ezra understood and practiced the dynamism of the Torah that both permitted and required interpretation.

2. Ezra and Nehemiah worked according to an imperial grant from Persia; Persian authorities financed and authorized the restoration of Jerusalem and its worshiping community. This activity was consistent with Persian policy in general. For Jews specifically, Judaism would thus be a cultic community, confined to worship matters without claim or pretense to political capacity. Judaism, since that time, has characteristically had to accommodate itself to the practical reality of imperial overlords who are regularly indifferent or hostile to its peculiar religious claims, so that the Persian imperial reality as the context of Ezra's accomplishment became something of a characteristic mark of Judaism.

3. While Ezra and Nehemiah were authorized by Persia and prepared to accommodate Persian imperial perception, they were also members and representatives of the exilic community of Jews who had been deported to Babylon and who had developed an influential and learned diaspora Judaism. This particular community of Jews came to dominate among the many alternative and competing modes of Judaism, so that one practical effect of Ezra's work was to give preeminence and privilege to Babylonian Jews in the recharacterization of Judaism. Ezra and Nehemiah likely were members of an urban elite derived from the "good

fig" exilic community of Jeremiah 24. They present themselves in the tradition as the primary heirs to Israelite covenantalism and continue the Torah accents reflected in Deuteronomy and in the tradition of Jeremiah. Their positive commitment to Torah is a decision appropriate to a circumstance of displacement. Judaism thus had resources to maintain itself in any dislocation. The leadership of Ezra symbolizes this accomplishment, which perhaps was elementally enacted by him.

References: Blenkinsopp, Joseph, *Ezra-Nehemiah* (OTL; Philadelphia: Westminster Press, 1988); Brueggemann, Walter, "Always in the Shadow of the Empire," in *The Church as Counter-Culture,* ed. Michael L. Budde and Robert W. Brimlow (Albany: SUNY Press, 2000): 39–58; Grabbe, Lester L., *Judaism from Cyrus to Hadrian: Sources, History, Synthesis: The Persian and Greek Periods,* Vol. 1 (Minneapolis: Fortress Press, 1991); Klein, Ralph, "Ezra and Nehemiah in Recent Studies," in *The Mighty Acts of God: In Memoriam G. Ernest Wright,* ed. Frank M. Cross et al. (Garden City, N.Y.: Doubleday, 1976): 361–76.

■ ■ ■

Faith The central theological construct of the Old Testament is covenant—a passionate, interactive relationship between YHWH and YHWH's people. That relationship is presented as an interaction between two free and committed partners amidst all of the vagaries of historical reality. Thus, that the primary and defining issue of that covenantal relationship is fidelity is not surprising. Both parties have sworn primary allegiance to the other, and faithfulness concerns the ways in which that sworn allegiance is enacted, YHWH toward Israel and Israel toward YHWH. (See, for example, Ezek. 11:20; 14:11.)

The primary vocabulary for fidelity uses two terms that occur frequently together, *hesed* and *'emeth,* rendered "steadfast love and faithfulness," and eventually "grace and truth" (John 1:14). The two terms together bespeak the utter reliability of one covenant partner (first of all, YHWH) to the other. The psalmist celebrates YHWH's practice of "steadfast love and faithfulness" in every circumstance (Ps. 25:10); Israel and every individual Israelite can count on the attentive fidelity of YHWH in every circumstance (Pss. 40:10; 57:3; 61:7; 85:10; 89:14; 115:1; 138:2). The core claim of Israel's faith is that YHWH is utterly reliable. This utter reliability became the subject of Israel's most exuberant doxologies and the ground of appeal in Israel's most earnest complaints.

The two terms function together and have a merged meaning, but each term may also be taken alone. *Hesed* (rendered as "mercy" [KJV]; "steadfast love" [NRSV]) is covenantal love according to previously uttered covenantal vows and promises. Distinguished from an initiating act of love, *hesed* concerns the long-term sustenance of a relationship already underway. In Psalm 103, the term is employed in verses 4, 8, 11, and 17 in a variety of different ways. The usage in verse 4 is coupled with "mercy" to characterize YHWH's primal propensity. In verse 8 the term stands in a cluster of terms that appears to be quoting from an older creedal affirmation in Exodus 34:6–7. In verse 11, the term stands alone and implies YHWH's generous readiness to forgive and restore a broken relationship; but in verse 17, the term pertains only to people who are obedient in covenant. These several uses suggest some of the ways in which the notion of YHWH's faithfulness can be interpreted and given nuance.

The second term, *'emeth,* rendered

"faithfulness," is of course a close synonym and holds interest in two particular ways: *'Emeth* is the Hebrew word from which we receive our term "amen," that is, "Yes, it is so." Moreover, we render this term "believed," as in Genesis 15:6 and Habakkuk 2:4 (KJV), verses that became crucial in the struggles of the Reformation concerning the meaning of "justification by faith." Von Rad, on the basis of Isaiah 7:9, Exodus 14:13–14, and related texts, has proposed that Israel's notion of "faith" derives directly from dangerous contexts of war, when Israel learned to rely completely upon the utterly reliable God in the face of threats beyond their own coping. That is, YHWH's faithfulness is an affirmation Israel makes that has arisen out of real-life circumstance in which the reliable presence and engagement of YHWH was said and known to make a concrete difference.

Because fidelity is a covenantal term, Israel is also expected to know and honor its covenantal commitments to YHWH, and so to practice faithfulness through obedience. Familiar references to Israel's covenantal obligation include two prophetic texts:

For I desire *steadfast love* and not sacrifice,
the knowledge of God rather than
burnt offerings.
(Hos. 6:6, emphasis added)

He has told you, O mortal, what is good;
and what does the LORD require of you
but to do justice, and to love *kindness,*
and to walk humbly with your God?
(Mic. 6:8, emphasis added)

Israel's faithfulness to YHWH is enacted by obedience to Torah. Obedience, however, requires more than merely following specific commands. Obedience means, rather, engaging in a life that embraces the large intentions of YHWH, which are marked by compassion, mercy, and forgiveness.

The same language of fidelity operates in human transactions, whereby people who have commitments to each other, or who are bound in friendship, are held to accountability. A prime example is the relationship between David and Jonathan, in which David promises to remain faithful to Jonathan and his family in times to come. Clearly Jonathan secures the oath from David because the two of them are engaged in risky, high-stakes political intrigue:

"If I am still alive, show me the *faithful love* of the LORD; but if I die, never cut off your *faithful love* from my house, even if the LORD were to cut off every one of the enemies of David from the face of the earth." (1 Sam. 20:14–15, emphasis added)

In 2 Samuel 9:1, the narrative returns to David's solemn oath to Jonathan and evidences David's attentiveness to his long-standing obligation to Jonathan, thus exhibiting David as reliable. See also 2 Samuel 10:2, wherein David undertakes fidelity in the international realm. In both cases, cynical self-interest could mark David's enactment of fidelity.

Israel's remarkable account of reliability and fidelity of course evokes an awareness that such faithfulness is always at risk; Israel can speak as well about unfaithfulness and infidelity, even on YHWH's part. Thus the Psalms of lament are cries of need and protest that summon YHWH to enact a foresworn faithfulness. In Psalm 89:49, for example, our defining word pair is employed to assert that Israel can discern no evidence of YHWH's attentive reliability in its present crisis and in fact concludes that YHWH is not actively faithful. One of the most astonishing qualities of Old Testament faith is that it entertains the thought—out of its experience of suffering—that YHWH is, on occasion, absent, silent, or negligent in violation of oaths of fidelity, and Israel is, for that reason, exposed and in jeopardy. Psalm 44 voices a harsh example of this sentiment; Israel characterizes its suffering and accuses YHWH of having abused Israel (vv. 9–16). Israel moreover has been faithful to YHWH (vv. 17–18), so that the only conclusion is that YHWH has not kept faithfulness. In the face of the accusation, however, Israel finally, in verse 26, appeals precisely to YHWH's reliability as the only basis of Israel's hope and expectation. Thus, even where it is not experienced, YHWH's faithfulness is the ground of hope and expectation that YHWH will again be faithful as YHWH has sworn to be. In a parallel way, Israel is often accused, through the prophets, of unfaithfulness to YHWH. Even as the covenant is celebrated when both parties act faithfully, either party—Israel in complaint and YHWH through the prophets—can thus accuse the other of having violated the covenant. Restoring covenant, when Israel violated it, depended upon Israel's repentance and YHWH's readiness to forgive for the sake of the relationship.

"Faith" concerns attentive engagement in a promissory relationship. Only rarely does the Old Testament suggest that "faith" is a body of teaching that Israel is to "believe." Israel's faith does not necessarily lack normative substance nor is it vacuous, but the relationship is more elemental than the substantive teaching which reflects upon that relationship. That in the Old Testament faith regarded as "trust in" is more elemental than "assent to" is a matter often discounted in formal theological articulations, but "trust" is not to be understood primarily in emotive terms. Trust is a practice that

entails obedience to Torah and its specific requirements. Israel's fidelity to YHWH, not unlike fidelity in marriage, thus consists of concrete acts that take the other party with defining seriousness.

While the notion of faithfulness admits of immense variety in the Old Testament, the key point is not to be missed: what is known of YHWH and what keeps YHWH and Israel connected to each other is a mutual, elemental loyalty in the prospect of a shared life of well-being. This notion of fidelity, so pivotal in biblical faith, is a peculiar treasure in the contemporary world that often wants either (a) to dissolve relational fidelity into a contractual matter that limits and eliminates personal loyalty, or (b) to flatten fidelity into certitude as if a defining relationship could ever be merely or mainly cognitive. The mutual passion of the covenant partners for each other and the will for rehabilitation of the relationship prevent both dissolution into contract and flattening into cognition.

Israel's great joy and confidence is that the One who upholds its life and the life of the world is completely trustworthy; Israel proposes to live a trustworthy life in response. That affirmation on the part of Israel is a great responsibility for Israel in societal relations and a ground for defiance in a world indifferent to relationality. In its deepest moment of loss, Israel tenaciously asserted confidence that the data do not support:

> The *steadfast love* of the LORD never ceases,
> his mercies never come to an end;
> they are new every morning;
> great is your *faithfulness*.
> (Lam. 3:22–23, emphasis added)

Out of that deep, abiding, recurring conviction—about the character of God in the midst of the world, and precisely from that poem—the church boldly sings:

Great is Thy faithfulness, O God my
 Father,
There is no shadow of turning with Thee;
Thou changest not, Thy compassions they
 fail not;
As Thou hast been Thou forever wilt be.
Great is Thy faithfulness!
Great is Thy faithfulness!
Morning by morning new mercies I see;
All I have needed Thy hand hath
 provided;
Great is Thy faithfulness, Lord, unto me!

References: Heschel, Abraham, *The Prophets* (New York: Harper & Row, 1962); Lindström, Fredrik, *Suffering and Sin: Interpretations of Illness in the Individual Complaint Psalms* (Stockholm: Almqvist & Wiksell, 1994); Rad, Gerhard von, *Old Testament Theology* vol. 2 (San Francisco: Harper and Row, 1965), 155–64; Sakenfeld, Katharine Doob, *Faithfulness in Action; Loyalty in Biblical Perspective* (OBT; Philadelphia: Fortress Press, 1985); idem, *The Meaning of Hesed in the Hebrew Bible* (Missoula: Scholars Press, 1978); Snaith, Norman H., *The Distinctive Ideas of the Old Testament* (London: Epworth Press, 1944).

The Fall The "fall" is a dominant motif in classical Christian theology, deriving from Paul's discussion of Adam and Christ in Romans 5:12–21 and 1 Corinthians 15:21–22, 45–49. In these texts, Paul contrasts the significance of Adam (who introduces sin into the world) with Christ (who is God's final antidote to the sin of Adam). The term "fall" suggests a universal, irreversible fall from a relationship with God into a state of corruption, degradation, and deprivation in which human persons are completely helpless and have hope only because of the powerful intervention of God in Christ. In this reading, the power of sin entered into the world through Adam and is, so to say, "in the human genes," passed down from generation to generation. The notion of "fall" asserts a profound understanding of human sin that is matched in Christian theology by a profound notion of grace given in the gospel of Jesus Christ.

The doctrine of the fall is grounded in the narrative of Genesis 3, wherein the initial couple, Adam and Eve, disobeys the command of the creator and is consequently expelled irreversibly from the garden of paradise. The narrative is complicated by the role of the serpent who lured the human couple into disobedience, which perpetually seals the negative destiny of humanity short of the gospel. The narrative offers no explanation for the origin or character of the serpent, who is a given of the narrative.

This doctrine of inherited human corruption has received great play in Christian theology, largely through the immense influence of Augustine and to a lesser extent Martin Luther. In the Old Testament, however, Genesis 3 itself says nothing about any inherited corruption, for the narrative seems to be only one among many that portray the troubled interaction between God and humanity. Genesis 3 appears to be of no special importance, or does it introduce a major theme that dominates or overrides other narratives that follow. In general the Old Testament does not adhere to such a profound or dread-filled notion of human sinfulness as does classical Christian theology. The Christian reading (or overreading) of Genesis 3 exemplifies one way in which an interpretive tradition can take on a life of its own and impose itself on a text. In Jeremiah 31:29–30 and Ezekiel 18:1–4, the prophetic tradition is at some pains, in a particular historical context, to resist any notion that one generation of the faithful inherit guilt from another (see also Deut. 24:16).

While Paul was the major interpreter to make the fall central to Christian faith—and confessions of sin central to Christian liturgy—Paul should not be presumed to have articulated the matter of inherited sin *de novo*. In any case the apocryphal book of 2 Esdras, perhaps dated just after 70 C.E. and in the same world as Paul's writings, articulates the grief that the faithful know in pondering the hopelessness of the human predicament:

"Better never to have come into existence than be born into a world of wickedness and suffering which we cannot explain! . . . We are all of us sinners through and through. Can it be that because of us, because of the sins of mankind, the harvest and the reward of the just are delayed? . . . O Adam, what have you done? Your sin was not your fall alone; it was ours also, the fall of all your descendants. What good is the promise of immortality to us, when we have committed mortal sins; or the hope of eternity, in the wretched and futile state to which we have come. . . . [W]e have made depravity our home." (4:12, 38–39; 7:48–50, 54 NEB)

Tracing literary dependencies is not possible, but one can see the deep dismay of the Jewish world in which Paul articulated the faith of the church.

The contrast between Old Testament understandings of obedience and Christian understandings of sin and grace may provide an important interface and difference of accent between Judaism and Christianity. As Ricoeur has shown, Genesis 3 is the kind of text that is immensely generative of fresh interpretation. At the same time, some contemporary scholars insist that Paul's categories, which have come to dominate classical Christian theology, may have been misunderstood or reified in subsequent interpretation. The matter is a difficult one, but no doubt fresh exchange between Jews and Christians will provide critical ground for a reconsideration of long-established interpretive assumptions.

References: Barr, James, *The Garden of Eden and the Hope of Immortality* (Minneapolis: Fortress Press, 1993); Barth, Karl, *Christ and Adam* (New York: Harper & Row, 1957); Donfried, Karl P., *The Romans Debate* (Peabody, Mass.: Hendrickson Publishers, 1991); Ricoeur, Paul, *The Symbolism of Evil* (Boston: Beacon Press, 1967); Stendahl, Krister, "The Apostle Paul and the Introspective Conscience of the West," in *Paul among Jews and Gentiles* (Philadelphia: Fortress Press, 1976).

Fertility Religion   The phrase "fertility religion" of course does not occur in the Old Testament, but it does appear often in the interpretive literature of Old Testament study, most often as "Canaanite fertility religion." The topic appears here because (a) a great deal is at stake in a proper understanding of the topic, and (b) the scholarly history of "fertility religion" in twentieth-century Old Testament study is a telling exercise in scriptural interpretation.

The sharp contrast between Yahwism (covenantal, Israelite faith) and Baalism (Canaanite religion) is as old as Elijah's contest at Mt. Carmel (1 Kgs. 18). A convergence of two matters in the 1930s led Old Testament scholarship to place enormous accent in the twentieth century on the struggle between Yahwism and Baalism [see BAAL]. First, in 1929 a French archeological expedition discovered a huge deposit of Late Bronze Age clay tablets at the ancient city of Ugarit (= modern ruin, Ras Shamra). Those tablets, when deciphered and translated, have proved to be the most important resource for understanding Canaanite religion, the religion practiced by the dominant culture in the land of Canaan during Israel's premonarchial and monarchial periods. Baal is prominently represented in these tablets as a fertility god. He was worshiped in Canaan as the god responsible for the return of spring, the growth of crops, and the gift of rain that produced good crops in an otherwise arid climate. Scholars appeal to these documents for "Canaanite fertility religion." The Old Testament in its earlier period carries on an endless polemic against Baal and insists that worship of Baal is a false commitment when loyalty should be given only to YHWH.

Second, at the very time when the Ras Shamra tablets had been translated and gained scholarly attention in the 1930s, Hitler's aggressive ideology of "Blood and Soil" religion that issued in Aryan racism confronted the German church. The very soil of Germany, according to the ideology of National Socialism, matched by Aryan blood, produced the "master race."

In the generative and daring climate of theological interpretation in the 1930s, asserting a religious equivalency between "Canaanite fertility religion" known through these tablets and Nazi ideology—faced immediately and with great risk by the church—was relatively easy (and surely not wrong). The deep crisis of the German Evangelical Church escalated the interpretive contrast made in Old Testament studies between Yahwism and Baalism. The key figure in this interpretive maneuver was Karl Barth, the towering theological force in the Confessing Church's resistance to Hitler. Early on, Barth had condemned "religion" in general—by which he referred to a cultural practice of meaning that lacked both a dimension of transcendence and a radical ethic—and "natural theology" in particular, by which he meant the notion that "nature" may reveal God to us. Barth was adamant that the faith of the church, given in the biblical text, did not disclose a God "in nature," but that God is self-revealed only through specific events in the histor-ical process. Younger Old Testament scholars, notably Gerhard von Rad, joined Barth in this polemic contrasting "natural religion" (seen in National Socialism and in Canaanite fertility religion) with what came to be called the "historical religion of the Old Testament." The latter is the claim that God is revealed through distinctive, one-time historical happenings (e.g., the exodus) and not in the routines and regularities of the seasonal cycle. Against "fertility religion," YHWH, the God of Israel, was known to be a God who "acted in history."

In retrospect, this drastic and defining contrast was clearly an important interpretive maneuver, in that the church, under deep ideological assault, could find standing ground outside the totalistic system of National Socialism. This drastic contrast between a god of fertility and the God of history was in retrospect an overstated contrast that served the interpretive requirements of the German Confessing Church well, but did not fully reflect the claims of the Old Testament text.

In Old Testament studies, Claus Westermann, a close associate of von Rad, initiated a reconsideration of the contrast that dominated Old Testament study at mid-twentieth century. Westermann, of course, agreed that Israel's God is one who delivers in concrete historical events. He went beyond that settled claim, however, to insist that the God who delivers is also the God who blesses [see BLESSING]. In his massive study of the creation texts in Genesis, Westermann comes to the conclusion that "blessing" is a function of the creator God, and that the foundational act of blessing is the authorization and instigation of fruitfulness of a quite material kind: reproductive generativity of land and people, of plants and animals. Thus the commanding imperative "bring forth" in Genesis 1:24 is a typical case of the blessing for fertility given by the creator God who is a fertility God and who enacts the very fertility wrongly assigned to Baal.

By the end of the twentieth century, scholarship had retreated from its simplistic preoccupation with "history" and had toned down the harsh contrast between Canaanite and Israelite religion. Of course in saying that YHWH is a "fertility God," assigning to this fertility God all of the ignoble features found in Baal is neither necessary nor possible, for this God who fructifies the earth and all its creatures is a transcendent sovereign who, unlike Baal, calls to radical neighborly obedience and makes promises that are enacted in the historical process.

In retrospect, separating YHWH from all of the wonders of fertility was a loss, because this separation led, in Old Testament studies, to neglecting creation themes. In the interest of enunciating that sharp contrast, interpretation tended to neglect the rich textual evidence for the claim that YHWH is indeed the creator God who makes possible all generativity and productivity:

> Genesis 8:22, a promise by YHWH, assures that the cycle of the seasons is reliable and guaranteed.

> Isaiah 62:4, emphasis added, another promise by YHWH, asserts that the land will be "married," loved, and made fruitful:

> You shall no more be termed Forsaken,
>   and your land shall no more be termed Desolate;
> but you shall be called My Delight Is in Her,
>   and your land *Married;*

> for the LORD delights in you,
>   and your land shall be married.

> The term "married" (as indicated in the footnote in NRSV) is "Beulah land," and "Beulah" is a developed form of the word "Baal," so that YHWH has "Baalized" the land, that is, made it fertile.

> The celebration of YHWH's food-giving capacity in lyrical poetry is surely related to the God of blessing and fertility (Pss. 104:27–28; 145:15–16; Isa. 55:10).

> Above all, Hosea 2, under the metaphor of divorce and remarriage, portrays YHWH as the Lord of fertility. In the negative part of that long poem (vv. 2–13), under the rubric of divorce, the assertion is made that YHWH gave grain, wine, and oil, the staples of agricultural productivity (v. 8), and that YHWH will withhold grain, wine, wool, and flax (v. 9) because Israel has disobeyed. YHWH is clearly the ruler of the agricultural processes and determines in freedom when life-sustaining produce will be given and not given. The latter part of the poem under the rubric of remarriage reverses the tone of harshness and shows YHWH willingly restoring Israel's life in the land (vv. 14–23). In verses 16–17, YHWH rejects the title of "Baal," because Israel has tried to treat YHWH as Baal might be treated, a gross misconstrual of YHWH. But then in verses 21–23, YHWH is the God who revivifies the earth and causes it to produce grain, wine, and oil as signs of full covenantal restoration.

Barth's polemical categories were exceedingly powerful and indispensably important in the "church struggle" of the 1930s. Now, in a very different context, the either/or of "nature" or "history" is not so helpful a distinction, because YHWH is shown to be, in Israel's testimony, the Lord of both. Because of YHWH's sovereignty over creation, blessings of the earth are intimately connected to obedience to Torah requirements, a connection of course not inherent in Baalism. This linkage is succinctly put in Hosea 4:1–3, wherein the violation of the commandments (vv. 1–2: "faithfulness," "loyalty," "knowledge of God," "swearing, lying," "murder," "stealing," and adultery," "bloodshed") lead inescapably to the dismantling of creation, the reversal of Genesis 1 (v. 3: the loss of "wild animals . . . birds . . . even fish").

The concept of "fertility religion" in an inadequate sense made God to be completely immanent in the reproductive processes, without a transformative will that could go beyond the status quo. Reconsideration of this matter (a) has been in part the result of feminist awarenesses of the maternal, sustaining role of the God of the Bible and (b) has in turn evoked and fostered a much broader horizon in feminist hermeneutics. To be sure, some forms of feminism go so far toward immanentism as to require critique. That approach, however, should not cause us to resist learning from feminist interpretations that pay attention to the God of fruitfulness who is at the same time Lord of history and practitioner of covenant with all the demands and joys pertaining thereto.

References: Barr, James, *Biblical Faith and Natural Theology: The Gifford Lectures for 1991* (Oxford: Clarendon Press, 1993); Brueggemann, Walter, "The Loss and Recovery of Creation in Old Testament Theology," *Theology Today* 53 (July 1996): 177–90; Habel, Norman C., *Yahweh Versus Baal: A Conflict of Religious Culture* (New York: Bookman Associates, 1964); Harrelson, Walter, *From Fertility Cult to Worship: A Reassessment for the Modern Church of the Worship of Ancient Israel* (Garden City, N.Y.: Doubleday, 1969); Rad, Gerhard von, "The Theological Problem of the Old Testament Doctrine of Creation," in idem, *The Problem of the Hexateuch and Other Essays* (New York: McGraw-Hill, 1966), 131–43; Westermann, Claus, *Blessing in the Bible and the Life of the Church* (OBT; Philadelphia: Fortress Press, 1978); idem, "Creation and History in the Old Testament," in *The Gospel and Human Destiny*, ed. Vilmos Vajta (Minneapolis: Augsburg Publishing House, 1971), 11–38; idem, *What Does the Old Testament Say about God?* (Atlanta: John Knox Press, 1979); Wright, G. Ernest, *God Who Acts: Biblical Theology as Recital* (SBT 8; London: SCM Press, 1952).

Festivals   Festival occasions in ancient Israel were an unsettled mix of popular folk religion (drawing much from its cultural environment) and self-conscious theological intention. The interaction of these two forces reached no stable form, but was endlessly renegotiated and reconfigured.

The purpose of festival occasions was to give public, dramatic articulation to the identity of Israel as the people of YHWH and YHWH as the God of Israel; to celebrate the distinctiveness of that relationship; to inculcate the young into that communal identity; and to imagine the world through the lens of that particular identity. Obviously each particular festival had its own origin and purpose, but all of them served to assert a theologically self-conscious distinctiveness, for as Neusner has written of contemporary Jewish practices, "All of us are Jews through the power of our imagination" (212). Religious festivals enabled the community to step out of a normal, taken-for-granted world to live, for the occasion, in an alternative world that is construed through the theological memory articulated in the cadences of word and act peculiar to that community.

The "calendar" of festivals in ancient Israel most likely emerged slowly and remained flexible. An effort was made, however, to order and regularize the festivals into three major events, as reflected in the several calendars of Exodus 23:14–17; 34:18–26; Leviticus 23; Numbers 28–29; and Deuteronomy 16:1–17. The most prominent of these festivals is *Passover*, which came to be linked to the exodus and thus served to incorporate new generations into the identity of Israel that emerged from that memory (see Exod. 12–13). The other two festivals—of Weeks and Booths—may have arisen from agricultural cycles but were drawn into the orbit of Israel's historical memory. Agricultural festivals subsequently connected to Israel's historical memories most likely serve to attest to and enact the claim that YHWH is the benevolent sovereign over both the regularities of "nature" and over the crisis times of history.

While these three festivals are the most important and dominant in Israel's formal calendars, Israel's capacity for festival was clearly left open, so that new festivals could be instituted as time and circumstance required. Of these, the most important is *Yom Kippur,* a day of reconciliation (Lev. 16; 23:26–32). At the edge of the Old Testament, Esther 3:7 and 9:20–32 legitimate the festival of *Purim,* a celebration of Jewish identity in circumstances of risk and jeopardy [see PURIM]. Not mentioned in the Old Testament but germane to our topic is the festival of *Hanukkah,* instituted in the second century B.C.E. when the Jerusalem temple was rededicated after its violation through the abuses of Hellenistic intruders. The name of the festival derives from the verb "dedicate" (*ḥnk*). Because Judaism is a historical faith, these later festivals serve to keep defining memories derived from critical moments dynamically available in the community.

Related to our topic is the formation of "the five scrolls" (Megilloth) in the latter part of the canon of the Hebrew Scriptures, whereby each of the five scrolls is related to and used in liturgic celebration of a particular festival. Thus the scrolls function to script the imagination of the community for specific Holy Days:

Ecclesiastes: Feast of Booths

Esther: Purim

Song of Solomon: Passover

Ruth: Pentecost (= Feast of Weeks)

Lamentations: Ninth of Av (the time of the destruction of the temple)

The connection between text and festival decisively impacts the interpretive environment for each of these books. Moreover, in the Christian canon, these five scrolls have been distributed through the canon, apparently on a "historical basis," thus nullifying any interest in the liturgical connection.

The festivals function as vehicles for an alternative imagination of the world through faith. The several tensions of (a) historical memory and agricultural cycle, (b) popular religion and intentional theology, and (c) stable ordering and flexible development are never resolved but characterize the ongoing process of celebration of a distinct theological identity. The Christian liturgical calendar functions similarly, revolving around the three great festivals of Christmas, Easter, and Pentecost.

References: Albertz, Rainer, *A History of Israelite Religion in the Old Testament Period,* vols. 1 and

2 (OTL; Louisville, Ky.: Westminster John Knox Press, 1994); Neusner, Jacob, *The Enchantments of Judaism: Rites of Transformation from Birth through Death* (New York: Basic Books, 1987); Vaux, Roland de, *Ancient Israel: Its Life and Institutions* (New York: McGraw-Hill, 1961), chaps. 17–18; Gadamer, Hans-Georg, *The Relevance of the Beautiful and Other Essays* (Cambridge: Cambridge University Press, 1987).

Forgiveness   The issue of YHWH's forgiveness of Israel's sin is a complex and important one for faith in the Old Testament. Israel was not overwhelmed with a deep and pervasive sense of guilt, as Christian stereotype sometimes suggests in its reference to an alleged "legalism." Israel nonetheless cared intensely about a full, functioning relationship with YHWH and was aware that sin violated that full and free relationship and therefore must be addressed. In such recurring awareness and circumstance, YHWH, as the affronted party when Israel violated covenant, was the only one who could forgive sin and restore relationship. For that reason YHWH's capacity for forgiveness is crucial for the future of Israel. YHWH's capacity for forgiveness is not to be understood in a formulaic way but must be set amidst all the risks, complexities, and openness of a multidimensional relationship. Nor is YHWH to be understood as either relentlessly "rigid and unforgiving" or an automatic source of grace. Rather in a serious, ongoing relationship with Israel YHWH is the senior partner who always has options and alternatives available when dealing with a wayward companion (see Hos. 2). Among the pertinent facets to that open and complex relationship are the following:

1. Forgiveness usually (but not always) depends on repentance, a resolve to reverse course and resubmit to YHWH's governance in new and obedient ways. The long prayer of Solomon in 1 Kings 8:33–53 thus petitions for forgiveness but in every case makes repentance a precondition. (See also Ezek. 18 with its accent on "turning.")

2. Guilty Israel benefited greatly from powerful intercession, whereby noted leaders addressed YHWH on behalf of Israel and persuaded YHWH to forgive. The foremost examples are the remarkable prayers of Moses in Exodus 32:11–13, 32; 34:9 and Numbers 14:13–20, but see negatively Jeremiah 15:1.

3. While forgiveness may be understood as a judicial act whereby a judge simply asserts forgiveness, in other contexts forgiveness is a cultic act dependent on priestly activity and a sacramental transaction (see Lev. 4:20, 26, 31, 35; 5:16, 18). These texts express complete confidence in reconciling sacramental activity that is never explained but enacted. The extreme case is Yom Kippur, the Day of Atonement (Lev. 16), but the texts indicate that alongside that dominant instance were regular practices of forgiveness via priestly activity.

4. The matter of forgiveness pertains to the whole community of Israel as an entity, but forgiveness is also an important religious agenda for individual members of the community of Israel. The public agenda of forgiveness is especially pertinent in the exile of the sixth century when the immense loss of Jerusalem was understood as punishment for sin. The announcement of forgiveness for Israel is an important element in the poetic declarations of exilic Isaiah, as in Isaiah 40:1–2 and especially 55:7.

The more personal, intimate dimension of forgiveness is voiced especially in the so-called penitential Psalms (Pss. 6, 32, 38, 51, 102, 130, 143), of which Psalm 51 is the best known. In that Psalm the speaker fully acknowledges guilt and seeks a pardon. The prayer of confession apparently is offered in confidence that YHWH can and will forgive. The prospect of YHWH's forgiveness is confidently voiced in Psalm 130:3–4. Psalm 32 exhibits an acute discernment of the destructive power of sin (vv. 3–4) and the assurance of forgiveness that occurs in and through full and candid acknowledgment (vv. 5–6). Indeed these Psalms exhibit an understanding of sin and forgiveness that is as penetrating and sophisticated as any contemporary "therapeutic" understanding that forgiveness is possible and on what condition.

5. In some texts, YHWH is unable and unwilling to forgive sin (see Deut. 29:20; 2 Kgs. 24:4; Lam. 5:22). These cases are, to be sure, extreme, and they are linked to a Deuteronomic verdict of judgment concerning the failure of the royal establishment in Jerusalem [see DEUTERONOMIC THEOLOGY]. This harsh interpretive judgment on Jerusalem, which constitutes a philosophy of history, stands in rough continuity with older case law that issued harsh judgments concerning adultery (Deut. 22:22), murder (Deut. 19:11–13), or disobedience (Deut. 21:18–21). No general principle of "unforgivable sin" is present here, but simply an acknowledgment that, in this covenantal relationship, limits exist beyond which Israel cannot push YHWH. This dynamic suggests, of course, that in the Old Testament, covenant—not grace—is the defining category of faith, with grace a subset.

The sin of Jerusalem so profoundly condemned in these texts, however, is the same sin that is freely forgiven, according to the prophets, two generations later (Isa. 40:1–2; 55:7; Jer. 31:34; Ezek. 36:22–33). Thus YHWH's refusal to forgive is not a "principle" but a timely judgment that eventually became "not yet," because there is "a time to love, and a time to hate"

(Eccl. 3:8). What is appropriate in the relationship depends upon YHWH's sense of timing as presented in the texts; YHWH may, in a given circumstance, forgive or not forgive (see Lam. 3:42).

6. Some of YHWH's declarations are unqualified, unconditional assertions of forgiveness that exhibit YHWH's generosity and graciousness in full. Perhaps the most dramatic is in Jeremiah 31:34:

I will forgive their iniquity, and remember their sin no more.

The act of forgiveness to the generation of exiles is paradigmatic for Israel's faith. This act permits Israel to take up a new life with openness to the future that YHWH will yet give.

Along with a *cultic-sacramental* understanding of forgiveness that depends upon priestly action and a *juridical* model that depends on a judge-announced verdict, an *economic* dimension also exists to forgiveness: forgiveness of debts. Miller has observed that in Isaiah 61:1, the phrase "to proclaim liberty" (*drr*) refers to economic restoration and the cancellation of debts, as in the Year of Release and the Jubilee (see Lev. 25:10; Isa. 58:6, and the quote of the text in Luke 4:18–19). Forgiveness is, in this imagery, an economic transaction in which debts (first of all economic, but perhaps then many other kinds of debts) are forgiven. This usage is the one likely reflected in the familiar Lord's Prayer that the church prays: "Forgive us our debts as we have also forgiven our debtors" (Matt. 6:12).

This rich array of nuances of meaning suggests that partners of this God need neither grovel in fear and guilt nor complacently assume any cheap grace. Forgiveness is a function of the restoration of mutual fidelity, and forgiveness therefore happens according to the disposition of the parties toward each other in a particular time and circumstance.

Terminology for forgiveness in the Old Testament focused upon YHWH who forgives, for Israel confesses: "Against you, you alone, have I sinned" (Ps. 51:4). That transaction with YHWH, however, is a potential model for human transactions of forgiveness, especially the strong forgiving the weak and creditors forgiving debtors. When understood as the breaking of vicious cycles of alienation and hostility, forgiveness clearly becomes an urgent public issue in contemporary life. In some of the most intractable issues in the world today—whites and blacks in the United States, Catholics and Protestants in Northern Ireland, Palestinians and Israelis in the Middle East—acts of forgiveness matter crucially. Forgiveness should not be reduced to private and personal matters or slotted simply as psychological-therapeutic concerns, important as those are.

In the contemporary world, two remarkable acts of forgiveness can serve as models: One, the Truth and Reconciliation Commission in South Africa was a largely successful mechanism for beginning again in a public way. That commission depended upon truth-telling, for without truth-telling (as Ps. 32 makes clear) no new way into the future an emerge. The other model, "Jubilee 2000," concerned the cancellation of third-world debt as a matter of breaking the vicious and destructive cycles of domination and deprivation.

The theological root of forgiveness in the character of YHWH has immense implications for the life of the world. God's willingness to forgive makes possible and authorizes the practice of neighborly forgiveness. Israel will make no cleavage between the love of God who forgives and the love of neighbor who must be forgiven.

References: Heyward, Carter, and Anne Gilson, eds., *Revolutionary Forgiveness: Feminist Reflections on Nicaragua,* Amanecida Collective (Maryknoll, N.Y.: Orbis Books, 1987); Jones, L. Gregory, *Embodying Forgiveness: A Theological Analysis* (Grand Rapids: Eerdmans, 1995); Miller, Patrick D., "Luke 4:16–21," *Interpretation* 29 (1975): 417–21; Patton, John, *Is Human Forgiveness Possible? A Pastoral Care Perspective* (Nashville: Abingdon Press, 1985); Ringe, Sharon, *Jesus, Liberation, and the Biblical Jubilee: Images for Ethics and Christology* (OBT; Philadelphia: Fortress Press, 1985); Sakenfeld, Katharine, "The Problem of Divine Forgiveness in Numbers 14," *CBQ* 37 (1975): 317–30.

■ ■ ■

Glory The term "glory" bespeaks an aura of splendor and power, a capacity for sovereignty. The term in Hebrew, *kbd,* literally means "heavy." A person possessing "glory" was a person of weightiness, influence, power, prestige, and gravitas. While the term was used to refer to "weighty" human persons, as with many terms it was transposed into a theological term and came to testify to YHWH's splendor, majesty, and unrivaled power.

Like its near synonym, "holiness," the term "glory" is pulled in two different directions in Old Testament usage, in the priestly and Deuteronomic traditions. In the priestly traditions, the term alludes to the cultic presence of YHWH in Israel, a presence known in a brightness of light that "shines" visibly, as in Psalm 50:2 [see PRIESTLY TRADITION]. Von Rad has suggested that a *theology of glory* is to be contrasted with *name theology,* the two occurring respectively in priestly and Deuteronomic traditions, and accenting in turn the visual and the auditory. YHWH's presence is understood in the priestly tradition as a palpable, almost material presence, so that in Exodus

24:15–18 at Sinai and Exodus 40:34–38 with reference to the tabernacle, the presence is overwhelming and fills a great deal of space.

In a related tradition, Ezekiel takes up the notion of glory in order to testify to YHWH's coming and going, and absence and presence in the Jerusalem temple. Thus in Ezekiel 10:18–19, the glory departs from the temple, borne on the wings of cherubim to exile in Babylon. The careful yet expansive wording of the text suggests that the prophet is seeking to say what is unsayable about God's power. In the complementary passage of Ezekiel 43:1–5, the glory returns to the temple. While glory is essentially visual, Ezekiel's report also includes auditory experience of God's glory. The glory seen (or heard) in the holy place indicates YHWH's accessible, available presence for Israel. At the same time, however, the presence of YHWH is always portrayed as free, able to come and go, not a prisoner in a cultic scheme.

The God known in the cult, however, was not a benign, passive presence, and for that reason, the same term, "glory," is used in a much more dynamic way to witness to YHWH's engagement in contests for power and sovereignty. YHWH lives in a world where other gods also claim sovereignty and must from time to time engage challengers and demonstrate the ability to defeat other gods, thus claiming unrivaled sovereignty. The term therefore has something of a military connotation, and is sometimes linked to the ark, a fixture of Israel's military practice in which the glory of YHWH is perceived as attached to the ark (see Num. 10:35–36). In Israel's doxologies, YHWH is said to receive glory in worship from other worshipers, which include Israel, perhaps the nations, and other gods who are defeated and who concede YHWH's sovereignty (Pss. 29:1–2, 9; 96:4; 97:6–7). Indeed, in Psalm 19:1, the heavens and the earth become glad witnesses to the aura of sovereignty that is evident everywhere in the world. In a worship context, YHWH is seen to possess glory, but YHWH also receives glory from those who acknowledge and salute YHWH's majestic splendor and who surrender their own claims to YHWH's claim that is manifestly beyond challenge or competition.

YHWH's evident glory (or aura of sovereignty), however, is not confined to worship but is enacted in the life of the world. Thus in Exodus 14:4, 17, the exodus is said to be an exercise through which YHWH "gains glory" over Pharaoh, that is, evidences power to subdue and defeat Pharaoh, a would-be rival. First Samuel 4–5 includes a cunning word play on *kbd*. The defeat of Israel (and of YHWH), embodied in the capture of the ark, is summarized as "Ichabod," "the *kabod* has departed." But then the narrative reverses field. In 1 Samuel 5:6, 7, and 11, YHWH's hand is said to be "heavy," and the same term *kbd* is used; YHWH's sovereignty is back in play and is fully visible to the Philistines and to their God, Dagon, who is defeated and humiliated by YHWH's superior power. YHWH's claim to sovereignty, moreover, is sore tested in the exile when the Babylonian gods seem more powerful and capable of defeating YHWH. According to the poet, however, YHWH is unperturbed and concedes nothing to the divine opponents who want to usurp or share power:

> I am the LORD, that is my name;
>   my glory I give to no other,
>   nor my praise to idols.
>
>   (Isa. 42:8)

> My glory I will not give to another.
>   (Isa. 48:11; see 46:1–7)

In every contest for power, the text characterizes YHWH as having power completely beyond challenge; no would-be rival is capable of competition. Thus the one endlessly praised, honored, and "glorified" in the temple is the one who has earned, established, and demonstrated unrivaled, legitimate sovereignty in the real conflicts and contests of the world. The one who "sojourns" in the midst of Israel is the one surely worthy of praise and obedience.

Christians are so familiar with the term in worship that "glory" receives little attention. The term famously shows up on the lips of divine messengers in the birth announcement of Jesus in the Lucan narrative, whereby divine messengers assert that God's "aura of sovereignty" is linked to this newly birthed baby (Luke 2:14). Christians moreover regularly sing "Glory be to the Father and the Son and the Spirit," whereby the church gladly and without reserve cedes to and acknowledges the full sovereignty of the God named as Trinity who warrants praise and obedience. The high claim made for Jesus in the early church is that in Jesus of Nazareth is visible "his glory, the glory as of a father's only son, full of grace and truth" (John 1:14). Such a deep claim is only understandable when one engages the cultic and narrative traditions of Israel through which YHWH's legitimate rule is established and attested.

References: Balthasar, Hans Urs von, *The Glory of the Lord* vols. 1–3 (San Francisco: Ignatius Press, 1982–86); Brueggemann, Walter, *(I)chabod toward Home* (Grand Rapids: Eerdmans, 2002); Rad, Gerhard von, *Studies in Deuteronomy* (SBT 9; Chicago: Henry Regnery Co., 1953), chap. 3; Terrien, Samuel, *The Elusive Presence: Toward a New Biblical Theology* (New York: Harper and Row, 1978).

■ ■ ■

Hannah The Old Testament is convincedly patriarchal; men dominate much of the literature. As a predictable consequence, women play only tangential roles and for the most part modern readers are left with only traces of their presence and importance. Some notable exceptions exist, however, as in the narratives of Hagar, Ruth, and Esther, and recent feminist studies have called attention to the important roles of women in the text that conventional patriarchal interpretation missed. Even so, the patriarchal hegemony in the text, as in most interpretation, is obvious. In this book, I include comment on four prominent women— Miriam, Hannah, Jezebel, and Huldah— to go along with the four crucial men I cite: Moses, David, Elijah, and Ezra. I suggest that each of the men took on a larger-than-life metaphorical significance in the traditioning process. Hannah, Miriam, Jezebel, and Huldah, I suggest, also have metaphorical significance even as they have, at the same time, experienced sustained marginalization in the traditioning process. The extensive literature on these several subjects from a feminist perspective is crucial reading in order to understand the work and costs of the patriarchal traditioning process.

Hannah, whose name means "grace," is known only in the text of 1 Samuel 1–2, and so one might judge her a marginal figure in the Old Testament. I focus on her as a representative woman figure, however, for three reasons.

First, Hannah is the mother of Samuel, who was born to her as a gift of God out of her barrenness. In this role, Hannah may be taken as a representative of all the barren women in Israel who give heirs and sons to Israel, including Sarah (Gen.

11:30), Rebekah (Gen. 25:21), Rachel (Gen. 29:31), and the wife of Manoah (Judg. 13:2). To see her in the context of these other "mothers in Israel" is to notice that her narrative also includes the recurring features of rivalry between wives and the dedication of a son given late to the service of the Lord. The case of Hannah is noteworthy, however, for, we are told, she was given a son because she was the embodiment of piety and because she prayed steadfastly and insistently for the gift from God. She did not wait passively but initiated an assertive petition to YHWH. She is thus a model for vigorous faith. Moreover, her son Samuel is, after Moses, the "great man" in Israel who authorizes and institutes the monarchy that is eventually focused on the great David (1 Sam. 16:1–13; see Jer. 15:1). Whereas Samuel is the transitional figure between tribal and royal Israel, Hannah is his mother and must persist through the vagaries of her condition to give such a son who makes Israel's future possible.

Second, Hannah is the beginning point of the books of Samuel, the figure through whom the narrative begins a new epoch in Israel's life. We may imagine that the true and only subject of that literature is David; in order to introduce David, however, Samuel is necessary. In turn, in order to introduce Samuel, his mother Hannah is necessary to the narrative. Hannah, though, is as far back as the narrator can regress, for behind her is nothing except her barrenness, which forms the matrix of the upbeat royal tale to be told. She is a vulnerable recipient of God's gift, in order to demark the entire narrative that follows as the gift of God. Thus her name, "grace," characterizes the entire tale of God and monarchy, a tale of "grace alone."

Third, the entire story of Hannah can be seen as a story of how a woman of silence becomes a woman of buoyant, confident, grateful, efficacious voice. At the outset Hannah does not speak, so depressed is she (1 Sam. 1:7–8). She then utters a silent prayer on her trembling lips (v. 13). As she becomes pregnant, she utters the name of the child and offers him gladly to Eli in payment of her vow (vv. 20–28). As the narrative moves into chapter 2, she sings a bold Yahwistic song, the "Song of Hannah" (2:1–10). She now is an exuberant, energized voice of praise to YHWH, a voice that through her son will impinge decisively upon the future of Israel.

Clearly the Song of Hannah belongs to the traditional material of Israel's celebrative singing, evidenced in the parallel of Psalm 113. As the song is now placed on her lips, however, Hannah sings the primal theme of David's story, a story of the way in which the last become first and the lowest are exalted. That theme from the lips of Hannah is taken up in the "Magnificat," the Song of Mary, whereby Luke introduces the most radical theme of his gospel account, a theme of social transformation wrought by God (Luke 1:46–55). Thus Hannah serves as either the source, or more likely, the mediator of Israel's most revolutionary song. In her singing, Hannah enlists in the bold assertion of Israel's faith by paralleling the daring singing of Miriam (Exod. 15:20–21) and Deborah (Judg. 5:1–31). Hannah's song, moreover, is taken up in Christian liturgy and is the most used song of all in the liturgic life of the church. Thus Hannah, a vulnerable, hopeless, barren woman, becomes a sign and metaphor of YHWH's grace-filled reversal that is wondrously given in the life of Israel and, as Mary anticipates, in the life of Jesus. No wonder Israel's most dangerous song is on her lips. Hannah is the voice of Israel's deepest hope, a hope reiterated in the singing faith of the church.

References: Brueggemann, Walter, "1 Samuel— A Sense of a Beginning," *ZAW* 102 (1990): 33–48; Klein, L. R., "Hannah: Marginalized Victim and Social Redeemer," in *A Feminist Companion to Samuel and Kings,* ed. A. Brenner (Sheffield: Sheffield Academic Press, 1994), 77–92; Meyers, Carol, "The Hannah Narrative in Feminist Perspective," in *Go to the land I Will Show You,* ed. J. E. Colesin and V. H. Matthews (Winona Lake, Ind.: Eisenbrauns, 1996), 117–126; Miller, Patrick D., *They Cried to the Lord: The Form and Theology of Biblical Prayer* (Minneapolis: Fortress Press, 1994), 237–39; O'Day, Gail R., "Singing Woman's Song: A Hermeneutic of Liberation," *Currents in Theology and Mission* 12/4 (August 1985): 203–6; Willis, John T., "The Song of Hannah and Psalm 113," *CBQ* 25 (1973), 139–54.

Ḥerem The Hebrew term here is variously translated as "exterminate," "utterly destroy," "utterly devote," and "annihilate." As a noun, *ḥerem* is translated as "ban, devoted thing," by which is meant the object of extermination. The term refers to what is set apart exclusively for the deity to claim and so etymologically is connected to the more familiar word "harem," the wives or women exclusively reserved for the ruler.

Perhaps including a Hebrew word in such a book as this seems odd, but the word is reflective of a problematic dimension of Israel's most elemental faith. In Hebrew *ḥerem* functions as something of a technical term, even though the technical aspect is not easily recognized in familiar translations. The term refers to the religious requirement that everything that Israel captures or gains in war—booty as well as people—is to be "utterly destroyed," offered up to YHWH in conflagration or some other mode of killing (thus acknowledging YHWH to be the real victor in war). Nothing that a conquering Israel gained from war was to be retained, either as valued war booty for

profit or as a spared human being. This practice, sanctioned in the instruction of Deuteronomy 20:16–18, is of interest because (a) Torah provides an unambiguous instruction in this regard and (b) such practice is authorized in the name of the God of Israel.

The authorized wholesale slaughter of enemies is closely linked to the claim of YHWH's sovereignty, so that *ḥerem* expresses the total sovereignty of YHWH, who presides over and claims exclusively all that is conquered. According to this claim, anything spared or kept for the benefit of Israel would detract from the fact that the victory belongs solely to YHWH, who fights for Israel. (This practice can be perceived as a concrete, brutal way of demonstrating YHWH's later assertion, "My glory I will not give to another" [Isa. 48:11].) The authorization reflects a dimension of Israel's faith (and of Israel's God) that bespeaks profound violence rooted in a claim of sovereign authority beyond any rational legitimacy. The theological root of the instruction is profoundly problematic, as Schwartz has suggested, in seeing exclusive theological claim as a warrant for violence.

The instruction in Deuteronomy provides little rational or practical explanation. The contrast between the authorization of *ḥerem* for conquered enemies close at hand (Deut. 20:16–17; see Num. 21:2–3; Deut. 2:34; 3:5–6; 7:2; Josh. 6:17–21) and the more humane treatment of conquered enemies who are "very far from you" (Deut. 20:14–15) may indicate a rationale. This distinction suggests that the practical consideration, nowhere made explicit, is that the survival of such peoples close at hand might be a theological temptation and seduction away from Israel's peculiar identity as the people of YHWH. Nothing of that explanation, however, is voiced in the text, and the rationale remains an inference.

In any case, the instruction and practice of *herem* seem to have pertained only to a most primitive dimension of Israel's political and ideological development during a time when Israel, according to its memory, struggled most deeply for survival in the midst of hostile neighbors (Josh. 2:10; 10:28–40; 11:11–21). As political and military practices in Israel became rationalized in the monarchy according to reasons of state, this more primitive practice was doubtlessly superseded. (Thus, in the narrative of 1 Kgs. 20, King Ahab spared his enemy, the Syrian King Benhadad, and in v. 42 is placed "under ban" [*herem*] by the prophet for not implementing *herem*. King Ahab certainly understood that reasons of state precluded such an act toward a rival, sometime-enemy state.) This practice does not generally pervade Old Testament assumptions about military conduct; rather *herem* belongs to one slice of Israel's tradition.

The most extensive narrative account of the practice of *herem* occurs in 1 Samuel 15. On the basis of Exodus 17:8–16 and Deuteronomy 25:17–19, the old tradition of Israel took the Amalekites as the paradigmatic enemy toward whom Israel was enjoined to practice a policy akin to ethnic cleansing at every opportunity. The narrative of 1 Samuel 15 exhibits King Saul compromising that practice of *herem* by saving the life of the Amalekite king and some Amalekite booty at, says he, the behest of his people. A commonsense judgment, uninformed by harsh ideology, must have suggested to some, perhaps including Saul, that the destruction of perfectly good cattle was irrational and economically stupid. That commonsense judgment, according to the narrative, is profoundly opposed by the established authority of Samuel who, in this case, represents the voice of the old radical tradition of YHWH's exclusive, even violent claim to all war booty.

This simple, quickly accomplished negation of Saul as king on the basis of the violation of the old ideological commitment no doubt served the larger purpose of the tradition in disposing of Saul as a way to make room for David as king. Irony marks appeal to the old practice of *herem*, however, on three counts:

1. Saul is condemned because he "listened to the people" who urged salvage in violation of *herem* (1 Sam. 9; 24), even though Samuel himself had earlier yielded to public opinion against his clear theological mandate in the matter of kingship (1 Sam. 8:7, 22).

2. Saul's confession of sin for not killing the Amalekite (1 Sam. 15:24) is rejected, whereas David is readily forgiven when he confesses killing Uriah (2 Sam. 12:13).

3. Saul is condemned for seizing and saving Amalekite booty (1 Sam. 15:14–15), whereas David does the same thing and his practice is accepted without negative judgment, even without comment (1 Sam. 30:18–20).

The practice of *herem*, as exemplified in this narrative of 1 Samuel 15, evidently occupied a prominent ideological place in Israel's self-discernment. This ideological claim is unstable, however, and is open to more than one interpretation, depending upon the circumstance and the interpretive requirement of the case.

Stern opines that although such a primitive practice may have existed in ancient Israel, in the final form of the text, appeal to the practice is made not for the sake of actual violent destruction, but as an exclusive theological claim for sovereignty that is ideological but well removed from actual practice. That is, the conversion of old memory into canonical claim constitutes a residue of theological claim that has left behind actual practice. That explanation of how these texts might now be understood theologically is credible. Such an interpretive maneuver, however, does not permit us to disregard or explain away an elemental violence rooted in YHWH's claim of sovereignty.

References: Gunn, David M., *The Fate of King Saul: An Interpretation of a Biblical Story* (JSOT-Sup 14; Sheffield: JSOT Press, 1980); Schwartz, Regina M., *The Curse of Cain: The Violent Legacy of Monotheism* (Chicago: University of Chicago Press, 1997); Stern, Philip D., *The Biblical Herem: A Window on Israel's Religious Experience* (Brown Judaic Studies; Atlanta: Scholars Press, 1991).

High Place   "High Place" is a conventional translation of the Hebrew term *bamah*, which means "high" or "raised." The term's usage indicates a place of worship, so that a high place is taken to be a shrine or sanctuary in an elevated location. Whether the elevation was natural or artificially constructed, however, is not known. In fact, we know nothing of the exact nature of these shrines or what was done there, although the assumption is that general worship activities (such as sacrifices and the utterance of oracles) took place.

Apparently high places were local, rural, or village shrines, extensive in number and operated by local priesthoods without connection to or supervision by any external authority. In the narrative of 1 Samuel 9:1–10:16, for example (where the NRSV regularly translates *bamah* as "shrine"), the "high place" is unexceptional. One might readily go there for guidance by a "man of God"; moreover, sacrifices are regularly conducted there.

The notion of "high place" would not be particularly interesting to us if we attended only to the uses of the term that treat the phenomenon as routine and unexceptional. What evokes our attention is the fact that in the Deuteronomic tradition, the most self-conscious theological trajectory in the Old Testament, the high places are subjected to sustained and harsh criticism [see DEUTERONOMIC THEOLOGY]. The Deuteronomic tradition simply assumes, in contrast to other narrative accounts, that the high places are profoundly objectionable and must be destroyed. We are not told why they are objectionable, except that they do not conform to the rigorous theological insistences of that tradition, and we can guess that any rural shrine with a local rural priest might accommodate itself to the folk religion of the community, which in this case would be Canaanite religion, perhaps even "Canaanite fertility religion" [see FERTILITY RELIGION]. Thus the objection of the Deuteronomist may be to the syncretism of the practice and the compromise of Yahwism in violation of the First Commandment (Deut. 5:6–7; 6:4–9).

Solomon with his people worshiped at high places (1 Kgs. 3:2–4), and Rehoboam and Jehoram are said to have built high places (1 Kgs. 14:23; 2 Chr. 21:11). Among the most important narratives about such a place of worship is Genesis 22, Abraham at Mt. Moriah. Evidently such an installation was not generally perceived as objectionable. Judean kings who instituted cultic reform, moreover, regularly stopped short of destroying the high places (1 Kgs. 15:14; 22:43). Perhaps they did not remove them because their reforms were not radical. Perhaps acting against local shrines was politically risky. Or perhaps the high places were not judged to be objectionable because the rigor of the Deuteronomist was not widely shared, certainly not in royal circles.

In any case, the two great royal reforms of Hezekiah (2 Kgs. 18:4, 22; 2 Chr. 31:1;

32:12) and Josiah (2 Kgs. 23:5–9) did indeed find the high places objectionable and destroyed them [see REFORM OF HEZEKIAH, REFORM OF JOSIAH]. These two reforming kings are remembered as the most zealous of reformers, or conversely they are made to seem, in the narrative, as agents for Deuteronomic theology. That theology is profoundly committed to the urging of the book of Deuteronomy, which provides for the worship of *one God* (Deut. 6:4) in *one place* (Deut. 12:2–12), presumably Jerusalem.

Theologically we may conclude that the program of reform is undertaken to enforce the "YHWH alone" requirement of the First Commandment in its most stringent form (Exod. 20:2–3; Deut. 5:6–7). A frequent suggestion, however, is that the closure of all village shrines and the centralization of all authorized worship in Jerusalem was likely not simply a disinterested act on the part of the reforming kings. At the very least, these actions gave Jerusalem a monopoly on worship and greatly enhanced the city and the king who presided there. Beyond that, some scholars propose that centralizing worship was also a royal stratagem to control the money that flowed through the institutions, to the benefit of the royal budget.

The high places are of interest to us (even though we do not know much about them), because they call attention to the immense religious pluralism of the Old Testament text. In some texts, the high places are routinely accepted as a venue for conventional worship. In other texts, the same sort of shrine evokes harsh polemic and repression. When we read the text in the church, we are likely to be drawn to the stringent Deuteronomic objections and so align ourselves as readers with the reforming kings. No doubt the final form of the text intends us to do just that. Such an account bespeaks

a concern for the purity of religious practices.

At the same time, the Deuteronomic condemnation of high places is not consistent in the text; the voice of condemnation is only one advocacy among many. The fact that the text gives quite varied impressions about the high places suggests that when we are confronted in the Bible with pluralistic judgments (as we often are), we may pay great attention to the way in which we adjudicate those voices and the grounds on which we accept one claim rather than another. (In what we now call "culture wars" in our contemporary society—concerning different lifestyles and other personal choices, and in the church concerning different kinds of music and styles of worship—we are perhaps meeting firsthand the same difficult disputes that Israel faced over high places. In both that ancient case and in contemporary cases, these disputes are strongly felt, and in the end a great deal is at stake in adjudicating the matter.) We may not innocently imagine that one view is clearly "correct," for every view is an advocacy in the presence of others. In the Old Testament text, the Deuteronomic tradition appears to have the last word, but not the only word.

References: Albertz, Rainer, *A History of Israelite Religion in the Old Testament Period I: From the Beginnings to the End of the Monarchy* (OTL; Louisville, Ky.: Westminster John Knox Press, 1994); Barrick, W. Boyd, "What Do We Really Know About 'High Places'?" *Svensk Exegetisk Arsbok* 45 (1980): 50–57; Emerton, John A., "The Biblical High Place in the Light of Recent Study," *Palestine Exploration Quarterly* 129 (1997): 116–32; Miller, Patrick D., *The Religion of Ancient Israel* (Library of Ancient Israel; Louisville, Ky.: Westminster John Knox Press, 2000); Vaux, Roland de, *Ancient Israel: Its Life and Institutions* (New York: McGraw-Hill, 1961).

History Israel, the people of the Old Testament, lived fully under the conditions of history and subject to the vagaries, risks, and possibilities of history. Moreover, the God of the Old Testament is presented as effectively and decisively engaged in the history of Israel and the history of the world. On both counts—the people of Israel and the God of Israel—faith in the Old Testament is deeply connected to history. Inescapably the critical study of the Old Testament has long been understood as a historical project.

The term "history," when used in Old Testament studies, is immensely complex and in the end is an imprecise and elusive notion. In fact, the "history" in Old Testament studies can have at least three quite different meanings:

1. *Remembered history.* "History" is what is recorded and written about the past. This notion of history may pertain to modern, critical scholarship whenever various scholars, with great critical learning, present their version of Israel's past in the ancient period. The notion of "recorded and written" may also refer to "histories" within the Old Testament itself, so that scholars refer to the "Deuteronomic History" (consisting of Joshua, Judges, Samuel, and Kings) or to the "Chronicler" as historian (consisting of 1 and 2 Chronicles). [See THE CHRONICLER, DEUTERONOMIC THEOLOGY.] To be sure, the ancient versions and the modern critical versions of the past are very different, for the modern versions make use of critical methodologies not available to the ancients. These two kinds of presentations of the past nonetheless have in common that they are "versions," that is, they are renderings of the past that are shaped by and filtered through the perspectives and imagination of the ones who record and write. While different "versions" of the past (ancient or contemporary) may more

or less nearly appropriate the "actual past," every "version," ancient and modern, is a version that cannot claim to be objective or leanly factual. Imagination, as a constitutive force, is inescapably at work in piecing together various kinds of data into a credible narrative account of the past.

2. *Actual history.* Quite distinct from what is recorded and written, the term "history" may also refer to what happened. This dimension of meaning is in play when one seeks to exhibit the reliability of the Bible by claiming that its testimony squares with actual events. Such an appeal often assumes that if the Bible is shown to be "historically reliable," we may then assuredly count on its theological validity. Or put negatively, undermining "historical reliability" may be an effort to question the theological validity of the Bible. This often-assumed connection is much more problematic than is often recognized.

In fact, what happened is remote from us and to some great extent unrecoverable, because we lack access to what would count as verifiable data. As recently as fifty years ago, critical scholars tended to assume that the essential story line of the Bible was an accurate guide to what happened, so that the two were related to each other in intimate and trustworthy ways. In the last two generations, however, new methodologies, perspectives, and ways of framing the question have resulted in a strong scholarly propensity to conclude that the biblical evidence itself is a poor and unreliable guide to what happened, because interpretive purposes and tendencies shape the biblical evidence and thus make it untrustworthy.

The emerging consensus of critical scholarship thus appeals primarily to nonbiblical evidence in its attempt to recover what happened. Particular attention is paid to archeological evidence and to nonbiblical textual evidence, much of which comes from outside of ancient Israel.

Current methods have led some scholars in the last decade to conclude that no historical evidence exists for much of what is purported in the Old Testament, and that reliable historical evidence is noticeably lacking for what is reported as having happened prior to the seventh, sixth, or fifth centuries; some scholars would push the matter to as late as the second century. This more recent scholarship, completely guided by "objectivist" procedures and assumptions, needs to be taken with great seriousness. For all its claim of objectivity and its sober assessment of the data, however, this scholarship also fails the test of "objectivity" and in fact is minimalist in its assumptions before the data is considered. As a consequence, this scholarship is yet another version of the past. At least three factors may be generative in this minimalist account of Israel's past:

(a) The project is based upon Enlightenment epistemology, which from its inception has been and continues to be concerned with eliminating from consideration any religious dimension to what happened, even though the text itself includes a vigorous religious dimension to its historical narrative. Enlightenment epistemology constitutes an immense problematic, because what happened is measured by what is credible to a certain modern rationality that is impatient with texts that have arisen from outside of that rationality, as is of course the case with the biblical text.

(b) The perspective of some minimalist scholars is profoundly shaped by earlier personal experiences of religious authoritarianism. In some cases, minimizing the historical claims of the Bible is probably a reaction to authoritarianism that is itself no part of the biblical claim but is easily elided into it. When such a link is operative, even if hidden and unrecognized, then of course the claim of "objectivity" is hardly appropriate in assessing such scholarship. Determining when skepticism is a legitimate scholarly stance and when it slides over into an emotively propelled ideological stance is not easy.

(c) Because the "historical claims" of the Bible are sometimes used in modern Israeli political claims for the "promised land," occasional "scholarly" debunking of these claims occurs, a debunking designed to deflate the ideological use of the biblical text in contemporary political dispute. I do not suggest that this approach is a major component in the current questioning of the historicity of the Bible, but it at least needs to be noted as a representative example of the way in which interest operates in the midst of scientific interpretation.

3. *Confessed history.* A very different notion of history is operative wherein biblical interpreters make the claim—after the claim of the Bible itself—that God acts in history. This sort of affirmation, now seen to be enormously problematic, was powerfully influential a generation ago in biblical interpretation. By the phrase scholars simply meant that in Israel's scriptural narration of the exodus (Exod. 1–15) or the taking of the land (Josh. 1–12), presented as events that really happened, for example, the narrated events included the decisive agency of YHWH as a character in the action, without whom the narrative account itself makes no sense. That is, one could hardly imagine the exodus event, as treasured in Israel, as a happening that did not involve the decisive agency of YHWH.

In the last generation of scholars, the

problematic of this claim that makes YHWH a central "historical character" has been recognized, not only by those who seek a nontheistic account of what happened, but by serious theological interpreters who recognize the difficulty of the "category mistake" of "God/history." The theological, "evangelical" presentation of what happened (as remembered "saving events" that fund Israel's life of faith) cannot appeal to "historical events" in which God has not been decisively engaged. Such a definitive theological claim is endlessly problematic to believers in the Bible who seek to make their faith intelligible—to themselves and to their children—according to the rational intellectual assumptions of the modern world.

Thus the term "history" moves in many directions and hosts immense ambiguities. The interrelatedness of these three uses of the term likely constitutes not only a difficult problem but also important work for the ongoing community of biblical interpretation. One can, as a scientific skeptic, simply bracket out the third use and portray Israel's "history" according to modern commonsense capacities. Such a horizon, however, not only fails to satisfy theologically serious biblical interpreters; it also offers a history that is remote from the testimony of the community whose past we claim to recover. That is, a recovered past without the presence of God in the midst of it is a past that would have been of no interest to those who shaped and preserved the biblical narrative.

How the matter of (a) remembered history, (b) "actual" history, and (c) confessed history is to be adjudicated remains to be seen. Scholarship is currently in a "minimalist" posture; but given the fact that this perspective is a rather abrupt reversal

of the "maximalist" projection of a generation ago, we may anticipate that the present stance will, sooner or later, give way to other hypotheses. The problem is difficult, and one should neither imagine any easy resolution nor discount the problematic by *ad hominem* dismissals. While skepticism is now the order of the day, an older fideism is not now an available option among scholarly interpreters. Nonetheless, in my judgment, in the end skepticism is not intrinsically a superior stance, though it may serve better for some interpreters with their particular personal histories and consequent intellectual assumptions. Fideism as an alternative—a readiness to believe—cannot for that matter claim any privilege in the church as against the skepticism of the academy.

As is regularly the case, the Bible eludes our categories of explanation. After we have pondered what happened according to either the narration of the text (remembered history) or our best scientific reconstruction (actual history), we find that the Bible itself, never claiming to be "history" in any modern sense, remains uncompromising in its testimony to its central Character. "History/God" may be a "category mistake," but it is a category mistake on which the synagogue and the church have staked their faith. Paying the cost of "correcting categories"—whereby everything interesting and dangerous is explained away—is hardly appropriate.

References: Barth, Karl, "The Strange New World Within the Bible," in *The Word of God and the Word of Man* (New York: Harper & Brothers, 1957), 28–50; Buber, Martin, "The Man of Today and the Jewish Bible," *On the Bible: Eighteen Studies,* ed. N. N. Glatzer (New York: Schocken Books, 1968), 1–13; Davies, Philip R., *In Search of "Ancient Israel"* (Sheffield: JSOT Press, 1992); Dever, William G., *What Did the Biblical Writers Know and When Did They Know It?* (Grand

Rapids: Eerdmans, 2001); Finkelstein, Israel, and Neil Asher Silberman, *The Bible Unearthed: Archeology's New Vision of Ancient Israel and the Origin of Its Sacred Texts* (New York: Free Press, 2001); Halpern, Baruch, *The First Historians: The Hebrew Bible and History* (San Francisco: Harper & Row, 1988); Lemche, Niels Peter, *Ancient Israel: A New History of Israelite Society* (Sheffield: JSOT Press, 1988); idem, *The Israelites in History and Tradition* (Library of Ancient Israel; Louisville, Ky.: Westminster John Knox Press, 1998); Thompson, Thomas L., *Early History of the Israelite People: From the Written and Archaeological Sources* (Leiden: Brill, 1992); Van Seters, John, *Abraham in History and Tradition* (New Haven, Conn.: Yale University Press, 1975); idem, *Prologue to History: The Yahwist as Historian in Genesis* (Louisville, Ky.: Westminster/John Knox Press, 1992); Whitelam, Keith W., *The Invention of Ancient Israel: The Silencing of Palestinian History* (New York: Routledge, 1996); Yerushalmi, Yosef Hayim, *Zakhor: Jewish History and Jewish Memory* (Seattle: University of Washington Press, 1982).

Holiness   The notion of "holiness" characterizes what is deepest, most inscrutable, most marvelous, and most demanding in Israel's faith. With a certain elasticity of meaning, the term becomes a vehicle for some characteristic tensions in that faith. Unlike almost every other theological usage in Israel's vocabulary of faith, this term was not derived from daily life and preempted for theological usage. As a consequence, "holiness" has no reference point outside of its theological use and is more difficult to characterize.

The term is used both to assert separateness of a palpable, material kind and righteousness of a moral kind. These two accents do not appear to be clearly distinct or mutually exclusive; one use likely contains nuances of the other. But the term does function differently in different traditions. In the priestly traditions of Exodus-Leviticus-Numbers and in the

parallel uses in Ezekiel, "holiness" refers to what is separated from common use and therefore pure and reserved for careful religious use (see Ezek. 22:26). The term is closely related to the land, for these traditions assume that the land of Israel is held precariously and is in jeopardy if contaminated or polluted. Holiness as the antithesis of pollution is a strategy for land preservation. Thus the "holiness" materials oppose mixing and confusing matters and thereby "profaning" them (as in Lev. 19:19). These traditions specify purity for priests, festivals, sacrifices, food, and sexual relationships. Such an accent on holiness as purity might have become especially important to the community when its identity was under threat, so that careful distinctions were made in order to secure the identity, well-being, and cohesion of the community.

As a subset of the priestly tradition, Leviticus 17–26 is regarded by scholars as a distinct tradition that is preoccupied with holiness, and has been dubbed the "Holiness Code." This set of commandments is preoccupied with purity to preserve the well-being of the community and its land. The commandments cover aspects of community life concerning food, farming, prostitution, care for the aging, holy priests, holy festivals, and holy sacrifices.

Leviticus 18:22 and Leviticus 20:13, two prohibitions concerning some form of homosexuality, hold some present-day interest. These prohibitions are part of a long catalogue of sexual affronts, and the two lists of sexual affronts occur in the larger catalogue on holiness. Today, these specific verses are most often taken out of context and transposed into a category issue (e.g., heterosexual versus homosexual), while the large and primitive palpable notion of holiness is completely disregarded.

In other, specifically prophetic uses, holiness has to do with the right ordering of social relationships, that is, the practice of neighborly righteousness. In this usage the community must overcome not the threat of impurity but of injustice in socioeconomic and political spheres. The entire accent of prophetic faith on the practice of justice and respect for the disadvantaged thus belongs to the sphere of the holy. In enacting neighborly relations, Israel fulfills its vocation as a holy people. The idea of "separateness" is still on the horizon, but now the distinctiveness of Israel lies not only in careful cultic distinctions but in the quality and character of social relationships. The difference in nuance is acute among the several Old Testament traditions. (Without much adjustment one can see how the difference in nuance still operates in the church under the contemporary labels of "liberal" and "conservative," sentiments grounded in and informed and legitimated by one dimension or another of "holiness.")

Holiness refers to the very character of God but also to all that belongs to God and specifically to Israel as YHWH's "holy" people. The awesome vision of YHWH in Isaiah 6:1–8 is a defining portrayal of YHWH's holiness wherein the majesty, awe, and sovereignty of YHWH are on the lips of the heavenly beings who are moved almost beyond speech at the vision and presence of YHWH and who can only sing in response, "Holy, holy, holy" (v. 3). Note that this vision of holiness evokes in the prophet a sense of his own "uncleanness" and that of his people. The tradition of Isaiah is focused upon YHWH's holiness and understands the God of Israel to be beyond all the conventional categories of tradition or religion. God is unutterably beyond the reach of Israel and is unapproachable in splendor beyond any intimacy, yet the prophet Hosea, pondering the mercy of YHWH, can speak of "The Holy One in your midst" (Hos. 11:9). The God beyond reach in splendor has condescended to be a decisive presence and a decisive difference in Israel's life and future.

The term "holy" also referred to religious objects and religious practices. Such objects, in the horizon of Israel, had no intrinsic holiness but were "holy to YHWH"—belonging to, devoted to, and existing for YHWH, and deriving their character as "separate" through this attachment to YHWH. Thus God made the seventh day holy (Gen. 2:3), but that day is holy precisely because it is given over to the purposes of YHWH, and the same holds true for the holy tabernacle, the holy temple, and holy priests. In characterizing its holy objects and holy places, moreover, Israel devised a system of gradations in the construction of tabernacle and temple, whereby some zones of holiness are more intensely holy than others, depending upon nearness to YHWH.

Most of all Israel should be recognized as "a priestly kingdom and a holy nation" (Exod. 19:6). Such phrasing signifies that Israel, at Sinai, is given over irreversibly to the purposes, intentions, and commands of YHWH. Israel's holiness derives from YHWH and occupies that status and identity only in and through that relationship.

The status of Israel (and of every other object marked as "holy to YHWH") depends upon that relationship. Two temptations are consequent to such a holy relationship. On the one hand, Israel may come to imagine its intrinsic holiness, possessing that status and character on its own, without reference to YHWH. On the other hand, Israel may seek to separate itself from YHWH, renounce its special status, and seek to be "like other nations" (as in 1 Sam. 8:5, 20). The first temptation is one of idolatry. The second is one of profanation. Either idolatry or profanation is an easier way to live, for holiness in relation to YHWH is an endlessly demanding process of responsiveness in obedience and communion.

We can identify two contemporary temptations with regard to holiness. First, in a technological society, the demands of God's holiness are difficult to meet, because those demands entail yielding in awe and wonder. A technological consciousness wants to explain, control, and master, so that thereby what is central to faith is emptied of sacramental power and respect. Second, in an attempt to counter the deep "emptying of holiness" by technological control, myriad attempts are now made to separate the "sacred" from the "profane," to delineate protected zones for religious practice and sensibility. That bifurcation of "sacred and profane," however, must not be confused with what is holy, for the holiness of YHWH as understood in Israel requires yielding and redefining all of life, not only some zones while abandoning other spheres of life to human manipulation. The manifold efforts to encompass the holiness of YHWH into zones of sacredness attests to the overwhelming requirements made by YHWH's holiness and the endless capacity of resistance to those requirements expressed as the manufacture of idols that are weak and banal replicas of the "real thing." The reality of God's holiness, according to Israel's attestation, admits of no such management of the one who defies all such management.

References: Belo, Fernando, *A Materialist Reading of the Gospel of Mark* (Maryknoll, N.Y.: Orbis Books, 1981); Douglas, Mary, *Purity and Danger: An Analysis of the Concepts of Pollution and Taboo* (London: Routledge & Kegan Paul, 1969); Gammie, John G., *Holiness in Israel* (OBT; Minneapolis: Fortress Press, 1989); Houston, Walter, *Purity and Monotheism: Clean and Unclean Animals in Biblical Law* (JSOTSup 140; Sheffield: JSOT Press, 1993); Jenson, Philip Peter, *Graded Holiness* (JSOTSup 106; Sheffield: JSOT Press, 1992); Knohl, Israel, *The Sanctuary of Silence: The Priestly Torah and the Holiness School* (Minneapolis: Fortress Press, 1995); Miller, Patrick D., *The Religion of Ancient Israel* (Louisville, Ky.: Westminster John Knox Press, 2000), chap. 4; Wells, Jo Bailey, *God's Holy People: A Theme in Biblical Theology* (JSOTSup 305; Sheffield: Sheffield Academic Press, 2000).

Hope   The Old Testament voices the oldest, deepest, most resilient grounding of hope in all of human history, a hope that has been claimed by both Jews and Christians but that is also operative beyond those traditions in more secular modes. The hope articulated in ancient Israel is not a vague optimism or a generic good idea about the future but a precise and concrete confidence in and expectation for the future that is rooted explicitly in YHWH's promises to Israel [see PROMISE]. In those promises, which are text specific, YHWH has sworn to effect futures of well-being that are beyond the present condition of the world and that cannot, in any credible way, be extrapolated from the present. The remarkable act of hope that permeates the Old Testament lies in the fact that the promises Israel heard and remembered link together the character and intent of YHWH, the creator of heaven and earth, with the concrete, material reality of the world. YHWH's promises characteristically do not concern escape from the world but transformation within it.

Israel's hope is based on the character of YHWH, who utters promises and whose utterances Israel has found to be reliable. Indeed the very nature of YHWH, as confessed by Israel, is to make promises and to watch over those promises to see that they come to fruition (see Josh. 21:43–45). Thus the Old Testament is an ongoing process of promise-making and promise-keeping.

YHWH's promises tend to be clustered in four particular portions of the Old Testament text, the ancestral narratives, the covenant blessings in Leviticus and Deuteronomy, the prophets, and the Psalms.

1. The ancestral narratives of Genesis 12–36 are replete with promises (a) that YHWH will give land to Israel and cause Israel to prosper in the land where fertility is assured, and (b) that the nations will be blessed (see Gen. 12:1–3; 28:13–15).

2. The promises take a different form in the covenant blessings related to the Sinai traditions (Lev. 26:3–13; Deut. 28:1–14). Unlike the promises of Genesis, the blessings are part of a quid pro quo arrangement, so that the promises to Israel are assured when Israel obeys the commandments. In this tradition, the commands are the condition of hope.

3. The prophetic promises look beyond the present and anticipate a new arrangement of the world "in the days to come" [see THE DAY OF THE LORD]. These promises are not predictions but are rather acts of faithful imagination that dare to anticipate new futures on the basis of what YHWH has done in the past. While the promises occur at various places in the prophetic literature, they are particularly clustered in the exilic materials, such as Isaiah 40–55, Jeremiah 30–33, and Ezekiel 33–48.

4. In the Psalms we may identify two rhetorical practices of hope. First, in the great "Psalms of Enthronement" (Pss. 93; 96–99), the coming rule of YHWH is celebrated and welcomed by all of creation:

Let the heavens be glad, and let the earth rejoice;

let the sea roar, and all that fills it;
let the field exult, and everything in it.
Then shall all the trees of the forest sing for joy
before the LORD; for he is coming,
for he is coming to judge the earth.
He will judge the world with righteousness,
and the peoples with his truth.
(Ps. 96:11–13)

This large public doxology is matched by the second rhetorical practice, a much more intimate practice of faith in which individual Israelites voice complete hope for the future because of their unqualified confidence in YHWH:

The LORD is my light and my salvation;
whom shall I fear?
The LORD is the stronghold of my life;
of whom shall I be afraid?
(Ps. 27:1; see 30:4–5)

All of these texts and their various images attest to Israel's conviction that YHWH has promised and intends to enact a new well-being for Israel and the world. YHWH's promise characteristically concerns peace, security, prosperity, fruitfulness, righteousness, and justice, which will come in the earth, not because of any claim the earth has, but because the one who utters promises in the hearing of Israel is the creator of heaven and earth who is known in Israel to be reliable. Thus in the wondrous promises of Isaiah 2:2–4, Isaiah 11:1–9, and Micah 4:1–4, YHWH promises that the present earth will be healed by YHWH's own fidelity. Israel is therefore certain that YHWH will overcome every impediment and defeat every resistance to the well-being that YHWH intends for the world.

As the Old Testament develops, Israel's hope in YHWH is verbalized in two particular ways. On the one hand, Old Testament faith is *messianic,* believing that YHWH will dispatch and empower a particular human agent who will enact the new age that YHWH has promised. Thus, hope is "this worldly," inside the present ordering of creation. On the other hand, Old Testament faith also developed in an *apocalyptic* mode, a cataclysmic hope that YHWH will effect YHWH's new world without any human agency. Despite their differences, both traditions attest to the coming "rule of YHWH" in which all of creation will be ordered for YHWH's intent of peace, security, and justice. The later traditions of the Old Testament do not choose between these modes of faith, but hold them together in tension.

Israel's capacity to trust these promises of YHWH is the substance of faith. Trust in YHWH's promises is not a particularly "religious" undertaking, but rather concerns living differently in the world. As the Old Testament looks beyond itself to what YHWH will yet do, that powerful expectation for God has been addressed variously by Jewish and by Christian interpretive traditions. No single tradition has a monopoly on the promises of YHWH, and no single tradition is the designated custodian of hope.

A strong case has been made that a defining mark of a postindustrial, technological world is despair, the inability to trust in any new and good future that is promised and may yet be given. Insofar as despair marks the current social environment of faith, to that extent hope is a distinctive mark of faith with dangerous and revolutionary social potential.

References: Gowan, Donald E., *Eschatology in the Old Testament* (Philadelphia: Fortress Press, 1986); Rad, Gerhard von, *Old Testament Theology,* vol. 2 (San Francisco: Harper and Row, 1965); Westermann, Claus, *Prophetic Oracles of Salvation in the Old Testament* (Louisville, Ky.: Westminster John Knox Press, 1991); idem, "The Way of the Promise through the Old Testament," *The Old Testament and Christian Faith: A Theological Discussion,* ed. Bernhard W. Anderson (New York: Harper and Row, 1963), 200–24; Wolff, Hans Walter, *Anthropology of the Old Testament* (Mifflintown, Pa.: Sigler Press, 1996), 149–55; Zimmerli, Walther, *Man and His Hope in the Old Testament* (SBT Second Series 20; Naperville, Ill.: Alec R. Allenson, n.d.).

Huldah The Old Testament is convincedly patriarchal; men dominate much of the literature. As a predictable consequence, women play only tangential roles and for the most part modern readers are left with only traces of their presence and importance. Some notable exceptions exist, however, as in the narratives of Hagar, Ruth, and Esther, and recent feminist studies have called attention to the important roles of women in the text that conventional patriarchal interpretation missed. Even so, the patriarchal hegemony in the text, as in most interpretation, is obvious. In this book, I include comment on four prominent women—Miriam, Hannah, Jezebel, and Huldah—to go along with the four crucial men I cite: Moses, David, Elijah, and Ezra. I suggest that each of the men took on a larger-than-life metaphorical significance in the traditioning process. Hannah, Miriam, Jezebel, and Huldah, I suggest, also have metaphorical significance even as they have, at the same time, experienced sustained marginalization in the traditioning process. The extensive literature on these several subjects from a feminist perspective is crucial reading in order to understand the work and costs of the patriarchal traditioning process.

Huldah, a prophet, is mentioned only twice in the Bible, in 2 Kings 22:14–20 and the parallel passage in 2 Chronicles 34:22–28. She is thus a marginal figure in the tradition. I cite her—along with Miriam,

Hannah, and Jezebel—as a representative woman because of the important role she plays in her single appearance as a prophet. A prophet is one deemed to have peculiar authority and direct access to the will of God delivered through prophetic oracles. In an intensely patriarchal society such as ancient Israel was, this woman's acceptance as a divine spokesperson is of no small matter. (Notice that Miriam is termed a prophet in Exod. 15:20; see also Neh. 6:14.)

Huldah is, moreover, involved in what is presented as the pivotal event in the Deuteronomic account of Israel's royal history, reiterated in the same way in the Chronicles account of Judah's royal history. That pivotal event is the finding of the scroll in the temple, taken to be a version of Deuteronomy, and the derivative reform that King Josiah initiated. This event, by this king, is without a doubt the decisive event in the history of Israelite religion as presented in this textual tradition. Nor is there doubt that Josiah is the key king in this theological rendition of Israel's past. Given the cruciality of the event as it is remembered, that in 2 Kings 22:14 the closest advisors to the king turned immediately and directly to Huldah in order to receive prophetic comment on the scroll is immensely important. Huldah is obviously an important, highly visible person and is, moreover, connected by marriage to one who occupied a royal office. She is a reliable public figure, a known quantity in the circles of Judean royalty.

The oracle that she offers in response to the ominous tone of the scroll shows her, as rendered by the Deuteronomists, to be an articulate representative of the core covenantal tradition (2 Kgs. 22:16–20): "She is part of the royal court, and her importance is indicated by the fact that an official delegation of high-ranking govern-

ment officers is sent to inquire through her. Josiah apparently recognizes her as a Mosaic prophet, who is capable of interceding with Yahweh. In keeping with Deuteronomic ideas about the proper functions of Mosaic prophets, her oracle validates the book, revives the old Ephraimite religious traditions, and sets in motion the Deuteronomic reform" (Wilson, 220).

The oracle is in two parts, reflecting Huldah's capacity as an authorized theological interpreter. First, she reiterates a core conviction of the Deuteronomists that Judah, under failed royal leadership, is headed toward disaster (vv. 16–17). Second, though, she offers a promise to the good King Josiah, related to his identity as a keeper of the Torah.

The single oracle by which Huldah is known is predictable Deuteronomic theology, and she may not be an independent voice in the tradition at all but rather a mouthpiece (historically or literarily) for a theological tradition, rooted in Mosaic covenantal faith, that stands in critical opposition to royal policy. Even if so, however, the historians found it useful and compelling to place the tradition's crucial verdict on the lips of an authorized woman. Huldah thus embodies a conviction in Deuteronomic Israel that the divine word that defines the future may indeed be carried and uttered by an authorized woman who can utter the "Thus says the LORD" of Israel's God: "Hulda[h] herself may have had connections with the bearers of the Ephraimite traditions. If so, then her stereotypical speech and behavior simply reflect the expectations of her support group and are not completely the result of Deuteronomic editing" (Wilson, 223).

Reference: Wilson, Robert R., *Prophecy and Society in Ancient Israel* (Philadelphia: Fortress Press, 1980).

The Hymn   The hymn is one of Israel's most prominent and most used liturgical expressions. It is Israel's characteristic way of resituating its life in glad response to YHWH, the subject of the hymn. Hymns occur in various places in the narrative books of the Old Testament (as in Exod. 15:21; 1 Sam. 2:1–10) and occupy a dominant position in the book of Psalms (as in the concluding corpus of Pss. 145–150).

The genre of hymn likely emerged in a world of polytheism, in which the advocates for a particular God sang in ways that flattered, enhanced, and magnified that one God in contrast to other gods who were not praised. William Albright and his students, Frank Cross and David Noel Freedman, early on paid attention to poetic antecedents in the Canaanite collection of Ugarit, noting that poetic discourse stood at the beginning of Israel's theological articulation and was deeply rooted in polytheistic antecedents. As Israel's faith moved toward monotheism, this act of contrasting "our God" and "other gods" became unimportant, and hymns of praise became simply lyrical articulations of celebration, amazement, and gratitude toward the God named in the hymn. The initial impetus for a hymn of praise may have been a specific, concrete act of transformation credited to God—for example, a victory in war that was understood as an act of divine deliverance (thus Exod. 15:21). The inexplicable, surprising act of deliverance (in Exod. 15:21 rescue from Egyptian slavery) is named and credited to God's intervention.

In the rhetorical development of hymnic practice, Israel's praise moved from specific acts of intervention on God's part to characteristic acts, the sorts of things God does all the time. In Hebrew grammar these claims for God are expressed in participles, verbs for ongoing action:

> The LORD sets the prisoners free;
> the LORD opens the eyes of the blind.
> The LORD lifts up those who are bowed
>   down;
> the LORD loves the righteous.
> The LORD watches over the strangers;
> he upholds the orphan and the widow,
> but the way of the wicked he brings to
>   ruin.
>
> (Ps. 146:7c–9)

As hymns developed, God's characteristic actions, for which Israel had a stable inventory, became God's own attributes, the markings of God's own character and disposition, which were evidenced in actions:

> The LORD is gracious and merciful,
> slow to anger and abounding in
>   steadfast love.
> The LORD is good to all,
> and his compassion is over all that he
>   has made.
>
> (Ps. 145:8–9; see 103:8)

The primal data for such praise was the evidence of God that was known and remembered in Israel's own tradition. The hymn, however, pushed beyond Israel and issued in a summons for other peoples to join in the praise of the God of Israel (see Pss. 67:3–5; 117:1). The ground for such praise may emerge in Israel's own life, but the inference of such a summons is that what Israel knows of God may also be known and enacted everywhere beyond Israel, so that the hymn functions to assert the cosmic, universal claim for God who's "got the whole world in his hands."

Hymns are acts of lyrical self-abandonment whereby the singing congregation moves its attention beyond the community itself to the God who warrants all attention. The hymn, moreover, is a poetic act that surges beyond close description and engages in emancipated hyperbole—a mode of articulation in which emotional commitment matches cognitive substance about God (that is, serious theological claim). Thus, praise is testimony to God as true God and commitment on the part of the singing community to order its life in glad trust and obedience to this God.

The hymn is a primal carrier of Israel's best faith, a faith that knows the unutterable reality of God, who outdistances all our explanatory modes of speech. Thus in the New Testament's most forceful testimony to the God known in Jesus of Nazareth, the evangelical voices must finally break beyond narrative testimony or explanatory theological formula to lyrical self-abandonment. Consider Paul's attempts to formulate the mystery of God's unimaginable graciousness:

> O the depth of the riches and wisdom and knowledge of God! How unsearchable are his judgments and how inscrutable his ways! (Rom. 11:33)

Such an assertion is not in any way an argument, but rather a glad, exuberant, amazed doxology about the God who is beyond all our reasoning. In the same way, when the book of Revelation wants to characterize the wondrous coming rule of God in heaven and on earth, the only way to speak is in hymnic exuberance:

> "You are worthy, our Lord and God,
>   to receive glory and honor and power,
> for you created all things,
>   and by your will they existed and were created."
>   (Rev. 4:11; see 5:9–14)

In contemporary usage, the hymn—as exuberant hyperbole beyond explanation that refocuses life away from "us" to the God who is due all our attention—is a primal act of faith. Such doxology is a crucial

resource in the life of the church, for it is a lyrical, communal counter to the power of technique—in all kinds of electric control—that wants to thin, flatten, and isolate life so that nothing is left of life but "us." Against such a temptation that empties the world of everything of God, hymns are a crucial counterassertion that the world is to be received in awed gratitude for the mystery of God that is present in and presides over the world.

References: Brueggemann, Walter, *The Psalms and the Life of Faith* (Minneapolis: Fortress Press, 1995), 112–32; Cross, Frank M., and David Noel Freedman, *Studies in Ancient Yahwistic Poetry* (Grand Rapids: Eerdmans, 1997); Freedman, David Noel, *Pottery, Poetry and Prophecy: Studies in Early Hebrew Poetry* (Winona Lake, Ind.: Eisenbrauns, 1980); Hardy, Daniel W., and David F. Ford, *Praising and Knowing God* (Philadelphia: Westminster Press, 1985); Jacobson, Rolf, "The Costly Loss of Praise," *Theology Today* 57 (2000): 375–85; Miller, Patrick D., *They Cried to the Lord: The Form and Theology of Biblical Prayer* (Minneapolis: Fortress Press, 1994), 178–243.

■ ■ ■

Image of God   Although the notion of "image of God" occurs in only three texts in the Old Testament (Gen. 1:26–28; 5:1; 9:6), this concept has become enormously important in subsequent theological interpretation. The Bible is powerfully opposed to the creation of any likeness of God, and Judaism is a powerful force against any iconic construction: "While various proposals have been put forward to identify central elements of discontinuity or uniqueness in Israel's religion, the most likely candidates are the initial demands of the Decalogue, the claim of exclusive worship by Yahweh, and the aniconic requirement" (P. Miller, 211–12).

Thus the Second Commandment holds:

> You shall not make for yourself an idol, whether in the form of anything that is in heaven above, or that is on the earth beneath, or that is in the water under the earth. You shall not bow down to them or worship them. . . . (Exod. 20:4–5)

This prohibition pertains in its broadest expanse both to images of YHWH and to idolatrous representations of other gods. YHWH cannot be made into an image, because YHWH's freedom would be thereby limited and YHWH's sovereignty diminished. Moreover, the Deuteronomic-prophetic traditions regularly urge and authorize the destruction of signs and symbols that compete with and detract from YHWH (Exod. 34:13; Deut. 7:5; 16:22; 2 Kgs. 3:2; 10:26–27; 11:18). In Daniel 2–3, the image of Nebuchadnezzar looms large as an offensive alternative to YHWH that must be resisted. Distinctions can be made between the images of YHWH and the images of other gods, but the prohibition pertains to both and is uncompromising.

All the greater reason, then, to be astonished that in the priestly creation narrative of Genesis 1:26–28 and in the derivative texts of Genesis 5:1 and 9:6, human persons ("male and female") are in the image of God [see PRIESTLY TRADITION, SEXUALITY]. The most important reference is in Genesis 1:26–28 wherein the man-woman creature is unlike all other creatures because those human creatures resemble the character of YHWH. The text (perhaps deliberately) does not tell us wherein the "likeness" consists; the most plausible hypothesis is that the human person is placed among all the other creatures in order to attest to and enact the rule of God. The analogue to which appeal is often made for this interpretation is that of a governing sovereign who cannot be everywhere present in the realm, but who erects statues of himself/herself as witness and reminder of who the real sovereign is. By analogue, the invisible God has placed human creatures in creation so that, upon seeing the human creature, other creatures are reminded of YHWH's rule. Thus the text in Genesis 1 immediately goes on to speak of "dominion," so that the human creature not only exhibits the rule of YHWH, but in fact enacts it on behalf of and in the place of the sovereign God who is not visibly present to the other creatures. Thus "image of God" is a phrase designed to celebrate and enhance the dignity and authority of human persons who are "little lower than the angels" (Ps. 8:5–8). With the gift of dominion intrinsic to human personhood comes immense responsibility, for the work of humankind is to care for the earth even as the Creator has already begun to care, to protect and enhance the earth as God's creation. The notion of image thus serves well the theme of human responsibility for the well-being of the earth, a charge that, according to this reasoning, God has turned over to the Chief Creature.

The second use of "likeness" attests to the claim that the narrative of alienation in Genesis 3 has not caused human persons to forfeit their character or identity as image (Gen. 5:1) [see THE FALL]. That is, if Genesis 3 is taken, as in classic Christian tradition, as "fall," not even this deep verdict of sinfulness erodes the image. The third use of "image," in Genesis 9:6, attests, in a parallel form, that the identity and character of image is not diminished or nullified by the flood, as it was not by "the fall." The mark of "God's likeness" is thus definitional for humankind and beyond eradication; failure cannot eliminate the mark. Humankind bears that mark of identity, authority, and responsibility to perpetuity. Much church theology powerfully contradicts this remarkable affirmation about personhood by giving primary accent to human's sinfulness and low estate. Moreover, Genesis 9:6 is a statement of the inordinate value and worth of human persons who, because of this character and identity, must not be killed. This statement is of great importance in the valuing of human life—every human life—in a technological, uncaring, and brutalizing society where life is cheap. This verse thus serves as the culmination of the sequence from Genesis 1:26–28, drawing an uncompromising protective line against doing harm to this creature of all creatures.

Remarkably these three texts are the only Old Testament texts on this theme. They have, however, functioned powerfully in derivative theological tradition. First, the phrase "image of God" is important in the New Testament in an attempt to provide an adequate understanding of Jesus. While "image" language was not elevated into the orthodox christological formulae as was "Son," the New Testament witnesses to Jesus as the true image of God, wherein we know all that we can know of God:

Whoever has seen me has seen the Father.
(John 14:9)

In the rule of Jesus the rule of God is present and seen:

In their case the god of this world has blinded the minds of the unbelievers, to keep them from seeing the light of the gospel of the glory of Christ, who is the image of God.
(2 Cor. 4:4)

He is the image of the invisible God, the firstborn of all creation.
(Col. 1:15)

But second, the phrase not only refers to Jesus, but functions derivatively to refer to the new humanity of all those who are in Christ.

Do not lie to one another, seeing that you have stripped off the old self with its practices and have clothed yourselves with the new self, which is being renewed in knowledge according to the image of its creator.
(Col. 3:9–10)

You were taught to put away your former way of life, your old self, corrupt and deluded by its lusts, and to be renewed in the spirit of your minds, and to clothe yourselves with the new self, created according to the likeness of God in true righteousness and holiness.
(Eph. 4:22–24; see Rom. 8:29; 1 Cor. 11:7; 15:49)

In both Judaism and Christianity, the phrase provides a theological basis for the intense valuing of human life. Every human person—including the unattractive, the unacceptable, the disabled, the unproductive—is entitled by his or her very existence to the dignity and worth befitting the creature who alone among the creatures bears the irreducible markings of dignity and dominion from the Creator's own grant.

Special notice should be taken of recent feminist literature on this subject, for the decree for "male and female" stands as a powerful witness, in the ancient and contemporary worlds, against the patriarchal assumption that women are second-class creatures. The first utterance of image in the Bible is an utterance of a jointly assigned status and character "little lower than the angels."

References: Barr, James, "The Image of God in the Book of Genesis—A Study of Terminology," *The Bulletin of the John Rylands Library* 51 (1968/69): 11–26; Bird, Phyllis, *Missing Persons and Mistaken Identities: Women and Gender in Ancient Israel* (OBT; Minneapolis: Fortress Press, 1997), chaps. 6–8; Borresen, Kari E., *Image of God: Gender Models in the Judaeo-Christian Tradition* (Minneapolis: Fortress Press, 1995); Miller, J. Maxwell, "In the 'Image' and 'Likeness' of God," *JBL* 91 (1972): 289–304; Miller, Patrick D., "Israelite Religion," in *The Hebrew Bible and Its Modern Interpreters*, ed. Douglas A. Knight and Gene M. Tucker (Philadelphia: Fortress Press, 1985), 201–37; Raschke, Carl A., and Susan D. Raschke, *The Engendering God: Male and Female Faces of God* (Louisville, Ky.: Westminster John Knox Press, 1996); Stendahl, Krister, "Selfhood in the Image of God," in *Selves, People and Persons: What Does It Mean to Be a Self?*, ed. Leroy S. Rouner (Notre Dame, Ind.: University of Notre Dame Press, 1992), 141–48; Trible, Phyllis, *God and the Rhetoric of Sexuality* (Overtures to Biblical Theology; Philadelphia: Fortress Press, 1978).

■ ■ ■

Jerusalem Jerusalem dominated the political imagination of ancient Israel, and that locale continues to inform a good deal of contemporary political energy for both Jews and Christians. The city—anciently termed Jebus—was an old city long before Israel, but entered Israel's horizon of history and faith when David conquered it and made it irreversibly the "city of David" (2 Sam. 5:6–10). Archaeologists have determined which parts of the "old city" functioned as "the city of David" (never "the city of Israel") and which parts were in fact "Zion." The city was never part of Israel or Judah and remained the private property of the House of David. While such distinctions may be made, in Israel's theological discourse "Zion" and "city of David" refer to the entire urban scene that took on such immense importance in the faith and for the future of Israel.

Jerusalem is historically important in the Old Testament for two reasons: (1) the city became the seat of the Davidic dynasty when David moved his entourage from Hebron (2 Sam. 5:5), after which his dynasty lasted for an astonishing four hundred years; and (2) the city was the seat of Solomon's temple, which became the focus and legitimator of Israel's political-economic success and the pivot of much of Israel's hope for the future that YHWH would give. In the liturgic imagination of Israel, the dynasty of David and claims for the temple are paired as the two defining commitments YHWH has made to Israel:

> [H]e chose the tribe of Judah,
>> Mount Zion, which he loves.
> He built his sanctuary like the high
>> heavens,
>> like the earth, which he has founded
>> forever.
> He chose his servant David,
>> and took him from the sheepfolds . . .
>> to be the shepherd of his people Jacob,
>> of Israel, his inheritance.
>> (Ps. 78:68–71)

Over time the imaginative-interpretive significance of Jerusalem far outstripped its concrete political function, for the city became the seat of much of Israel's faith, both in the present as the place where YHWH dwells (1 Kgs. 8:12–13) and for the future when it will become the center of YHWH's promised, splendid newness. The interaction and tension between concrete political reality and deep theological hope that exceeds concrete reality are among the wonders of faith that the city of Jerusalem guaranteed.

Three renditions of Jerusalem occurred in the liturgical imagination of Israel:

1. Jerusalem, the temple, and all of the city of David are understood as a present liturgical reality where YHWH dwells

and where Israel may enter into YHWH's presence. In the city of David, YHWH's commitments to Israel were affirmed and YHWH was regularly celebrated as King and Creator, especially in the great Hymns of Enthronement (Pss. 93; 96–99). As a consequence, Jerusalem was a place of pilgrimage to which serious worshipers of YHWH returned regularly in great joy and expectation (Ps. 122:1). In Jerusalem, the faithful contemplated beholding God, though knowing precisely what such phrasing means is difficult (see Pss. 11:7; 17:15; and less directly 73:17).

Jerusalem is the place where Israel's best assurances of faith are gathered, where dwells YHWH, who guarantees the life of Israel. The cruciality of the city for the politics as well as the faith of Israel is best expressed in the Songs of Zion, of which the best known is Psalm 46:

> God is our refuge and strength,
> a very present help in trouble. . . .
> There is a river whose streams make glad
> the city of God,
> the holy habitation of the Most High.
> God is in the midst of the city; it shall
> not be moved;
> God will help it when the morning
> dawns. . . .
> The LORD of hosts is with us;
> the God of Jacob is our refuge.
> (Ps. 46:1, 4–5, 7;
> see Pss. 48; 76; 84; 87)

This glorious affirmation of safety and well-being is richly theological. Note, however, that this liturgical claim also has the rather obvious ideological function of making YHWH the guarantor and patron of the Davidic house, which dwells in the city, so that in the high days of ancient "Zionism," separating the liturgical-theological and the political-ideological components, which were fully merged,

was almost impossible. Such a merger was the goal of hegemonic power in its quest for legitimacy. Thus the theological claim for the city came to political fruition in the crisis of 705–701 wherein King Hezekiah, at the behest of the prophet Isaiah, was able to resist the Assyrian assault (Isa. 37:22–38).

2. The defining crisis of Jerusalem and the great nadir of Old Testament faith was the destruction of the city and the temple in 587 B.C.E. at the hands of the Babylonians. This disaster is understood in the text as either the intended punishment of YHWH, for whom Babylon is only the instrument (thus fulfilling long-standing prophetic warnings), or as the victimization of helpless Jerusalem at the hands of the Babylonians, who practice extreme oppression and brutality. Either way, the Old Testament gives voice to Jerusalem's immense loss, whereby the core assurances of faith were profoundly shattered. This loss is given full articulation in the book of Lamentations, which grieved the humiliation of the city, and in Psalms 74, 79, and 137, all of which voice the bitterness and bewilderment of displaced people. Thus the opening lines of Psalm 137:1, "By the waters of Babylon—there we sat down and there we wept," is a leitmotif for exilic faith in its deep and hyperbolic longing for Jerusalem as true home. The juxtaposition of the Songs of Zion (Pss. 46, 48, 84, and 87) and the Songs of Grief (Psalms 74, 79, and 137) bespeak the nearly unbearable jarring that is definitional for Old Testament faith.

3. Out of exile emerged a deep hope for a restored, renewed, rebuilt Jerusalem, for YHWH would not finally abandon what came to be regarded as YHWH's true home and the epicenter of all creation (see Zech. 1:14; 8:2–8). The "historical" recovery of Jerusalem is reflected in the prophetic utterances of Haggai and

Zechariah 1–8 and in the concrete though modest restoration led by Ezra and Nehemiah. The lyrical hope for "New Jerusalem" continued, however, even though the visible evidence of the city in shambles was to the contrary.

In exile, and perhaps especially for the exiles, a deep, determined, lyrical anticipation emerged that Jerusalem would be restored to a new glory that would exceed all that was remembered from the ancient, glorious days of Solomon. Jeremiah in exile thus contemplated a wondrous return and rebuilding of the city (Jer. 31:4–14). In a more sacerdotal cast, Ezekiel anticipated the return of YHWH in glory to the temple (Ezek. 43–44), so that the new name of the city will be "The LORD is There" (Ezek. 48:35), thus contradicting the present experience that YHWH is absent from the city. Most eloquently, belated Isaiah imagines a new Jerusalem commensurate with YHWH's "new heavens" and YHWH's "new earth" (Isa. 65:17–25). This wondrous poem details a new urban regime, which YHWH will give in coming days, marked by complete well-being, absence of every threat, immediate access to God, and reconciliation of every aspect of its life:

> Before they call I will answer,
> while they are yet speaking I will hear.
> The wolf and the lamb shall feed together,
> the lion shall eat straw like the ox;
> but the serpent—its food shall be dust!
> They shall not hurt or destroy
> on all my holy mountain, says the
> LORD.
> (Isa. 65: 24–25)

A dimension of this hope is no doubt exclusivist, that Jerusalem will be home to Jews who have been displaced too long. Alongside that affirmation, however, in what may be the more expansive vision of the coming Jerusalem that YHWH will give, Jerusalem is projected to become the pilgrimage center for all nations who will come there to study Torah, for Torah will provide the clue to coming world peace:

> Many peoples shall come and say,
> "Come, let us go up to the mountain of the
> LORD,
> to the house of the God of Jacob;
> that he may teach us his ways
> and that we may walk in his paths."
> For out of Zion shall go forth instruction
> [Torah],
> and the word of the LORD from
> Jerusalem. . . .
> [T]hey shall beat their swords into
> plowshares,
> and their spears into pruning hooks;
> nation shall not lift up sword against
> nation,
> neither shall they learn war any more.
> (Isa. 2:3–4; see Mic. 4:1–4)

This vision of coming Jerusalem makes no mention of special Jewish status or restoration of Davidic rule, for in this text transcendence of such Jewish particularities is envisioned in coming time. At the same time, however, Israel's Torah is precisely the center of the new vision of peace. Thus the hopes of Israel, without clarity about detail, hold together both a particular Jewish future and a large human future that is a gift to the world from the God of the Jews through the City of David.

In the horizon of the Old Testament, the promised Jerusalem of course never comes to concrete fruition. While the city has greatly recovered, the ancient hope clearly remains unfinished business, so that Jerusalem remains an open-ended invitation for a city that God as maker and builder is yet to construct. In contemporary Zionism, the Jerusalem yet to be is a place anticipated as deeply safe for Jews as Jews pray for the "peace of Jerusalem." In a different way, Jerusalem functions as a reference in Christian tradition that hopes for the coming rule of God when God will be all in all:

> And I saw the holy city, the new Jerusalem, coming down out of heaven from God, prepared as a bride adorned for her husband. And I heard a loud voice from the throne saying,
>> "See, the home of God is among mortals.
>> He will dwell with them as their God;
>> they will be his peoples,
>> and God himself will be with them."
> (Rev. 21:2–3)

In somewhat different cadences, Jews and Christians have found "Jerusalem" to be a way of speaking about God's ultimate fulfillment of God's promises to creation. These different cadences draw on ancient memories, but at the same time express confidence in YHWH's future-generating, city-restoring capacity. In different cadences and yet in a common voice, Jews and Christians, surely joined by Muslims, pray for the peace of Jerusalem, for when Jerusalem has peace, the world will have become more fully the world YHWH intended from the outset. That new Jerusalem will hold ancient memories, old disputes, and deep scars, but ancient Israel also knows that YHWH's newness—even when marked by memories, disputes, and scars—will take concrete form and leave God's people in unutterable joy. All of these characteristics are carried by this one city— old, destroyed, rebuilt, awaited . . . and promised!

References: Brueggemann, Walter, "A Shattered Transcendence? Exile and Restoration," in *Biblical Theology: Problems and Perspectives,* ed. Steven J. Kraftchick et al. (Nashville: Abingdon Press, 1995), 169–82; Hoppe, Leslie J., *The Holy City: Jerusalem in the Theology of the Old Testament* (Collegeville, Minn.: Liturgical Press, 2000); Hess, Richard, and Gordon Wenham, *Zion, City of Our God* (Grand Rapids: Eerdmans, 1999); Ollenburger, Ben C., *Zion, The City of the Great King: A Theological Symbol of the Jerusalem Cult* (JSOTS 41; Sheffield: Sheffield Academic Press, 1987); Porteous, Norman W., "Jerusalem-Zion: The Growth of a Symbol," in *Verbannung und Heimkehr: Beitrage zur Geschichte und Theologie Israel's im 6. und 5. Jahrhundert v. Chr.,* ed. Arnulf Kuschke (Tubingen: J. C. B. Mohr, 1961), 235–52; Rad, Gerhard von, "The City on the Hill," in *The Problem of the Hexateuch and Other Essays* (New York: McGraw-Hill, 1966), 232–42; Roberts, J. J. M., "The Davidic Origin of the Zion Tradition," *JBL* 92 (1973): 329–44.

Jezebel The Old Testament is convincedly patriarchal; men dominate much of the literature. As a predictable consequence, women play only tangential roles and for the most part modern readers are left with only traces of their presence and importance. Some notable exceptions exist, however, as in the narratives of Hagar, Ruth, and Esther, and recent feminist studies have called attention to the important roles of women in the text that conventional patriarchal interpretation missed. Even so, the patriarchal hegemony in the text, as in most interpretation, is obvious. In this book, I include comment on four prominent women— Miriam, Hannah, Jezebel, and Huldah— to go along with the four crucial men I cite: Moses, David, Elijah, and Ezra. I suggest that each of the men took on a larger-than-life metaphorical significance in the traditioning process. Hannah, Miriam, Jezebel, and Huldah, I suggest, also have metaphorical significance even as they have, at the same time, experienced sustained marginalization in the traditioning process. The extensive literature on these several subjects from a feminist perspective is crucial reading in order to understand the work and costs of the patriarchal traditioning process.

Unlike the other three women I discuss as representative types—Miriam, Hannah, and Huldah—Jezebel is a metaphor for all that is evil and rejected in ancient Israel.

Jezebel must be understood in the context of the Omride dynasty and the way that dynasty is remembered in Israel. The Omride dynasty, which enjoyed considerable economic and political success, consisted in its founder, Omri, his son Ahab, and his two sons in succession, Ahaziah and Jehoram (876–842). From the interpretive perspective of the Bible, however, the dynasty was the very antithesis of serious Yahwism, and as a consequence receives a sustained polemical treatment that is expressed particularly by Elijah and in a lesser way by Micaiah and Elisha.

The pivotal drama of the contest at Mt. Carmel (1 Kgs. 18) is seen as a dispute between two religious loyalties, YHWH and Baal (1 Kgs. 18:21) or perhaps YHWH and Asherah (see 1 Kgs. 16:31–33). Uncertainty aside, the religious dimension of that deep dispute is intimately and clearly linked to competing social theories, that is, notions of economic and political perspective. The religious contest of 1 Kings 18 is thus certainly connected to the dispute over land (and competing theories of land) in the narrative of chapter 21. In the end, the Omri dynasty was routed and assassinated by the Yahwistic purists who used violence to purge a rejected (religious, economic, political) system and so to recover a "pure" Yahwism (see 2 Kgs. 9–10).

Jezebel, a foreigner and princess of the royal house of Sidon, married into the Omri dynasty as the wife of Ahab (1 Kgs. 16:30–31), and presumably was the mother of Ahaziah (1 Kgs. 22:52) and Jehoram (2 Kgs. 3:2). The dynasty of Omri sought a strategic peace with its neighbor, the city–kingdom of Sidon, for Omri desperately needed commercial access to a seaport and Sidon, situated in the Mediterranean Sea, provided that. The marriage of the Omride Ahab to Jezebel was thus a great diplomatic achievement for Omri. At the same time, that Jezebel, when she came to the court in Israel, would bring her own practices and religious connections was not unexpected. (See, comparably, 1 Kgs. 11:1–8.) Another occurrence was normal, for the queen mother to play a prominent role in royal politics, and Jezebel is portrayed as an especially strong force in the political environment of Samaria, capital city of the Northern Kingdom.

The Deuteronomic Historian maintains a powerful polemic against "foreign wives" who invariably import, with their arrival in Israel, alien religious convictions and alternative socioeconomic, political notions that are incongruent with Israel's covenantal traditions, which the Deuteronomists so champion. (See a generic polemic in 1 Kgs. 11:1–8.) That Jezebel of the Sidonian royal house brought with her to Israel royal assumptions about entitlement and privilege that were inimical to Israel's covenantal faith and practice is entirely credible. Because the Omri dynasty demonstrated a readiness to marry "a foreign princess," her religious-social propensity seems to have found ready acceptance in royal circles of Northern Israel; she did not need to convince those in the royal entourage who already looked askance at rigorous Yahwism.

The contest at Mt. Carmel (1 Kgs. 18) and the account of Naboth's vineyard (1 Kgs. 21) bring the dynasty (and Jezebel) face-to-face with Elijah, perhaps the most radical Yahwistic spokesperson in the entire tradition. Their encounter is the most polemical in all of scripture. The outcome of that encounter, reported from a Deuteronomic perspective, is a harsh condemnation of and death sentence on the Omride dynasty (1 Kgs. 21:19–26), a sentence violently enacted in 2 Kings 9:30–37, reported as a vindication of Elijah and as an act of devotion to YHWH, an act that eliminated, so the narrative goes, the threat and seduction of Baalism.

Jezebel is inescapably a part of that intense dispute. She is to be understood primarily as a "foreigner" who intrudes foreign ideology into the life of Israel. She is, perhaps, a harbinger of the later rejection of "foreign wives" by Ezra and Nehemiah in their attempt to "purify" emerging Judaism (Ezra 9:1–4; Neh. 13:23–27; see the danger of a "foreign woman" already in the Joseph narrative (Gen. 39). Thus Jezebel is a "point person" for a systemic dispute that runs throughout the tradition.

The polemic against Jezebel is probably more acute because she is not only "foreign," but a "foreign woman," so that the weight of patriarchy is also mobilized against her. Thus Ahab is "urged on by his wife Jezebel" (1 Kgs. 21:25), perhaps suggesting the voice of a temptress. That role, then invested with a kind of sexual allure, is likely reinforced by the report of 2 Kings 9:30, that "she painted her eyes, and adorned her head. . . ."

Thus the fundamental systemic dispute is intensified by the actions of a woman who "seduces" her husband and sons and eventually all of Israel. This characterization of her as a temptress is reflected in Christian tradition in Revelation 2:20, where she beguiles to fornication, although even that rhetoric in Revelation is not particularly about sexuality. In any case, the accent upon sexuality, as reflected in the pop song of Frankie Laine, detracts from the much more important systemic dispute that concerns an elemental struggle for faith. Laine's song, popular in the fifties, talked about eyes that promised paradise, and said, "Jezebel . . . it was you!"

On both counts of systemic dispute and belated sexual portrayal, Jezebel embodies all that is evil and distorted, in contrast with the prophet Elijah who stands boldly for a Yahwism that the Deuteronomist regarded as pure.

This sharp and total contrast is surely the intent of the biblical text. I would have settled for it, moreover, except for the recent study of Phyllis Trible. She of course notices the total contrast affirmed in the text. But then Trible's shrewd and playful analysis shows that Elijah and Jezebel are two of a kind and do the same sorts of things:

> The ironies in his victory [Elijah's victory at Mt. Carmel] leave the reader to ponder who has triumphed over whom at Mount Carmel. Elijah against Jezebel; Jezebel against Elijah. Winner and loser exchange identities to expose the futility of the contest. . . . From elevated positions the two characters behave in similar ways. . . . Elijah shows no fear in taunting Ahaziah; Jezebel shows no fear in taunting Jehu. Yet the outcomes diverge radically. Elijah wins. Ahaziah dies "according to the word of YHWH that Elijah had spoken" (1:7). Jezebel loses. Jehu orders her murdered. But long before that happens, Elijah disappears. . . . Elijah and Jezebel, beloved and hated. In life and in death they are not divided. Using power to get what they want, both the YHWH worshiper and the Baal worshiper promote their gods, scheme, and murder. A reversal of the context in which their stories appear illuminates the bond between them. In a pro-Jezebel setting Elijah would be censured for murdering prophets, for imposing his theology on the kingdom, for inciting

kings to do his bidding, and for stirring up trouble in the land. . . . By contrast, Jezebel would be held in high esteem for remaining faithful to her religious convictions, for upholding the prerogatives of royalty, for supporting her husband and children, and for opposing her enemies until death. . . . No wonder each threatens the life of the other (Trible, 8, 14, 17–18).

Trible's analysis is of course against the grain of the text, for the text is unrelenting in its contrast of "absolute good" and "absolute evil" in this pair. Her analysis, however, makes us aware that Jezebel could be read differently. She was what she was. Baal worship could likely have had wide support and momentum in Northern Israel and that Jezebel was not exceptional in her adherence to Baal, which is likely attested by the harsh protest of the text through the championing of Elijah and by the presence of 450 prophets who served Baal. The militant Yahwism of Elijah (and the text) likely represents a detrimental and quite minority opinion in Israel. As we have her now in the text, however, Jezebel is made a carrier of an ideology that draws her profoundly beyond any sympathy in Israel or even any attempt to understand her. The negation to which she is subject in the text is the consequence of a deep ideological dispute. No doubt in the end even that dispute is given a harsher nuance by her role as a woman. She invites an extremity of interpretation and has received an extreme interpretation in full measure.

References: Brodie, Thomas L., *The Crucial Bridge: The Elijah-Elisha Narrative as an Interpretive Synthesis of Genesis-Kings and a Literary Model for the Gospels* (Collegeville, Minn.: The Liturgical Press, 2000); Camp, Claudia V., "1 and 2 Kings," in *The Woman's Bible Commentary*, ed. Carol A. Newsom and Sharon H. Ringe (Louisville, Ky.: Westminster/John Knox Press, 1992), 103–4; Renteria, Tamis Hoover, "The

Elijah/Elijah [sic] Stories: A Socio-cultural Analysis of Prophets and Peoples in Ninth-Century B.C.E. Israel," in *Elijah and Elisha in Socioliterary Perspective*, ed. Robert B. Coote (Atlanta: Scholars Press, 1992), 75–126; Rofé, A., "The Vineyard of Naboth: The Origin and Message of the Story," *VT* 38 (1988): 95–102; Toorn, Karl van der, *Family Religion in Babylon, Ugarit and Israel: Continuity and Changes in the Forms of Religious Life* (Leiden: Brill, 1996); Trible, Phyllis, "Exegesis for Storytellers and Other Strangers," *JBL* 114 (1995): 3–19.

Jubilee   The "Jubilee" is a radical ethical-economic practice sanctioned for Israel in the Torah teaching of Leviticus 25. The term "Jubilee" itself is derived from the Hebrew term *ybl*, and is apparently related to the ram's horn that was blown to signal the occasion of the Jubilee. The Torah teaching provided that every forty-nine years ("seven times seven" of the "year of release," on which see Deut. 15:1–18), land was to be returned to its original owners who may have lost the land amid the normal risks of the economy. The proposed, commanded practice was profoundly radical, for it aimed to disrupt and curb the normal processes of the economy. Some lands were ultimately not to be treated according to conventional economic transactions, but were finally to be defined by the more elemental claims of family inheritance.

The sociology of the jubilee year is rooted in a family and land structure that treats the land as an inalienable family inheritance (on which see 1 Kgs. 21). That inalienable family inheritance belongs not to a private individual or to a "nuclear family," but to a subset of the clan, what is called in the Old Testament "the father's house." That small economic unit was enormously vulnerable to the rough and tumble of the economy, and so the land is guaranteed for the survival and protected for the well-being of that small kinship unit against the vagaries of more strident economic transactions. For this reason Naboth refuses to deal with Ahab concerning his inherited land (1 Kgs. 21).

While the practice is rooted in tribal sociology, in the Old Testament Jubilee is understood theologically as a command of YHWH, the God who makes promises of inheritance and who wills the protection of the weak and vulnerable from the power of the strong and rapacious. Thus the Jubilee is a convergence of preservative economics and covenantal theology; the God of covenant commands this radical economic practice.

Scholars have used great energy to answer the question of the historicity of the festival: did it happen? Regarding this particular practice, the question of historicity is endlessly posed and, in my experience, no other teaching in the Bible is questioned as this one is about its historicity. I believe the question is asked because we recognize intuitively that of all the commands of YHWH, this Torah teaching is the most dangerous and demanding for it subverts and undermines all of our conventional assumptions about the organization of community life. In fact historians cannot demonstrate that the festival was practiced in ancient Israel, though some hints emerge, as perhaps in Nehemiah 5. Of course much in the covenantal imagination of ancient Israel cannot be verified historically. Nonetheless, a teaching such as that of Jubilee stands in the text as a daring act of ethical imagination concerning an alternative future for the community. As such, the text is important, whatever may be our judgment about its historicity.

In the end, what counts is that the Torah has preserved this radical act of social imagination, which is said to be rooted in YHWH's deepest covenantal commitment. Whether "historical" or not, the command stands as the most extreme ethical vision of Israel's covenantal memory, endlessly inviting reconsideration, even in economies that have become complex and postindustrial.

Ringe urges that the ministry of Jesus, especially in the Gospel of Luke, enacts the Jubilee. Luke 4:18–19 is a quote from Isaiah 61:1–4, and in both texts, the phrase "the year of the Lord's favor" is taken to be an allusion to Jubilee.

The extent to which and the way in which Jubilee is pertinent to a contemporary postindustrial economy requires immense moral imagination. If, however, the provision for Jubilee is understood as a curb on economic rapaciousness, then transposing that old Torah instruction into a contemporary economic concern is not difficult. The power of the global economy is currently dangerously destructive of local economies that are vulnerable to its force. The old text of Leviticus poses the contemporary question of whether economic power is to be curbed in the interest of maintaining and enhancing the human fabric of society. Of great interest is that in the year 2000, the turn of the millennium, a broadly based initiative was undertaken to secure the cancellation of third-world debt. Known as Jubilee 2000, the initiative met with some important success. It may be taken as an indication of a way in which the old clan practice—framed as divine command—may continue to require careful attention in a belated economy where "the neighborhood" is endlessly in jeopardy from the power of the economy. Such an option for the economy requires not only theological passion but hard and shrewd economic analysis as well. The text itself shows this community of faith well able to work at the interface of theological passion and economic analysis.

References: Daly, Herman E., and John B. Cobb Jr., *For the Common Good: Redirecting the Economy Toward Community, the Environment, and a Sustainable Future* (Boston: Beacon Press, 1994); Harris, Maria, *Proclaim Jubilee! A Spirituality for the Twenty-First Century* (Louisville, Ky.: Westminster John Knox Press, 1996); Kinsler, Ross, and Gloria Kinsler, *The Biblical Jubilee and the Struggle for Life* (Maryknoll, N.Y.: Orbis Books, 1999); Lowery, Richard H., *Sabbath and Jubilee* (St. Louis: Chalice Press, 2000); Meeks, M. Douglas, *God the Economist: The Doctrine of God and Political Economy* (Minneapolis: Fortress Press, 1989); Neal, Marie Augusta, *A Socio-Theology of Letting Go: The Role of a First World Church Facing Third World Peoples* (New York: Paulist Press, 1977); Ringe, Sharon H., *Jesus, Liberation, and the Biblical Jubilee: Images for Ethics and Christology* (OBT; Philadelphia: Fortress Press, 1985); Weinfeld, Moshe, *Social Justice in Ancient Israel and in the Ancient Near East* (Minneapolis: Fortress Press, 1995); Wright, Christopher J. H., *God's People in God's Land: Family, Land, and Property in the Old Testament* (Grand Rapids: Eerdmans, 1990); Yoder, John Howard, *The Politics of Jesus: Vicit Agnus Noster* (Grand Rapids: Eerdmans, 1972).

■ ■ ■

Kingship   Kingship was a very old idea and institution in the world in which ancient Israel emerged. Governance by a single, completely authorized human ruler was the dominant mode of societal power in the ancient world, yielding only slowly to democratic processes. The theory of human kingship was characteristically grounded in a notion of a divine king, a god-ruler who presided over all earthly affairs, sometimes with a subordinated, advisory council of lesser gods.

Israel appropriated from its cultural context both the idea of divine kingship and the institution of human kingship. YHWH, the God of Israel, is affirmed as "maker of heaven and earth" (as in Gen. 14:19), as "God of gods and Lord of lords, the great God, mighty and awesome" (Deut. 10:17), who presides over all earthly affairs and, in a polytheistic world, over all divine affairs as well. The divine kingship of YHWH, moreover, is regularly celebrated in the hymnic liturgies of the Jerusalem temple (see Pss. 93:1; 96:10; 97:1; 98:6; 99:1) wherein YHWH is acknowledged to be fully sovereign. Perhaps such hymnody is essentially an act of hope, looking to the full establishment of that governance and to the defeat of all rivals in time to come; or it may be that the liturgic act of hymnody is itself understood as an effective act of enthronement whereby Israel's liturgy of praise causes YHWH to become king, so that YHWH is "enthroned on the praises of Israel" (Ps. 22:3).

Either way, the full authority of YHWH as unchallenged ruler in Israel and over the world means that all powers of chaos, evil, or death are diminished; YHWH alone kills and makes alive (Deut. 32:39), does *shalom* and causes woe (Isa. 45:7). YHWH as king is a "lover of justice," who intends that the world be well ordered (Ps. 99:4; Isa. 61:8) and who acts to create justice in the world, especially for the weak and vulnerable (Ps. 146:7–10).

That divine kingship, however, came to seem to some in Israel to be remote from the daily exigencies of lived life and inadequate for the crises Israel inevitably faced. While YHWH may be "king" from the exodus (Exod. 15:18) who wills Israel to be YHWH's own "priestly kingdom" (Exod. 19:6), very soon in Israel efforts were made to establish a human king who would attend to urgent military, economic, and judicial matters. Human kingship would seem, in the ancient world, to be a practical necessity. That institution, however, was resisted on two grounds by some in ancient Israel who argued that (1)

YHWH is king and a human king is an unnecessary rejection of YHWH's own rule, and (2) a human king is characteristically and inescapably unjust and exploitative (1 Sam. 8:10–17). The vigorous debate over the institution of human kingship pitted those who regarded YHWH's "direct rule" as adequate against those who, perhaps more pragmatically, found stable human governance a political necessity (1 Sam. 7–15).

After Saul's failed kingship (see 1 Sam. 13–15), attention in Israel's narrative focuses on David (1 Sam. 16–1 Kgs. 1), his greater son Solomon (1 Kgs. 3–11), and David's long-standing dynasty, which ended in 587 B.C.E. (1 Kgs. 14–2 Kgs. 25). David, no doubt supported by a contrived royal ideology, proved to be a winsome leader and an effective military commander. He was duly anointed as king, an act of "sacramental" authorization (1 Sam. 16:1–13). Note that "anointing" is from the Hebrew verb *mšh*, from which comes the noun "messiah," the *anointed* agent of YHWH. So, with the coming of David, the tension over human kingship evaporated into a durable loyalty toward David and his family.

In what must be an ominous irony, David receives great attention in the text. The book of Psalms (see Pss. 2, 72, 89, 110, 132), together with the oracle of 2 Samuel 7:1–17, provides powerful theological and liturgical support for the kingship of David as an enactment of YHWH's will. Alongside that authorization, however, the narratives of 2 Samuel offer an artistic portrayal of the shabby life of David and his family (see 1 Kgs. 15:4–5). The testimony of the text makes no effort to harmonize these narrative accounts with the lyrical affirmations of the Psalms. No doubt the juxtaposition of a realistic narrative and liturgical ideology attest to the deep ambivalence felt in Israel toward the monarchy.

The tradition of the Sinai covenant, which stands in tension with the high claims of the royal dynasty, insists that kings in Israel should be subject to the Torah. Specifically the Torah commands the king to obedience and seeks to curb royal avarice (Deut. 17:14–20). The judgment of the long narrative account of monarchy in 1 and 2 Kings is that, on the whole, the monarchy in Israel failed because of inattentiveness to Torah requirements. In the end, the failure of kingship is the basis for the destruction of Jerusalem and the deportation of its leading citizens (2 Kgs. 21–25; Ezek. 34). The royal failure to keep Torah is expressed as self-serving, self-indulgent power that failed to practice covenantal modes of justice and righteousness, a task assigned in the liturgy to the kings (see Ps. 72). Thus the dynasty comes to a sorry end with deportation and displacement, topped by the humiliating surveillance of Jehoiachin, the last of the Davidic kings (2 Kgs. 25:27–30).

One of the hallmarks of Old Testament faith, however, that the cataclysmic events of 587 did not finish the monarchial dream of Israel. None doubted that, in those events of destruction and termination in 587, the sovereign power of YHWH, the divine king, was operative, for the disaster was understood as the work of YHWH's administration. Beyond that, however, Israel wondered about human kingship and about YHWH's solemn promise to the house of David that the lineage of David is guaranteed by YHWH to perpetuity (see Ps. 89:38–51).

The Davidic king, the one anointed and authorized to be YHWH's agent on earth, had in 587 failed. The promissory oracle of YHWH to the House of David, however, persists (2 Sam. 7:1–17). For that reason, even amidst its deepest defeats, Israelites trusted that in due course YHWH would restore kingship and raise up a newly anointed king, a "messiah" who would effectively enact YHWH's will in the world. The prophetic materials of the Old Testament teem with promises and expectations that, in the face of present-tense failed Davidic kings, a future anointed king, a coming "messiah," will rule rightly (Isa. 9:2–7; 11:1–9; Jer. 23:5–6; 33:14–16; Ezek. 34:23–24; Amos 9:11–12; Zech. 9:9–10).

As practical, immediate hopes for the restoration of a Davidic king failed in the Persian period, the prophetic-poetic anticipation of a coming king (messiah) was eloquently and courageously voiced in the face of the data. Alongside the continuing hope for a future David, Cyrus the person, an outsider to Israel, is remarkably called "Messiah" in Isaiah 45:1. The anticipation is that the coming, awaited Davidic king, rooted in old promises from YHWH, will effectively rule on behalf of YHWH in time to come. The outcome of such governance is that the earth will be restored—socially, politically, economically, environmentally—as the rule of God, that is, the "kingdom of God."

The twofold affirmation of *divine king* and *human king* persists from the Bible into Jewish and Christian hope. In both evolved traditions, the expectation is that God will establish God's rule, and so Christians regularly pray, "Thy kingdom come . . . on earth as it is in heaven" (see Matt. 6:10). Both Jews and Christians, moreover, expect a coming messiah who will humanly enact God's will in the word. In Jewish tradition that coming human one is unnamed and yet to be recognized. In Christian tradition, of course, "messianic" conviction revolves around Jesus of Nazareth. The early church hosted the question, "Are you the one who is to come?" (Luke 7:20). The church, moreover, regularly asserts in Holy Communion, in an act of exuberance, ". . . until he comes." The identity of Jesus as Messiah, as the promised, anointed one of God, of course divides Jews and Christians decisively, even though both await a coming messiah.

References: Frick, Frank, *The Formation of the State in Ancient Israel* (Sheffield: JSOT Press, 1985); Gray, John, *The Biblical Doctrine of the Reign of God* (Edinburgh: T. & T. Clark, 1979); Halpern, Baruch, *The Constitution of the Monarchy in Israel* (Chico, Calif.: Scholars Press, 1981); Roberts, J. J. M., "In Defense of the Monarchy: The Contribution of Israelite Kingship to Biblical Theology," in *Ancient Israelite Religion: Essays in Honor of Frank Moore Cross*, ed. Patrick D. Miller Jr. et al. (Philadelphia: Fortress Press, 1987), 377–96; Whitelam, Keith, *The Just King: Monarchical Judicial Authority in Ancient Israel* (Sheffield: JSOT Press, 1979).

■ ■ ■

The Lament   The lament is a stylized form of speech—usually poetic—and was a preferred and characteristic way of petitionary prayer in Israel. Though such lament prayers occur elsewhere in the Old Testament, fully one-third of the book of Psalms are laments. The lament is a daringly assertive way for Israel to address God in its need and ask (or expect or demand) that God should and must respond decisively to alleviate or overcome the need. The Old Testament regularly assumes that Israel's forceful petition is a proper, legitimate form of prayer and that Israel has a right and an obligation to ask of God in insistent ways. Moreover, the assumption is that God has a legitimate obligation to answer the prayer, because God's own people, who are bound to God in a covenant of mutual fidelity and commitment, are offering it. On rare occasions the prayer is a sad lament in a mood of resignation. Much more often, the prayer is a protest or complaint that actively expects a good resolution from God.

This stylized form of prayer is often in the voice of an individual speaker who prays as a member of the community but who, at the same time, speaks from an intimate personal relationship with God. Such personal prayers may petition God out of illness or social isolation or perhaps prison. Sometimes the prayer expresses guilt and asks forgiveness, but much more often the prayer voices loyalty to YHWH and seeks a responding loyalty from YHWH.

In somewhat varied form, lament prayers may be offered in the voice of the community when the entire community is caught up in a public crisis such as war or drought. Most particularly in the Old Testament, such communal laments are concerned specifically with the destruction of the Jerusalem temple in 587 B.C.E. at the hands of the Babylonians. This profound concern is expressed in Psalms 74 and 79 and in the collection of poems in the book of Lamentations. Such poems express sadness at loss; righteous indignation at the destroying enemy; and a deep, confident yearning for God's positive intervention.

The most interesting and perhaps most important recurring feature of this form of prayer is that while it characteristically begins in need, sadness, or dire strait, these same prayers characteristically end in praise, celebration, and confidence that God has acted or will act. Thus, the plea of Psalm 13:1–4 is matched in verses 5–6 by praise. In Psalm 22, verses 1–21a are followed by resolution in verses 21b–31. Psalms 39 and 88 are important exceptions to the usual pattern, for these psalms include no positive resolution; they are included in the collection as an act of candor, a recognition that God may character-istically, but not automatically, answer prayer. The fact that these demanding prayers, filled with imperatives addressed to God, are characteristically answered suggests four important interpretive points:

1. These prayers are real prayers and not merely psychological acts of catharsis whereby the speaker "feels better" by expressing need out loud. These prayers are seriously addressed to God, who is expected to answer.

2. The prayers, some of them savage in their urgency, are acts of hope uttered in confidence that God will hear and act in response. This point is of great significance, for conventional Christian piety tends to regard such abrasive speech toward God as affrontive and beneath the dignity of polite faith. These prayers reflect the awareness of Israel that in serious conditions of need, faith demands not politeness toward God but full candor about need expressed toward the God "from whom no secret can be hid."

3. The fact that these prayers characteristically end in joyous resolution indicates that in Israel's horizon of speech, they are effective prayers that do indeed habitually evoke a transformative response from God who intervenes to change circumstance. That is, a passionate realism exists about them that challenges "modern" faith. That realism—real prayer prayed in real hope to a real God who makes real answer—suggests that Israel understood its prayer as real communication and not pious role-play.

4. In the pervasive practice of the church—in liturgical prayer and in personal devotion—these prayers have nearly disappeared from the horizon of faith, which is an immensely important development. Likely they remain unused because (a) they are too raw, candid, and abrasive for "nice Christians," and (b) they are too robust in hope for modern

people who do not expect a God who hears and acts. The toning down of a prayer to less demanding form constitutes a loss of realism, candor, and robustness in much prayer.

Studying and using these psalms likely suggests to us that in its own ancient idiom, Israel had long understood the interactionist dynamics that belatedly has taken the form of twelve-step programs. Prayer in this recurring pattern is as psychologically discerning as it is religiously daring and demanding. These psalms reflect real engagement of every dimension of life with the God who attends to and rules over every dimension of life.

References: Anderson, Gary A., *A Time to Mourn, A Time to Dance: The Expression of Grief and Joy in Israelite Religion* (University Park: Pennsylvania State University Press, 1991); Brueggemann, Walter, *The Message of the Psalms: A Theological Commentary* (Minneapolis: Augsburg Publishing House, 1984), 51–121; idem, *The Psalms and the Life of Faith* (Minneapolis: Fortress Press, 1995), 33–111, 217–34, 258–82; Fisch, Harold, "Psalms: The Limits of Subjectivity," in *Poetry with a Purpose: Biblical Poetics and Interpretation* (Bloomington: Indiana University Press, 1988), 104–35; Miller, Patrick D., *They Cried to the Lord: The Form and Theology of Biblical Prayer* (Minneapolis: Fortress Press, 1994), 55–177; Westermann, Claus, *Praise and Lament in the Psalms* (Atlanta: John Knox Press, 1981).

Land Land is a defining theme in Old Testament tradition. The Old Testament is preoccupied with the concrete particularity of land, thereby assuring that Israel's faith is in touch with the public, material, sociopolitical-economic aspects of living in the world. For that reason, one cannot consider the faith of the Old Testament or the God of the Old Testament without at the same time being concerned with socioeconomic analysis, for land is not

just a "good idea," but actual real estate that evokes and hosts profound hope, imaginative social policy, deep moral conflict, savage acts of violence, and acute communal disappointment.

According to the tradition of the Old Testament, God's first encounter with Abraham and Sarah (who were to become the progenitors of Israel) concerned land (Gen. 12:1). Indeed, the entire ancestral narrative of Genesis is preoccupied with God's promise of land and, derivatively, with the presence of an heir who will carry the land promise into the future. This ancestral promise of land—in a sure oath from God—is defining for all events that follow in the Bible (see Gen. 15:18–21). Israel lives in the conviction that sooner or later it will receive a secure land. The ancestral promise is matched in the Mosaic tradition, which is organized around God's deliverance from Egypt (he "brought us out") in order that "he [may bring] us into" the good land (see Deut. 26:8–9). The exodus is completed by the entry into the land of promise, which is the initial goal and intent of the exodus (see Exod. 3:7). The traditions of both ancestors and Moses root Israel in promises about and anticipation of the land that will be God's gift to Israel [see HOPE; PROMISE].

The promise and anticipation of land, rooted in God's resolved generosity toward Israel, came to fruition in ancient Israel in less than glorious ways. Two aspects of the tradition are important here. First, the account of the entry into and conquest of the land in the book of Joshua are saturated with violence. The land that YHWH promises and gives is also taken by Israel in a vigorous onslaught. The violence that entails burning the cities and killing their inhabitants, moreover, is sanctioned and authorized by the God of the promises, so that God's own life and character are embedded in narratives of violence. When the promises of land are understood in theological innocence, the matter is easy enough. The geopolitical "facts on the ground" are very different, though, because the land is not empty, waiting for the new inhabitants whom God dispatched. In fact "Canaanites" who have long been there already occupy and regard the land as their own. The gift of land thus entails the displacement of an entrenched population that is violently denied its own ("rightful"?) place in the land. The land promise thus cannot be separated from the violence that enacts and makes theological claims concrete [see VIOLENCE].

Second, while the land was said to be governed for a time by "judges" who emerged in times of crisis and ordered by "militiae" that arose in emergency, the long-term governance of the land was according to royal authority, specifically the Davidic dynasty. While the dynasty that presided over the land of promise for what the story recounts as four hundred years was duly authorized by divine oracle (2 Sam. 7:1–17), in fact the monarchy introduced into Israel a theory of land management and economic policy that was inimical to the deepest promises of the ancestors and the deepest hopes of the Mosaic tradition. Counter to traditional communitarianism, the monarchy introduced into Israel a systemic practice of surplus wealth that inevitably produced rapacious, antineighborly economic practice. Thus the land of promise became the land of coveting abusiveness; 1 Kings 12 provides one dramatic protest against the new royal land policy practiced by Solomon and inherited by Rehoboam.

Such a guiding theory of land possession evoked a steady stream of polemic and protest from poetic speakers who came to be styled "prophets." For three centuries, from Elijah to Jeremiah, these prophetic voices—soon to be streamlined into a "prophetic tradition"—spoke harshly against royal policies and warned that such rapacious practices would eventually lead to the forfeiture of the land that YHWH gave to Israel according to covenantal stipulations. The long history of monarchy in the books of Kings, moreover, characterizes the royal policies and conduct that led to land-loss at the hands of invading Babylonian armies. A characteristic prophetic assertion was that Nebuchadnezzar and the Babylonians acted at YHWH's behest, so that imperial invasion was praised as the equivalent of divine judgment. The outcome is that with the destruction of Jerusalem, the people who had so long awaited the land of promise were now again made landless.

The great articulation of land theology in the Old Testament is found in the book of Deuteronomy. The importance of the collection of sermonic addresses and commandments is to assert the nonnegotiable conditions of land possession, conditions that are worked out in policy and public action but that are understood theologically as the commandments of YHWH. At the center of this land-ethic is the "year of release" in Deuteronomy 15:1–18, which provides canceling debts among the poor in the community so that they may participate viably and with dignity in public. This same legal provision is writ large in the provision of the jubilee year in Leviticus 25. These laws on the year of release and jubilee year have the intention of curbing an unfettered economy by subordinating economic transactions to the needs and requirements of the civic community [see JUBILEE]. Thus the covenantal stipulations provide for a theory of land management that is immediately pertinent in the contemporary world of uncurbed market forces. The covenantal tradition of Moses and the prophets knows that no community can hope to occupy land peaceably and justly unless the claim of the neighbor is honored in the face of exploitative possibility. Israel's own sad experience is taken to attest to the truth of that advocacy.

The story of the early part of the Bible thus is the movement from land anticipation to land governance and finally to land loss, culminating in the deportation and displacement from the land, signaled as "exile." Remarkably in this tradition preoccupied with land, the exile is the defining signature event of ancient Israel. The exile, moreover, became the matrix in which the ancient promises of land were reiterated afresh. Thus the great prophetic traditions of Isaiah 40–55, Jeremiah 30–31, and Ezekiel 33–48 all assure exilic Israel that God will once again give land to Israel as it was first given to the heirs of the ancestors (see Isa. 49:19–20; 51:2–3; Jer. 31:12–14, 38–40; Ezek. 37:13–14; 47:13–14). With these utterances the gift of land is again in prospect. Again YHWH guarantees, and again Israel is to trust the promise and receive the gift.

The actual restoration of the land and the rebuilding of the destroyed city of Jerusalem after the deportation are, in fact, much more modest than this expansive poetry suggests. The initial return to Jerusalem featured the reconstruction of the temple (see Haggai; Zech. 1–8). Then in the mid-fifth century under Ezra and Nehemiah, a modest political restoration and resumption of ordered life in the land took place. While much less than the grand prophetic promises, the concrete reality was enough to provide a basis for enduring hope of a fuller, greater restoration yet to come, a hope that marks the emerging life of Judaism. Four conclusions can be drawn from this long history of land promise, land governance, land loss, and land restitution.

1. Israel's hopes are for the full appearance of the governance of God over the earth, of which the Jewish community will be a primary beneficiary. That is, the full fruition of God's promises are in prospect and not in hand. This defining anticipation of God's rule has provided the phrase "kingdom of God." The phrase is a hope that God's neighborliness will, soon or late, be fully enacted in the earth, so that all may dwell peaceably and securely.

2. The land promises are decisively important in the ongoing life of Judaism and are especially important for Zionism, an intensely political movement within Judaism that struggles for the full restoration of the "land of promise" to the Jewish community. This deep theological promise, now transformed into a political agenda, has legitimated the current state of Israel, which occupies the old "territory of promise" and nurtures a vision of "Greater Israel." A case can be made that the violence of ancient Israel against the Canaanites in securing the land is currently replicated in the policies of the State of Israel concerning the Palestinians.

3. The land promises, of course, come to a different fruition in Christian tradition. The tendency of Christian interpretation has been to "spiritualize" land promises, so that they no longer apply in the first instance to the real estate of the "land of promise." To be sure, talk of "heirs" in the rhetoric of the early church is reminiscent of the ancestral promises (see Rom. 8:15–17; Gal. 4:1–7; Heb. 6:17). That rhetoric, however, now characteristically pertains to an assurance of God's faithful presence more than to territory. Christians, moreover, pray that "your kingdom come . . . on earth as it is in heaven," a petition that God's rule shall be fully effective and visible in the earth (Matt. 6:10). Such spiritualization and

making cosmic of the land promises, however, has not caused Christianity to lose its sense that the defining promises of God are in important ways this-worldly promises for an earth marked by peace and justice. Thus the materiality of land promises survives in Christian anticipation, but often without appreciation of the particularity of the specific land of Israel.

4. Taken most largely, the biblical perspective on land is an acknowledgment that none can live without the security, dignity, and well-being that come with land; faith in the God of the Bible, moreover, concerns a commitment to the just sharing of land, its produce and its guarantees. Taken negatively, this tradition stands as an important critique of the massive enterprise of colonialism in the modern world whereby imperial powers have occupied and confiscated lands not their own. Taken positively, the land promises of the Bible are a generic affirmation of liberation movements whereby disadvantaged landless people receive back (take back) their own lands too long denied them. Construed most broadly and without denying the particularity of the tradition, the biblical perspective affirms (a) that none can live humanly without guaranteed land or its socioeconomic equivalent, and (b) that the God of the Bible is precisely concerned with such issues, and with the power arrangements and systemic practices that either guarantee or deny such land holdings. The linkage of God and land makes the biblical tradition endlessly revolutionary in its social function. Every attempt to reduce the Bible to an otherworldly subject fails precisely on this accent on land.

References: Berry, Wendell, *The Gift of Good Land: Further Essays Cultural and Agricultural* (San Francisco: North Point Press, 1981); Brueggemann, Walter, *The Land: Place as Gift, Promise, and Challenge in Biblical Faith* (OBT; Philadelphia: Fortress Press, 1977); Davies, W. D., *The Territorial Dimension of Judaism* (Berkeley: University of California Press, 1982); Habel, Norman C., *The Land Is Mine: Six Biblical Land Ideologies* (OBT; Minneapolis: Fortress Press, 1995); O'Brien, Conor Cruise, *God Land: Reflections on Religion and Nationalism* (Cambridge: Harvard University Press, 1988); Stevenson, Kalinda Rose, *The Vision of Transformation: The Territorial Rhetoric of Ezekiel 40–48* (SBL Dissertation Series 154; Atlanta: Scholars Press, 1996).

Listening   "Listening" is a peculiarly freighted notion in the faith of ancient Israel. Beyond the ordinary aspects of auditory communication, listening—expressed in the familiar Hebrew term *Shema'*—pertains to the peculiar covenantal bonding that is affirmed between YHWH as the commanding sovereign and Israel as the responding subject. "Listening" is thus not simply an auditory exercise, but it involves singular attentiveness of the covenant partners to each other, to whom each is pledged in solemn oath. Thus to "listen" means to "obey," to take with utter seriousness the will and intention of the other, as when we say of a wayward child, "The problem is that you do not listen!"

The beginning point of this covenantal attentiveness is in the Shema' of Deuteronomy 6:4–9, often termed the creed of Judaism. These verses are called "the Shema" because they begin with the weighty imperative, "Listen," with which YHWH, the sovereign, addresses Israel with the elemental commands of Sinai faith. This commanding address uttered by the God of Sinai asserts that YHWH is the only God whom Israel may serve, trust, or obey; obedience to YHWH is an act of "love"—that is, singular devotion and covenantal fidelity. In the theology of Deuteronomy, this one imperative in

Deuteronomy 6:4, reinforced by the imperative "love" in verse 5, implies attentiveness to all of the commandments that are remembered in chapter 5 (the Ten Commandments) and all the derivative commandments that follow in Deuteronomy 12–25. More than that, the next generation of Israel is to be saturated with the requirements of faith, so that YHWH's commandments intentionally and zealously define all of life. The term "listening" thus carries all of the weight of Israel's most intense commitment to Torah, characterizing Israel as a covenanted people whose purpose, character, and raison d'être involve responsiveness to YHWH's will and purpose (see Deut. 5:1, 27; 9:1; Jer. 2:4; 11:2, 6; 13:11).

The truth of Israel's life, as Israel reflects upon it, however, is that Israel characteristically did not listen to YHWH, did not respond in obedience. The Old Testament does not reflect much on whether Israel could not or would not listen, but in fact did not (see 2 Kgs. 17:14; 18:12; Jer. 5:21, 7:13; 13:10). Thus the initial Shema' provides the premise for the pervasive indictment of Israel that is found in both Deuteronomic and prophetic traditions. The term is employed both to propose a working covenant with a responsive Israel and to reflect on a broken covenant with an unresponsive Israel. Special attention may be given to Isaiah 6:9–10 (see also Matt. 13:14–15; Mark 4:12; Luke 8:10; John 12:37–43; Acts 28:26–27):

"'Keep listening, but do not comprehend;
keep looking, but do not understand.'
Make the mind of this people dull,
    and stop their ears,
    and shut their eyes,
so that they may not look with their eyes,
    and listen with their ears,
and comprehend with their minds,
    and turn and be healed."

In this text, Israel is asserted to have failed to hear because YHWH, in judgment upon Israel, had willed Israel not to hear.

Remarkably the same rhetoric, with the same verb, Shema', in an imperative, is used in reverse form as well. That is, in its urgent petitions Israel addresses YHWH and "compels" YHWH to "listen" to the cries of need on its lips. As YHWH addresses Israel in an imperative, so Israel may address YHWH in an imperative (1 Kgs. 18:37; 2 Kgs. 19:4; Pss. 4:1; 13:3; 20:1; 55:2; 60:5; 69:16; 140:6; 143:7). Whether the imperative on the lips of Israel carries the same force as the utterance of YHWH is not clear, but the grammatical form of imperative is the same and, in the moment of urgent need, the petition of Israel assumes a "commanding" tone, at least, toward YHWH.

In its gratitude, moreover, Israel regularly announces that YHWH did hear the imperative and therefore the urgency of the crisis was overcome (see 1 Sam. 7:9; Pss. 3:4; 18:21; 22:21; 34:4). One can argue that even the pivotal exchange of Exodus 2:23–25 reports YHWH responding to the urgent petition of the slave community in a way that begins the entire drama of the exodus. That Israel, as the lesser party in the covenant, can address YHWH, the great sovereign, and can "command" YHWH's attention is a wonder of biblical faith. YHWH is responsive to the commanding need of YHWH's covenant partner.

To be sure, the readiness of YHWH to hear Israel's petition assumes a working context of fidelity. YHWH is indeed inclined toward Israel, but YHWH is also the God of Sinai who has requirements and expectations, and who will not be mocked. Thus, the occasions and circumstances when Israel is not heard and YHWH refuses to respond (see 1 Sam. 8:8; Job 30:20; Jer. 7:16; 14:12) are not wholly surprising. YHWH has engaged with Israel to be sure, but YHWH also has a sovereign purpose and so is not endlessly available as an automatic reactor to Israel.

Finally, one may notice that as YHWH is a hearing God, so Israel knows as well that the "idols" are incapable of hearing, because they are in fact not free and real agents (see 1 Kgs. 18:26; Pss. 115:6; 135:17). YHWH is contrasted with the idols as a real partner who is capable of responsive engagement.

We do not know what kinds of transactions were involved in such "hearing" between human creatures and the creator of heaven and earth. Perhaps occasions of directness occurred; certainly authorized human agents mediated much of the activity. Either way, hearing is a distinctive and peculiar discipline and trait of covenant. To listen is to open self, beyond autonomy and self-sufficiency, to the commanding authority of another (see SABBATH). The modern "turn to the subject," the inordinate preoccupation with "I," means that self-announcement has largely displaced responsive listening as an assumption of human life. While that modern turn is unmanageable, ancient Israel already likely understood that a preoccupation with self-announcement is futile. They called such a habit "idolatry," an attempt to have life outside the commanding limitations of another. That Israel (and all of humanity) is addressed is a profound claim of Israel's faith. All the rest is the struggle to respond appropriately.

References: Fishbane, Michael, "Deuteronomy 6:20–25/Teaching and Transmission," in *Text and Texture: Close Readings of Selected Biblical Texts* (New York: Schocken Books, 1979), 79–83; Janzen, J. G., "On the Most Important Word in the Shema," *Vetus Testamentum* 37 (1987): 280–300; McBride, S. Dean, "The Yoke of the Kingdom: An Exposition of Deuteronomy 6:4–5," *Interpretation* 27 (1073): 273–306; Miller, Patrick D., "The Most Important Word: The Yoke of the Kingdom," *Iliff Review* 41 (1984): 17–30; Terrien, Samuel, *The Elusive Presence: Toward a New Biblical Theology* (San Francisco: Harper & Row, 1978).

Love Not unexpectedly the Old Testament incorporates the gamut of emotions, thereby including many dimensions of love. Of special note is that Israel's poets identify a rich variety of love in the life and person of YHWH, who is fully available as a character in Israel's life. Of course, those beings who are in the image of this God—all human persons—also have various capacities for love.

Although not a primary accent of the text, romantic live is in evidence in the Old Testament, especially in the Song of Solomon, which is an intensely erotic love poem. The poem exuberantly celebrates erotic interaction between a man and a woman, thus affirming both the goodness of creation and sexuality as a part of good creation. Traditional theological interpretation has understood these poems as an intensely emotional interaction between God and God's people or, in Christian tradition, between Christ and the church (on the latter, see Eph. 5:25), which is profoundly important. God in this tradition is fully capable of intimate engagement and is as committed to God's people in intense ways as is any lover toward the beloved. That relationship of covenantal fidelity is one of passion, because God is passionately committed. In the more self-consciously theological tradition of Deuteronomy, this aspect of the covenantal relationship is voiced with the verb *hŝq*, "to be emotionally attached" (Deut. 7:7; 10:15). This passion of God for Israel then evokes the intense rage of YHWH toward Israel when Israel is unfaithful, precisely because such exposed emotional commitments push the lover to extremes, sometimes negative and destructive, a negation still rooted in profound passion. The text indicates that YHWH, in the hands of Israel's poets, is fully capable of such extremity (see Ezek. 16:40–43).

More central to the theological enterprise is covenantal love, a mutual commitment of trust, regard, and obedience between two partners. The primary term for love, 'ahav, is found in documents of political treaties (Moran); in such usage, while perhaps containing a measure of emotion, the term clearly refers to a solemn, public commitment of fidelity that covenant partners make to each other. This language used concerning David is surely political in intent: Saul loves David (1 Sam. 16:21); Jonathan loves David (1 Sam. 18:1); Israel and Judah love David (1 Sam. 18:16); all his servants love David (1 Sam. 18:22). Thus YHWH in covenanting love chooses Israel to be covenant partner whom YHWH will protect; Israel in response promises to love YHWH fully by way of obedience to Torah commands. The core command of Moses to Israel is thus to listen and love, obey and recite (Deut. 6:4–7; see Exod. 20:6; Deut. 5:10). To love is to obey the commands of the final political authority. The language of "love" is used to speak of a solemn, public covenantal commitment that contains formal, concrete requirements that move beyond emotion and intentionality to enforceable obligation.

That notion of formal mutual obligation, however, is never devoid of passion. Thus, in Hosea 2:19–20, the poem can speak of this relationality as a marriage betrothal. Jeremiah, in an especially poignant usage, speaks of a parent-child relationship (31:20; see Hos. 11:8–9), and Isaiah presents explicitly maternal language in 66:13. The poets are driven to use as figures for this love relationship the most intense interpersonal relationships, because the formal relationship of command and obedience has within it a passion that motivates and endures through every vicissitude.

A subset of covenantal love is derivative commitment to neighbor love, best known in the terse command of Leviticus 19:18: "You shall love the life of your neighbor as you love your own life." While this provision is not devoid of emotion, the primary accent is upon public obligation, in a neighborly, covenantal framework, to care for and enhance the well-being and dignity of neighbor.

While these covenantal commitments and obligations tend to focus on YHWH and Israel and upon Israelite to Israelite, evidence is also present of a reach beyond that covenant community. Thus Deuteronomy 10:18 asserts that YHWH "loves the strangers" (along with the widow and orphan). YHWH, moreover, "love[s] justice" (Isa. 61:8; Ps. 99:4). That is, YHWH's covenantal relationship pertains especially to people who are vulnerable and lack full standing in a patriarchal society. In Leviticus 19:34, moreover, in the same chapter as the "neighbor command," the Torah reaches beyond "neighbors" to concern for aliens:

> The alien who resides with you shall be to you as the citizen among you; you shall love the alien as yourself, for you were aliens in the land of Egypt; I am the LORD your God.

At its best, the social vision of ancient Israel, rooted in YHWH's own character, reaches beyond the contained community of faith or of ethnicity to those outside that community who, by their very existence, warrant neighborly solidarity. Thus, the neighbor question posed to Jesus in Luke 10:29 haunted and preoccupied Israel from early on. The command to love (act in solidarity), rooted in YHWH's own character, moves against the more tamed passion to remain exclusive and discriminating toward outsiders.

The other primary term for "love" is *hesed*, which is often translated "steadfast love, loving-kindness." This term refers to the fulfillment of covenant obligations, based on a previously made pledge, to a partner in covenant by acting in ways consistent with loyalty and solidarity. Thus Rahab is celebrated for doing *hesed* toward Israel (Josh. 2:12; see 6:17), and David keeps his vow to Jonathan (1 Sam. 20:14–17; 2 Sam. 9:1) and to the Ammonites, but just barely (2 Sam. 10:1). Unlike *'ahav, hesed* bespeaks reciprocity inside an already established covenant relationship; one who commits such an act of solidarity either establishes a new relationship of fidelity that evokes obligation or fulfills an already extant obligation. The term pertains to human transactions of solidarity, fidelity, and obligation. In Israel's purview, however, YHWH is also one who acts in faithfulness on the basis of sure oaths of fidelity (see Exod. 20:5–6; 34:6–7; 2 Sam. 7:11–16).

The outcome of such rhetoric is the recognition that social life depends upon maintaining and fulfilling already embraced obligations. This characteristic biblical rhetoric, which is saturated with covenantal assumptions, is powerfully contrasted with the practice of the late modern world where everything is reduced to commoditization and advantage. In such a world, no durable fidelities sustain public life. The contemporary tension between a tradition of covenantal fidelity and electronic commoditization is thus as acute as can be imagined. Concluding that these obligations are "the ways of life and of death" (as in Deut.

30:15–20) is not an overstatement. "Death" comes not by fierce assault and punishment, but by the erosion and loss of the human fabric of fidelity that is indispensible for healthy, sustainable human life.

References: Heschel, Abraham J., *The Prophets* (New York: Harper & Row, 1962); Moran, William L., "The Ancient Near Eastern Background of the Love of God in Deuteronomy," *CBQ* 25 (1963): 77–87; Sakenfeld, Katherine Doob, *Faithfulness in Action: Loyalty in Biblical Perspective* (OBT; Philadelphia: Fortress Press, 1985); idem, *The Meaning of Hesed in the Hebrew Bible* (Missoula, Mont.: Scholars Press, 1978); Snaith, Norman H., *The Distinctive Ideas of the Old Testament* (London: Epworth Press, 1955); Weinfeld, Moshe, "The Covenant of Grant in the OT and in the Ancient Near East," *JAOS* 90 (1970): 184–203.

■ ■ ■

Messiah   The noun "messiah" derives from the Hebrew verb translated "anoint" (*mŝh*). The act of anointing consists in being especially designated by God for a particular task through an anointing by oil, an act freighted with deep symbolic significance. The "anointed" (= messiah) is the one designated in such sacramental fashion with special powers and authority for a special God-given task.

In the earlier traditions, the notion of being anointed—that is, of being "messiah"—may pertain to a variety of roles and functions including priest (Exod. 28:41; 29:7; 30:30) or prophet (1 Kgs. 19:16), because all such designees were summoned to a particular God-given task that required special empowerment and authorization. A particular case of interest is the familiar assertion of Isaiah 61:1, in which "the servant" is anointed to the task of justice. Whether the anointed is in a prophetic or royal role is not clear, but the convergence of anointing, spirit, and task in this case is paradigmatic.

The act of anointing and the title "messiah" are in the end of interest to us because the act and the title pertain to David and to the kings in the Davidic line after him [see DAVID; KINGSHIP]. The anointing of David in 1 Samuel 16:12–13 is of singular importance in Israel's presentation of its memory, for this empowering, authorizing act, accompanied by the rush of YHWH's spirit, definitively shapes Israel's future. After David (on whom see also 1 Sam. 16:21; 2 Sam. 19:21), see the royal anointments of Solomon (1 Kgs. 1:39), Joash (2 Kgs. 11:12), and Jehoahaz (2 Kgs. 23:30). We may assume, moreover, that the other kings of the dynasty were also anointed, in appropriate ritual fashion, even if not mentioned in the narrative. The act of anointing was a recurring liturgical authorization and legitimation of royal power. Thus the act designated a member of the Davidic line, and, in the first instance, referred to a present-tense king.

Only in the prophetic tradition, and apparently in light of the destruction of Jerusalem and the historical termination of the Davidic line, did Israel begin to hope for a restoration of the Davidic throne and the coming of an "anointed one," a messiah, who would right the world and bring well-being to an abased, displaced, abandoned Israel. These prophetic anticipations of a coming king/messiah are expressed throughout the text (Isa. 7:10–17; 9:2–7; 11:1–9; Jer. 23:5–6; 33:17–18; Ezek. 34:23–24; Amos 9:11; Mic. 5:1–2; and Zech. 9:9–10).

As Judaism was freshly reorganized after the exile, an expectation of political revival under Davidic rule was one strand of hope and apparently of possibility. These prophetic anticipations were pushed into the future. While becoming a com-

munity preoccupied with Torah obedience, Judaism did not cease to be a people of deep hope, confident that a human, political agent would come to reassert power at YHWH's behest.

This hope, while grounded in specific textual traditions and historical memories, was quite open-ended, so that its fulfillment was open to a variety of interpretations. One such option is stated in Isaiah 45:1, wherein Cyrus, the Persian, is reckoned as YHWH's messiah who will come to emancipate Israel from Babylon. That this title which had become profoundly Davidic is now utilized to refer to a Gentile king is remarkable. Indeed some scholars think that the David expectation is now reassigned to the awaited Persian.

Alongside this remarkable turn of usage, we may note three other strands of expectation:

1. The Dead Sea Scrolls speak of a messiah to come, so that the hope is linked to the fervent expectations of that sectarian community. The community of the Scrolls variously anticipated two messiahs, a king and a priest, a dual hope perhaps already inchoately expressed in Jeremiah 33:19–22.

2. In 135 C.E., the revolution of Bar Kochba, which led to a decisive Roman incursion against the Jews, was based on a messianic claim. This particular messianic clan was not unique, for during this period of restless expectation such claims readily arose.

3. Christians, in seeking to understand and interpret Jesus in relation to older tradition, saw in him the fulfillment of messianic expectations. Thus in asking the question, "Are you the one who is to come . . . ?" (Luke 7:19–20), the old question of messianic expectation is raised and applied to Jesus. Clearly from Luke 7:22, no straightforward answer is given. Jesus' actual ministry did not conform con-

cretely to conventional messianic expectation, for it lacked the political-military dimension that belonged to a recovery of Davidic power. Christians should recognize that messianic expectations in Judaism vary widely. The notion of messiah takes many forms among Jews, and many religious Jews in ancient times and in contemporary faith do not expect or await the messiah.

When, however, we recognize that the standard Greek translation of "messiah" is "Christ" (Christos), that "Jesus the Christ," as in Peter's confession of Mark 8:30, is a primal messianic interpretation of Jesus in the early church becomes readily apparent. In that entitlement of Jesus, the early church (a) secures a place for Jesus in terms of a key expectation of Judaism, and (b) radically and inescapably reinterprets what Judaism has meant by "messiah." The notion of Jesus as messiah became a ground for his crucifixion at the hand of Rome, for "messiah" as a Davidic leader was a revolutionary, political threat that Rome could not countenance. The connection of Jesus and his ministry to the old Davidic expectation defined Jesus in a certain way, while also inviting great risks for his ministry. In much subsequent interpretation, the notion of messiah-Christ has been spiritualized and made otherworldly, and has drawn away from its inherent political dimension. That political dimension, however, is not ever completely lost to the title, for the "messiah" always cares about the public questions facing Jews. For that reason Jesus' initial self-announcement in the Gospel of Luke (4:18–19) cites Isaiah 61:1–4 with its messianic reference ("anointed"), its reference to the power of the spirit, and the task of social restoration and emancipation.

This New Testament interpretation of Jesus has capitalized fully on Israel's expectation of coming messiah. However, Jesus' ministry did not in fact accomplish the social transformation characteristically expected of messiah, so it became inescapable in Christian interpretation that the task would await a return of messiah to complete the messianic work. Thus Christians await the return of messiah. Jews, who do not recognize Jesus as messiah, continue to await messiah's coming. This distinction is a deep, demanding issue between Jews and Christians, while also an important ground of commonality, for Jews and Christians in fact wait together for messiah who is to come. Elie Wiesel writes of a conversation that Martin Buber, great Jewish theological interpreter, had with Christian clergy. They had asked Buber why Jews did not accept Jesus as messiah. Buber answered:

> What is the difference between Jews and Christians? We all await the Messiah. You believe he has already come and gone, while we do not. I propose that we await Him together. And when He appears, we can ask Him: "were you here before?" . . . And I hope that at the moment I will be close enough to whisper in his ear, "For the love of heaven, don't answer."
>
> (Weisel, 354–55)

Just so!

References: Charlesworth, James H., *The Messiah: Developments in Earliest Judaism and Christianity* (Minneapolis: Fortress Press, 1992); Klausner, Joseph, *The Messianic in Israel, from Its Beginning to the Completion of the Mishnah* (New York: Macmillan, 1955); Mettinger, T. N. D., *King and Messiah* (Lund: LiberLäromedel/Gleerup, 1976); Mowinckel, Sigmund, *He That Cometh* (Nashville: Abingdon Press, n.d.); Neusner, Jacob, *Messiah in Context* (Philadelphia: Fortress Press, 1984); Ringgren, Helmer, *The Messiah in the Old Testament* (SBT 18; Chicago: Alec R. Allenson, 1956); Wiesel, Elie, *Memoirs: All Rivers Run to the Sea* (New York:

Knopf, 1995); Wise, Michael, *First Messiah: Investigating the Savior before Jesus* (San Francisco: Harper, 1998).

Miracle   The Old Testament, in song and narrative, bears witness to transformative events in the world that are said to occur because of the force and intention of God's presence, purpose, and power. Our modern term for such freighted, inexplicable events is "miracle," by which we mean an event beyond our capacity to explain or understand. The Old Testament has no single term for "miracle" but rather uses a cluster of terms, all of which refer to God's inexplicable—but undoubted—capacity to transform. In the doxology of Psalm 145, a number of such terms cluster:

> One generation shall laud your works to another,
> and shall declare your mighty acts.
> On the glorious splendor of your majesty,
> and on your wondrous works, I will meditate.
> The might of your awesome deeds shall be proclaimed,
> and I will declare your greatness.
> They shall celebrate the fame of your abundant goodness,
> and shall sing aloud of your righteousness.
>
> (vv. 4–7)

Here in one brief poetic unit are the terms *work, mighty acts, glorious splendor, wondrous works, awesome deeds, greatness, fame, goodness, righteousness*. To be sure, each of these terms has its own particular connotation and can be readily distinguished from the others. Taken alone, not all of them mean "miracle." When they are grouped together in a celebrative doxology, however, the cumulative effect is more than the precise meaning of any or all of the terms. All of them, and deriva-

tively each of them, refer to God's power and presence causing a disturbance and a transformation in the midst of human life.

In its doxologies and narratives, Israel is awed by the events to which it bears witness. At the same time, however, Israel is not embarrassed by such events nor by the primary theological significance attached to them. Neither does Israel seek to explain or rationalize that to which it testifies. Israel, in its testimonial modes, can take such "turns" in life as evidence of God's powerful engagement, which evokes endless glad, exuberant retelling from generation to generation. Whereas Israel has no epistemological problem with miracle, modern scientific rational consciousness has acute misgivings about an intrusive power for transformation. As a result, the common modern definition of miracle is "an event that violates natural law," thus making "miracle" by definition a category that is odd and problematic, to be explained rather than celebrated.

Israel did not begin with "natural law" or any modern, scientific notion of the world. Israel is not seeking to be "scientific," but is engaged in immediate, direct, unfiltered religious sensibility that attests to what it has experienced and subsequently to what it remembers. Thus "miracle" will not, in the horizon of this faith, be submitted to or measured by any external rationality. The best formulation known to me for the expression of such religious immediacy is that of Martin Buber: "The concept of miracle which is permissible from the historical approach can be defined at its starting point as *an abiding astonishment*" (Buber, 75–76).

Note that this characterization completely eludes modern scientific explanation or resistance. Israel simply knows that certain events loaded with mystery beyond human management evoke amazement because the community recognizes intuitively the presence of something "surpassing." That amazement, moreover, is not exhausted in the testimony, but lingers and becomes a reference point to which the community endlessly returns. Such abiding astonishment simply will not be contained in or flattened by human management. Central to Israel's faith is that it lives in a world where such transformations occur and linger with power and compelling attractiveness, thus requiring retelling, remembering, and rehearing.

Israel's articulation of a miracle-infused world requires rich patterns of doxology, for exuberant singing beyond self toward the wonder of God is a perfect human response to God's self-embodying wonder. In Israel's patterned doxology, moreover, certain turns are the primal miracles to which the community always returns and by which it measures all other turns. In the memory of Israel, events that have no rational explanation include the exodus deliverance and the gift of the promised land. According to the tradition, the claim of this memory is made concrete and tangible by the ongoing reference to the jar of manna (Exod. 16:31–36) and the tablets preserved in the ark (1 Kgs. 8:9). In larger scope, the creation itself dazzles Israel and evokes awe and wonder in response to creation as a sign of God's splendor, beauty, and power. On a smaller scale, the prayers of Israel focus on local, immediate concerns, sometimes expressed as thanks for turns accomplished and sometimes petitions for deliverance yet to be wrought according to remembered miracles.

"Miracle" bespeaks the dominant power of God. In some attestations, Israel praises God for God's own direct work. Occasional human persons in the horizon of Israel are so fully invested with God's transformative power that the human agent also accomplishes such turns. Along with Moses and Elijah, Elisha is surely a prime example of a God-empowered human agent. Israel remembered his "great things" in sum (2 Kgs. 8:4) but also recalls specifically that he delivered food to a bereft widow (2 Kgs. 4:1–7), that he raised a dead boy to life (4:8–37), that he transformed dangerous food into nourishment (4:38–41), and that he fed a hungry multitude (4:42–44). The narrative does not explain or even express curiosity about his deeds, but seems to accept that the transformative power of God is concretely enacted in the midst of the human process. Quite clearly, these great things of Elisha generate abiding astonishment, for these quite concrete deliverances have come to constitute scripture in Israel. Israel attests to the wonder-working God who refuses to leave the world to its own inadequate resources.

The intellectual problem of miracle is acute. A common strategy has been to measure miracle by scientific norms. An alternative practice might be to recognize the limitation and relatively small scope of scientific rationality, to take in a different mode so much of life that operates beyond the canon of our common explanations. Israel's attestation is so bold and so odd because it is a people unafraid of amazement and gratitude. Thus the reiterated refrain of Psalm 107:

Let them thank the LORD for his steadfast love,
   for his wonderful works to humankind.
(vv. 8, 15, 21, 31)

Israel has seen and knows and tells, ceaselessly astonished.

References: Brueggemann, Walter, *Abiding Astonishment: Psalms, Modernity, and the Making of History* (Louisville, Ky.: Westminster/John Knox Press, 1991); Buber, Martin, *Moses*

(Atlantic Highlands, N.J.: Humanities Press International, 1946); Culley, Robert C., *Studies in the Structure of Hebrew Narrative* (Philadelphia: Fortress Press, 1976).

Miriam The Old Testament is convincedly patriarchal; men dominate much of the literature. As a predictable consequence, women play only tangential roles and for the most part modern readers are left with only traces of their presence and importance. Some notable exceptions exist, however, as in the narratives of Hagar, Ruth, and Esther, and recent feminist studies have called attention to the important roles of women in the text that conventional patriarchal interpretation missed. Even so, the patriarchal hegemony in the text, as in most interpretation, is obvious. In this book, I include comment on four prominent women— Miriam, Hannah, Jezebel, and Huldah— to go along with the four crucial men I cite: Moses, David, Elijah, and Ezra. I suggest that each of the men took on a larger-than-life metaphorical significance in the traditioning process. Hannah, Miriam, Jezebel, and Huldah, I suggest, also have metaphorical significance even as they have, at the same time, experienced sustained marginalization in the traditioning process. The extensive literature on these several subjects from a feminist perspective is crucial reading in order to understand the work and costs of the patriarchal traditioning process.

Miriam appears in only a few texts in the Old Testament, though we may note the verdict of such a traditional scholar as Martin Noth "that at one time much more was told about her which is now completely lost" (182). Our discussion of course must focus on what remains of the memory of Miriam that has survived a long, complicated traditioning process.

She is remembered as a sister of Moses and Aaron and is grouped with them as part of an important leadership team in ancient Israel (Mic. 6:4). This mention indicates her prominence at some point in the tradition.

The primary evidence of Miriam's prominence is in Exodus 15:20–21, where she sings a celebrative song about the exodus victory of YHWH over Pharaoh. This brief poem is commonly taken as the oldest poem in Israel concerning the exodus, and the verse places her as a foremost articulator of Israel's primal narrative faith tradition. Moreover, the longer song attributed to Moses in Exodus 15:1–18 begins with a quote from Miriam, suggesting that the male leader has preempted her initiative (perhaps not unlike the way in which the male testimony to the resurrection of Jesus verified but in fact preempted the initial witness of the women at the tomb [John 20:1–10]).

The other key element in the tradition is her dispute with Moses in Numbers 12, whereby she suffers leprosy as a punishment for her disputatious challenge to Moses' authority (see Deut. 24:9). This narrative suggests one of two possibilities. Miriam may have been a formidable challenge to Moses in a time when Mosaic authority was not a settled fact, so that she presented a genuine alternative to his leadership and was, as a consequence, censored in the finally determinedly Mosaic text. The other interpretation is that she was at least important enough that concerns of a later time were projected on to her. Either way she represents in the tradition an alternative to what became Moses' final authority.

The literature suggests that, whatever her historical significance, Miriam is subject to the vagaries of a traditioning process that did not treat her well. Recent feminist study makes clear that she continues to function as a powerful force below the surface of the text. A recent publication by Angel is an imaginative act suggesting the ways that later Midrashic tradition might have portrayed her. Well beyond her historical significance, Miriam is clearly a generative metaphor for ongoing interpretive work that precludes any simple, settled patriarchal closure. She is a durable presence that attracts interpretation, which, in turn refuses to let her be silenced.

References: Angel, Leonard, *The Book of Miriam* (Oakville, Ont.: Mosaic Press, 1997); Bach, Alice, "De-Doxifying Miriam," in *A Wise and Discerning Mind: Essays in Honor of Burke O. Long,* ed. Saul M. Olyan and Robert C. Culley (Providence, R.I.: Brown Judaic Studies, 2000), 1–10; idem, "With a Song in Her Heart: Listening to Scholars Listening for Miriam," in *A Feminist Companion to Exodus to Deuteronomy,* vol. 6, *The Feminist Companion to the Bible,* ed. Athalya Brenner (Sheffield: Sheffield Academic Press, 1994), 243–55; Burns, Rita, *Has the Lord Indeed Spoken Only Through Moses? A Study of the Biblical Portrait of Miriam* (Atlanta: Scholars Press, 1987); Noth, Martin, *A History of Pentateuchal Traditions* (Englewood Cliffs, N.J.: Prentice-Hall, 1972); Trible, Phyllis, "Bring Miriam Out of the Shadows," *Bible Review* 5/1 (February 1989): 13–25, 34.

Money   The theological question of "money" does not concern the history of coinage but rather how faith perceives and practices the economy. The context of much of the Old Testament is an agrarian economy that was interested in land and other forms of real property rather than money per se. Indeed the transition from an economy of land to an economy of money probably permits us to identify a critical tension in the Old Testament. From the outset, the Old Testament does not speak with a single voice about economics. The great variation indicates conflicting and disputed claims, even as they continue to reappear in the ongoing work of biblical interpretation.

On the one hand, the tribal economy of what is remembered of early Israel was of necessity a neighborly economy in which peasant farmers depended upon one another, and in which every member of the agricultural community likely lived with the threat of poverty. (See, for example, Exod. 22:1–15.) Given this economic situation, the emergence of a somewhat distributive economic practice—whereby members of the community shared what wealth they had with needier members of the community—is not surprising.

While such a distributive sense of justice may have actually been agrarian practicality, in the Old Testament this practice becomes a covenantal requirement rooted in the very character of YHWH. Seen in this way, we may recognize that something of YHWH's character, as understood in these early traditions, arises from the concrete reality of society, and the accompanying acknowledgment that the community owes special attention to the needy and vulnerable who are characteristically listed as the widow, orphan, and alien (see Deut. 24:17–21). In Zechariah 7:9–10, the poor are added to the conventional triad. In this ethic, the economically substantive in the community are obligated to share wealth with the economically disadvantaged. That obligation does not simply depend upon "charity," but is written into "law" as a public, systemic requirement. This approach is most formidably articulated in the "year of release" (Deut. 15:1–18) and the "year of jubilee" (Lev. 25) [see JUBILEE].

The warrant for such an economic obligation, moreover, is found in the character of YHWH, who is the one who enacted the initial "year of release" from Egyptian slavery (see Deut. 15:15), a notion that is familiarly voiced in the First Commandment: "I am YHWH your God who delivered you from the house of bondage." This God loves sojourners and all such vulnerable people (see Deut. 10:18). Israel is enjoined to imitate YHWH in enhancing the neighbor. This public obligation rooted in YHWH's character toward widow, orphan, and sojourner gives warrant for the recent declaration of "God's preferential option for the poor."

On the other hand, as Israel remembers its past, the economy was severely disrupted and transformed with the rise of the monarchy and the culminating opulence of Solomon. Society was reorganized away from simple agrarian neighborliness so that Israel became "like all the nations" in the accumulation of surplus value for some and the consequent stratification of society (see 1 Sam. 8:5, 20 and the intervening verses). In short, Solomon came to embody legitimated acquisitiveness. This characterization results from his remarkable commercial activity (1 Kgs. 9:26–28), his building program (1 Kgs. 7:1–8), his arrangements for tax collection (1 Kgs. 4:7–19), his arms program (1 Kgs. 9:17–19), his program of forced labor (1 Kgs. 5:13–18; 9:20–22), and his extravagant living (1 Kgs. 4:20–28), all of which came to be consolidated and legitimated in the elaborate temple that featured great quantities of gold (1 Kgs. 6:20–22; see 10:14–22). By linking an opulent temple to the rest of his opulence, Solomon was able to claim YHWH's approval and patronage for all of his acquisitiveness. In the economy privileged elite emerged who easily and readily forgot any neighbor ethic. The end result was likely a retributive theory of money in which those who possessed it were known to deserve it and those who lacked it deserved that as well.

Knowing how historically specific any of these memories are is difficult; more likely our text presents stark models that are without the nuance of reality. In terms of models for the economy then, we see that two different economic theories are set side by side, both having their advocates, both preserved in the text, each no doubt claiming divine legitimacy for its perspective.

In part the two economic models sketched out above are the outcome of different social settings and class distinctions. The advocates themselves, however, claim more than that. They assert that the legitimacy of a distributive economy or a retributive economy is rooted in YHWH's own character and will, so that the economic questions ultimately become theological questions—a dispute about YHWH's will. The linkage of economic and theological issues inescapably calls to mind its echo, albeit stated in reverse, in the aphorism of Karl Marx:

> The criticism of heaven is thus transformed into the criticism of earth, the criticism of religion into the criticism of law, and the criticism of theology into the criticism of politics. (Marx, 22)

The connection of economics and theology is evident in the critique of Solomon's economic opulence in 1 Kings 11:1–18; his love of "other gods" is reported to have led him away from obedience to YHWH, but his love of other gods is articulated in his labor practices, his extravagance, and his political alliances made in the form of marriages. Thus "other gods" refers not simply to a religious practice but to a perspective on life that embraces the economic. This shrewd linkage made in the text is a parallel to the arrangement of the Decalogue:

First Commandment	You shall have no other gods before me. (Exod. 20:3)
Tenth Commandment	You shall not covet your neighbor's house. (Exod. 20:17)

The First Commandment and Tenth Commandment together suggest that obedience to YHWH imposes a curb on acquisitiveness. Solomon is critiqued in the text for violating the First Commandment in the form of coveting. Thus the old Sinai foundation for a distributive ethic stands as a critique of an alternative that Solomon, as given in the text, fully embodies.

Given the sharp delineations about the economy in these particular models, three perspectives on the economy can illuminate Israel's disputatious concern about money:

1. The prophets maintain a steady critique of the royal economy and continually assert the cause of justice, which includes care for the vulnerable and unprotected (see Isa. 1:17; 32:7; Jer. 5:26–29). The prophets insist that the forfeiture of a neighborly economy will lead to the forfeiture of the covenant. The wealthy cannot enjoy the guarantees of YHWH unless those guarantees are extended to the marginal (see Amos 8:4–8).

2. Some psalms explicitly give voice to the poor, who appeal to YHWH against the rapaciousness of the wealthy. The poor in these poems claim some entitlement from YHWH but are themselves helpless to receive that entitlement. In their pleas, they also reflect a vested social interest, for a convention in these pleas is to equate "the rich" with "the wicked," on the assumption that the accumulation of wealth is inescapably the accumulation of ill-gotten wealth:

In arrogance the wicked persecute the poor—
  let them be caught in the schemes they have devised.
                        (Ps. 10:2)

"Because the poor are despoiled, because the needy groan,
  I will now rise up," says the LORD. . . .
You, O LORD, will protect us;
  you will guard us from this generation forever.
On every side the wicked prowl,
  as vileness is exalted among humankind.
                        (Ps. 12:5, 7–8)

3. The wisdom materials in the book of Proverbs reflect a different perspective:

One thing they have in common: the existence of poverty—that is, the presence in society of a number of poor persons—is taken for granted. Like disease, poverty is regarded as a misfortune to which human beings generally are liable. . . . [S]ome attempt is made to discern its causes; but nowhere is any possibility of eliminating it envisaged. There is no notion that it is due to a flaw in the organization of society which can be corrected, nor any perception that impoverished individuals might be helped in such a way as to restore the~~i~~ prosperity and to a proper place in the life of the community. . . . The voice that is inevitably missing in the book is that of the poor—that is, of the totally destitute—themselves. All those who speak in the book have material possessions. . . . (Whybray, 113)

Even with the variety of nuances, on balance the Proverbs reflect a general commitment to the economic status quo, so that the rich and the poor live side by side. But no overriding claim is advanced for the poor, and no particular judgment is made upon the wealthy. In a world of "deeds and consequences," in the

Proverbs the rich become rich by diligence and YHWH blesses them (Prov. 10:4), and the poor receive their reward for laziness (Prov. 12:24, see 10:15). A qualification appears that money without right action is no gain, but this nuance is within the larger assumption of retribution (see Prov. 11:18, 28). This view does not advocate individualism, for the poor are on the horizon of the creator (Prov. 14:31; 17:5). Rather, the view entertains no notion of social transformation or radical change, so that social relations are given and must be endured.

The wisdom tradition, in that general perspective, also includes the following notes:

Both Gowan and Whybray call attention to Proverbs 30:7–9:

Two things I ask of you;
    do not deny them to me before I die:
Remove far from me falsehood and lying;
    give me neither poverty nor riches;
    feed me with the food that I need,
or I shall be full, and deny you,
    and say, "Who is the LORD?"
or I shall be poor, and steal,
    and profane the name of my God.

The text takes a middle way and recognizes that either poverty or wealth may be seductive and corrupting. This saying suggests that one's life cannot finally be defined by economics.

Psalm 49, commonly recognized as a wisdom psalm, asserts that economic gains are short-term and inconsequential, because in the long run,

Mortals cannot abide in their pomp;
    they are like animals that perish.
                                    (vv. 12, 20)

The effect of the Psalm is to debunk the pretensions and self-importance that come with wealth, because "you can't take it with you."

Ecclesiastes 6:1–6 includes wealth— and its endless desires—among the vanities that are eventually futile and unfulfilling.

Out of this array of contending views, we may perhaps draw the following conclusions:

1. Money (or wealth in any form) warrants tough, critical attention and is seen in all traditions of the Old Testament to be freighted with significance and fraught with problems.

2. Every view of money is likely deeply situated in a concrete social context and is therefore not without specific social interest. In assessing any biblical claim about money, one must ask, "Who is speaking?"

3. All traditions agree that in one way or another, money is deeply linked to the reality of YHWH, so that no autonomous economy can have a life of its own. Whether the view of money is transformative or supports the status quo, whether distributive or retributive, the economy is clearly an articulation of the theological reality of YHWH's gifts and YHWH's demands.

In the end, the Old Testament sees that money is a vehicle for faith, yet finally penultimate. The pursuit of "commodity" is subordinated to the practice of "communion." In speaking of obedience to the Commandments, the psalmist can aver:

More to be desired are they than gold,
    even much fine gold;
sweeter also than honey,
    and drippings of the honeycomb.
                                    (Ps. 19:10)

The term "desired" translates *ḥmd*, usually rendered "covet." YHWH's life and YHWH's command are finally the proper objects of coveting; all other coveting is finally misguided and destructive. Attentiveness to YHWH and YHWH's generosity evokes a glad response of gratitude expressed economically. David nicely sums up this characteristic response of faith in his statement that has given rise to a standard Christian utterance at the presentation of an offering, an economic gesture toward YHWH:

For all things come from you, and of your own have we given you. (1 Chr. 29:14)

References: Borowitz, Eugene B., *Judaism after Modernity: Papers from a Decade of Fruition* (New York: University Press of America, 1999), chap. 19; Gowan, Donald E., "Wealth and Poverty in the Old Testament: The Case of the Widow, the Orphan, and the Sojourner," *Interpretation* 41 (1987): 341–53; Haughey, John C., *Virtue and Affluence: The Challenge of Wealth* (New York: Sheed and Ward, 1997); Lang, Bernhard, "The Social Organization of Peasant Poverty in Biblical Israel," *JSOT* 24 (1982): 47–63; McLellan, David, *The Thought of Karl Marx: An Introduction* (London: McMillan, 1971); Sider, Ronald J., ed., *Cry Justice: The Bible on Hunger and Poverty* (New York: Paulist Press, 1980); Whybray, R. N., *Wealth and Poverty in the Book of Proverbs* (JSOTSup 99; Sheffield: Sheffield Academic Press, 1990).

Monotheism Monotheism, as presented in classical Western Christian theology, is an intellectual claim that only one God presides over all existence. Such an intellectual claim is, as conventionally articulated, of little interest for the Bible and has caused endless mischief in understanding the Bible. The reason that such a claim, from the perspective of the Bible, is uninteresting and mischievous is that the Bible articulates YHWH as a fully func-tioning person marked by immense complexity and interiority that are characteristically excluded in conventional rational understandings of "the one God." The biblical question is not the number of gods [one!], but the practice and character of YHWH in an assumed world of contested polytheism, the ways in which this God (among others) is known, and the ways in which Israel is related to this God. This claim of "one God" is to be distinguished from henotheism, a common assumption in the ancient world that each god presided over his or her own territory, but was limited to that territory (see 1 Sam. 26:19).

The Old Testament, in its final form, certainly ends up with an affirmation that "YHWH alone is God." This affirmation is clearest in exilic Isaiah (43:11; 48:12). That confession made in doxological form is not an intellectual or rational conclusion; rather the assertion is a faith confession with the quite practical intent of permitting displaced Israel in exile to continue to "trust and obey" in terms of its most elemental faith commitments. That Israel arrived at this affirmation (in response to immediate need) provides a point from which to consider Israel's faith up to "doxological monotheism" and Israel's faith in the wake of "doxological monotheism."

Contemporary scholarship typically considers the question of monotheism in the Bible from a historical perspective, studies the sequence of statements that constitute Israel's confession of faith, and tries to understand that sequence in terms of historical context.

A rough scholarly consensus now exists that YHWH appears in the memory of Israel among many other gods, in a rich world of lively polytheism, a world of gods under the presiding governance of El (El Elyon), the High God. YHWH may have been understood initially as a quite subordinate agent in the world of the gods, perhaps from the outset allied with and committed to Israel. Israel, in its interpretive traditions, continued over time to reformulate its testimony about YHWH: the subordinate God of Israel began to be assigned greater and greater domains of governance, until YHWH was assigned, in Israel's testimony, the preeminent place, occupying the role in theological imagination that El long held as the presiding officer of the divine council [see DIVINE COUNCIL].

Israel did not, until very late, deny or nullify the existence of other gods. Rather Israel characteristically insisted upon the covenantal exclusiveness of YHWH in relation to Israel. While other gods may have indeed existed, Israel was not free to trust or obey them, because Israel at Sinai had signed on exclusively with YHWH. Thus the "jealousy" of YHWH is a function of covenantal exclusiveness (see Ezek. 16:41–42). Israel's sin that evokes YHWH's wrath is the compromise of that oath of singular allegiance reflected in the First Commandment of Exodus 20:2–3.

While insisting upon the legitimacy of its exclusive claim of YHWH, Israel was also preoccupied with making the negative claim that the other gods were powerless, could not deliver on their promises, and therefore did not deserve any attention or devotion. This claim was made in song and narrative by exhibiting the futility of Dagon before YHWH (1 Sam. 5) and the silence of Baal at Mt. Carmel (1 Kgs. 18:26–29), and by observing that the gods of Babylon must be carried (Isa. 46:1–2). While these gods may exist in a shadowy way, they were weak and helpless (Pss. 115:4–8; 135:15–18); they are sharply contrasted with YHWH, who is full of power and who merits Israel's complete trust and full obedience:

Their idols are like scarecrows in a
     cucumber field,
   and they cannot speak;
they have to be carried,
   for they cannot walk.
Do not be afraid of them,
   for they cannot do evil,
   nor is it in them to do good.

There is none like you, O LORD;
   you are great, and your name is great in
     might.
Who would not fear you, O King of the
     nations?
   For that is your due;
among all the wise ones of the nations
   and in all their kingdoms
   there is no one like you. . . .
But the LORD is the true God;
   he is the living God and the everlasting
     King. . . .
                              (Jer. 10:5–7, 10)

While anticipation of a more final monotheism is present in the traditions of Elijah and Hosea, only in the sixth-century traditions did this expectation become explicit. Remarkably, in Israel's most despairing context of exile, Israel's poet made the most extravagant case for YHWH:

Before me no god was formed,
   nor shall there be any after me.
I, I am the LORD,
   and besides me there is no savior. . . .
I am God, and also henceforth I am He;
   there is no one who can deliver from
     my hand;
   I work and who can hinder it?
                              (Isa. 43:10–13)

This doxological claim is practical and polemical, amounting to the dismissal of the imperial gods of Babylon and consequently the discrediting of Babylonian imperial authority.

In taking up this doxological claim of Israel, which had immediate pastoral, existential force, the dominant tradition of Western Christian theology over time transposed a vigorous, relational affirmation into a flat principle of certitude that is largely devoid of the vitality of the biblical doxology. In turn this transposed affirmation, under pressure from rational, philosophical formulation, issued into settled absolute theological propositions largely lacking in doxological force. The most familiar of these formulations is the insistent claim of the catechism that God is "omnipotent, omnipresent, and omniscient." While of course logically defensible, such a formulation is remote from the ways in which biblical faith is given as confessional statement, characteristically in a life-or-death context of gratitude and obedience.

Thus, on the near side of doxological monotheism—that is, after the claim for YHWH was established in exilic Isaiah—more interpretive work needed to be done about monotheism. Israel insisted that YHWH was to be understood, not as a transcendent sovereign who is unimpinged upon, but rather as a fully personal God who is known to be related to Israel and whose own life and power are relative to Israel and to the life of the world.

As McFague has understood, monotheism runs a great risk of becoming so flat and thin that it becomes idolatry, the reduction of God away from all vitality in order to have a God that is settled, fixed, and predictable. Israel's rhetorical strategy to keep monotheism from becoming idolatry was to articulate the thick singularity of YHWH in a rich panoply of metaphors, each of which functioned to disclose something of YHWH, but none of which was permitted to dominate or eliminate others. Various families of metaphors were used for the utterance of "the one God" of Israel, including military, judicial, familial, medical, artistic, agricul-

tural, and political, in almost endless variety (Brueggemann, 229–66). The richest metaphors for YHWH tended to emerge in times of deep crisis; the most stunning are in the traditions of Hosea (when Northern Israel fell), Jeremiah (when Judah fell), and Second Isaiah (when exile ended). In each case, the poet strained the imagination in order to disclose fully something of YHWH that is peculiarly poignant for and germane to the particular crisis.

These rich metaphors offer a sense of the equally rich interiority of YHWH's own life, an interiority of fidelity and contestation in which YHWH must endlessly adjudicate the claims of Israel and the claims of YHWH's own position among the other gods. As Heschel has shown, the rich interiority of YHWH, expressed successfully only by the daring poets, is peculiarly marked by pathos that exhibits YHWH's own suffering, which in time became the ground for newness in Israel and in the life of the world.

The rich metaphors of monotheism offered in the text mean that Israel attests to one God, but this God will not be slotted in or domesticated by conventional theological formulations. This monotheism is the articulation and enactment of a God who comes and goes, who wounds and heals, who judges and saves in ways that defy all preconceived patterns. Such a restless God, evident in the texts of doxological monotheism, is often too rich and wild for institutional faith, which thrives on control and certitude. Institutional forms of theology thus endlessly yearn to limit, narrow, and flatten the rich metaphorical field that this God inhabits and where this God is known in Israel.

In the end, Israel can confess,

Hear, O Israel: The LORD is our God, the LORD alone. (Deut. 6:4; see Mark 12:29)

"YHWH is one" or "YHWH alone": Either way that stark affirmation is a large umbrella under which lives the thick poetic utterance of Israel's testimony. YHWH is the one, the only one, who is known in Israel as warrior, king, mother, doctor, artist, rock—one, but one in rich, varied ways. Readers of the Bible may attend to this testimony and resist the familiar, traditional ways of containing. In that way, confession of monotheism becomes a practical matter wherein the God who is richly available in complexity is the counterpart to a covenantal community also richly available in complexity.

The primal confession of Deuteronomy 6:4 permitted Israel to stand strong in its covenantal identity in dangerous contexts. In contexts of faith-under-threat, rational propositions about the nature and number of gods help not at all. What counts for Israel is always confidence in a rich rhetoric of fidelity and passion that it found to be utterly reliable because it spoke of the One Israel knew in its own life.

References: Banks, Robert, God the Worker: Journeys into the Mind, Heart, and Imagination of God (Valley Forge, Pa.: Judson Press, 1994); Brueggemann, Walter, Theology of the Old Testament: Testimony, Dispute, Advocacy (Minneapolis: Fortress Press, 1997), 229–313; Edelman, D. V., ed., The Triumph of Elohim: From Yahwisms to Judaisms (Grand Rapids: Eerdmans, 1996); Heschel, Abraham, The Prophets (New York: Harper & Row, 1962); Johnson, William Stacy, "Rethinking Theology: A Postmodern, Post-Holocaust, Post-Christendom Endeavor," Interpretation 55 (2001): 5–18; McFague, Sallie, Metaphorical Theology: Models of God in Religious Language (Philadelphia: Fortress Press, 1982); Miles, Jack, God: A Biography (New York: Knopf, 1995); Sanders, James A., "Adaptable for Life: The Nature and Function of Canon," in Magnalia Dei: The Mighty Acts of God: Essays on the Bible and Archaeology in Memory of G. Ernest

Wright, ed. Frank Moore Cross et al. (Garden City, N.Y.: Doubleday, 1976), 531–60; Schwartz, Regina M., The Curse of Cain: The Violent Legacy of Monotheism (Chicago: University of Chicago Press, 1997); Smith, Mark S., The Early History of God: Yahweh and the Other Deities in Ancient Israel (San Francisco: Harper & Row, 1990).

Moses   In a book of theological themes such as this, mentioning personalities may seem a bit odd. I do so, however, with four men from the tradition—Moses, David, Elijah, and Ezra—because in each case that individual person embodies a crucial theological claim of the Old Testament.

The historical questions about Moses are exceedingly difficult, due to the complexity of the literature itself and to the seeming lack of "historical evidence" about him. On balance, critical scholarship now offers a near consensus that we have no compelling evidence for the existence or history of Moses outside the biblical text itself. Thus we are concerned here only with the Moses offered in the biblical tradition.

Moses is the human agent whom YHWH dispatched to enact in the historical arena the founding miraculous narrative events of Israel. The juxtaposition of "human agent" and "miraculous events" is a stunning one, for conventional interpretation reads these Moses-dominated events (exodus, sojourn, Sinai) as divine happenings. In fact, however, Moses as human agent stands front and center in these memories of Israel, so that they are wrought through his obedience and courage:

Moses is the human perpetrator of the exodus. In Exodus 3:7–9, YHWH resolves to save Israel from Egyptian slavery; in verse 10, however, YHWH dispatches Moses to do the direct confrontation work of liberation. Moses, in the end, sings the triumph over Pharaoh and his armies (Exod. 15:1–18). The tradition reassigns to him the "Song of Miriam" (Exod. 15:21), which becomes the first verse of his song [see MIRIAM]. This preemption is a measure of the cruciality of Moses who takes up a lot of space in the tradition.

Moses is the responsible agent for Israel's wilderness wandering; he presides over Israel in the wilderness in order to sustain Israel and bring Israel to the land of promise (Exod. 16–28; Num. 10–36; Deut. 1–3).

Moses presides over the Sinai encounter with YHWH and becomes the means whereby YHWH's commandments are known in Israel, and thus is a mediator of divine revelation (Exod. 19; Num. 10; more specifically see Exod. 20:18–21).

Moses is the decisive intercessor who prays to YHWH on behalf of Israel and who boldly challenges YHWH (Exod. 32:11–14; Num. 11:11–15; Num. 14:13–19; see Jer. 15:1).

Each of the complex traditions of text poses immense problems and each in itself constitutes an enormous field of study; the main points are nonetheless readily apparent.

In this brief discussion, I will consider a different aspect of the memory of Moses: Moses' role in the book of Deuteronomy. The book of Deuteronomy is clearly well removed from Sinai and purports to be a belated representation of the Sinai commandments by Moses for a later time and place. That is, Deuteronomy, in the mouth of Moses, is the first commentary on the Sinai commandments (see Deut. 1:5). Deuteronomy begins with a reiteration of the Ten Commandments of Sinai with some slight modifications (Deut. 5:6–21). What follows is a corpus of commands that Braulik and Kaufman take to be ordered according to the Decalogue, so that the corpus of Deuteronomy is an ordered exposition of the commandments. The statement of Deuteronomy 5:22–33 indicates that Israel accepts the durable authority of Moses as the principal interpreter of the commands of Sinai.

The dynamic process of interpretive movement from Sinai to Deuteronomy strikes me as the most important theological dimension of Moses in the memory of Israel. The interpretive vitality that runs through Deuteronomy—rooted in but moving well beyond Sinai—is intimately attached to the person of Moses in the memory of Israel. But of course all that tradition assigns to Moses is a long, complicated interpretive traditioning process that extends far beyond any historical person. Thus Moses became the cipher for the dynamism of the entire interpretive process. The initial Torah of Sinai is the material out of which Judaism fashioned an ongoing canonical process of authorized rootage and contextual extrapolation. This dynamism so characteristic of Judaism is evident in the Torah itself, for the Torah in the book of Deuteronomy is itself a process of ongoing interpretation. The continuing authority of Moses is evident in the phrase "Moses' seat," which is subsequently occupied by scribes and Pharisees, the normative interpreters of the tradition (Matt. 23:2).

What Moses enacts in the Torah itself is what the Pharisees and their descendants in rabbinic Judaism practiced as oral Torah—the ongoing process of discerning what resides in the authoritative tradition beyond what is written. One aspect of the same process in Christian interpretation is what is called *"sensus plenior,"* a conviction that the text would, upon further interpretation, always yield a "fuller meaning," or as poignantly asserted in the old Puritan adage, "God has yet more light to break forth from his Word." That "yet more light" in the canonical horizon is carried by Moses, the normative, quintessential interpreter. In Christian tradition, the same process is evident in Jesus' saying, "It was said of old . . . but I say to you" (Matt. 5:21, 27, 31, 33, 38, 43).

The interpretive function of Moses runs well beyond any historical question and draws our understanding toward the rooted, open-ended vitality of the tradition in both its narrative and legal genres. The old historical-critical hypothesis of Pentateuchal "documents" sought to point to this dynamism, though expressed in rather wooden, nineteenth-century interpretive categories.

References: Braulik, Georg, *The Theology of Deuteronomy: Collected Essays of Georg Braulik* (vol. 2 of Bibal Collected Essays; trans. Ulrika Lindblad; N. Richland, Tex.: Bibal Press, 1977); Brown, Raymond E., *The Sensus Plenior of Sacred Scripture* (Baltimore: St. Mary's Seminary, 1955); Brueggemann, Walter, *Theology of the Old Testament: Testimony, Dispute, Advocacy* (Minneapolis: Fortress Press, 1997), 567–90; Buber, Martin, *Moses: The Revelation and the Covenant* (Atlantic Highlands, N.J.: Humanities Press International, 1988); Coats, George W., *Moses: Heroic Man, Man of God* (JSOTSup 57; Sheffield: Sheffield Academic Press, 1988); Crüsemann, Frank, *The Torah: Theology and Social History of Old Testament Law* (Edinburgh: T. & T. Clark, 1996); Kaufman, Stephen, "The Structure of the Deuteronomic Law," MAARAV 1 (1979): 105–58; Levinson, Bernard M., *Deuteronomy and the Hermeneutics of Legal Innovation* (Oxford: Oxford University Press, 1997); Neusner, Jacob, *What, Exactly, Did the Rabbinic Sages Mean by "The Oral Torah"? An Inductive Answer to the Question of Rabbinic Judaism* (Atlanta: Scholars Press, 1998); Olson, Dennis T., *Deuteronomy and the Death of Moses: A Theological Reading* (OBT; Minneapolis: Fortress Press, 1994); Rad, Gerhard von, *Old Testament Theology*, vol. 1 (San Francisco: Harper and Row, 1962), 289–96.

■ ■ ■

Neighbor The "neighbor" is a central preoccupation of Old Testament ethics. Best known of course is the imperative of Leviticus 19:18: "You shall love your neighbor as yourself." The term "neighbor" (*ra'*) can also be translated "brother" and refers to a fellow member of a socioeconomic or perhaps ethnic community in which members are pledged to care for and bound to look after each other's interests.

The notion of "neighbor" likely arose in small, face-to-face communities, such as a tribe, clan, or "father's house." Such groups may have been based on kinship or may have been intentional groups bound together by common social interest or vision. While a theological understanding of the imperative is evident in Leviticus 19:18 with the concluding formula, "I am YHWH," the "neighbor" is no doubt the one at hand with whom one must deal politically and economically, whatever may be one's theological passion.

The verb of the imperative, "love," does not first of all refer to emotional attachment but to obligation that takes social, political, and economic form. Thus the command serves to insist upon communal solidarity and the curbing of private interest that operates at the expense of the community. The large textual unit of Leviticus 19:13–18, moreover, addresses social obligation between members of the community who are not social "equals." Reference to the deaf, the blind, and the poor requires that the strong, wealthy, and able must take the neighbor need of the weak as seriously as they take their own need.

One can understand the idea of "neighbor" in a quite restrictive way, thus limiting social horizon and social obligation to an in-group of land owners who control the law-making process. In such a usage, the scope of neighborliness is limited and may be understood restrictively as applying only to landed males. Thus, for example, in Exodus 20:17, the imperative provides protection for the goods of the neighbor—wife, house, slaves, and animals—the neighbor evidently another landed male.

The question of the scope of neighborliness is endlessly open-ended in the ethics of the Old Testament. Certainly exclusionary statements limit neighborliness to a select company (see Deut. 23:1–8). One may, moreover, sell to a foreigner endangering meat that is prohibited to an insider (Deut. 14:21), as well as charge interest to foreigners who are not protected by neighborly requirements (Deut. 23:20). But other statements open the horizon of neighborliness much more expansively, pertaining even to those with disordered genitalia (see Isa. 56:3–7). This provision is of particular interest because it negates the earlier teaching of Moses in Deuteronomy 23:1. In Leviticus 19:34, it is commanded:

> The alien who resides with you shall be to you as the citizen among you; you shall love the alien as yourself, for you were aliens in the land of Egypt; I am the LORD your God.

The term rendered "alien" is *ger* (sojourner), a welcomed outsider, one who is more welcomed than a "foreigner" (*nkr*)

(see Deut. 10:19). But even the affirmation of the "sojourner" hints at an openness eventually toward the "foreigner."

The ongoing interpretive process in both Judaism and Christianity is the struggle to enlarge the circle of neighborliness, a process reflected in the answer of Jesus to the question of the lawyer (Luke 10:29–37). That process is ongoing and keenly disputatious in contemporary Christian interpretation. In any case that inclusiveness is unmistakably at the core of Old Testament ethics, made durable by the commanding, "I am YHWH" at the conclusion of the imperative. Justice of a covenantal kind requires a disciplined look beyond self-interest to neighbor-interest that is as valid and legitimate as one's own.

References: Birch, Bruce C., *Let Justice Roll Down: The Old Testament, Ethics and the Christian Life* (Louisville, Ky.: Westminster/John Knox Press, 1991); Douglas, Mary, "Justice as the Cornerstone: An Interpretation of Leviticus 18–20," *Interpretation* 53 (1999): 341–50; Gerstenberger, Erhard S., *Leviticus: A Commentary* (OTL; Louisville, Ky.: Westminster John Knox Press, 1996), 268–72; Malamat, Abraham, "'You Shall Love Your Neighbor as Yourself': A Case of Misinterpretation?" *Die Hebraische Bibel und ihre zweifache Nachgeschichte: Festschrift für Rolf Rendtorff zum 65. Gebürtstag*, ed. Erhard Blum et al. (Neukirchen-Vluyn: Neukirchener Verlag, 1990), 111–15; Mollenkott, Virginia, and Letha Scanzoni, *Is the Homosexual My Neighbor?* (San Francisco: Harper & Row, 1978).

■ ■ ■

Persia   The empire of Persia, a people that occupied what is now Iran, dominated the history and politics of the Near East from the time of Cyrus (550–530), its first great leader, who defeated the power of Babylon, until its defeat by Alexander the Great in 333. Thus, for two centuries the Persian empire was the defining power in the region. Until recently, not much was known about the impact of the Persians on the community of ancient Israel and scholars did not pay much attention to it. Lately, however, scholars are considering the prospect that the period of Judaism under Persian hegemony was the generative period in shaping Judaism and in the formation of what became the Old Testament.

The dominant feature of Persian policy that concerns the Old Testament is a new policy toward conquered peoples. The Persians reversed the oppressive imperial policies that Assyria and Babylon imposed and instead fostered local autonomy of religion and government, local permits limited only by the requirements of taxation and conformity to imperial interests. This more or less benign policy toward local initiative, moreover, is given a quite positive spin in the Old Testament, so that the contrast between brutal Babylon and benign Persia is perhaps overstated there. Nonetheless, Persian policy over time permitted the Jewish deportees in Babylon to return home to Jerusalem.

We may identify three defining points of contact between Persian imperial power and emergent Judaism. First, the initial victory of Cyrus over Babylon is extravagantly celebrated in the poetry of exilic Isaiah and is perceived as a great act of emancipation of God's people at the behest of YHWH. Thus Isaiah 44:28 identifies Cyrus as "my shepherd" (that is, a "king" designated by YHWH) and 45:1 astonishingly identifies Cyrus as "anointed" (= messiah). This is a Yahwistic interpretation of the imperial upheaval, whereby the Persian displacement of Babylonian power is lined out as a "mighty act" on the part of YHWH. This interpretation of course reflects the readiness of ancient Israel to redescribe its world with reference to YHWH. Cyrus's new policy did indeed permit a return of deportees who could enact some local autonomy.

Second, Cyrus's second successor, Darius (522–486), sponsored the rebuilding of the Jerusalem temple, which Babylon had destroyed in 587. Cyrus had authorized the rebuilding is authorized by (2 Chr. 36:23; Ezra 1:2–4; 6:3–5) that Darius undertook. This construction of the Second Temple is reflected in the prophetic materials of Haggai and Zechariah 1–8. Scholars believe that the Jerusalem temple, paid for with Persian funds, had a dual social function as a center of Jewish life and also as an administrative and tax-collecting center for the Persians. Judaism thus enjoyed a small zone of autonomy, but well within the confines of Persian oversight.

Third, under Artaxerxes a new initiative was undertaken that featured the new leadership among the Jews of Ezra and Nehemiah. The date of the mission is uncertain because the identity of Artaxerxes, the authorizing Persian ruler, is uncertain. In any case, during the fifth century Ezra the scribe and Nehemiah the builder worked to restore the city of Jerusalem and to re-form Judaism as a people of the Torah. With reference to the events of Nehemiah 8, Ezra is reckoned in Jewish tradition to be the founder of Judaism and the most important figure after Moses.

The capacity of Israel's faith to adjust to the durable power of the Persian empire is of immense importance for the future of Judaism:

1. The returning deportees in the fifth century, represented by Ezra and Nehemiah, constituted a self-conscious elite

subcommunity of Jews with important connections to Persian imperial power. The formation of a dominant strand of Judaism thus represents the voice and interests of a power elite in Jerusalem that was concerned to protect its own interpretive interests from would-be competitive voices within Judaism.

2. Judaism as a client-community under imperial patronage—perhaps, as Weinberg has proposed, a "citizen-temple community"—was an important learning experience for Judaism. It provided the forms and images through which Judaism was to learn about its survival and faithfulness in a political, social environment that had little sympathy for its faith claims. That is, Judaism learned a kind of pragmatism toward political power that served it well.

3. During this period, the Torah (Pentateuch) reached its final form. Indeed the Torah can be perceived precisely as a document designed to adjudicate the faith claims of Israel amidst imperial reality. Thus, Judaism in the Persian period gave decisive shape to the Old Testament, a blending of passionate faith and political realism. An increasing number of scholars accept the view that the Persian period is the matrix of the completed Torah and, conversely, that the Torah serves Judaism precisely in this context.

References: Balentine, Samuel E., *The Torah's Vision of Worship* (OBT; Minneapolis: Fortress Press, 1999); Berquist, Jon L., *Judaism in Persia's Shadow: A Social and Historical Approach* (Minneapolis: Fortress Press, 1995); Grabbe, Lester L., *Judaism from Cyrus to Hadrian: Sources, History, Synthesis: The Persian and Greek Periods*, vol. 1 (Minneapolis: Fortress Press, 1991); McNutt, Paula, *Reconstructing the Society of Ancient Israel* (Louisville, Ky.: Westminster John Knox Press, 1999); Weinberg, J. P., *The Citizen-Temple Community* (Sheffield: Sheffield Academic Press, 1992).

Plague   While the term "plague" may generically suggest destructive epidemics that beset specific communities, in the Bible it refers particularly to upheavals in the environment wrought by the creator as an act of sovereignty and judgment.

Of its two characteristic uses, the best known are "the ten plagues" that dominate the exodus narrative in Exodus 7–12. These several disasters (including frogs and gnats, flies and boils—culminating in the death of the firstborn) occurred in order to assert and establish YHWH's power over the realm of Pharaoh, where Pharaoh thought that he himself was sovereign. The purpose of the sequence is that Pharaoh may come to "know" (= acknowledge) YHWH as sovereign to whom he must submit, as he does in his astonishing confession of Exodus 10:17.

The second use concerns a recurring fourfold pattern of "pestilence, sword, famine, and captivity," a cluster of threats that are said to be YHWH's characteristically ferocious manifestation of sovereignty over recalcitrant subjects (see Jer. 15:2; 24:10; 32:24). In Leviticus 26 and Deuteronomy 28 (and see also 1 Kgs. 8:31–53; Amos 4:6–11), these four most cited threats belong to a larger stock of curses that function as negative sanctions whereby the sovereign enforces treaties and covenants to which assent has been given. This fourfold pattern shows up, belatedly and famously, in the book of Revelation as the Four Horsemen of the Apocalypse, culminating a long tradition of such usages (Rev. 9:18), all of which signify the terrifying judgment of the coming sovereign.

The most important point is that the plagues must be understood theologically, that is, with reference to YHWH. Attempts have been offered, such as that by Hort, to explain the plagues as natural phenomena. This effort is unhelpful, first because the cause-and-effect chain of explanation that must be proposed defies credibility. Second, even if the naturalistic explanation were convincing, it would miss the characteristic intention of the biblical narrative, which is to attest to and enact YHWH's sovereignty over those parts of creation that are resistant to that rule.

Fretheim has been especially helpful, suggesting that the Exodus narrative is concerned not just with punishment of Pharaoh and the liberation of Israel, but with the celebration of YHWH as the creator and as governor of all that is. The several plagues exhibit YHWH's capacity to mobilize endless facets of creation in order to effect defeat and liberation, and thus we may take them to be "negative miracles," that is, wonders that in a destructive way evidence YHWH's power, such as the "tumors" brought upon the Philistines in 1 Samuel 5–6.

Such a claim requires a contemporary reader to understand the plagues within the intent of Israel's rhetoric, which prefers to call these upheavals "signs and wonders," signs of YHWH's governance [see RETRIBUTION]. Two texts—Exodus 10:1–2 and Psalm 105—make the point plainly. The plague cycle in the book of Exodus is as extended as it is clearly because YHWH "hardens the heart of Pharaoh" in order to make Pharaoh more resistant, and so to require more manifestations of YHWH's power. The narrative suggests the reason that the sequence of plagues is extended through the hardening of Pharaoh's heart:

"Go to Pharaoh; for I have hardened his heart and the heart of his officials, in order that I may show these signs of mine among them, and that you may tell your children and grandchildren how I have made fools of the Egyptians and what signs I have done

among them——so that you may know that I am the LORD." (Exod. 10:1–2)

The grandchildren will see that YHWH has routed Pharaoh and so acknowledge YHWH in full sovereignty.

This doxological intention of the plague cycle is made unmistakable in Psalm 105:

They performed his signs among them,
   and miracles in the land of Ham.
He sent darkness, and made the land dark.
. . . .
He turned their waters into blood,
   and caused their fish to die.
Their land swarmed with frogs,
   even in the chambers of their kings.
He spoke, and there came swarms of flies,
   and gnats throughout their country.
He gave them hail for rain,
   and lightning that flashed through their
      land.
He struck their vines and fig trees,
   and shattered the trees of their country.
He spoke, and the locusts came,
   and young locusts without numbers;
. . . .
He struck down all the firstborn in their
      land,
   the first issue of all their strength.
            (vv. 27–36; see Ps. 78:42–53)

By the conclusion of the sequence both needy Israel and recalcitrant Egypt know (= acknowledge) the true sovereign who will tolerate no resistance and brook no rival (see Exod. 8:10; 9:14; 11:7).

References: Brueggemann, Walter, "Pharaoh as Vassal: A Study of a Political Metaphor," *CBQ* 57 (1995): 27–51; Fretheim, Terence E., "The Plagues as Ecological Signs of Historical Disaster," *JBL* 110 (1991): 385–96; Hort, Greta, "The Plagues of Egypt," *ZAW* 69 (1957): 84–103, and *ZAW* 70 (1958): 48–59; McCarthy, Dennis J., "Plagues and the Sea of Reeds: Exodus 5–14," *JBL* 85 (1966): 137–58.

Prayer   Prayer in the Old Testament is an interactive conversation—a drama, a dialogue—in which both parties have a role. Its defining premise is the character of YHWH, who is characteristically known as and trusted to be the one named in the great doxologies and memories of Israel, the one who has intervened actively on behalf of Israel and who has pledged abiding loyalty to Israel. The other party to the dialogue of prayer is Israel, who is the prime beneficiary of YHWH's goodness and who has sworn faithful obedience to YHWH and to YHWH's Torah commands.

In some prayers Israel speaks as a community. At other times, the speaker is an individual member of the community. Sometimes this speaker of prayer is an identifiable leader of Israel who prays on behalf of Israel, but more often, a nameless member of the community of Israel speaks a quite personal and intimate prayer, but always as a member of the community and always in the context of Israel's doxological tradition and Israel's memory of its past with YHWH. Prayer is thus an activity that has as its characteristic premise the reality of covenant in which these two parties have sworn enduring allegiance to each other. This dialogical reality as the assumption, context, and practice of prayer has been given its most popular expression in Martin Buber's *I and Thou*, a characteristically Jewish affirmation that the life of Israel (and more broadly the life of the individual human person for whom Israel is a representative) is always derived from and related to this God who can be addressed in prayer.

Israel's prayer may be understood in terms of the condition of the covenant, that is, whether it is functioning well or not. When the covenant is functioning well, Israel engages in praise of YHWH.

While praise is an address to YHWH and is abundantly evidenced in the Psalms, it is not commonly treated under the rubric of prayer. When the covenant is in good condition, prayer may be an act of trustful intimacy and confidence.

But Israel also engages YHWH when the covenant is in disarray and is not functioning well, when the parties are experiencing some alienation. Then prayer is an attempt to reach across the breach that has arisen in the dysfunction of covenant. Because Israel's faith is largely defined in juridical categories, reaching across this breach is cast juridically in terms of guilt and failure. Most familiar to us are prayers of confession in which Israel accepts responsibility for the failure of covenant and acknowledges its own guilt and failure. The best known of such prayers is Psalm 51, placed by tradition on the lips of David.

Most remarkable, however, is Israel's readiness to entertain and express the thought that the failure of covenant is not its own but YHWH's. Most often these prayers suggest not YHWH's active failure, but rather YHWH's neglect, silence, or absence (see Pss. 13:1–3; 35:17, 22–23; 71:12; 77:7–9). The one who prays is not, however, typically preoccupied with guilt or accusation, but simply in a desperate state, pleading that YHWH will be attentive to help, heal, save, or rescue, because the prayer is no longer able to act effectively for one's self. This mood and context suggest that the center of Israel's prayer is characteristically petition in which Israel speaks in an imperative and "cries out" to seek God's active presence and intervention. The imperative may be a petition on behalf of one's self or intercession for another or the community. Either way, an urgent address to YHWH is voiced in confidence based on a history with YHWH and a mood of trustful intimacy.

The imperative petition can most likely be understood by itself as the rawest, most elemental form of prayer. The petition was highly stylized in Israel, accompanied by an address to God ("my God") and suggesting motivations or reasons that YHWH should heed the imperative and answer effectively. The motivations may include a statement of dire need (Ps. 3:1–2), an appeal to YHWH's past fidelity to Israel (Ps. 22:3–5), or an appeal to YHWH's reputation for splendor and majesty (Ps. 7:6–8). The motivations seem designed to persuade YHWH to act, and they appeal in part to YHWH's obligation to Israel but also to YHWH's pride and sense of YHWH's proper role and reputation.

The conversation Israel has with YHWH is open to every issue that may occur in human life, in the conviction that the God of covenant is relevant to and adequate for every circumstance. Israel's prayers concern public needs, such as support in war or intervention in drought, as well as intimately personal issues of illness, family alienation, or a sense of abandonment. Indeed, the Psalms are a collection of the rich deposit of Israel's prayer practice. They include prayers that must have been used on High Holy Days in public; they also include more intimate prayers that were characteristically offered in less public arenas. Outside the Psalms, moreover, prayers occur throughout the narrative of the Old Testament, so that reports of lived life include concrete references to YHWH voiced by the most representative figures in Israel's memory, including the following:

Abraham in his demanding petition on behalf of Sodom (Gen. 18:22–32)

Jacob at the moment of his deep fear in the face of his brother Esau (Gen. 32:9–12)

Moses' intervention on behalf of Israel in the face of YHWH's anger (Exod. 32:11–14; Num. 14:13–19)

David, who consolidates the large promises of YHWH just made to him in an oracle (2 Sam. 7:18–29)

Solomon, who prays in summary fashion that YHWH can override every situation of curse (1 Kgs. 8:31–53)

Hezekiah, who prays that YHWH will be more than adequate in the face of the Assyrian threat (Isa. 37:16–20).

The prayers of women are especially to be noted as Miller has observed, including the prayer of Hagar (Gen. 21:15–19), the prayer of Hannah (1 Sam. 1–2), and the remarkable prayer of Psalm 131.

This rich array of examples suggests that Israel was characteristically and self-consciously a praying people; every part of its life was addressed confidently and passionately to YHWH's rule and will. This defining reality for Israel suggests that:

1. Israel's prayer is real address to a real partner in anticipation of a real response. Israel's presentation of itself suggests a history of prayer's effectiveness. One of the dazzlements of covenantal prayer is that imperatives addressed to YHWH can evoke a real response. The dominant scholarly hypothesis is that through a human mediator, the petitions of Israel evoked a "salvation oracle" that offered an assurance of YHWH's presence and help. This quality of theological realism is evident in the prayers of acknowledgment and thanks that Israel utters after a prayer has been effective:

I waited patiently for the LORD;
    he inclined to me and heard my cry.
He drew me up from the desolate pit,
    out of the miry bog,
and set my feet upon a rock,
    making my steps secure.
                   (Ps. 40:1–2)

Then they cried to the LORD in their
    trouble,
    and he delivered them from their
    distress.
          (Ps 107:6; see vv. 13, 19, 28)

I love the LORD, because he has heard
    my voice and my supplications.
Because he inclined his ear to me,
    therefore I will call on him as long as I
    live.
                 (Ps. 116:1–2)

2. At the same time, Israel knows that YHWH is not an automaton whose reaction to prayer is a given according to the petition. The drama of the book of Job shows that Job receives a divine answer to his many protests (Job 38–41), but not the user-friendly response on the terms Job had sought. Moreover Psalm 88 is a startling acknowledgment on the part of Israel that prayer may indeed go unanswered even after passionate repetition (see also Ps. 89:46–49). Thus, while YHWH is passionate, loyal, and attentive to Israel, YHWH deals with Israel (and with Israel's prayers) with the freedom to answer as YHWH wills, or not at all. Israel may have confidence in its prayers, but no ground for complacency or for taking YHWH for granted.

3. Israel's sustained practice of prayer demonstrates a trustful theological innocence. Modern, scientifically oriented, technologically conditioned people (such as many of us are) find that innocence difficult to trust. As a consequence, prayer is regularly adjusted in the modern world:

either the prayer becomes anemic and does not really ask anything (in the confident suspicion that nothing would in any case be given), or prayer is transposed into a psychological act of catharsis so as to make us feel better, or prayer becomes a group process of sharing. The innocence of this ancient faith is not readily appropriated among us, but we could begin by acknowledging that our conventional reductionisms of prayer are pale, inadequate shadows of prayer as Israel practiced it. Recovering that innocence begins not simply in prayer, but in the redescription of the God of Israel who is the God of the church, the one known as present in the deepest cadences of faithful rhetoric.

References: Balentine, Samuel E., *Prayer in the Hebrew Bible: The Drama of Divine-Human Dialogue* (OBT; Minneapolis: Fortress Press, 1993); Boyce, R. N., *The Cry to God in the Old Testament* (Atlanta: Scholars Press, 1988); Clements, Ronald E., *In Spirit and in Truth: Insights from Biblical Prayers* (Atlanta: John Knox Press, 1985); Greenberg, Moshe, *Biblical Prose Prayer As a Window to the Popular Religion of Ancient Israel* (Berkeley: University of California Press, 1983); *The Living Pulpit* 2/3 (July–September 1993); Miller, Patrick D., "Prayer and Divine Action," *God in the Fray: A Tribute to Walter Brueggemann,* ed. Timothy Beal and Tod Linafelt (Minneapolis: Fortress Press, 1998), 211–32; idem, "Prayer as Persuasion: The Rhetoric and Intention of Prayer," *Word & World* 13 (1993): 356–62; idem, *They Cried to the Lord: The Form and Theology of Biblical Prayer* (Minneapolis: Fortress Press, 1994); Newman, Judith, *Praying by the Book* (Atlanta: Scholars Press, 1999); Reif, Stefan, *Judaism and Hebrew Prayer: New Perspectives on Jewish Liturgical History* (Cambridge: Cambridge University Press, 1995).

Priestly Tradition The phrase "priestly tradition," commonly used among scholars, is important to know because the phrase recurs in interpretive books about the Old Testament. During the intense period of historical-critical study of the Old Testament in the eighteenth and nineteenth centuries (accomplished mostly by German Protestant researchers), scholars were able to identify and isolate different literary-theological sources in the text. In those days these sources were regarded as distinct "documents" that were subsequently edited together, though today we might prefer to call them "voices" in the text rather than "documents." The precise dating and location of such sources is much in dispute, but different voices do apparently have a say in the text's final form.

Among these sources, perhaps the defining one for the shape and witness of the Pentateuch is "the priestly tradition," a name assigned by scholars to a series of texts (both narratives and commandments) that have common characteristics: the narratives tend to be concerned with cultic institutions, and the commandments assigned to this assumed source are preoccupied with cultic holiness, that is, with questions of purity and the ritual performance of purity. In identifying and understanding this material, the German Protestant scholars who shaped critical categories of understanding likely were using the term "priestly" in a pejorative way, operating with a deep bias in favor of ethical considerations and an equally deep antipathy toward cultic matters, which they considered primitive and magical. The presumed source was thus understood as an expression of late and "degenerate" Judaism; this attitude, so crucial and influential in the history of scholarship, reflects a common Christian stereotype of Judaism. In a secondary way, this Protestant nomenclature may have suggested a polemic against Roman Catholicism, which was viewed as equally "priestly" in its devotion to "punctilious"

ritual practices that were perceived as primitive and magical. More recent and mature understanding, somewhat free of the biases of liberal Protestantism, is able to recognize that the priestly tradition articulates a lively, thoughtful, generative voice of faith in Judaism that both provides a rich world of theological symbolism and sustains an ethical practice and a passionate vision of reality.

The priestly tradition, in its final form, likely reflects the theological needs and perceptions of the community of faith in the exile, a time when the source, and perhaps the entire Pentateuch, reached its final form. In an influential study, Mary Douglas has proposed that an accent on "purity" (and related cultic considerations) is a characteristic agenda of a community under deep social threat; the articulation of a cultic world of imagination is a serious offer of an ordered world of well-being, cultically situated, as an alternative to an exilic world that is perceived as hostile and chaotic. Exilic Jews, profoundly displaced, probably experienced the world around them in this hostile and chaotic way; a cultic vision of alternative reality (presided over by a reliable God) provided a way to maintain a distinct and confident faith identity in an profoundly alien environment.

Surely, however, the tradition that was finally shaped in exile drew upon and valued much older traditions, for a cultic focus on purity and cultic identity had undoubtedly been a mode of faith in all seasons of Israel's life. The cultic agenda of purity was not simply a reactive or defensive measure in the exilic faith of Israel, but was in deeply rooted ways a characteristic manner of being Israel. The faith of Israel was expressed as a public ethic, yet an ethic sustained and fed by a vigorous cultic life in which the mediated presence of YHWH was a symbolically secured certainty.

The great narratives that form a part of the priestly tradition include: (a) the creation narrative of Genesis 1:1–2:4a, which concludes with the authorization of the Sabbath as the culmination of creation and as the defining institution of Jews in exile and for all subsequent Judaism as well; (b) the portions of the flood narrative that are preoccupied with the distinction of "clean and unclean," a distinction that pervades the priestly tradition (Gen. 7:1–16) and the ultimate promise of covenantal loyalty on the part of YHWH concerning the reliable order of the entire cosmos (Gen. 9:8–17); (c) the narrative of Genesis 17 that takes circumcision as a sign of the covenant, even as circumcision became a decisive sign for Jews in exile; (d) the promise of the land in Genesis 35:9–15, which served as a powerful source of hope for displaced exiles; and (e) the self-disclosure of YHWH together with a promise of land in Exodus 6:2–9. These narrative texts show the ways in which the tradition is resituated to meet the particular needs of displacement.

The much more extended part of the priestly tradition, however, appears in the body of instruction that the canonizing process places at Sinai in the mouth of Moses. This material includes Exodus 25–31 and 35–40, all of Leviticus, and Numbers 1:1–10:10, and it provides for Israel an alternative world of cultic imagination that is an adequate, suitable place where the Holy God of Sinai is willing to sojourn. The careful provision made for holy practices—holy place, holy people, holy activities—yields the profound theological affirmation that even in exilic displacement Israel can host the Holy God who accepts the "prepared place of holiness" as an adequate residence so that God may be palpably present even in the exile. This extended material of command, marked by exactitude, precision, punctiliousness, and repetition, focuses on being careful and attentive to the reality, wonder, and danger of the presence of the Holy God.

Exodus 25–31 provides *instructions for the construction of a tabernacle* with its "mercy seat," a habitat for YHWH's gracious presence. Blenkinsopp and Kearney have noticed that this material is ordered into seven speeches by Moses, culminating in a command about Sabbath. The seven speeches correlate with the seven days of creation in Genesis 1:1–2:4a, which also culminate in the Sabbath. Given the parallel, one can conclude that the tabernacle was to be constructed as a cultic replica and embodiment of an ordered creation, made available in the midst of the chaos of exile.

Exodus 35–40 *enacts the instruction* of Exodus 25–31, culminating in 40:34–38, assuring that the "place prepared" is one that adequately houses the glory of YHWH. The "glory" witnessed, according to the priestly tradition, in Exodus 24:15–18 is now transferred from the awesome mountain to the tabernacle to be regularly and reliably available to displaced Israel.

Leviticus 1–7 provides a highly stylized *catalogue of sacrifices to be practiced* in Israel. While that inventory no doubt brings together many cultic practices that arose and were practiced incidentally and ad hoc, the sum effect of the list is to provide regular, reliable means for communion with YHWH, both to celebrate and maintain life-giving contact with YHWH's holiness and to conduct restorative acts when the relationship is in jeopardy. Specifically Milgrom has demonstrated that what are conventionally termed "sin offerings" in older translations are in fact rituals of purification and purgation of what in Israel impedes or endangers the relationship of Israel to YHWH.

Leviticus 11–16 offers a rich list of *practices of purification* designed to prepare Israel for hosting YHWH's holiness. We may mention especially Leviticus 16 and its provision for a Day of Atonement (Yom Kippur). Israel has authorized for this day, by the goodness of YHWH, an annual festival of forgiveness and reconciliation, an occasion of ritual symbolic practice for restoring life with YHWH.

Scholars view Leviticus 17–26 as a distinct subtradition within the priestly materials. These chapters are conventionally dubbed the "Holiness Code" because of the sustained *emphasis upon Israel's holiness*:

> You shall be holy, for I the LORD your God am holy. (Lev. 19:2)

Milgrom has argued that the Holiness Code pertains only to the land of Israel: the land must be pure in order that YHWH may be present there. We may notice three items:

1. Leviticus 18 and 20 contain a list of sexual taboos, violations of holiness that will preclude YHWH's holiness in Israel. These texts have been prominent lately because of the church's preoccupation with homosexuality. However these chapters are concerned with matters of ritual purification and not great matters of morality. Ironically, church conservatives who care most about the issue of ritual have conventionally scuttled the old ritual laws of the Old Testament and have valued only moral laws that are retained in Christian tradition. These chapters in Leviticus, however, clearly occur in a context of ritual holiness; they are concerned only with cultic propriety, which is generally said to be "overcome" in the New Testament faith.

2. In Leviticus 19:18, Israel preserved the teaching of "love of neighbor" that Jesus identifies as the second great commandment (Mark 12:31). (See also the remarkable teaching of Lev. 19:33–34 that situates the "alien" among "the neighbors.") Mary Douglas (1999) has shrewdly suggested that, in the architectural arrangement of these chapters, Leviticus 18 and 20 (on sexuality) provide the framing for Leviticus 19 on justice; the central accent on justice is consequently the dominant theme to which all else in these chapters is subservient. The effect of such a judgment is to subsume sexual concerns under the concern for justice.

3. Leviticus 25 is the central text in the Bible on the radical proposal for the year of jubilee, surely a primal practice of justice that characterizes Israel's economic vision. That this provision is situated in the Holiness Code indicates the way in which cultic practice may issue in radical social vision.

The priestly tradition, or the priestly editors, were likely the final editors of the Tetrateuch (Genesis to Numbers) who gave final form to these chapters. The large "scheme" for ordering the material of these extended chapters is a series of formulae of "the generations" (*toledôt*) that are intentionally and strategically placed to give shape, coherence, and continuity to originally quite disparate materials (see Gen. 2:4; 5:1; 6:9; 10:1; 11:10; 11:27; 25:12; 25:19; 36:1; 37:2). Scholars suggest that this recurring formula provided an important way through which the entire memory of Israel, ordered through a priestly lens, established a reliable, stable past. That past in turn issued in YHWH's commands that require holiness and narratives that report on holiness as present within Israel. The tradition thus mediates a sense of stability and equilibrium rooted in YHWH's own "stability" that borders on the static. The literature seeks such a stability and equilibrium, if exile is its final context, as a profound counter to an exilic world of disequilibrium and instability. In that milieu, Israel clearly did not object to embracing an order that was nearly static.

This quite intentional, self-conscious textual tradition is not incidental or late or "degenerate," but is rather the voice of a lively, generative intentional theological tradition that provided imaginative resources for sustaining Israel in what must have been an environment of deep jeopardy. The extreme "thinness" of ethical teaching when taken by itself, so prized in early critical study, may be seen at the beginning of the twenty-first century to be inadequate in a situation of deep social and therefore religious crisis. Human action (even as obedience) is thus not sufficient for human life unless set deep within a network of thick symbols that have priority over human possibility. The priestly tradition provides exactly such sacramental depth for Israel and is a recurring matrix for Torah-keeping, covenantal faith.

Commenting on two extrapolations from this defining tradition is in order here. First, the tradition of Ezekiel is closely linked to that of the priestly tradition, so that the voice of that book is likely situated in the matrix of the priestly tradition. Ezekiel is concerned with the failure of the temple (chaps. 9–10) and with revitalizing the temple as a place for the holiness of YHWH (chaps. 40–48). Specifically, Ezekiel 22:26 may be taken as a hint of a preoccupation with the holiness issues that dominate the priestly tradition (see also 36:22–32; Hag. 2:10–14):

Its priests have done violence to my teaching and have profaned my holy things; they have made no distinction between the holy and the common, neither have they taught the difference between the unclean and the clean, and they have disregarded my sabbaths, so that I am profaned among them.

Second, the priestly tradition is a context for the New Testament formulation of faith. Specifically, the significance of Jesus in Hebrews 7–10 is formulated completely within the categories of the priestly tradition. To be sure, the letter to the Hebrews claims that the work of Jesus has "superseded" the claims of the priestly tradition of ancient Israel. At the same time, however, the claims made in this priestly idiom for Jesus make no sense at all unless informed by that priestly tradition and its categories. Thus, a disregard of the priestly tradition would likely leave us failing to appreciate the depth and power of the claim made for Jesus in this literature, from which the church has derived one of its primary formulations of the "work of Christ."

More generally, Christian rhetoric about "being saved by the blood" depends on the imagery and symbolic world of the priests. This priestly tradition funds the Christian tradition in decisive ways. Moreover, the need for sacramental sustenance in the thin, technical world at the beginning of the twenty-first century helps us to appreciate the intent and the claim of this powerful, resilient tradition from the priests. Perhaps we may claim as our own this odd tradition if we appropriate it from that season of displacement into our own coming season of displacement in a world hostile or indifferent to this trusting act of imagination.

References: Blenkinsopp, Joseph, *Prophecy and Canon: A Contribution to the Study of Jewish Origins* (Notre Dame, Ind.: University of Notre Dame Press, 1977); Crüsemann, Frank, *The Torah: Theology and Social History of Old Testa-*

ment Law (Edinburgh: T & T Clark, 1996), 277–327; Douglas, Mary, "Justice as the Cornerstone: An Interpretation of Leviticus 18–20," *Interpretation* 53 (1999): 341–50; idem, *Purity and Danger: An Analysis of the Concepts of Pollution and Taboo* (Boston: Ark Paperbacks, 1984), 41–57; Haran, Menahem, *Temples and Temple Service in Ancient Israel* (Oxford: Oxford University Press, 1978); Kearney, Peter J., "The P Redaction of Exod. 25–40," *ZAW* 89 (1977): 375–87; Knohl, Israel, *The Sanctuary of Silence: The Priestly Torah and the Holiness School* (Minneapolis: Fortress Press, 1995); Lohfink, Norbert, *Theology of the Pentateuch: Themes of the Priestly Narrative and Deuteronomy* (Minneapolis: Fortress Press, 1994); Milgrom, Jacob, *Leviticus 1–16* (Anchor Commentaries 3; New York: Doubleday, 1991); idem, *Studies in Levitical Terminology* (Berkeley: University of California Press, 1970); Rad, Gerhard von, *Old Testament Theology*, vol. 1 (San Francisco: Harper and Row, 1962), 77–84, 232–79.

Priests   As in other cultures, the faith community of the Old Testament recognized authorized priests who presided over the formal worship of the community. The purpose of the priesthood was to oversee, protect, and assure the effectiveness of the cultic apparatus as a way of guaranteeing YHWH's presence in the midst of Israel. As with every other priesthood and every cultus, Israel presumed that while occasional immediate contact with YHWH may occur in theophanies, for the most part the community relied upon the regularized mediations of priests. The intended effect of a faithfully regulated cult was to assure the order, life, and well-being of the larger community. That is, carefully regulated worship functioned as a generative source of power and imagination for reconstruing and reordering all of life. To that end, the priests in ancient Israel performed the characteristic tasks and roles of priests everywhere, which included:

1. The priests maintained the distinctions of "holy-profane, clean-unclean, pure-impure" that protected the ordered life of the community (see Lev. 10:10; Ezek. 22:26). The preoccupation with holiness in the book of Leviticus evidences the importance of this task, which derived from elemental religious assumptions but also pertained to matters of hygiene and the practical maintenance of health. The liturgic rendering of the book of Leviticus should be understood not as historical description, but as an imaginative proposal for an attentive world of meaning. Above all, however, maintaining such distinctions was crucially symbolic for a well-ordered world with YHWH at its center.

2. The priests delivered oracles whereby YHWH's will and purpose were authoritatively made known in the community. These oracles were thus a regularized channel of revelation from YHWH to Israel. Special equipment such as the Thummim and Urim (Deut. 33:8) or ephod (1 Sam. 23:6–12) was important in the reliable delivery of such oracles.

3. The priests enacted the sacrifices and offerings designed to celebrate, maintain, or restore well-being between YHWH and Israel. The routinized inventory of sacrifices in Leviticus 1–7 indicates the extensive practice of sacrifices and offerings that were available to Israel and the seriousness with which such actions were regarded. The actions are serious because YHWH's presence provides guarantees for the land, and the sacrifices are a part of the dramatic enterprise of making YHWH's presence possible and available.

4. The priests pronounced blessings. The familiar priestly blessing of Numbers 6:22–26 is a characteristic formulation whereby the priestly transmission of blessing is an authoritative, effective act mediating YHWH's force for well-being to a receptive, trusting congregation.

5. In what may be a peculiarly Israelite practice, the priests engaged in Torah instruction (Deut. 10:8). The priests of particular orders were charged with instruction of Torah—that is, they were educators in the normative traditions of faith (Deut. 33:10). Perhaps in early form the task was simply to identify matters of holiness and purity upon which the safety of the community depended. In the more developed tradition, such Torah instruction refers to the larger body of commands that needed interpretation and exposition. Thus the tradition of Deuteronomy, apparently connected to the Levitical priests, required exposition. In Nehemiah 8, moreover, the Levites assist Ezra—a scribe but also called a priest—in reading the Torah to Israel "with interpretation." The task of the priests was to make the tradition of command and instruction available and credible to the ongoing life of Israel by way of imaginative interpretation.

These several functions of the priests reflect Israel's self-characterization as a community evoked by and responsive to YHWH. The evidence for the priesthood in the Old Testament is quite ad hoc; no systematic formulation is offered. Scholars, however, have used great inventive energy in seeking to trace the history of priesthood in Israel, so that a rough consensus is now established among interpreters about that history. While incidental and ad hoc priests appear here and there in the text, in general one may identify several priestly lines (families and dynasties) that prevailed over the generations, had great authority, and exercised enormous power, through interpretation, in the public processes of politics. These several lines, moreover, were rivals and gave different nuances to their task, reflecting different notions of the faith, perhaps not unlike clergy of different denominations within the realm of Christianity.

In 2 Samuel 15:29 David apparently had two priests, Abiathar and Zadok. Scholars reckon that Abiathar represents a priestly line that is perhaps traced back to the shrine of Shiloh, but is in any case a representative of the old, radical covenant tradition. Zadok's origin is an enigma, but he may represent a line of priests less radical than Abiathar and more amenable to Canaanite adaptation. The two priests thus embody different, even competing priestly lines that are rooted in different places and have different perspectives and interests. In 1 Kings 1:7–8, this difference of orientation is made explicit as the two are respectively allied with sons of David who themselves reflect different perspectives. Because Solomon, Zadok's candidate for kingship, prevails in the contest for succession, Zadok becomes the dominant priest of the realm and Abiathar is banished from the courts of power (1 Kgs. 2:27). The reference in that verse alludes back to the anticipation of 1 Samuel 2:35, already an anticipation of the coming domination of Zadok—who is the "faithful priest"—and the diminishment of Abiathar and the priestly line he represents.

If one takes the Abiathar-Zadok rivalry as definitional, one may reach back to the tradition, as does Cross, to suggest that Abiathar is rooted in the old claims of the "Mushite" (Mosaic) priesthood and Zadok is linked to the priesthood of Aaron. In Exodus 32, from a perspective quite in contrast to that of 1 Samuel 2, Aaron is the disobedient priest and the Levites, linked to Moses, are the faithful who eliminate those led by Aaron (Exod. 32:25–29). The old rootage is thus connected to the later contest in the time of Solomon as "Moses-Levites" and "Aaron-Zadok."

If we reflect on the exile and postexilic traditions, Ezekiel 44 reflects the domination of Zadokites, for in verse 10 the Levites are assigned menial tasks and in verse 15 the descendants of Zadok are made the dominant authority over the restored temple. Many scholars believe that the Zadokites are the forerunners of the Sadducees in later Judaism, as the names seem related to each other.

Tracing with any certitude or precision the actual history of priesthood is not possible, for these texts are literary efforts to provide legitimacy and ideological force to competing claims. Unmistakably, though, the contestation of priestly authority (reflected in an earlier text like Exod. 32 and in a later text like Ezek. 44, and in what seem to be the concrete narratives around David and Solomon) indicates that the priestly office was situated in old and deep theological tensions regarding the character of Israel and its relation to YHWH. The Levites are, in Deuteronomy, the advocates of Torah, whereas the Aaron-Zadok line is much more concerned with cultic presence. This tension runs all through the life and memory of Israel; different cultic accents and different priestly authorizations are clues to defining theological tensions—tensions that have endlessly resounded throughout church history in disputes about sacraments, polity, and liturgy. These recurring tensions concern, in the end, the very dimensions of faith that constitute the life of the faith community. That tension notwithstanding, the priestly conduct of ritual nurtured a distinctive imagination of faith that contributed mightily to Judaism's survival and vitality. The rituals are endlessly crucial to Judaism and have historically lacked other sociopolitical supports.

References: Brueggemann, Walter, *Theology of the Old Testament: Testimony, Dispute, Advocacy* (Minneapolis: Fortress Press, 1997), 650–79; Cody, Aelred, *A History of Old Testament Priesthood* (Analecta Biblica 35; Rome: Pontifical Biblical Institute, 1969); Cross, Frank Moore, *Canaanite Myth and Hebrew Epic: Essays in the History of the Religion of Israel* (Cambridge: Harvard University Press, 1973), 195–215; Haran, Menahem, *Temples and Temple Service in Ancient Israel: An Inquiry into Biblical Cult Phenomena and the Historical Setting of the Priestly School* (Winona Lake, Ind.: Eisenbrauns, 1985); Miller, Patrick D., *The Religion of Ancient Israel* (Library of Ancient Israel; Louisville, Ky.: Westminster John Knox Press, 2000); Nelson, Richard D., *Raising Up a Faithful Priest: Community and Priesthood in Biblical Theology* (Louisville, Ky.: Westminster John Knox Press, 1993); Vaux, Roland de, *Ancient Israel* (New York: McGraw-Hill, 1961).

Promise   The promise of YHWH made to Israel constitutes a major component of Israel's faith and self-understanding. "The promise of God" was not a universal assurance nor a generic feeling about the future, but rather a precise utterance from the mouth of YHWH, given in the text, whereby YHWH has solemnly sworn to Israel to enact certain futures that are not "natural" developments or extrapolations from the present but are acts of power wrought through YHWH's sovereign will. Faith is understood in the Old Testament as Israel's confidence that YHWH's promises are reliable; in response, Israel is prepared to stake its future on that promise, even though it flies in the face of fact. Indeed Israel at its best is prepared to take specific practical steps in the present that make sense only on the basis of that promise (see Gen. 15:6 as the primal example).

The ancestral narratives of Genesis 12–50 are a primary locus of promise, and they may be seen as an engine that endlessly urges Israel into YHWH's future, which is well beyond Israel's sight or control. The promises to the ancestors, however, are preceded by the large promises that God makes to Noah (Gen. 8:21–22; 9:8–17). Already in the flood narrative, YHWH is disclosed as a promise-maker. The defining promise of YHWH to Israel is in Genesis 12:1–3 wherein YHWH promises to Abraham and Sarah a new land. Support of that defining promise is an assurance of an heir in the next generation to maintain that promise, a blessing, and a great name. Beyond a commitment to Israel's own life, YHWH also promises that through Israel the world of curse, featured in Genesis 3–11, will receive a blessing.

YHWH's mouthful of promise becomes a dominant motif for all that follows in the Bible. The promise is reiterated and reestablished with each successive generation, so that each new generation is understood as one that trusts the promise and carries the promise into the future (see Gen. 18:18; 22:18; 26:4; 28:13–15). The remarkable text of Joshua 21:43–45 constitutes an affirmation of promise fulfilled, thus attesting that YHWH keeps promises and that YHWH is a concrete agent known to be reliable.

A quite different promise, perhaps related to the ancestral promises in the history of tradition, is YHWH's promise made through Nathan to David (2 Sam. 7:1–16). That promise—celebrated in Psalm 89 and made conditional in Psalm 132—is the driving force behind Israel's monarchy and the key for the historiography of the Deuteronomic History. In that interpretive history, the oracle of promise to David limits the effect of YHWH's anger at Israel's recurring disobedience, a limit that holds until the last excruciating moment before the savage termination of the Jerusalem establishment. That destruction notwithstanding, Israel continued to find in YHWH's wondrous promise to David a ground for new possibility within history, even when all historical circumstance testified against such historical possibility.

In the exile of the sixth century and the destruction of Jerusalem, its temple, and its king, the promises of YHWH to Israel seemed voided (see Lam. 5:22). In such a context, that the great prophets of the exile (Isa. 40–55; Jer. 29–33; Ezek. 33–48) were able to assert new promises from YHWH precisely in a historical circumstance that contradicted any such promise is remarkable.

In the exile and thereafter, Judaism became a community coping with present circumstance but deeply committed to a new future whereby YHWH would enact pending promises. In a schematic way, one can identify two strands of faith in Judaism that are responsive to YHWH's durable promises. First, the promise of YHWH is *messianic*: a new king of the Davidic house will appear in time to come, thus posing the characteristic and recurring question, "Are you the one who is to come?" (see Luke 7:19). This promise, rooted in the old oracle of 2 Samuel 7, continued to be enlivening (as is evident in Isa. 9:2–7; 11:1–9; Jer. 23:5–6; 33:14–16; Hag. 2:6–7, 21–22; Zech. 3:8; 4:14; 6:10–13; 9:1–10). The promise is quite specific, assuring Jews that the fullness of God's promise for the future will be this-worldly well-being, enacted by a God-designated human agent.

A second, quite distinctive expectation for the future takes the form of *apocalyptic* hope, particularly expressed in Daniel. This more radical hope trusts that YHWH's sure newness will happen by YHWH's own decisive intervention, without reference to human agency and without confinement to present historical circumstance. A focal text for such an expectation is Daniel 7:13–14, a vision of a heavenly being, a Son of Man, coming on the clouds to do what cannot be accomplished by human agency or within present human history. The theological core of this hope is that the future is surely, decisively, and singularly in YHWH's own hand, to be enacted according to YHWH's own will.

These categories of messianic and apocalyptic do not exhaust or contain all of the promises. They are this-worldly promises enacted without human agency (see Isa. 2:2–4; 58:8–9, 11–12; Mic. 4:1–4).

This deep sense of the future continued to power Judaism. On the whole, the rabbis sought to temper or limit apocalyptic hope and awaited a coming messiah. At the same time, the early Christian movement is itself an act of hope, articulated in both messianic and apocalyptic modes.

Beyond the twin expectations of Judaism and Christianity, which have much in common, the modern ideology of progress in its secularized, distorted form is a mode of hope appropriated from the biblical tradition. In that secularized form, however, an open and good future is taken to be intrinsic to the historical process itself, a vague sense of the future shared in varying ways by Marxism and Enlightenment capitalism.

This capacity of faith to risk the future on YHWH's promise is well voiced in Hebrews 11, where a long line of the faithful are celebrated as having lived according to YHWH's promises. That wondrous recital ends, in vv. 39–40, with a bid that the present generation of the faithful should refuse to accept present circumstance and risk for the future that is sure in God's hands, a future anticipated as of personal, communal, and cosmic well-being. This vision of the future, shared by Jews and Christians, is a powerful antidote to despair that is rooted in God's own solemn utterance through which

God's own self is committed to a future of well-being for Israel and for the world.

References: Alt, Albrecht, "The God of the Fathers," in *Essays on Old Testament History and Religion* (Oxford: Blackwell, 1966), 1–77; Brueggemann, Walter, "Faith at the Nullpunkt," *The End of the World and the Ends of God: Science and Theology on Eschatology,* ed. John Polkinghorne and Michael Welker (Harrisburg, Pa.: Trinity Press International, 2000), 143–54; Gowan, Donald E., *Eschatology in the Old Testament* (Philadelphia: Fortress Press, 1986); Miller, Patrick D., "Syntax and Theology in Genesis 12.3a," in *Israelite Religion and Biblical Theology: Collected Essays,* ed. idem (JSOTSup 267; Sheffield: Sheffield Academic Press, 2000), 492–96; Mowinckel, Sigmund, *He That Cometh* (Nashville: Abingdon Press, n.d.); Rad, Gerhard von, *Old Testament Theology,* vol. 2, *The Theology of Israel's Prophetic Traditions* (San Francisco: Harper and Row, 1965); Westermann, Claus, *The Promises to the Fathers: Studies on the Patriarchal Narratives* (Philadelphia: Fortress Press, 1980); Wolff, Hans Walter, "The Kerygma of the Yahwist," *Interpretation* 20 (1966): 131–58.

Prophets   The prophecy that is central to the Old Testament is an ancient Near Eastern phenomenon. Before we come to the peculiar markings of Israelite prophecy, considering the matter more generically can be helpful. Psychologically, the prophets are people who have uncommon access to matters of God's will and purpose that are hidden to other humans. Anthropologically, the prophets of ancient Israel have much in common with other social manifestations, so that the peculiar knowledge of the prophet is not unlike that held by shamans in other cultures. Sociologically, the prophets are situated realistically among issues of social power, functioning as speakers and advocates for a variety of social interests that are said to be congruent with God's will and purpose. Israelite prophets, without much doubt, participate anthropologically, psychologically, and sociologically in the more general phenomenon of prophecy.

In Israel, prophetic figures appear from time to time seeming to be outside the conventional "presumed world" of stable social relationships. These prophets may enact or articulate a *novum* in Israelite society that is experienced as disruption or sometimes as transformation. As carriers of peculiar powers of insight and transformation, they refuse to be explained by or contained in more conventional modes of order, power, or knowledge. We may identify in ancient Israel prophets who receive "messages from God" in "ecstatic moments" (1 Sam. 10:9–13; 19:20–24), though eventually such ecstatic moments are transposed into "call narratives" wherein the subject's life is redefined and resituated according to God's purposes (see Isa. 6:1–8; Jer. 1:4–10; Ezek. 1–3). Some of the prophets are embedded in narratives, (especially Elijah [1 Kgs. 17–21] and Elisha [2 Kgs. 2–9]), though even in those cases, their utterances are usually the decisive factor in the narrative.

Alongside but later than these cases are prophets who are known primarily because of their oracular utterances, introduced characteristically by the formula, "Thus saith the Lord" (KJV). This formula intends to establish the authority of the speaker beyond any established authority, including the king. Over several centuries a variety of such holy utterances were voiced in Israel. Their words were treasured, remembered, and collected by other members of the community, collections that were edited and eventually became scrolls (books) of the Bible. As a consequence, these prophetic figures are best remembered and have often been termed "classical prophets," in contrast to the earlier prophets who received popular support, but were judged to be false and excluded from the canon (see Deut. 13:1–5; 1 Kgs. 18:40; Jer. 23:9–22, 28:1–17; Ezek. 13:1–19).

These prophets appeared ad hoc as the word of God and the spirit of God moved them. Subsequent tradition has more or less imposed an order on what must have been a scattered and unordered process:

1. The prophetic personalities (as much as they can be dated) tended to be clustered around *great public crises* in Israel:

In the eighth century: Amos, Isaiah, Hosea, and Micah

In the seventh century: Jeremiah, Zephaniah, Nahum, and Habakkuk

In the sixth century: more of Jeremiah, Ezekiel, and later Isaiah

As much as our knowledge permits, these utterances should be understood in the context of quite concrete sociopolitical emergencies.

2. While these several speakers are immensely imaginative and generative, they spoke in rather *characteristic oracular patterns*, as follows:

Speeches of judgment that indict Israel for disobedience of God's commands, and that sentence Israel to punishments congruent with the sanctions of covenant

Summons to repent and return to covenantal obedience

Promises of new gifts of well-being that God will give

The effect of these recurring modes of speech is to assert that all of the life of Israel-Judah is in the presence of YHWH's rule, and that every sphere of its life as God's people must come to terms with God's purposes. The poetic form of prophetic oracle is to engage in redescription, reconstrual, and reimagination of human life in the world as life lived before a sovereign, attentive God.

3. The characteristic forms of speech thus permit the wider generalization that for all the richness and variety of utterance, prophetic oracles tend to reiterate themes of *judgment and deliverance*. Judgment declared against a recalcitrant people will surely end in trouble. Deliverance is the news that in, through, and beyond judgment, God will work newnesses that are beyond perceived historical possibility. The themes of judgment and deliverance, taken by themselves, can be understood in flat and settled ways. In the midst of these articulations, however, the prophets daringly portray the interior life of God, whose sovereign authority is deeply qualified by compassion and pathos, so that what might be only the relation of lord and vassal is a much more profoundly complex relationship of troubled fidelity and mutuality. The complexity of the relationship uttered by the prophets matches the generative imagination of those who gave utterance.

Studies of the prophecies have devoted a great deal of attention to the original personalities whose names we know. Attention should also focus on the editorial process whereby the materials from these original personalities became edited, canonical books. What we have in the Bible are, at best, remembered personalities to which we have no direct access, but only the utterances that have now been shaped for subsequent theological use.

A major factor in the transposition from person to book is surely the work of the tradition of Deuteronomy, a sustained interpretive process, which apparently dominated the canonizing enterprise of the Old Testament that eventuated in the scribal tradition of later Judaism. Deuteronomy 18:15–22 asserts the coming of a prophet "like you" (Moses); the tradition thus anticipates a subsequent prophet who will do for Israel what Moses has done for Israel, that is, assure its fidelity to the covenant. While Jeremiah is a candidate in the tradition for the one like Moses, the same Deuteronomic interpretive tradition in 2 Kings 17:13 assumes (a) a deliberate succession of prophets, (b) all of whom said, "Turn." This interpretive presentation of the prophets is far removed from the actual personalities who appeared in Israel; they have now been transposed to serve a larger theological agenda—namely, that prophetic faith, through a series of speakers, continues the Mosaic function of forming and reforming Israel into YHWH's faithful covenanted people.

In this process of theological editing and interpretation, moreover, material that became "prophetic books" has been characteristically edited so that the twin themes of judgment and deliverance roughly dominate the text. These themes are particularly pertinent to the historical experience of ancient Israel in 587 B.C.E., when Jerusalem was destroyed and leading Israelite citizens were deported. God's judgment is seen to be the destruction of Jerusalem, and the subsequent deliverance is the restoration of the deported to Jerusalem and the formation of Judaism. That twin account, however, is not bound to that particular historical experience but has now become the defining theological thematic of prophetic faith. In every time and place, because human history stands under the rule of the covenant-making, covenant-insisting, covenant-ending God, judgment and loss occur at God's behest;

newness, moreover, comes through the generosity, fidelity, and compassion of that same God.

The process of moving from generative personalities to canonical scrolls culminates in the prophetic canon of the Hebrew Bible, the second part of the threefold canon. Eight "books" compose the prophetic canon. The first four—Joshua, Judges, Samuel, and Kings—are reckoned in Jewish tradition as "former prophets." That is, this literature is not "history," as Christians are wont to term it, but "prophecy," an act of reimagining the past/present/future according to the active reality of God. The other four "books" of the prophetic canon are Isaiah, Jeremiah, Ezekiel, and "the twelve" (minor prophets). While these books are no doubt seeded by generative personalities, they are a consequence and product of a long interpretive process over many generations, with each generation of interpreters making connections between the reality of God and its own life in the world.

The "prophets" have been poorly caricatured in much Christian interpretation, and these caricatures need to be unlearned. On the one hand, "the prophets" have been too often taken as "predictors," as in "Well, I'm no prophet but . . ." To be sure, the prophets anticipate the future that God will give. That capacity to know the future, however, is not because of any manipulating, future-telling procedures that ancient Israel decisively rejected (Deut. 18:9–14). Rather, the prophets know in deep and intimate ways about the character of God and so can anticipate God's constancy, which will be decisive in the future as in the past.

On the other hand, the prophets are taken as social activists, a peculiarly "liberal" temptation, as in the equation of "social action" with "prophetic ministry."

Social action that seeks to establish justice in the world is surely grounded in biblical warrants, but is more likely to be understood as "covenantal" rather than "prophetic." In fact, these prophets have remarkably little to say about specific issues, and they rarely urge particular action. They are primarily poets who bring the world to voice outside of settled convention. While the future is implied in their discernment of the reality of God and while justice is intrinsic to their characteristic utterance, the most important aspect of their speech is their reperception of the world as the arena of God's faithful governance. In that ancient community, these poets were characteristically countervoices, mostly unwelcome and resisted. (Note that this assertion is not true in every case; Wilson has identified "central intermediaries" who occupy permanent and legitimate places in established structures, for example, Nathan and Isaiah. Even these prophets, however, are remembered as having given utterances against established order [2 Sam. 12:1–15; Isa. 5:1–7].) The prophetic canon, where taken as scripture, continues to be a persistent voice of dissent, sketching out how differently life is to be lived when YHWH is viewed as the decisive Subject of the public processes of life. That voice of dissent knows about coming judgment in a narcotized society of disobedience; the verse knows as well about deliverance for a society paralyzed by despair. This tradition of utterance keeps alternative alive in any society that is shut down in either pride or in failure.

References: Barton, John, *Oracles of God: Perceptions of Ancient Prophecy in Israel after the Exile* (Oxford: Oxford University Press, 1986); Blenkinsopp, Joseph, *A History of Prophecy in Israel: From the Settlement in the Land to the Hellenistic Period* (Philadelphia: Westminster Press, 1983); Heschel, Abraham, *The Prophets* (New York:

Harper and Row, 1962); Koch, Klaus, *The Prophets: The Assyrian Period*, vol. 1 (Philadelphia: Fortress Press, 1983); idem, *The Prophets: The Babylonian and Persian Periods*, vol. 2 (Philadelphia: Westminster Press, 1984); Overholt, Thomas W., *Channels of Prophecy: The Social Dynamics of Prophetic Activity* (Minneapolis: Fortress Press, 1989); Rad, Gerhard von, *The Message of the Prophets* (New York: Harper & Row, 1962, 1965); Steck, Odil Hannes, *The Prophetic Books and Their Theological Witness* (St. Louis: Chalice Press, 2000); Wilson, Robert R., *Prophecy and Society in Ancient Israel* (Philadelphia: Fortress Press, 1980).

Purim   Purim is a spring festival in the Jewish calendar, celebrated on the fourteenth day of Adar. the festival is intimately linked to the book of Esther, which provides the biblical warrant for the celebration (Esth. 3:7; 9:18–28), and likely arose in the Persian period. As a holiday celebrated in the narrative of Esther, Purim replicates the imperial threat to Jewish identity and Jewish community, the heroic and cunning resistance of Jews to that imperial threat, and the wondrous rescue and vindication of Jews. The celebration of Purim, so named from the casting of "lots" that determined the fate of Jews, includes the reading of the book of Esther in the synagogue. Beyond that, however, the festival invites and enacts a carnival atmosphere of uninhibited behavior that celebrates and exults in emancipated Jewish identity and freedom. The celebration includes self-indulgent eating and drinking and costumes worn to reenact both the menacing threat to Jews and the vindication and emancipation of Jews from every threat.

A latecomer to the Jewish calendar, the festival reflects the threat Judaism faced in the Persian period, but more broadly it reflects the perennial threat of dominant culture against the Jewish community.

Thus Purim is an occasion, regularly celebrated, in which the full, emancipated, unafraid reality of Jewish identity is given full, public disclosure, an occasion that refuses to curb, limit, or silence Jewish identity or submit to conventional political requirements or social expectations.

Beal has best understood the radical deconstruction of social "normalcy" through the practice of carnival that is constitutive of the festival:

> The book of Esther plays on the borderlines between the ostensible and the inostensible: between overt power and covert power, between the public and the private, between identity and difference, between sameness and otherness, between the determined and the accidental, between disclosure and hiding. This is also where Purim plays. As carnival performance, Purim is a communal embodiment of the book *par excellence,* subverting authority, inebriating sobriety, blurring the lines between self and other, and laughing in the face of chillingly real historical possibilities. . . . Purim invites us to recognize, and even to celebrate, the otherness within us that we so often try to repress or hide. . . . Purim is, in this sense, a coming-out party. Purim crosses boundaries, and invites others to do the same. (*The Book of Hiding,* 123–24)

> It [Purim] is a time when the familiar becomes strange and the strange becomes familiar, a time when distinctions between self and other blur, as do the rules for social hierarchy that normally guarantee those distinctions. (*Esther,* x)

While Beal imagines the text powerfully beyond its primal Jewish context into other spheres of deconstruction, the Jewishness of this carnival must be accented. The festival attests to the powerful force of Jewish liturgy and imagination in resisting "the final solution" that the world is always seeking to impose upon Jews.

References: Beal, Timothy K., *The Book of Hiding: Gender, Ethnicity, Annihilation, and Esther* (New York: Routledge, 1997); idem, and Tod Linafelt, *Ruth, Esther* (Berit Olam; Studies in Hebrew Narrative & Poetry; Collegeville, Minn.: The Liturgical Press, 1999); Craig, Kenneth, *Reading Esther: A Case for the Literary Carnivalesque* (Louisville, Ky.: Westminster John Knox Press, 1995).

■ ■ ■

Redemption As is so often the case with biblical theological themes, the theme of "redemption" that looms large in Christian understandings of the Trinity and Christology has its origins in the ordinary practices of daily life. The theme has been used in two quite distinct ways: to redeem and to ransom.

The Hebrew term "redeemer" (*go'el*) refers, in its initial use, to the practice and maintenance of familial obligations. The "redeemer" is a member of the family, perhaps next of kin, who is responsible for protecting the honor of a family member and preserving family property that may be otherwise at risk (see Gen. 38:8). In Deuteronomy 19:4–6, for example, the blood redeemer acts to preserve family honor by retaliating for a death in the family, and in Jeremiah 32:6–15 and in the narrative of Ruth, Jeremiah and Boaz act to protect family property. In the Torah provision for jubilee, moreover, the kinsman must "redeem" the land for the sake of the family. In Deuteronomy 25:5–10, a brother must act to preserve the line and name of his brother. In a patriarchal society in which no resources or support were available for a woman without a husband or a son, the obligation to provide a male protector was of great moment.

The imaginative capacity of theological interpretation in ancient Israel transposed a concrete family practice into an expansive theological image. In that transposition, YHWH is portrayed as the "redeemer" of Israel—the next of kin who acts to preserve Israel's life and protect its future. Thus in Exodus 6:6–7 and 15:13, for example, the exodus event is brought under the metaphor of "redeemer" and YHWH functions to preserve Israel and secure Israel's release from being in hock to Pharaoh. (See Pss. 74:2; 77:15; 78:35; 106:10, all uses congruent with Israel's initial exodus recital.) Because the emancipation from Babylon is characteristically regarded as a "second exodus," that YHWH is again portrayed as Israel's redeemer in the act of transformative deliverance is not surprising (Isa. 41:14; 43:1, 14; 44:6, 22–24; 47:8; and many other uses). Israel construes that event as a transaction whereby Israel is preserved, protected, and returned "home" to well-being.

Israel's more personal rhetoric of faith also appeals to the same imagery. Israel, in need and at risk, petitions YHWH to act in a specific circumstance as redeemer:

Draw near to me, redeem me,
 set me free because of my enemies.
                    (Ps. 69:18; see Pss. 103:4;
                               107:2; 146:9)

Given this practice of piety, particular attention might be paid to Job 19:25, familiarly but erroneously read in Handel's *Messiah.* The "redeemer" in whom Job trusts is not likely God, but rather an unidentified agent in whom Job trusts to maintain Job's reputation against God, even after Job is dead. This usage is curious, but it reminds us that the concept of "redeemer" is not an innocent image, but a pivotal force in times of great risk and crisis.

A different set of images is evoked by a second term, "ransom" (*pdh*), which suggests the purchase of freedom by the payment of a price, or cash transaction. The most stunning case is found in those textual provisions that assume that the firstborn son belongs to God, whether to be bodily sacrificed or offered for a lifetime as a religious functionary. Remarkably, provision is made for a substitute: an animal that takes the place of the firstborn son in a sacrifice (Exod. 13:13–15; 34:20). This exchange is tantamount to a cash transaction and would be available only to those who had the necessary economic provision to pay for a substitute.

What was perhaps a not uncommon commercial transaction is, characteristically, transposed into a theological metaphor. Thus, in Isaiah 43:3–4, YHWH offers other peoples in exchange for Israel, in order to emancipate Israel. In Psalm 44:12, YHWH is chided for having sold Israel into slavery for too cheap a price. As with "redeem," the notion of "ransom" is used in terms of the exodus (Deut. 7:8; 9:26; 13:5; 15:15, 21), and again with reference to the liberation from Babylon (Isa. 50:2; 51:11). As the imagery is used for public "miracles" of YHWH, so also the same term is taken up in Israel's personal prayer (Pss. 31:5; 44:26; 55:18). The prayer of Israel is an anticipation that petition will move YHWH to pay what is required in order to release the petitioner from a restricted and unbearable situation. (The notion of "payment," when no longer taken as a metaphor, has come to cause immense mischief in a Christian understanding of redemption in Christ offered by Anselm in a "satisfaction theory.")

The metaphorical power of the words "redeem" and "ransom" is in each case quite distinct, one related to family obligation, the other to a commercial transaction of substitution. In the imaginative articulation of Israel's traditions of praise, confession, and petition, however, the two terms have coalesced and bear witness in a common voice. Israel's capacity for theological articulation is funded by the prior, nontheological use of the terms. We may believe that the theological uses continue to echo the prior specific nuances in the terms. When transposed into a larger interpretive vista, the terms bear witness to YHWH's capacity and readiness to intervene effectively against powers and circumstances that preclude a good life. Israel attests to such prior interventions by YHWH and continues to count on such like interventions by YHWH in present circumstances and in time to come.

References: Levenson, Jon D., *The Death and Resurrection of the Beloved Son: The Transformation of Child Sacrifice in Judaism and Christianity* (New Haven, Conn.: Yale University Press, 1993); Newsom, Carol A., "The Book of Job: Introduction, Commentary, and Reflections," in *NIB IV* (Nashville: Abingdon Press, 1996), 477–79; Perdue, Leo G. et al., eds., *Families in Ancient Israel* (Louisville, Ky.: Westminster John Knox Press, 1997); Stuhlmueller, Carroll, *Creative Redemption in Deutero-Isaiah* (Analecta Biblica 43; Rome: Biblical Institute Press, 1970); Unterman, J., *From Repentance to Redemption* (JSOTSup 54; Sheffield: Sheffield Academic Press, 1987).

Reform of Hezekiah Hezekiah (ca. 715–687) was one of the most distinguished and celebrated kings in ancient Judah. His reputation turns on (a) his defiant resistance to the Assyrian military threat against Jerusalem (2 Kgs. 18–19; Isa. 36–37; but see 2 Kgs. 18:13–17), and (b) his reform that purged and purified the religious practices of Judah (2 Kgs. 18:4; 2 Chr. 29:1–31:21). Hezekiah is well reported in the annals of the Assyrian kings; however, that account and the biblical narrative do not agree in every detail. For the most part, scholars regard the Assyrian documentation as a serious historical source.

The textual evidence for the Reform of Hezekiah is not without problems. Although only mentioned in Kings, commonly thought to be generally a more reliable historical source than the Chronicler, the reform is given great attention in 2 Chronicles, the historical reliability of which has often been in question [see THE CHRONICLER]. While one cannot be certain, in the case of Hezekiah, current scholarship credits the reliability of the report of the Chronicler and judges that Hezekiah did indeed institute a great reform in Jerusalem at the end of the eighth century, an anticipation of the reform a century later by his great-grandson Josiah (2 Kgs. 22–23) [see REFORM OF JOSIAH]. While the Reform of Josiah has received much more attention from scholars, Hezekiah's earlier effort marks an important point in the political history of Judah and in the history of its religion.

The Chronicler reports on the reform in highly stylized theological rhetoric. Among its primary features are these seven:

1. The Levites figure prominently in the reform and are its primary agents [see HOLINESS]. Commonly perceived as the carriers of Israel's most self-conscious covenantal traditions, the Levites may have played a major role in the constitution of Judaism in the fifth century, when the Chronicler likely wrote (see Neh. 8:7). Thus the reform is said to be grounded in Israel's deepest theological traditions.

2. The temple itself had become a compromised shrine with practices that were judged to be inimical to YHWH, the Lord of the temple (2 Chr. 29:16). (See Ezek. 8 for an extreme case of the later distortion of the temple.) Thus the reform is grounded in what may have been old

rules for holiness that we know from the book of Leviticus.

3. The appeal for reform is particularly expressed in the word "return" that eventually became a keystone for Deuteronomic theology [see DEUTERONOMIC THEOLOGY, REPENTANCE]. This self-conscious use of the term pertains to a deliberate resubmission to the commands of YHWH after a time of indifference and compromise. As in every serious theological reform, this one concerns return to fundamental theological commitments.

4. The focus of reform is a reengagement in covenant (2 Chr. 29:10). Hezekiah appeals to the old Mosaic tradition; the rhetoric of his utterance echoes the cadences of Deuteronomy, the quintessential covenantal document.

5. The Passover, hardly mentioned in the monarchial history, is the great festal occasion for return to and renewal of covenant (2 Chr. 30:1–9; see Deut. 16:1–8; 2 Kgs. 23:21–23). In Passover Judah reclaims its most elemental Yahwistic identity, and, as with Josiah, Hezekiah sets the festival in Jerusalem, thus bringing this defining festival under immediate royal supervision.

6. The reform is an instrument of centralization of worship and consolidation of royal authority. As the temple in Jerusalem had become a venue for compromised worship that is now corrected, so the country and village shrines in Judah were closed and destroyed, regarded as venues for unworthy and unacceptable religious practices [see HIGH PLACE].

7. Running through this narrative account is a recurring polemic against the North. In the fifth century (the likely date of the Chronicler), the recovered establishment of Jerusalem, led by Babylonian Jews who had returned, conducted an endless polemic against Jews in the north who were regarded as "less qualified"

Jews [see SAMARITANS]. The text likely includes some fifth-century polemic, but also reflects the perpetual tension between North and South. Jews in the north (Ephraim, Manasseh, Zebulon) reportedly mocked Hezekiah's summons to Passover in Jerusalem and "only a few . . . came" (2 Chr. 30:10–22; see v. 18). Hezekiah, however, is magnanimous in his readiness to have the recalcitrant Northerners pardoned.

Most important in this rendition is Hezekiah's quite intentional theological rhetoric that echoes Israel's most characteristic covenantal commitments:

> Do not now be stiff-necked as your ancestors were, but yield yourselves to the LORD and come to his sanctuary, which he has sanctified forever, and serve the LORD your God, so that his fierce anger may turn away from you. For as you *return* to the LORD, your kindred and your children will find compassion with their captors, and *return* to this land. For the LORD your God is gracious and merciful, and will not turn away his face from you, if you *return* to him. (2 Chr. 30:8–9 [emphasis added]; see v. 19 and 29:5–11)

This reference is of interest because it evidences the way in which the political process (either remembered from the eighth century or reclaimed in the fifth century) is deeply permeated with theological sensitivity. Hezekiah likely undertook reform for two quite practical reasons. First, such an act is a characteristic exhibit of royal piety in the ancient world, a way whereby the king asserts his theological credentials and enhances his legitimacy. Hezekiah no doubt would have intended and received such approbation (2 Chr. 31:20–21). Second, Hezekiah's entire public career is conditioned by the endless military threat of the Assyrian empire [see ASSYRIA]. From that we

may imagine that the reform and the appeal to the north are in part undertaken as a defiance of Assyria, for Assyria endlessly wanted to crush any independence on the part of Judah. Hezekiah may have been seeking to gain buffer territory toward the north.

Having acknowledged these pragmatic grounds for reform, as we now have the text as scripture, we may read the text as evidencing a stunning theological resolve to redefine the public processes of political life and the practice of political power in covenantal ways. In its present place in the text, the report of reform runs quickly past any pragmatism and celebrates Hezekiah as one whose faith devolved into visible, demanding public policy. The narrative reflects the conviction that the faithful management of religious symbols (temple, Passover) has immediate connections to the prospect of viable public life.

References: Albertz, Rainer, *A History of Israelite Religion in the Old Testament Period*, vol. 1, *From the Beginnings to the End of the Monarchy* (OTL; Louisville, Ky.: Westminster John Knox Press, 1994), 180–86; Moriarty, F. L., "The Chronicler's Account of Hezekiah's Reform," CBQ 17 (1965): 399–406; Myers, Jacob M., "The Kerygma of the Chronicler: History and Theology in the Service of Religion," *Interpretation* 20 (1966): 259–73; Rad, Gerhard von, "The Levitical Sermons in 1 and 2 Chronicles," in idem, *The Problem of the Hexateuch and Other Essays* (New York: McGraw-Hill, 1966), 267–80; Rosenbaum, J., "Hezekiah's Reform and the Deuteronomistic Tradition," HTR 72 (1979): 23–43; Vaughn, Andrew, *Theology, History, and Archaeology in the Chronicler's Account of Hezekiah* (Archaeology and Biblical Studies 4; Atlanta: Scholars Press, 1999).

Reform of Josiah   This phrase refers to the events remembered in 2 Kings 22–23 (see 2 Chr. 34–35), where it is reported that during a royal project for the restoration of the temple in Jerusalem, a scroll was found from which King Josiah instituted a major religious-political reform of the realm. To be sure, citing such a reported event in a survey of theological topics such as this book is a bit unusual. However, this remembered event is the pivotal interpretive mark of the Deuteronomic history, which in turn is perhaps the dominant theological presentation of Old Testament faith. This remembered event is thus crucial in the articulation of faith that became definitional for Jews and for Christians [see DEUTERONOMIC THEOLOGY].

In the ancient Near East, kings regularly engaged in restoration of temples. Royal devotion to the temple was taken to be an expression of great piety. The temple, moreover, was a powerful legitimating symbol for monarchy, so that concern for the temple was characteristically not an innocent act but in at least an indirect way, very self-serving. As noted, 2 Kings 22–23 reports that in 621 B.C.E. royal revenues were deployed to repair the temple, and during those repairs the scroll was found [see HULDAH]. It was immediately recognized as important and read aloud to the king, himself portrayed as a pious, responsive man of faith. When King Josiah heard the scroll, he recognized its serious insistence on Torah obedience. In response, he "tore his clothes" as a sign of penitence and instituted a major reform of public religious practice, which purged the realm of disobedience to Torah and compromise of loyalty to YHWH. Second Kings 23 specifies the reform and reports on the centralization of the Passover festival. To understand the reform, consider the widely shared scholarly consensus that the scroll was in fact some form of the book of Deuteronomy, thus the term "the Deuteronomic Reform." Josiah's effort at reform is thus an effort to conform his realm to the Torah requirements of the book of Deuteronomy, the clearest statement of covenantal theology in the Bible. That tradition includes an offer of covenantal requirements (Torah commandments) and covenantal sanctions (blessings and curses). Josiah's reform is thus a dramatic effort to reshape public life in Israel according to the intention of Torah authorized by Moses and rooted in Sinai.

The following five points in the history of interpretation of this event are important:

1. Nineteenth-century scholarship concluded that the scroll found in the temple was not in fact an old, once-lost scroll, as purported, but a "pious fraud," a deception by well-meaning religionists (perhaps Levites) who had brought the scroll south with them and hid it there after the fall of Samaria and the Northern Kingdom a century earlier. That scholarly judgment, widely held for a long period, denies antiquity for the scroll but does not doubt the theological seriousness or intentionality of the people who perpetrated the "fraud." That is, the "fraud" concerns the historical claim of antiquity while the seriousness of the scroll itself was not doubted.

2. Josiah's years of rule (639–609) occurred during a vacuum in imperial power in the Near East. The long-dominant power of Assyria had waned completely, and Babylon's power was only beginning (see 2 Kgs. 23:28–30). In that vacuum, Josiah could not only reassert the independence of Judah but could also take steps to reincorporate into his realm territories that had long been under Assyrian control, parts of the old kingdom of north Israel. The religious reform thus has more of a political motivation than the text itself suggests.

3. With the rise of sociological criticism in scripture study, reassessing the Reform of Josiah became possible. Claburn and more fully Nakanose have proposed that Josiah's reform was a major monarchial effort at centralization that confiscated the goods and produce of the agrarian society all around the city. Thus, the movement of Passover celebration to Jerusalem symbolized the power of the crown to require that all important actions, and therefore all important financial resources, be centered in the hands of and at the disposal of the crown and the urban elite related to the crown. This view suggests that the "pious fraud" now takes on the very different meaning, of providing a religious facade for what was in fact a calculated, perhaps cynical, financial usurpation by the crown. This perspective alerts us to the fact that biblical texts and the events they report should not be taken innocently or at face value.

4. With the recent rise of "minimalist" historical views, some scholars now suggest that the Reform in fact was not a historical event at all, but a literary creation devised by the Deuteronomists to advance certain ideological claims. This judgment is different from the old notion of "pious fraud," because that older view did not doubt the historicity of the event.

If the reported event is fiction, then we may ask what the intent of the fictional presentation might be. Perhaps after the long recital of wayward kings who violated Torah and thereby placed the public realm at risk of divine judgment (see 2 Kgs. 23:26–27), Josiah is presented in a counterrole, as the one true king who practiced Torah. This literary invention contrasts him to all the other kings (with the possible exception of Hezekiah) and places a good king, a Torah-keeping king, at the end of the history as a counterpoint to the bad kings and as a parallel to Joshua

at the beginning of the history. Thus, at the outset of the Deuteronomic narrative, the Torah is the only requirement for life in the land of promise:

"Only be strong and very courageous, being careful to act in accordance with all the law that my servant Moses commanded you; do not turn from it to the right hand or to the left, so that you may be successful wherever you go. This book of the law shall not depart out of your mouth; you shall meditate on it day and night, so that you may be careful to act in accordance with all that is written in it. For then you shall make your way prosperous, and then you shall be successful." . . . They answered Joshua: "All that you have commanded us we will do, and wherever you send us we will go. Just as we obeyed Moses in all things, so we will obey you. Only may the LORD your God be with you, as he was with Moses!" (Josh. 1:7–8, 16–17)

At the end, it is said of Josiah:

Before him there was no king like him, who turned to the LORD with all his heart, with all his soul, and with all his might, according to all the law of Moses; nor did any like him arise after him. (2 Kgs. 23:25)

These two figures, Joshua and Josiah, thus envelop Torah, so that the entire royal history of Judah and Israel is situated in the overriding claims and ultimate assurance of Torah. In such a deliberate and artful arrangement of texts, the "Still" of 2 Kings 23:26 is all the more stunning, for it is asserted that the disobedience of Torah (especially by Manasseh) would override the gains of the Torah-keepers. The soon-to-be destruction of Jerusalem is thus presented as a result of Torah violation. That the report on Josiah may be fictive gives free rein to such theological interpretation.

5. In any case, the scroll of 2 Kings 22

(matched by the scroll of Jeremiah in Jer. 36) initiates a "scroll movement" in Judah that became a process of canon-making; that movement advanced the notion of Judaism as a "people of the scroll." If this text of the Deuteronomic historian is a product of the exile, then the celebration of the Torah and the anticipation of a literary canon may be understood as an alternative reference point for the faith of Israel in light of the loss of both temple and kingship.

The narrative report of Josiah admits of a variety of historical, literary, theological, and ideological judgments; in the midst of all such judgments, the text stands as a pivot point in the process whereby Judaism emerged out of the memories and interpretations of ancient Israel as a scroll community.

References: Brueggemann, Walter, *1 & 2 Kings* (Smyth & Helwys Bible Commentary; Macon, Ga.: Smyth & Helwys, 2000); Campbell, Antony F., and Mark A. O'Brien, *Unfolding the Deuteronomistic History: Origins, Upgrades, Present Text* (Minneapolis: Fortress Press, 2000); Cazelles, Henri, "Jeremiah and Deuteronomy," in *A Prophet to the Nations: Essays in Jeremiah Studies,* ed. Leo G. Perdue and Brian W. Kovacs (Winona Lake, Ind.: Eisenbrauns, 1984), 89–111; Claburn, W. Eugene, "The Fiscal Basis of Josiah's Reform," *JBL* 92 (1973): 11–22; Lohfink, Norbert, "Die Bundesurkunde des Königs Josias," in idem, *Studien Zum Deuteronomium und zur deuteronomistischen Literatur,* vol. 1 (Stuttgarter biblische Aufsatzbände; Altes Testament 8; Stuttgart: Verlag Katholisches Bibelwerk, 1990), 99–165; Nakanose, Shigeyuki, *Josiah's Passover: Sociology and the Liberating Bible* (Maryknoll, N.Y.: Orbis Books, 1993); Nicholson, E. W., *Preaching to the Exiles: A Study of the Prose Tradition in the Book of Jeremiah* (Oxford: Blackwell, 1970).

Remnant "Remnant" refers to survivors after the catastrophe. The notion occurs occasionally in the Old Testament and is of immense importance even if at the edges of the literature. Whether natural or political-military, such catastrophes are characteristically connected, in the text, to the wrath and judgment of God.

The anticipation of a remnant after disaster is an ominous threat when uttered in the context of well-being and complacency. In such usage, the status quo, under judgment from YHWH, will be severely disrupted. This use of "remnant" means that "*only* a remnant" will survive—not more, not all who are currently alive and well. The most poignant imagery for the remnant is in Amos 3:12, where the remnant of Israel (and its capital city) is likened to the remnant of a sheep ("two legs or a piece of an ear") after the attack of a lion—not much remains (see also Amos 5:3; 9:1–4). In its most severely reduced form, the remnant that will survive is barely recognizable and in no good condition for the future (see 2 Kgs. 21:13–15; Isa. 17:4–6; Jer. 8:3; Ezek. 15:1–8).

The same language, however, can also function as a positive assurance: in spite of the severity of judgment, some will survive because of YHWH's compassion and attentiveness. The destruction will not be total, because God has curbed God's wrath and protected some from the catastrophe. That result of course is good news for those included in the remnant while at the same time *bad news* for all but the remnant. Perhaps the clearest case is that of Noah who, with his family, is a saved remnant from the flood (Gen. 8:15–18; 9:8–17). In Isaiah 54:9, moreover, the poet likens exile in the sixth century to the flood, so that a remnant of displaced Jews will be protected from that disaster of exile as was Noah in the flood.

The negative judgment and the positive assurance as dimensions of the notion of remnant attest to both the provisional, precarious quality of life in the world and the great extent to which life in the world depends upon God's disposition for good or for ill. "Remnant" is a way of speaking about both the judgment and the mercy of YHWH, who finally will determine the future of all of God's people.

The notion of remnant thus is an intensely theological one, for it places the future of God's people securely in God's governance. The term also has sociological-ideological force. The small group of returnees from exile in the sixth and fifth centuries understood themselves as the beloved, spared remnant of God who are thereby the sole legitimate carriers of the old traditions of Israel (see Hag. 1:12–14; 2:2; Zech. 8:6–12). In some later texts of Isaiah (1:25–26, 4:2–4) as well as the Ezra tradition (Ezra 9:8–15), the remnant is a way of self-understanding and self-differentiation for a quite particular community. This community knows itself to be under mandate to live a life of purity and obedience in response to the commands of Torah. These people are the ones who emerge in later piety as "righteous," who live by God's mercy and respond in glad obedience. The implied counterpoint is that people who do not share in such purity and obedience and who do not submit to the defining authority of this particular community are not of the saved remnant and have no share in Israel. Remnant can thus be turned ideologically into a principle of exclusion (see Isa. 56:3–7; see also 2 Kgs. 21:14 for an even more negative usage).

References: Campbell, J. C., "God's People and the Remnant," *Scottish Journal of Theology* 3 (1950): 78–85; Hasel, George, *The Remnant* (Berrien Springs, Mich.: Andrews University Press, 1974).

Repentance   The context of repentance is Israel's covenantal relationship with YHWH whereby Israel is bound in obedience to YHWH's Torah. Israel knows very well that the Torah requirements of covenant with YHWH can and may be fully obeyed. Of course, Israel also knows that Torah obedience is not fully kept, and therefore restoration in light of violated Torah is a major issue in covenantal faith.

Because the covenant is bilateral, that restoration to covenant may entail initiatives by both parties is not surprising. God's readiness to restore the covenant that Israel has broken is readily attested and takes two forms. God makes restored relationship possible by providing and authorizing a cultic apparatus of sacrifices whereby Israel may be forgiven and reconciled (see ATONEMENT); alternatively, YHWH may, by divine decree, simply assert forgiveness and restoration. Such actions include a "turning" on the part of YHWH, for which the usual verb is *nḥm*. That is, YHWH reverses field, ends anger and judgment, and reembraces Israel.

Restoring covenant, however, characteristically is not a one-sided effort on God's part; restoration requires Israel's full and intentional engagement. Israel's return to covenantal relations with YHWH comes through repentance. A certain symmetry exists in Israel's traditions. The priestly traditions focus on the cultic mechanisms that God gives as means of reconciliation, while the Deuteronomic tradition makes the most of repentance. The key term for repentance is *šûb*, to "turn," an image of walking on the way—the way of life, the way of Torah—which is a life of obedience. Sin is the violation of that way, and therefore repentance is to reverse course and resume one's walk on the way of Torah obedience (as in Ps. 1:6). Repentance is thus a deliberate act, a decision that involves a sustained, long-term resolve to act differently, according to YHWH's will and way as known in the Torah.

The tradition of Deuteronomy is very old, but its accent on turning seems particularly situated in the exile. Deuteronomic theology held that the displacement of exile happened because Israel had disobeyed Torah. For that reason, reversal of course in exile is the way out of exile, which is particularly evident in three texts from that tradition:

> When all these things have happened to you, the blessings and the curses that I have set before you, if you call them to mind among all the nations where the LORD your God has driven you, and *return* to the LORD your God, and you and your children obey him with all your heart and with all your soul, just as I am commanding you today, then the LORD your God will restore your fortunes and be compassionate on you, gathering you again from all the peoples among whom the LORD your God has scattered you. (Deut. 30:1–3, emphasis added; see Deut. 4:29–31; 1 Kgs. 8:31–53)

The same accent is evident in the tradition of Jeremiah, which is heavily impacted by and intimately connected to Deuteronomy. The final form of the book of Jeremiah is witness to the destruction of Jerusalem and the deportation to Babylon of leading members of Jerusalem society. Jeremiah is preoccupied with the question of the return of deported Jews to Jerusalem and the return of obedient Judaism to covenant with God. What is treated as a geographical problem of exile and homecoming is at the same time a theological issue of violation of covenant and restoration to covenant that only repentance and return to Torah obedience can accomplish.

A prime example of this accent in Jeremiah is in the extended poem of Jeremiah 3–4:

> *Return*, faithless Israel,
> says the LORD.

> I will not look on you in anger,
>   for I am merciful,
>   says the LORD
> . . . .
> *Return*, O faithless children,
>   says the LORD
> . . . .
> *Return*, O faithless children,
>   I will heal your faithlessness
> . . . .
> If you *return*, O Israel,
>   says the LORD,
>   if you *return* to me,
> if you remove your abominations from my
>   presence,
>   and do not waver,
> and if you swear, "As the LORD lives!"
>   in truth, in justice, and in uprightness,
> then nations shall be blessed by him.
>   and by him they shall boast.
> (Jer. 3:12, 14, 22; 4:1–2, emphasis added)

The final lines of this poem indicate the concrete substance of repentance that is entailed in restoration to covenant. The anticipation, moreover, is that such a return to Torah is likely to involve only a particular part of the community, that is, a remnant passionate enough about Torah faith that the remnant is willing to undertake the disciplines of obedience. Such a remnant is suggested in the notion of "good figs" who will be returned to the land and to the covenant:

> Like these good figs, so I will regard as good the exiles from Judah, whom I have sent away from this place to the land of the Chaldeans. I will set my eyes upon them for good, and I will bring them back to this land. I will build them up, and not tear them down; I will plant them, and not pluck them up. I will give them a heart to know that I am the LORD; and they shall be my people and I will be their God, for they shall *return* to me with their whole heart. (Jer. 24:5–7, emphasis added)

This remnant no doubt became the carriers of what emerged as a dominant strand of Judaism. The same notion of a faithful remnant is reflected in the penitential prayers of Nehemiah 9 and Ezra 9:

And you warned them in order to *turn them back* to your law. Yet they acted presumptuously and did not obey your commandments, but sinned against your ordinances, by the observance of which a person shall live. They turned a stubborn shoulder and stiffened their neck and would not obey. Many years you were patient with them, and warned them by your spirit through your prophets; yet they would not listen. Therefore you handed them over to the peoples of the lands. Nevertheless, in your great mercies you did not make an end of them or forsake them, for you are a gracious and merciful God. (Neh. 9:29–31, emphasis added; see Ezra 9:15)

The same accent is also voiced in other prophetic traditions that constitute responses to the crisis of exile:

For I have no pleasure in the death of anyone, says the Lord GOD. *Turn*, then, and live. (Ezek. 18:32, emphasis added)

Seek the LORD while he may be found,
    call upon him while he is near;
let the wicked forsake their way,
    and the unrighteous their thoughts;
let them *return* to the LORD, that he may
    have mercy on them,
and to our God, for he will
    abundantly pardon.
            (Isa. 55:6–7, emphasis added)

While it is a motif appropriate everywhere in a covenantal faith, repentance became a decisive theme in response to the exile. As a result, repentance became a leading motif of Judaism as it was organized after the exile, a community of faith attentive to Torah obedience on which the faithful would "meditate day and night" (Ps. 1:2).

A counterpoint to this theme is the occasional acknowledgment that God may also "repent," that is, change mind. In the uses related to YHWH, a different Hebrew term is used, *nḥm*, which has a somewhat different connotation. That motif allows God to take into account the changed stance of Israel or of any other creature bound to God in obedience. As pertains to Israel, Jeremiah asserts:

. . . but if that nation, concerning which I have spoken, *turns* from its evil, I will *change my mind* about the disaster that I intend to bring on it. . . . (Jer. 18:8, emphasis added; see also Gen. 6:6)

Beyond Israel, YHWH's new response to the people of Nineveh is one of repentance:

When God saw what they did, how they *turned* from their evil ways, God *changed his mind* about the calamity that he had said he would bring upon them; and he did not do it. (Jonah 3:10, emphasis added)

The response of God, in these cases, indicates a readiness to resume a relationship of mutual fidelity. That readiness, however, depends upon an intentionality and gesture of good faith on the part of God's partner. Israel's faith tradition understood that a serious relation with God, for all of God's generous sovereignty, eventually must be seriously embraced by God's partner. (On the important evidence of God's readiness and capacity to forgive without such repentance, see FORGIVENESS.) In this context, the Christian tradition understands that Jesus' initial public utterance makes the same accent:

"[R]epent, and believe in the good news." (Mark 1:15)

In this utterance that initiates his ministry, Jesus stands fully within the tradition of repentance in the Old Testament, and echoes that imperative with an urgency parallel to that of Israel's tradition.

References: Fretheim, Terence E., *The Suffering of God: An Old Testament Perspective* (OBT; Philadelphia: Fortress Press, 1984); Heschel, Abraham, *The Prophets* (New York: Harper and Row, 1962); Holladay, William L., *The Root SUBH in the Old Testament with Particular Reference to Its Usage in Covenantal Contexts* (Leiden: E. J. Brill, 1958); Hunter, A. Vanlier, *A Study of the Meaning and Function of the Exhortations in Amos, Hosea, Isaiah, Micah, and Zephaniah* (Dissertation, St. Mary's Seminary and University, Baltimore, 1982); Raitt, Thomas M., *A Theology of Exile: Judgment/Deliverance in Jeremiah and Ezekiel* (Philadelphia: Fortress Press, 1977); Unterman, Jeremiah, *From Repentance to Redemption* (Sheffield: Sheffield Academic Press, 1987.

Resurrection Only three clear attestations to the resurrection of the dead appear in the Old Testament (Isa. 25:6–10a; 26:19; Dan. 12:2; other texts that merit attention include Deut. 32:39; 1 Sam. 2:6; 1 Kgs. 17:17–24; 2 Kgs. 4:31–37; Hos. 6:1–3; Pss. 49:16; 73:24. Mitchell Dahood [xli–lii] almost alone among scholars has found much more evidence for such belief in the Psalms, but other interpreters have not followed him). These three references, moreover, are quite late in the formation of the Old Testament, seemingly falling at the edge of Israel's faith and occurring in texts commonly assigned to apocalyptic literature. They are statements of vigorous hope that, in God's own future, God will overcome the power of death:

> . . . he will swallow up death forever.
> Then the Lord GOD will wipe away the
>   tears from all faces.
>   (Isa. 25:7–8)

> Your dead shall live, their corpses shall
>   rise.

> O dwellers in the dust, awake and sing
>   for joy!
>   (Isa. 26:19)

Only in Daniel 12:2 is the notion of resurrection closely linked to judgment—that is, to punishment and blessing:

> Many of those who sleep in the dust of the earth shall awake, some to everlasting life, and some to shame and everlasting contempt.

These uses together suggest that the resurrection of the dead is an affirmation of faith that did not preoccupy early formulations of faith in Israel. In later developments, however, such a hope was expressed in order to assert the full sovereignty of God over all that is and all that will be. God's governance, moreover, is concerned with a final judgment. Israel has a deep conviction that God's sovereignty is morally concerned and takes moral criteria seriously in meting out the deserts of a new, full governance. Indeed, given the God of the Torah, a future life is inescapably concerned with God's response to obedience and disobedience, a concern as old as covenantal blessings and curses.

Perhaps resurrection (as a subset of apocalyptic thought) entered Israel's theological repertoire only later, as a result of non-Israelite influence. Already extant in Israel, though, were antecedent utterances and convictions that made resurrection faith an unsurprising extrapolation from what Israel characteristically believed. We may note three such antecedents:

1. Israel took over older Canaanite myths in which the "God of Life" (in Canaan, Baal; in Israel, YHWH) defeated the God of death, Mot [see DEATH]. This idea of combat against and victory over the power of death is evident in the taunt

of Hosea 13:14 (echoed in 1 Cor. 15:54–55) and voiced in the hope of Isaiah 25:6–10a.

2. Israel's most characteristic "prayer of lament" regularly moves from defeat to victory and celebration, from plea to praise. That movement signifies a conviction in Israel that YHWH has the power to defeat every negation. Israel has always known that God could defeat every negation of life. Thus the step from the defining structure of lament-to-praise (as in Ps. 30:11) to assert that YHWH can defeat "the final threat" is not a large step at all. The structure of the lament psalm from plea-to-praise provides the structure for death and resurrection, both word pairs revolving around YHWH's sovereignty over the powers of negation.

3. The experience and interpretation of ancient Israel understood exile as the nadir of life in abandonment and without God in the world. The hope that God will restore Israel from exile (voiced in Jeremiah, Ezekiel, and Isaiah) provides the format and rhetoric for resurrection of the dead; exile constitutes a deathlike disruption in Israel's life, a linkage made explicit in Ezekiel 37:1–14. An important antecedent to this text is Hosea 6:1–3, a text that was important for Christian antecedents of resurrection "on the third day."

From these various antecedents, which are definitional for Israel's faith, resurrection becomes an extreme and late articulation of the conviction shared everywhere in Israel that YHWH can govern all that threatens life in God's creation. Resurrection thus belongs to a wider order of God's power that includes, for Israel, creation from chaos, restoration from exile, forgiveness of guilt, birth from barrenness, and deliverance from slavery.

By the time of the New Testament, resurrection of the dead had become a com-pletely available conviction among Jews (see Mark 12:18–27). Most unfortunately, though, in modern uncritical Christian thought, resurrection has become a rather trivial, feel-good belief about "seeing one's loved ones again." A biblical sense of the resurrection of the dead is focused, in contrast to popular notions, on the sure power and fidelity of God in the face of every negation, including the ultimate negation of death. Trivialization of that conviction is an enormous temptation in an acculturated, comfortable church that seeks to rationalize faith so as not to disrupt anything "natural." In the end, nothing is "natural" about God's defeat of the power of death. That confident anticipation of victory is not "natural," but is welcomed by Israel in its conviction about God's sure rule over the future.

References: Barr, James, *The Garden of Eden and the Hope of Immortality* (Minneapolis: Fortress Press, 1992); Collins, John, "The Root of Immortality: Death in the Context of Jewish Wisdom," *Harvard Theological Review* 71 (1978): 177–92; Dahood, Mitchell, *Psalms III 101–150* (AB 17A; Garden City, N.Y.: Doubleday, 1970); Martin-Achard, R., *From Death to Life: A Study of the Development of the Doctrine of the Resurrection in the Old Testament* (Edinburgh: J. P. Smith, 1960); Schmidt, Werner H., *The Faith of the Old Testament: A History* (Philadelphia: Westminster Press, 1983), 268–77.

Retribution   The theological notion of retribution is the assumption or conviction that the world is ordered by God so that everyone receives a fair outcome of reward or punishment commensurate with his or her conduct. God is the guarantor of a moral calculus inherent in the world, so that "good people" (the obedient) prosper and "bad people" (the disobedient) suffer. Such an assumption functions to assure that (a) the world is morally coherent, (b) human conduct matters ultimately to the future of the world, and (c) human life is not lived amidst moral chaos. The reliable ordering of the world thus is taken to be essential to a certain moral-ethical perspective.

This general conviction is pervasive in Old Testament faith. One can distinguish between two systems of rhetoric (and therefore different articulations of faith) that bring this conviction to expression. A "hot" notion of retribution, found particularly in Deuteronomy and in the prophets, provides that God notices and responds to human conduct, often in anger because disobedience affronts God's own will and reputation, for which the flood narrative of Genesis 6–9 is a dramatic example:

> On the day I punish Israel for its
>   transgressions,
>   I will punish the altars of Bethel,
> and the horns of the altar shall be cut off
>   and fall to the ground.
> I will tear down the winter house as well
>   as the summer house;
>   and the houses of ivory shall perish,
> and the great houses shall come to an end,
>   says the LORD.
>   (Amos 3:14–15)

> Alas for those who devise wickedness
>   and evil deeds on their beds! . . .
> They covet fields, and seize them;
>   houses, and take them away;
> they oppress householder and house,
>   people and their inheritance.
> Therefore thus says the LORD:
> Now, I am devising against this family an
>   evil
>   from which you cannot remove your
>   necks;
> and you shall not walk haughtily,
>   for it will be an evil time.
>   (Mic. 2:1–3; see Deut. 30:15–20)

The decisive mark of this rhetoric is that YHWH is an active agent whose interven-

tion is evoked by obedience or disobedience and who personally oversees rewards and punishments. The entire system of rhetoric depends on the active agency of YHWH, who is the subject of the active verbs. See the same rhetoric more fully in the curse recitals of Leviticus 26:14–39 and Deuteronomy 28:15–68.

A second, "cool," very different pattern of rhetoric is also evident in the Old Testament, especially in the wisdom teaching of the book of Proverbs. This pattern is so different that Koch has insisted it is not really "retribution," but simply a system in which deeds have inherent in them the consequences that are sure to come from the act. The connection of deed and consequence is a part of the ordered reality of creation, which to the faith of Israel depends on and derives from the creator's watchful reliability. In this rhetorical pattern, no agent of reward or punishment appears, nor is pleasure, anger, or moral outrage articulated—only the inescapable outcome of the act itself.

These two systems of moral coherence— *act-reward or punishment* and *deed-consequence*—while very different rhetorically are essential equivalents that in different articulations perform the three functions noted above. To be sure, the different patterns of rhetoric make a great difference. The second system of deeds-consequences is likely more credible in a scientific era than is the hot claim of agency. Both ways of speaking, however, testify to the intractable linkage of act and outcome.

The two patterns of rhetoric together surely constitute the baseline of Old Testament ethics, the first set in the context of covenant and the second appealing to the reality of creation. As important as these claims are, however, they are not unproblematic. Ample evidence emerges in lived experience, well reflected in the text of the

Old Testament, that life is not lived according to these neat formulae; in fact, the disobedient often prosper and the obedient often suffer. Any claim for retribution inescapably leads to a crisis of theodicy, whereby lived experience contradicts neat explanatory systems. The crisis of theodicy is precisely voiced in the drama of Job, whereby an obedient man suffers deeply (see Job 31). The same problem occurs positively, whenever anyone prospers and declares in astonishment, "I do not deserve it," a registration of blessing beyond merit.

The Old Testament acknowledges this problem in the several texts that take up the issue of theodicy [see THEODICY]. With reference to the book of Proverbs (against which the book of Job protests), attention should be paid to the insight of von Rad. He recognizes that wisdom teaching assumes an unbreakable connection of deed and consequence, but he also observes (98–101) that a series of texts in the book of Proverbs readily acknowledges that the definitive claims and assumptions of wisdom concerning order are not adequate:

> The human mind plans the way,
>   but the LORD directs the steps.
> (Prov. 16:9; see 16:1, 2;
>   19:14, 21; 20:24; 21:30–31)

The wisdom teachers give no hint of how this awareness is reconciled with the more familiar teaching of commensurability. Nonetheless, the inclusion of these proverbs just cited indicates that the teachers recognized the complexity of the issue and refused simplistic closure to the question. The poem of Job may be precisely a meditation on this inscrutable contradiction that the wisdom teachers spelled out, which made every easy didactic conclusion, if not suspect, at least penultimate.

The issue of retribution (and its complexity in leading to issues of theodicy) is an especially urgent one in concrete practice:

1. In the Old Testament itself, the exile in the sixth century was powerfully interpreted—in 1 and 2 Kings and in some of the prophets—in terms of retribution. Jerusalem was destroyed and Israel was exiled as divine punishment for a long history of disobedience to YHWH: that statement is likely the normative comment in the Old Testament on the subject. As is evident, though, in Lamentations 3:40–57, the poetry moves from guilty perpetrator to innocent victim. Over time, any simplistic moral explanation of the crisis of the sixth century had to be opened to greater complexity and consequently less certainty.

2. A strong notion of retribution is only the baseline of Old Testament faith, which is open, as suggested here, to great variation and complexity. The uninformed Christian stereotype of the Old Testament (and of Jewish tradition more generally), however, has failed to notice the complexity present in the interpretive process. As a result, Christians who have not read the Old Testament often caricature it as offering a "God of wrath"—that is, an agent who eagerly presides over a closed system of merit. Such a misreading fails to recognize the practical awareness of the text that the complexity of experience overcomes simple explanation. The forceful affirmation of forgiveness in the Old Testament, and particularly in the exilic traditions, precludes any ill-informed Christian misinterpretation [see FORGIVENESS].

3. The notion of a tight system of retribution has been particularly important (and damaging) in understanding the Jewish Holocaust, as Rubenstein has seen from early on. Such a theory easily con-

cluded that the Holocaust punished the Jews for their waywardness. Any critical reflection must conclude that the Holocaust cannot be contained in any such theory. One must reckon at least with the demonic power of human evil; beyond that, one must notice the inscrutable reality in an event that defies every attempt at explanation.

While some notion of retribution is crucial for the ethical passion of the Old Testament, the reality of human life, the recognition of the fragility of human life, and the complexity of lived reality taken together require a serious critique of any simple theory of retribution. The ambiguity and complexity of lived reality admit of no such easy reading. The misery and splendor of human life fit no simplistic explanation, and therefore the Old Testament itself must endlessly revise any clean moral calculus that the text may prefer.

References: Brueggemann, Walter, *Old Testament Theology: Essays on Structure, Theme, and Text* (Minneapolis: Fortress Press, 1992), 1–44; Koch, Klaus, "Is There a Doctrine of Retribution in the Old Testament?" in *Theodicy in the Old Testament,* ed. James L. Crenshaw (Philadelphia: Fortress Press, 1983), 57–87; Miller, Patrick D., Jr., *Sin and Judgment in the Prophets: A Stylistic and Theological Analysis* (Chico, Calif.: Scholars Press, 1982); Rad, Gerhard von, *Wisdom in Israel* (Nashville: Abingdon Press, 1972); Rubenstein, Richard E., *After Auschwitz: History, Theology, and Contemporary Judaism,* 2d ed. (Baltimore: Johns Hopkins University Press, 1992).

Righteousness Righteousness, a key theological motif in the Old Testament, covers a broad range of meanings and pertains both to God's character and to human conduct. For purposes of theological interpretation, understanding righteousness in the context of covenant,

wherein every covenant member is obligated to "love God" and "love neighbor," is a useful approach.

Most importantly, righteousness is an ethical term used to mark people who live generatively in the community in order to sustain and enhance the community's well-being. The "righteous person" is characteristically one who invests in the community, showing special attentiveness to the poor and the needy. Such a communitarian ethic is variously sketched out in Psalms 15, 24, and 37, and Job 31. Characterizing the righteous, Psalm 112 declares:

> They rise in the darkness as a light for the
>   upright;
>   they are gracious, merciful, and
>   righteous.
> It is well with those who deal generously
>   and lend,
>   who conduct their affairs with justice.
> For the righteous will never be moved;
>   they will be remembered forever.
> They are not afraid of evil tidings;
>   their hearts are firm, secure in the
>   LORD.
> Their hearts are steady, they will not be
>   afraid;
>   in the end they will look in triumph on
>   their foes.
> They have distributed freely, they have
>   given to the poor;
>   their righteousness endures forever. . . .
>   (vv. 4–9)

People who regularly enact a communal ethic are those who are not greedy or self-sufficient, but who generously care for the neighborhood and are firm in devotion to YHWH.

"Righteousness" is regularly used in Proverbs to mark people who live with integrity and gravitas, who by their presence and their actions lend stability to the community (Prov. 10:2, 7, 11; 11:5, 6, 8, 10).

The prophets use the term specifically concerning the care of the poor, so that it has an economic component, but more generally "righteousness" refers to taking responsibility for the community (Isa. 5:7; Amos 5:7, 24; 6:12; Hos. 10:12). As Schmid has shown, the largest scope of righteousness concerns the good ordering of creation by the creator who wills life and well-being, so that to live responsibly is to conform to the limits and requirements that the creator ordained. Thus, righteousness becomes the primary mark of the coming rule of God (Isa. 9:7; 51:7; 60:17; 61:10–11; Jer. 4:2; 23:5; 33:15).

The antitheses of the righteous are the wicked, who are regularly characterized as selfish, greedy, and eventually destructive, because they do not care for the poor:

Like a cage full of birds,
    their houses are full of treachery;
therefore they have become great and rich,
    they have grown fat and sleek.
They know no limits in deeds of
    wickedness;
    they do not judge with justice
the cause of the orphan, to make it
    prosper,
    and they do not defend the rights of the
        needy.

(Jer. 5:27–28)

Psalm 10 moreover makes clear that a rapacious attitude toward the neighbor is intimately connected to a disregard for the character and governance of YHWH:

For the wicked boast of the desires of their
    heart,
    those greedy for gain curse and
        renounce the LORD.
In the pride of their countenance the
    wicked say, "God will not seek it
    out";
    all their thoughts are, "There is no
        God."

. . . .

Their eyes stealthily watch for the helpless;
    they lurk in secret like a lion in its covert;
they lurk that they may seize the poor;
    they seize the poor and drag them off
        in their net.
They stoop, they crouch,
    and the helpless fall by their might.
They think in their heart, "God has
        forgotten,
    he has hidden his face, he will never
        see it."

(vv. 3–4, 8b–11)

Every part of the Old Testament is insistent upon a covenantal, communitarian ethic that is rooted in the intention of the covenant-making God, who is the one who has ordered creation for communal well-being. The righteous are thus those people who guarantee life, and the wicked are those who bring the power of death into the community.

An ethical insistence on this, however, requires sanctions and enforcement, and for that reason the ethical term is at the same time a juridical term. In the covenantal imagination of Israel, every member of the community is held accountable for the enhancement or the diminishment of the community. The terms "righteous" and "wicked" are thus also translated as "innocent" (the ones who can justify their conduct) and "guilty" (the ones who have violated the ethic of the community and who merit punishment). This notion of accountability is evident in Psalm 1, which speaks of "the way of the wicked" (= characteristic conduct) who will "perish" and "the way of the righteous" (= characteristic conduct) who will prosper. The phrases "stand in the judgment" and "congregation of the righteous" probably came from court life (v. 5). When this language is taken up as theological-ethical language, the arena of adjudication is likely the cult, where the "righteous-innocent" and the "wicked-guilty" are sorted out according to communal norms of conduct that are taken to be the will of YHWH. Worship then becomes an arena where questions of righteousness are faced. This practice is evident, for example, in Psalms 15 and 24, where admission to worship is determined by adherence to the communal norms of Torah.

The juridical process in the cult finally appeals to YHWH, who is said to be a righteous God—one who gives reliable, fair judgment concerning obedience or disobedience of Torah. Indeed, the righteous judge is the creator who guarantees that the world (creation) operates in a reliable, ethically coherent fashion (see Gen. 18:25). This righteous judge can be counted on as the one

> who is not partial and takes no bribe, who executes justice for the orphan and the widow, and who loves the strangers, providing them food and clothing. (Deut. 10:17–18)

That YHWH is righteous toward orphans and widows means that this judge cannot be bought off by power, money, or influence.

At a minimum, YHWH is the guarantor of equitable judgment. Beyond that, however, YHWH is known as the one who actively intervenes to restore well-being; such active interventions are said to be "acts of righteousness," on which see Judges 5:11 ("triumphs"), 1 Samuel 12:7 ("saving deeds"), and Micah 6:5 ("saving acts"). All of these phrases render the Hebrew "righteousnesses" (plural), so that the entire history of miracles that constitutes the faith of Israel is taken as examples of YHWH's active interventions designed to restore to well-being creation and the covenantal community. In this usage, the term "righteous" runs beyond any popular notion of the "moral" and

opens to YHWH's marvelous saving power, so that YHWH's righteousness is constituted by YHWH's delivering salvation.

YHWH is taken to be the full embodiment of righteousness that makes life in the world possible, but two protests against YHWH's righteousness emerge. In Jeremiah 12:1–4, the prophet appeals to the righteousness of YHWH, perhaps in a sarcastic tone, in order to question whether YHWH does in fact act to guarantee justice and equity. The protest is actually a deep doubt that hovers around the edges of Israel's faith. In quite a different way, as one who affirms YHWH's predisposition toward generosity, Jonah is profoundly upset that it should extend to Israel's despised enemy, Assyria (Jonah 4:1–2). YHWH's righteousness may be doubted or the subject of disapproval. The elemental claim of YHWH's righteousness becomes the premise from which Israel may articulate a range of concerns that run from celebrative doxology to offended protest to righteous indignation. Through it all, YHWH is said to be steadfastly resolved to uphold the world in well-being.

YHWH's righteousness moves beyond a simple guarantee of equity to an active interventionism on behalf of well-being. One form of that interventionism is judicial: this notion of righteousness—the judicial capacity to declare as innocent those who are guilty, to justify the unjustifiable by decree—is the ground of a Christian understanding of grace (see Luke 18:14; Rom. 3:24; Titus 3:7). Genesis 15:6, reiterated in Galatians 3:6, became a primary text for this claim, and that inclination on YHWH's part to "justify" by forgiveness is powerfully attested in the Old Testament (see for example Pss. 103:8–14; 130:3–4). Thus the taproot of what became a key theological claim of

Christian faith, especially accented in Reformation teaching, is decisively present in ancient Israel's glad celebration of YHWH's generous adjudication on behalf of covenant partners.

References: Knierim, Rolf P., *The Task of Old Testament Theology: Method and Cases* (Grand Rapids: Eerdmans, 1995); Rad, Gerhard von, "'Righteousness' and 'Life' in the Cultic Language of the Psalms," in *The Problem of the Hexateuch and Other Essays* (New York: McGraw-Hill, 1966), 243–66; Schmid, H. H., "Creation, Righteousness, and Salvation: 'Creation Theology' as the Broad Horizon of Biblical Theology," in *Creation in the Old Testament*, ed. Bernhard W. Anderson (Philadelphia: Fortress Press, 1984), 102–17; Stuhlmacher, Peter, *Reconciliation, Law, and Righteousness: Essays in Biblical Theology* (Philadelphia: Fortress Press, 1986).

■ ■ ■

Sabbath   The root meaning of the term "Sabbath" is to "desist or stop." The seventh day, in the faith of Israel, was a day to stop productive work and normal activities. The observance of the seventh day likely has antecedents in Near Eastern culture and only late became definitive for the faith of Israel. Nonetheless, in the final form of the text of the Old Testament, Sabbath has become a defining mark of Jewish faith—a visible, regular discipline that distinguishes members of that faith community from the general culture in which it lives.

The Sabbath, according to the commands of Exodus 20:8–11 and Deuteronomy 5:12–15, has two quite distinct theological groundings. In the Exodus version, the Sabbath is authorized by the memory that on the seventh day of creation, God rested from the work of creation (Gen. 2:1–4a). Cessation and rest are thus grounded in the very structure of cre-

ation as ordered and blessed by YHWH. This same tradition of interpretation is likely the ground of Exodus 16:27–30 and Exodus 31:12–17. In Exodus 16, the Sabbath is observed in order to acknowledge that the sustaining gifts and presence of the creator are operative even in the wilderness that seemed beyond God's blessing of life. In Exodus 31, the Sabbath is the culmination of tabernacle construction in Exodus 25–31, thus a parallel to the Sabbath as the culmination of the creation in Genesis 2:1–4a. All three texts ground the Sabbath in God's ordering of the world for life.

A second, very different grounding for Sabbath is given in Deuteronomy 5, where the Sabbath rest of YHWH is contrasted to the demand for production on the part of Pharaoh. That is, exodus emancipation from the production quotas of Pharaoh is the warrant for the community of Israel also to act differently by Sabbath keeping as a refusal to give one's life over to productivity.

The defining character of Sabbath for faith is made clear in two other texts. In Amos 8:4–6, the prophet chides those in the commercial class for impatiently wanting to escape the Sabbath so that they can return to the exploitative practices that they have made inherent in commercial transactions. In a later text concerning the inclusiveness of emerging Judaism, Isaiah 56:3–7 astonishingly names Sabbath observance as one of two necessary conditions for admittance to the community. In this usage, everything is at stake in the Sabbath practice of a regular, disciplined, visible cessation of production.

The definitive character of this observance may be understood in two related ways. First, the festival of the Sabbath pertains to economic matters. The day is one of work stoppage:

[Y]ou shall not do any work—you, or your son or your daughter, or your male or female slave, or your ox or your donkey, or any of your livestock, or the resident alien in your towns, so that your male and female slave may rest as well as you. (Deut. 5:14)

Read in the context of exodus memory, the observance is an act of resistance against having one's life defined by one's productivity. More to life exists than the production that is the insatiable requirement in Pharaoh's realm. Second, as Tsevat has noted, the observance is a theological act. Sabbath is not merely rest from work, but a day to renounce autonomy and self-sufficiency:

Every seventh day the Israelite renounces his autonomy and affirms God's dominion over him. . . . In other words, God's dominion over space and His dominion over time are largely two aspects of the same thing: His dominion over man and especially over Israel. There is, therefore, nothing incongruous nor bold in the conclusion that every seventh day the Israelite is to renounce dominion over time, thereby renounce autonomy, and recognize God's dominion over time and thus over himself. Keeping the sabbath is acceptance of the sovereignty of God. (48–49)

The Sabbath day is thus a visible assertion of Israel's most elemental claim of having given life over to YHWH's will and purpose, and a renunciation of any will or purpose that conflicts with that holy vocation. The economic and theological dimensions of the observance are intimately connected to each other.

For good reason, great energy is currently invested in recovering the Sabbath in the contemporary world. In a consumer economy that is committed to endless growth and reducing everything to commodity, the competent can easily imagine that they are self-made, self-sufficient, and self-actualized, with no reference point beyond themselves. Thus, the old pressure to curb work (production) and to acknowledge that we do not produce our lives may now be matched by curbing consumption, the acknowledgment that life has not been handed over to us for our devouring. The contemporary capacity to redefine human society in terms of production and consumption, moreover, is reinforced by the expansive technology that seems to bring more and more of life under human control.

The social costs of recharacterizing human society in this manner are immense. Life comes to consist of an insatiable pursuit of goods, with prizes awarded to the most productive, while the less productive and the unproductive are treated to a casual kind of triage. Living is reduced to competing for endless goods, and neighborliness is completely scuttled; the prevailing attitude seems to be "without God everything is possible."

Sabbath provides a visible testimony that God is at the center of life—that production and consumption take place in a world ordered, blessed, and restrained by the God of all creation. Reordering social time around Sabbath is a visible declaration that all times are in God's hands and that human management of the forces of production and consumption is penultimate at best, limited by the love of God, who commands love of neighbor.

In Christian practice, the Sabbath day has been transposed from Saturday to Sunday in order to center the day as an Easter festival. Given that change, however, the significance, giftedness, and obligations of the Old Testament Sabbath continue to pertain to Christian practice.

References: Brueggemann, Walter, *Finally Comes the Poet: Daring Speech for Proclamation* (Minneapolis: Fortress Press, 1989), chap. 4;

Dawn, Marva J., *Keeping the Sabbath Wholly: Ceasing, Resting, Embracing, Feasting* (Grand Rapids: Eerdmans, 1989); Heschel, Abraham Joshua, *The Sabbath: Its Meaning for Modern Man* (New York: Farrar, Straus & Giroux, 1951); Lowery, Richard H., *Sabbath and Jubilee* (St. Louis: Chalice Press, 2000); Miller, Patrick D., "The Human Sabbath: A Study in Deuteronomic Theology," *The Princeton Seminary Bulletin* 6 (1985): 81–97; Peli, Pinchas H., *The Jewish Sabbath: A Renewed Encounter* (New York: Schocken Books, 1988); Plaut, W. Gunther, "The Sabbath as Protest: Thoughts on Work and Leisure in the Automated Society," in *Tradition and Change in Jewish Experience*, ed. A. Leland Jameson (Syracuse, N.Y.: Syracuse University Press, 1978), 169–83; Tsevat, Matitiahu, "The Basic Meaning of the Biblical Sabbath," in *The Meaning of the Book of Job and Other Biblical Studies: Essays on the Literature and Religion of the Hebrew Bible* (New York: KTAV Publishing House, 1980), 39–52.

Sacrifice The community of faith in the Old Testament put great energy and attentiveness into the offering of sacrifices to God, material gestures offered Godward as a sign of the defining importance of God for the life of the community. While the particulars of Old Testament sacrifice are largely borrowed from surrounding culture and parallel practices in other cultures (perhaps as food for the gods), the sacrifices that Israel offered to God are to be understood theologically according to the particular character of this God and according to the peculiar covenantal relation that God has enacted with Israel. The several sacrificial practices thus are to be understood as vehicles and instruments designed to celebrate, affirm, enhance, or repair that defining relationship.

Israel's linkage to this God was from the outset likely given expression by the offering of sacrifices—that is, the dedication of one's best vegetable and animal produce as a gesture of loyalty and gratitude and as recognition of sovereignty. Over time, what may have been random and spontaneous gestures made to God were ordered and regimented into a coherent system, as reflected in Leviticus 1–7. That regulated system may be taken as an indication that sacrifice as material gesture of loyalty was of defining importance in the working of Israel's faith—a practice that made a hidden relationship concretely visible and available, so that the material offerings constitute a mode of interaction and communion.

All of the sacrificial gestures articulate YHWH's cruciality for the life of Israel. Some of the offerings are "sacrifices of well-being" that affirm the good order of the relationship with God (Lev. 7:28–36). Some are restorative offerings in a relationship that has been disrupted. These types of gestures may include purification offerings (Lev. 4) and guilt offerings (Lev. 5). Some of them, as the tithe, acknowledge YHWH's ownership of the land and entitlement to its produce (Deut. 14:22–29), and some are acts of gratitude for the concrete generosity of God in particular circumstance (Lev. 7:12–15).

We may in particular notice three matters of interest:

1. As Levenson has indicated, on occasion the extreme sacrifice to God was of one's child (Exod. 22:28–29; 34:19–20; Isa. 30:30–33; Jer. 19:5; Mic. 6:6–8; Judg. 11:29–40; 2 Kgs. 3:26–27). This practice, to the extent that it occurred, need not be explained away as an embarrassment or rationalized. Rather, such an act, barbaric as it may strike us, indicated the depth of urgency about ceding what is of worth over to God.

2. The enactment of sacrifice is the giving over to God what is costly and valued. In an agrarian economy, agricultural produce would qualify. In Deuteronomy 14:24–26, however, the actual produce can

be transposed into money if that is more practical, so that we begin to see, for pragmatic reasons, the linkage of money to sacrifice. This connection has come to have immense implications for subsequent religious acts in an economy of surplus wealth.

3. On the Day of Atonement (Yom Kippur), the text provides for a particular, periodic occasion of forgiveness and reconciliation (Lev. 16) [see ATONEMENT].

The sacrifices are taken to be efficacious—that is, they do what they say they do in terms of celebration, enhancement, reparations, and restoration. The interpretive stance of liberal Protestantism has often been a rationalistic suspicion and dismissal of such practice. Such an inclination will never permit the interpreter to appropriate either the wonder or the gravity of the claim that God has generously provided concrete mechanisms whereby the relation of God and God's people can be sustained with intentionality. For those engaged in sacrifices, suspicion of the practice is irrelevant and only positions the holder of the suspicion outside the wonder of the act.

Two developments in the sacrificial system of ancient Israel are important. First, a prophetic critique of sacrificial practice is recurrent in Israel's text (see Hos. 6:6). This critique is commonly assumed not to dismiss sacrificial practice per se, but to be a critique of the distorted practices that arise when sacrifice comes to occupy the entire field of religious activity and intention to the exclusion of other dimensions of obedience, or when the practice has become so routine and familiar as to be pro forma, without serious engagement or intentionality.

Second, texts such as Psalm 51:16–17 and Micah 6:6–8 show that concrete and material "sacrifice" becomes on occasion, metaphorical and relational. Imagining "a development" from the material to the metaphorical will not do. Rather, the practice of sacrifice is a deeply symbolic gesture that invites interpretation in a rich variety of directions. One cannot, however, escape the concrete materiality that stands at the center of the act, a deep bodily engagement by bodied creatures with the creator (see Paul's intriguing phrase, "your bodies as a living sacrifice" [Rom. 12:1–2]).

Concerning Christian interpretation, a useful approach begins with reflecting on the ways in which the New Testament has appropriated and adapted the Old Testament system of sacrifice. On the one hand, Romans and Hebrews agree that Jesus, as a sacrifice to God, has displaced an obsolete and failed system of Jewish sacrifice (Rom. 3:25; Heb. 9:23–10:18). On the other hand, however, the entire argument made for Jesus, as priest and as sacrifice, is cast in and dependent on the categories of Israel's sacrificial practice. Without taking seriously Israel's claim of efficaciousness through material gesture, the New Testament affirmation does not work. Moreover, the popular notion of Christian salvation—"Christ died for my sins" or "saved by the blood"—depends completely on the efficaciousness of a material gesture, a claim appropriated from the Old Testament. The Christian preemption of Israel's sacrificial system in order to make christological claims was brought to fruition in the classical formulation of Anselm as late as the eleventh century in his *Cur Deus Homo*. That formulation of the efficaciousness of Jesus as sacrifice has deeply penetrated the imagination of the church but at the same time has turned out to be problematic in a number of ways, for it invites uncritical notions of bribery, bargaining, and manipulation in a transaction of utter graciousness.

In any case, the offer of material goods treasured by self or community is a gesture of ceding life over to God in gratitude and in gladness. This primal theological claim is made dramatically in the practices that stand at the center of Israel's life with God.

References: Anderson, Gary A., *Sacrifices and Offerings in Ancient Israel: Studies in Their Social and Political Importance* (Atlanta: Scholars Press, 1987); Anselm, Saint, *Basic Writings: Proslogium, Monologium, Gaulino's in Behalf of the Fool,* trans. S. W. Deane (Chicago: Open House Press, 1962); Levenson, Jon D., *The Death and Resurrection of the Beloved Son: The Transformation of Child Sacrifice in Judaism and Christianity* (New Haven, Conn.: Yale University Press, 1993); Levine, Baruch, *In the Presence of the Lord* (Leiden: E. J. Brill, 1974); Milgrom, Jacob, *Leviticus 1–16: A New Translation with Introduction and Commentary* (AB 3; New York: Doubleday, 1991); Miller, Patrick D., *The Religion of Ancient Israel* (Louisville, Ky.: Westminster John Knox Press, 2000), chap. 3.

Salvation   The primal story line of the Old Testament is a sequence of events through which YHWH intervenes in the life of Israel in order to effect rescue, deliverance, and emancipation. These actions are nameable, concrete, and decisively transformative, and are termed "salvation" or "deliverance" (Isa. 52:7, 10; Pss. 27:1; 78:22). The one who acts in such a decisive way (regularly YHWH, but sometimes human agents at the behest of YHWH, as in Judg. 3:31; 6:14; 10:1) is said to be a "savior" (Hos. 13:4; Isa. 43:3, 11; 45:15, 21; 49:26), and the decisive verb is "save" (*yš'*; Judg. 3:9; Isa. 49:25; 63:9). This language bespeaks transformative power of immense proportion so that salvation can also be understood as a victory over negating powers that are now defeated by the greater power of YHWH. (Derivative from the verb are the names Joshua, Isaiah, Hosea, and belatedly, Jesus.)

The primary story line of great public events of rescue wrought by YHWH on behalf of Israel constitutes a rather standard recital, sometimes termed a "credo"— the defining and most characteristic testimony Israel gives to its faith, a sequence of events in which YHWH is said to be transformatively engaged (see Pss. 105, 106). Most important of these events is the exodus event in which YHWH saved Israel from the overriding and abusive power of Pharaoh (Exod. 6:6). Beginning with the exodus, Israel then tells of the guidance of God in the wilderness and the gift of the good land, altogether framing something of a salvation history. To that narrative recital can then be added other events that Israel peculiarly values. From a critical perspective, connecting the named deity, YHWH, with the active verb to save is difficult, for we are not told how or in what way YHWH enacts the verb. This connection, however, is decisive for Israel's faith; in Israel's doxological rhetoric, the connection poses no problem but in fact is the most important faith claim that Israel can utter. The outcome of the doxological claim is that YHWH is known and confessed to be the God who saves (which, incidentally, is the precise meaning of the name Elisha: "God saves").

YHWH's saving action is characteristically in response to the cry of Israel, as evident in the initiating exodus encounter of Exodus 2:23–25, in the regular pattern of the book of Judges (as in Judg. 3:7–10), and in the highly stylized presentation of Psalm 107.

This normative recital of miracles provides the narrative in which YHWH is embedded and by which YHWH is to be known in Israel. Moreover, the recital identifies Israel as the peculiar beneficiary and subject of YHWH's saving capacity, marking the world as a place that is open to YHWH's powerful transformative intention.

This narrative recital of rescue that characterizes YHWH as savior, Israel as YHWH's people, and the world as YHWH's realm fully occupied Israel's doxological imagination. As a consequence, the rest of Israel's life in the world could be redescribed according to these normative narrative characterizations. Thus, in the sixth century when Israel was "miraculously" delivered from Babylon at the behest of Persia, this turn in Israel's life is understood doxologically as the work of the saving God (Isa. 43:12). In parallel fashion, the more intimate personal experience of Israel was also understood through the rhetoric of deliverance. Israelites regularly petitioned YHWH for rescue from personal circumstance (Pss. 3:7; 6:4; 7:1; 22:21) and, after deliverance, regularly thanked YHWH for deliverance (Pss. 34:6–8; 107:13–16, 19–22).

The large scope of "salvation" that is comprehended in Israel's doxological rhetoric is a crucial point. "Salvation" in the Old Testament is often said to be "material"—that is, concerned with lived, concrete, sociopolitical issues. Such a claim is made for the Old Testament, however, in response to frequent Christian claims that salvation is something spiritual and otherworldly. In reality, the Old Testament knows no such dualism as material-spiritual, and regards every aspect of life—personal and public, present and future—as open to YHWH's saving capacity. Thus "salvation" is deliverance from any and every circumstance or any negative power that prevents full, joyous, communal existence.

"Pharaoh" is a convenient cipher in Israel for every power that precludes the life God would have Israel live, even though the pressure of negation may take many forms, including illness, imprisonment, isolation, poverty, unfair judicial procedure, or even neighborly slander. Moving into a different set of categories—to speak of enslavement to death or even the power of the law, or in more contemporary categories, guilt and despair—as forces that actively preclude well-being is relatively easy. In such extrapolations, one must yet maintain the connection to the real life: the daily, lived reality where the terms for salvation have their primal setting.

In the Psalms, that active negating power that God must overcome is often termed "the enemy," but the term is left open and undefined. Any negating power or circumstance may be termed "enemy," even as we casually speak of "the war on poverty" or "the war against cancer," wherein poverty or cancer is viewed as the enemy that precludes a full life. The glad affirmation of Israel is that YHWH—the saving one—has in the past, can always, and will in the future overcome every impediment to well-being. The world in which salvation is to be enacted is a world of contesting, conflicting powers. Israel acknowledges these threatening powers but finally affirms that YHWH is stronger than every such power; YHWH is therefore to be praised as the one who makes new life possible. YHWH's rescue is the victory that in Christian parlance becomes the subject matter of "gospel," the announcement of God's rescue from death-dealing powers (see Isa. 40:9–11; 52:7–8 on "goodness" in a concrete situation of threat).

References: Brueggemann, Walter, Theology of the Old Testament: Testimony, Dispute, Advocacy (Minneapolis: Fortress Press, 1997), 173–81; Croft, Steven J. L., The Identity of the Individual in the Psalms (JSOTSup 44; Sheffield: Sheffield Academic Press, 1987), 15–48; Rad, Gerhard von, The Problem of the Hexateuch and Other Essays (New York: McGraw-Hill, 1966), 1–78;

Westermann, Claus, *What Does the Old Testament Say about God?* (Atlanta: John Knox Press, 1979), 25–38.

Samaritans The name "Samaritans" refers generically to the people located around the city of Samaria, the capital city of the northern kingdom. In 722–21, that city and its political kingdom were destroyed by the Assyrian armies under Sargon (2 Kgs. 17:5–6). As a part of standard imperial procedure, the Assyrians deported some leading inhabitants of that city and kingdom and replaced them in the territory of Samaria with other peoples, non-Israelites, from other places that Assyria had also conquered. This policy of deportation and replacement assured that no serious resistance to or rebellion against the empire would occur.

More specifically, "Samaritan" refers to this newer, non-Israelite population that came to occupy the environs of Samaria as a consequence of Assyrian policy. In 2 Kings 17:24–41, in a pejorative assessment of that population from the perspective of Jews within the environs of Jerusalem, this new population in the north is regarded as idolatrous, having compromised Yahwism with other religious practices and assumptions. The rivalry between the two religious communities is thus established, the biblical perception of which is, not surprisingly, from the angle of the Jerusalem community. The Jerusalem community regarded itself as the true carrier of Jewish faith and the alternative community as a dangerous heterodox departure from that faith, although the same fate of destruction and deportation came upon the south a century later at the hands of the Babylonians.

In the Old Testament itself, the other important clash between these two communities and its leaders is in the context of the reconstruction of Jerusalem under the leadership of Ezra and Nehemiah. In Ezra 4, the Samaritans are among those who actively hindered the rebuilding project; Sanballat, the Persian governor of Samaria, is portrayed as a major opponent of the Ezra movement and is castigated sharply in the Jerusalem record (Neh. 2:9–19; 4:1–7; 6:1–14).

In the later period of the Old Testament and beyond, the Samaritans emerged as a competing vision of Judaism that continued to flourish into the Christian period and survive as a small community even today. Of special interest is the fact that the Samaritans, as an alternative Jewish community, have preserved an alternative text of the Torah (Pentateuch) that is an important witness in establishing the most reliable text of the Hebrew Bible, and they do not recognize the prophets and writings as authoritative [see CANON].

For the Bible itself, the most important fact about the Samaritans is the schism that emerged between competing Jewish communities, both of which claimed to be the carrier of authentic Judaism; that our most familiar assessments of the rivalry are from Jerusalem's perspective is important. Two unsettled issues about the schism remain. First, the time of the break between these competing interpretive communities, culminating in the long-standing hostility between them, is not clear; likely the break occurred later rather than earlier in the Persian period. Second, whether the break was on religious or political or even ethnic grounds is also unclear, although eventually the break included all of these factors. The reason may have been political, even though it is cast, in our texts, as religious.

In any case, what interests a Christian reader of the Bible is the acute animosity that Jerusalem Jews expressed toward Samaritans in the New Testament. The kind of animosity that surfaces is that of a competing population dismissed as disqualified and unworthy, a dismissal that characteristically includes religious, political, and ethnic dimensions. The community gathered around Jesus, at the outset a particular version of Judaism, initially reflects some of this same consciousness toward the Samaritans (Matt. 10:5; Luke 9:51–52; John 4:9; 8:48); the tradition, however, also indicates an intentional break with such a long-standing posture of animosity as the community around Jesus reaches out toward the otherwise despised Samaritans (Luke 10:25–27; 17:11–19; John 4:39–42; Acts 8:25). Acts 1:8 assumes that the Samaritans are welcome candidates for the gospel. This tradition eventually urged a generosity toward "cousins" who had long been demonized, a demonization already present in the initial, programmatic text of 2 Kings 17.

References: Coggins, R. J., *Samaritans and Jews* (Atlanta: Scholars Press, 1975); Crown, A. D., ed., *The Samaritans* (Tübingen: J. C. B. Mohr [Paul Siebeck], 1989); Purvis, J., "The Samaritans and Judaism," in *Early Judaism and Its Modern Interpreters,* ed. R. A. Kraft and George W. Nicklesburg (Philadelphia: Fortress Press, 1986).

Satan The term "Satan" is a literal translation of the word from Hebrew. While in popular usage the term signifies a personal embodiment of evil (as in "the devil"), understanding the term and its use in the context of the Old Testament itself is important.

Long before acquiring theological importance, the term "Satan" meant "adversary," "antagonist," or "opponent," especially a military enemy (1 Sam. 29:4; 2 Sam. 19:22; 1 Kgs. 5:3; 11:14, 23, 25). In Genesis 26:21, the term refers to a competitor for economic advantage, an opponent who gives the traditional name to the place of dispute, Sitnah. The term also is used in judicial context to refer to an accuser or prosecutor, sometimes an unfair one (Pss. 38:21; 71:13; 109:4, 20, 29). In several later texts, the human adversary is evoked and designated by God, but these uses refer to ordinary societal transactions.

Characteristically, the Old Testament has no special or privileged theological vocabulary, but simply makes use of the ordinary language of daily experience. For the most part, the Old Testament affirms that God has the capacity, on God's own terms, to do good or to do evil (see Deut. 32:39; Isa. 45:7). In Isaiah 45:7, NRSV word pair "weal" and "woe" refer to conditions of well-being (*shalom*) and tribulation caused by God. Late in the Old Testament, however, Israel's theological imagination begins to split off the negative functions that were often assigned to God, and now locates them in a special agent, Satan, who does the negative work but who still is an obedient agent on God's behalf.

Three texts—Job 1–2, 1 Chronicles 21:1, and Zechariah 3:1–2—show this theological development wherein negatives are split off to a distinct agent. Best known is Job 1–2, wherein "Satan," an identifiable agent, discusses with and proposes to God a scheme whereby God may find out how serious Job is about faith. In the narrative that becomes the springboard for the poetry that follows, Satan is concerned not to destroy Job but to help God find out the truth. Satan is presented in terms of a judicial metaphor congruent with earlier, nontheological usage in the Psalms and plays the role of prosecutor or devil's advocate. In the final form of the book of Job, the proposed scheme works and God learns that Job utters "what is right." Satan has effectively served God's interest.

The most interesting use of the term "Satan" is in 1 Chronicles 21:1, which is related to 2 Samuel 24:1. In 2 Samuel 24:1, commonly regarded as the earlier text, God "incited" David to action that would bring God's harsh judgment upon David. Here, God does the negative work directly. By the later narrative of 1 Chronicles 21:1, however, Satan, a character who is not present in 2 Samuel 24, is the one who "incited" David. Now, Satan, a distinct agent, is assigned the negative role in the narrative over which God continues to preside. Satan is thus a role or function split off from God, likely in order to maintain the goodness of YHWH's character (see the same role in Num. 22:22, 32). In contemporary political terms, this functional split permits God to enjoy plausible deniability.

The third theological use, perhaps the latest, is Zechariah 3:1–2. Again Satan functions as a prosecutor, though we are not told the details of the case. In this instance, God "rebukes" Satan. The verb "rebuke" suggests that something of a tension has emerged between God and Satan; perhaps Satan has exceeded his mandate from God as a prosecutor, and God must remind Satan of God's enduring commitments that are not to be violated. This suggestion of tension anticipates later theological development through which Satan becomes a serious enemy of God and seeks to resist and negate God's purposes.

The Old Testament itself offers none of the material through which Satan emerges as the popular figure of tempter and devil. The propensity of Christians to read such a role in Genesis 3 is to project backward into the text from later texts. That entire development occurs later, after the Old Testament, perhaps under the impetus of an emerging religious dualism that has Persian origins, or per-haps from the dualism that emerged within Judaism in its apocalyptic traditions. This dualism asserts that good and evil are independent forces that stand opposed to each other, so that evil as a force is autonomous from the goodness of God. That developed dualism of course shows up much more prominently in the New Testament.

Two important matters are instructive from this strange trio of texts. First, the theological tradition develops and takes different forms in different contexts, with no single way to say things. A comparison of 2 Samuel 24:1 and 1 Chronicles 21:1 indicates how a narrative plot concerning God may be rendered in different ways. Second, negation and the force of evil constitute a difficult theological problem for Israel. Israel of course knows about that negation in the midst of its own life; but for that reason, finding an adequate way to speak whereby the force of evil is connected to God was not easy. No doubt this perplexity is why Israel, in the Old Testament and in ongoing traditions, perforce found it necessary to speak in more than one way about the tense issue of God and the negations of evil.

References: Brown, William P., *Character in Crisis: A Fresh Approach to the Wisdom Literature of the Old Testament* (Grand Rapids: Eerdmans, 1996); Day, P. L., *An Adversary in Heaven: Satan in the Hebrew Bible* (Atlanta: Scholars Press, 1988); Petersen, David L., *Haggai and Zechariah 1–8* (OTL; Philadelphia: Westminster Press, 1984), 187–202; Ricoeur, Paul, *The Symbolism of Evil* (Boston: Beacon Press, 1967).

Scribes   In the ancient world where the Old Testament emerged, the learned capacity to write was not democratically determined but rather was the special province of a learned, elite minority that no doubt belonged to a special social network which exercised enormous influence. The presence of scribes, not surprisingly, occurs characteristically in the midst of great concentrations of power, so that scribes are regularly attached to governmental or sacerdotal centers of administration. (Second Sam. 11:14 and 1 Kgs. 21:8 provide two negative examples of the ruthless use of writing skills in the service of exploitative royal power.) In these administrative centers, keeping records was important, and records commonly had to do with property, taxes, and debts, so that the management of writing was allied with the accumulation of power and the amassing of wealth.

The function of scribes as a learned guild was not, however, focused solely upon power; the function was preoccupied as well with the accumulation and preservation of knowledge. Scribes could thus be closely linked to the "wisdom teachers" who produced the collections of the book of Proverbs. Scribes may also have operated schools that were linked to the royal court and that served to nurture and advance the younger generation of the elite classes. Clearly the power of writing, in terms of knowledge and power, advanced the elite at the expense of the peasants in a way parallel to the ways in which computer access serves the "accessed" at the expense of the "underdeveloped."

Theological interest in the scribes concerns the more general task of generation and transmission of written materials when that task pertains precisely to the texts and scrolls that subsequently became the scriptures of Judaism. As learned men the scribes were custodians of religious scrolls and became the chief interpreters of the religious traditions of Judaism. Three particular scribes are, perhaps, representative. First, Baruch was closely linked to the prophetic personality

and career of Jeremiah and was responsible for the formation and preservation of the scroll that subsequently became the book of Jeremiah (see Jer. 32:12–16; 36:4–32; 45:1–2). The relation of Jeremiah and Baruch (whatever it was historically) may have been paradigmatic of the relation between the prophet who generates the scroll and the scribe who preserves the scroll that the prophet produced. "Baruch" was likely involved in a network of scribal families who cooperated in the production of religious scrolls around the Deuteronomic movement, which became the beginning of the canonizing process whereby Judaism became a religion of the book.

Second, Ezra is a scribal figure who is credited with the founding of Judaism and is regarded in rabbinic tradition as second only to Moses in his importance for the faith of Jews (see Ezra 7:6). His role is as preeminent teacher and interpreter of the Torah scroll. In the dramatic event reported in Nehemiah 8, Ezra together with the elders reads and interprets "the book of the law of Moses," recommitting the Jewish community to the Torah scroll, which at that point was in some settled form. By this act Ezra reconstitutes Judaism as a community committed to a covenant with God mediated by the scroll.

Third, Ben Sira, a scribe in the second century B.C.E., writes of his work as though it is a characteristic social role:

> How different it is with the man who
>   devotes himself
>   to studying the law of the Most High,
> who investigates all the wisdom of the
>   past,
>   and spends his time studying the
>   prophecies!
> He preserves the sayings of famous men
>   and penetrates the intricacies of
>   parables.

He investigates the hidden meaning of
    proverbs
and knows his way among riddles.
The great avail themselves of his services,
    and he is seen in the presence of rulers.
. . . .
He will have sound advice and knowledge
    to offer,
and his thoughts will dwell on the
    mysteries he has studied.
he will disclose what he has learnt from
    his own education,
and will take pride in the law of the
    Lord's covenant.
Many will praise his intelligence;
    it will never sink into oblivion.
The memory of him will not die
    but will live on from generation to
    generation.
                              (Sirach 39:1–4, 7–9)

By the second century B.C.E., when
Judaism had only diminished political
power, scribes had become experts on Jewish religious life, preserving and teaching
the treasured authoritative scrolls. Beyond
that, scribes interpreted and therefore
developed and added to the tradition in a
generative way. In postbiblical Judaism,
the scribal office continued to attend to the
contemporary importance of ancient religious texts in a way that made Judaism
into a community of dynamic interpretation, causing Judaism at the same time to
be deeply grounded in tradition and enormously flexible and adaptable to new circumstance.

In Christian tradition, the scribes are
commonly linked with the Pharisees as
the two social forces concerned with inter-
pretating the normative tradition (see
Matt. 5:20; 23:13, 15, 23, 25, 27, 29). While
the word pair is often used pejoratively in
early church teaching, their repeated
mention indicates that they are the recognized and pivotal figures in ongoing Jewish
interpretation. While Christian stereotypes
may portray the scribes as punctilious
and destructive in their teaching (as in
Matt. 23), the Gospel of Matthew can also
appreciatively recognize scribes as pivotal
for the mediation of old tradition into
new, faithful formulation:

> "Therefore every scribe who has been
> trained for the kingdom of heaven is like the
> master of a household who brings out of his
> treasure what is new and what is old."
> (Matt. 13:52)

The fact that knowledge and power are
the characteristic issues for scribal interpretation—and as such they were easily
distorted and seduced, as in Jeremiah
8:8—readers today have no reason to conclude that the scribes were characteristically so. In the emerging forms of Judaism
that lived in a hostile environment, the
scribes, with great learning—both rooted
and imaginative—ensured that faith remained a vital, substantive energy among
Jews.

References: Davies, Philip R., *Scribes and
Schools: Canonization of the Hebrew Scriptures*
(Louisville, Ky.: Westminster John Knox Press,
1998); Dearman, J. Andrew, "My Servants, the
Scribes: Composition and Context in Jeremiah
36," *JBL* 109 (1990): 403–21; Fishbane, Michael,
Biblical Interpretation in Ancient Israel (Oxford:
Clarendon Press, 1985); Muilenburg, James,
"Baruch the Scribe," in *Proclamation and Pres-
ence: Old Testament Essays in Honour of Gwynne
Henton Davies*, ed. John I. Durham and J. R.
Porter (London: SCM Press, 1970), 215–38.

Sexuality The Old Testament provides a
foundation for a healthy understanding
and practice of human sexuality, while also
offering a picture of human sexuality that
is deeply distorted as a result of patriarchal
assumptions. Therefore, what one finds in
the Old Testament largely depends upon
which of these motifs is accented.

The creation texts of Genesis 1–2 provide the basis for the claim that sexuality is understood in the Old Testament as a healthy, joyous gift of God as a dimension of creation. In the first creation narrative, "humankind" ('adam) is created as "male and female" and blessed by God to have dominion and to multiply (Gen. 1:26–28) [see BLESSING, IMAGE OF GOD]. The particular phrasing understands "male and female" together as constituting the meaning of "human." They are presented as fully equal and commensurate, both of whom together are in the image of God— that is, bearing God's good intention for the future of humanity.

The case is more complex in the second creation story, because the woman is from "the rib" of man and is therefore subordinate and derivative (Gen. 2:22) and because the woman is to be the "helpmate" (traditional rendering) for the man (Gen. 2:18). Both of these notations have led to a strong interpretive tradition that subordinates woman to man, defining her as a lesser, dependent creature. The conclusion of the narrative in Genesis 2:24–25 together with the poetry of verse 23, however, bespeak a solidarity that does not admit of subordination. One must take into account a long interpretive tradition running from Augustine to Karl Barth that struggles with the issue of subordination of woman to man. One must also, however, distinguish between that powerful interpretive tradition and an understanding of the text itself that does not unambiguously support subordination. Readers can find here, as does Phyllis Trible, grounds for equality and symmetry, even though enough hints of subordination permit that reading as well.

Regarding the second creation narrative, in Genesis 3 both the man and woman are placed under curse (vv. 16–19). Against popular misreading, the

violation that is read in Christian tradition as "the fall" is not related to any sin of sexuality [see THE FALL]. If Genesis 3 asserts that the human condition is pervasively distorted and that human life is now alienated from God (the substance of Christian teaching about "the fall"), then human sexuality participates in that distortion and alienation, but the case does not turn on sexuality per se; God-given sexuality would be part and parcel of the distortion from which no part of human life is exempted. If the "image of God" in Genesis 1:26–28 entails healthy human sexuality of male and female, then in Genesis 5:3 and 9:6 the "image of God" is nullified by neither "the fall" nor the flood. This quality of human personhood is affirmed even through such defining disruption.

The healthy, affirmative rendering of human sexuality given in the two creation stories is vigorously celebrated and underscored in the Song of Solomon, a series of love poems that render human love in romantic, erotic terms, without shame and without any alienation. It has been suggested that the Song of Solomon is the fullest articulation of creation theology in the Bible, for two human creatures are portrayed in God's image fully together in trust, delight, and well-being, a full enactment of God-given fidelity and joy.

A move from Israel's foundational poetry to Israel's law is a sobering turn. Carolyn Pressler and Harold Washington have demonstrated the way in which the laws in Deuteronomy 20:14, 22:13–20, and 24:1–5 "construct" sexual roles of man and woman that are profoundly sexist. While evidences of partnership exist, for the most part the laws articulate the woman as the property of the man, certainly subordinate and without equal entitlement. The prohibition against coveting (Exod. 20:17, Deut. 5:21) thus parallels "wife" to "field," indicating the two prize possessions that are to be honored and respected as the man's possession. Indeed, adultery committed by a man is not adultery if with an unmarried woman. The act is only adultery if it is committed with the wife of another man, whereby the affront is fundamentally against the husband of the woman, for in the act the relationship of the other man with his wife is disrupted, and he is subject to social shaming (Lev. 20:10; Jer. 5:8; 7:9; 9:2; 29:23). To be sure, in some texts the woman is also in adultery, but that is characteristically in collusion with the man who violates her husband (Hos. 3:1; 4:13–14; Ezek. 16:32; 23:27). While the evidence is not singular that adultery is a male "prerogative," the primary evidence points in that direction.

The prostitute often constitutes the female counterpart to adultery (see Lev. 21:9; Deut. 22:21), but even with that illegitimate female freedom, adultery is defined in terms of male prerogative. Of prostitution, Phyllis Bird writes:

> It is a product and sign of the unequal distribution of status and power between the sexes in patriarchal societies, which is exhibited, among other ways, in asymmetry of sexual roles, obligations, and expectations. This may be seen in the harlot's lack of a male counterpart. Female prostitution is an accommodation to the conflicting demands of men for exclusive control of their wives' sexuality and for sexual access to other women. The greater the inaccessibility of women in the society due to restrictions on the wife and the unmarried nubile women, the greater the need for an institutionally legitimated "other" woman. The harlot is that "other" woman, tolerated but stigmatized, desired but ostracized. (200–201)

In the cases of Leviticus 21:9 and Deuteronomy 22:21, the violation of the "father's house" is at stake, so that even the woman's action is defined by the impact upon male prestige. Bird reviews the narratives of three prostitutes, Tamar (Gen. 38), Rahab (Josh. 2), and the harlot in 1 Kings 3. In each case Bird shows that, in terms of the narrative itself, the harlot is made into a hero; the underlying social subtext is nonetheless shame and disapproval of those women in their assigned social roles.

In this connection, worthy of mention is the "loose woman" (in some translations "foreign woman") in Proverbs who is regarded as a threat to the well-being of a son who is being instructed (Prov. 2:16; 5:3, 20; 6:24; 7:5). Much foolishness has been written about this woman as a mythic reference. The threat, however, is much more mundane and concrete: simply that a woman from another culture with other faith commitments will mislead and corrupt. The solidarity of the family is to be protected at all costs. Sexuality is thus considered not in terms of individual entitlements or freedom, but in terms of the solidarity and well-being of the family as an integral part of a larger community of social solidarity. Yoder, moreover, has shown that this polemic against a dangerous woman has a central economic dimension; the issue needs to be framed in terms of social power, all of which is in the hands of men. In the characterization of either of these deviations, harlotry or adultery, the central preoccupation is shame, and the commandments are designed to protect the family from shame's erosive power.

In current church discussion, a great deal of energy is directed to matters of homosexuality, but for all of the discussion, the Old Testament gives the issue remarkably little attention. The narratives of Genesis 19 and Judges 19, often cited in this context, do not pertain because they in fact concern gang rape. With particular reference to Sodom in the narrative of Genesis 19, the prophetic uses of the term (Isa. 1:9–10; 3:9, Jer. 23:14; Ezek. 16:46–56) indicate the wide possibilities for interpreting the Genesis narrative. The two important texts regarding homosexuality are Leviticus 18:22 and 20:13. In both cases, the case appears unambiguous, providing that the perpetrator of a male homosexual encounter is to be executed in order to protect the cohesion and integrity of the community.

Having said that the cases are clear, the matter does not end there. First, these two verses cannot be taken to address only homosexuality, but rather occur in long catalogues of offenses that threaten the community; the texts enumerate an immense variety of threatening interactions. These two texts clearly hold to a rigorous husband-wife relationship in which any third-party connection warrants death, surely reflecting a community under deep anxiety about its cohesion.

Second, Leviticus 18 and 20 are a part of a larger text (Lev. 17–26), dubbed by scholars as the "Holiness Code," in which every aspect of life is to be ordered rigorously according to certain requirements so that YHWH shall not be offended and driven away.

The two commands of Leviticus 18:22 and 20:13 cannot be taken out of context, but belong as a part of the larger teaching. Current preoccupation with these texts—taken out of context—is almost ludicrous, because the urgency about them often comes from people who would characterize any other part of the Holiness Code as being remote from reality. Leviticus 18 and 20 are not moral teachings but are ritual requirements, if a delineation of long standing in Christian interpretation of Old Testament law is to be honored.

Finally, two larger interpretive questions need addressing. First, the Bible is culturally conditioned and cannot be taken in its detail as an absolute teaching to be indiscriminately normative in every culture. Of course the Bible is for Christians the only guide in matters of faith and morals. That formulation, however, has always included reference to the long, carefully developed, still dynamic interpretive tradition of the church. In the matter of sexuality, the Bible surely represents a traditional, patriarchal assumption that is not easily transferable to a post-Enlightenment culture which knows about personal freedom as an ingredient in any viable relationship. To take the text seriously is to struggle with it in relation to a church tradition still under construction and in relation to contemporary culture, for texts always "mean" differently in new contexts.

The interpretation urged here is not an attempt at a "liberal" dismissal of problematic texts, but rather an insistence upon a sound interpretive principle that the Bible must be read afresh in every new circumstance. This principle can readily be tested with a moment's consideration of a biblical teaching on money rather than sexuality. According to Deuteronomy 23:19–20, no interest shall be charged on loans to members of the community. Of course, in the modern economy we would adjust that teaching to say that this command was for a folk culture of face-to-face relations and thus does not pertain in a complex urban economy, which is the point exactly. We necessarily make allowances for new context; interpretation is the process of making allowances in order to determine not what a text meant but what it means.

In the church we readily do make allowances about the Bible and issues of morality, even concerning sexuality in the cases of adultery and divorce. The suggestion here is simply that ethical extrapolation from the Bible—a crucial interpretive act in the church—is important on every issue, including sexuality. But we must pay attention to the interpretive process and avoid picking and choosing the issues about which we are absolute. In the end, no biblical claims can simply be pronounced absolutely without the struggle of context and interpretation.

The Old Testament writers clearly understood that sexual relations are the most intimate, treasured, costly, and demanding of all relationships. Precisely for that reason, Old Testament texts—at their most poignant—appeal to the husband-wife relationship as the most elemental metaphor through which to speak about the covenantal YHWH-Israel relationship:

Jeremiah 2:2 speaks of that covenant, when it functions properly, as a honeymoon period:

I remember the devotion of your youth,
  your love as a bride,
how you followed me in the
    wilderness,
in a land not sown.

Hosea 2:19–20 uses the same imagery to speak of a restored, reconciled relationship:

And I will take you for my wife forever; I will take you for my wife in righteousness and in justice, in steadfast love, and in mercy. I will take you for my wife in faithfulness; and you shall know the LORD.

Between honeymoon and reconciliation, though, the same imagery is used to speak of fickleness, betrayal, and infidelity in relation to YHWH (Isa. 57:3; Jer. 3:8; Ezek. 23:37; Hos. 2:4). Already in Exodus 34:15 the worship of other gods is "prostitution." In Isaiah 54:5–6, Israel in exile is likened to a woman "cast off" by her husband. The purpose of such rhetoric is to accent the seriousness of the affront and the deep offense that brings shame on the husband, YHWH.

Most spectacularly, Jeremiah uses the imagery by transposing the patriarchal marriage command of Deuteronomy 24:1–4 for a remarkable invitation from YHWH for restoration in Jeremiah 3:1–4:4. In the old Mosaic teaching, a cast-off wife cannot return to her husband. In the prophetic transposition of Jeremiah, YHWH, the offended husband, is willing to violate the old protocols of the Sinai Torah for the sake of the relationship. Jeremiah uses the imagery precisely to communicate the pain and wonder of the restoration of an unfaithful partner, a restoration rooted in hurt and eager love. Indeed, one may suspect that had the poet not been able to use such radical imagery, the matter might at its depth have been left unsaid.

Having acknowledged that positive use of the imagery, we should also note, following Renita Weems and Carol Dempsey, that the husband-wife imagery in reference to YHWH's rule is hazardous, for this imagery in the Old Testament is not symmetrical. YHWH is characteristically the good husband and Israel is the fickle, condemned wife who deserves punishment and rejection, thus dangerously reinforcing the propensities of patriarchy.

Using husband-wife imagery theologically brings us one more time to the Song of Solomon, which concerns the erotic love of a man and a woman. A long interpretive tradition also understands the poetry to be about the intense love between God and Israel, or in Christian transposition, between Christ and his church. While critical interpreters resist such allegorical impulse, pondering a faith that must resort to the most erotic imagery to speak about a covenantal relationship that operates at the deepest levels of trust and intimacy is useful indeed. Such a way of reading Israel's relationship to YHWH pushes behind and beneath any contractual, legal model. The outcome of such usage is a relationship glorious in its intimacy and costly in its brokenness.

The Bible understands that sexuality is the ultimate arena of cost and joy; for that reason, sexual imagery is appropriate to Israel's most treasured relationship. The church surely has demanding work to do—in a profane society that reduces everything to commodity—in order to recover such a way of speaking about what is most intimate as well as ultimate. Church people in the Reformed tradition certainly need to pay great attention to the mystical tradition of interpretation kept alive mostly by Roman Catholics. After all, Bernard of Clairvaux, who probed deepest into this theological drama of love in the Song of Solomon, was a major force in forming John Calvin's faith.

References: Bird, Phyllis A., *Missing Persons and Mistaken Identities: Women and Gender in Ancient Israel* (OBT; Minneapolis: Fortress Press, 1997); Day, Peggy L., ed., *Gender and Difference in Ancient Israel* (Minneapolis: Fortress Press, 1989); Dempsey, Carol J., *The Prophets: A Liberation-Critical Reading* (Minneapolis: Fortress Press, 2000); LaCocque, Andre, *Romance She Wrote: A Hermeneutical Essay on the Song of Songs* (Harrisburg, Pa.: Trinity Press International, 1998); Pressler, Carolyn, *The View of Women Found in the Deuteronomic Family Laws* (BZAW 216; Berlin: de Gruyter, 1993); Selinger, Suzanne, *Charlotte von Kirschbaum and Karl Barth: A Study in Biography and the History of Theology* (University Park, Pa.: Pennsylvania State University Press, 1998); Trible, Phyllis, *God and the Rhetoric of Sexuality* (OBT; Philadelphia: Fortress Press, 1978); Washington, Harold C., "Violence and

the Construction of Gender in the Hebrew Bible: A New Historicist Approach," *Biblical Interpretation* 5 (1997): 324–63; Weems, Renita J., *Battered Love: Marriage, Sex, and Violence in the Hebrew Prophets* (OBT; Minneapolis: Fortress Press, 1995); Yoder, Christine Roy, *Wisdom as a Woman of Substance: A Socioeconomic Reading of Proverbs 1–9 and 31:10–31* (BZAW 304; Berlin: DeGruyter, 2001).

Sin   Old Testament faith has a broad and deep notion of sin commensurate with its all-pervading conviction about God, but that conviction about God precedes any thought of sin. God, who creates, governs, and wills a world of well-being with and for all of God's creatures, forms the context for sin; sin is the violation of God's will for that world of well-being willed by the creator God.

The vocabulary for sin in the Old Testament focuses on three terms, though other uses are present as well:

1. Sin as deficit, failure, or mistake (*ht'*)
2. Sin as recalcitrance and rebellion (*pš'*)
3. Sin as moral violation (*'wn*)

Each term has a distinct rootage; for practical purposes, however, they may be treated as synonyms, as in Exodus 34:7, where they are cited in sequence:

> . . . forgiving iniquity (*'wn*) and
>   transgression (*pš'*) and sin (*ht'*),
> yet by no means clearing the guilty (*nqh*),
> but visiting iniquity (*'wn*) of the parents
> upon the children . . .

Each term may retain its particular nuance, but generically all the terms concern a human disruption of a proper relation with God. (In the wisdom teaching, "foolishness" is a term used for failure to respect the ordering of creation that cannot be circumvented, a failure that has dire consequences because such acts run against the nonnegotiable ordering of creation, as in Prov. 10: 21; 12:15–16; 13:19–20.)

In the Old Testament, sin is profoundly God-centered. Its premise is that human persons are creatures of God, made by God and for God to live in glad, obedient responsiveness to God. Sin is a distortion or violation of that proper ordering of creatureliness through a refusal to be dependent and responsive. Creatureliness may have within it the seeds of sin, but the Old Testament is clear that sin is not an inescapable product of creatureliness. A characteristic confusion of creatureliness and sin in Christian interpretation of the Old Testament is reflected in the church's familiar Ash Wednesday formula, "Remember that you are dust and to dust you will return." The reference to "dust" acknowledges creatureliness and finiteness (as in Ps. 103:14), but that formula in the Lenten environment of the church is often taken to mean, "Remember, you are a sinner."

The distortion and violation of creatureliness is fundamentally a distortion of a relationship with God—a refusal to be in a relationship of glad praise, thanks, and obedience. In the Old Testament that relationship is properly ordered and guided by the commands of Torah, most centrally the Ten Commandments. Thus sin devolves into a violation of Torah instructions, which has permitted a Christian stereotype and distortion of the Old Testament as a religion of law or a religion of rules. In fact the commandments are articulations of a relationship, so that no wedge may be driven between the commands of the God of Sinai and the relationship offered by God the creator. The violation of command is a disordering of the relation to the creator and to the creator's will for the creature.

In broad outline the commands of Torah cluster around two concerns, though rich, varied detail emerges in working out the shape of those concerns. On the one hand, a relationship with the creator God evokes a concern for holiness (purity, cleanness), for

You shall be holy, for I the LORD your God am holy. (Lev. 19:2)

On the other hand, the Torah commands are concerned for the practice of societal justice in political and economic terms, so that "love of God" inescapably mandates concern for the neighbor, particularly for the disadvantaged or needy neighbor (see Prov. 17:5; Mark 12:28–31). In this latter trajectory, sin against the neighbor (violation of interdependence and solidarity with the neighbor) violates a relationship with the creator God.

In the Old Testament, sin is serious business and has serious, practical, discernible consequences. The basis of a covenantal existence with God is the premise that obedient living leads to well-being and disobedience leads to trouble and death (see Deut. 30:15–20), which is the undoubted assumption of a biblical, covenantal ethic. For the most part the consequences of misconduct are produced in the very process of violation and do not characteristically involve the wrath or rage of the creator God; the act of the wayward creature tends to issue its own sanction.

This core conviction, however, which assures moral coherence and moral significance to human conduct, is at the same time endlessly problematic. As the poem of Job insists, lived human experience is not all contained in and explained by such simple cause-and-effect moral calculus. Indeed Lindström (1994) has shown that many of the psalms which voice trouble and suffering do not acknowledge—indeed do not even hint at—sin or guilt. Thus, while taken seriously, sin does not and cannot function as the great moral explanation for all troubles.

Sin, then, is neither the defining mark of human personality nor the defining characteristic of life with God, but sin is still to be confessed and acknowledged. Psalm 51 famously confesses sin and seeks pardon. Psalm 32 shrewdly and knowingly observes that denied sin causes disability, even somatic symptoms (vv. 3–4). Acknowledged sin, however, permits forgiveness and restoration to life (v. 5). While taking sin seriously, Israel knows that the reality of God's receptivity and generosity abound well beyond sin, so that sin is at best penultimate and in the end not theologically important or even interesting. Precisely because sin in the Old Testament is theocentric—focused on the reality of God—God is the one who keeps sin from being any defining reality in the creaturely world.

God's capacity to deal effectively with sin is a celebrated certitude in the Old Testament. On the one hand, God is said to be, by a sovereign act, willing and able to pardon and forgive (see Jer. 31:34). On the other hand, God has generously given priestly mechanisms whereby the worship procedures of Israel give concrete, available, institutional ways for forgiveness and rehabilitation (as in Lev. 1–7). Israel did not choose between simple assertions of forgiveness and institutional forms of rehabilitation. God gave opportunities for both, and both are necessary to meet the complicated realities of guilt and alienation.

Much of Christian Old Testament interpretation has given a privileged influence to Genesis 3 and to a notion of "original sin"—that is, "sin in principle." This reading of Genesis 3 emerged in early Judaism and further developed in a Christian theological trajectory that runs from Paul to Augustine to Luther. However, a careful interpretation of Genesis 3 does not yield such an ominous reading, and nowhere in the Old Testament itself is such a notion of elemental sinfulness articulated as a normative statement. Such a reading is a belated caricature of the Old Testament made through the development of Christian self-understanding. Two unfortunate outcomes from such an overreading of the text are worth noting here. First, in much of Western Christianity, sinfulness and guilt theologically dominate self-understanding. Second, a Christian stereotype of Jews as legalists has been imposed on the text. In fact, while considering sin seriously, the Old Testament takes the gracious self-giving of God *more* seriously and assigns it more decisive importance. Thus the psalmists—in Psalm 130, which is often cited in order to assert sinfulness—do exactly the opposite by celebrating God's good forgiveness that is the context for voicing sin and being forgiven:

> If you, O LORD, should mark iniquities,
>   LORD, who could stand?
> But there is forgiveness with you,
>   so that you may be revered.
>   (Ps. 130:3–4)

The Torah intends to leave members of the Torah community free of the disability of sin and well able to live "a new and righteous life":

> Surely, this commandment that I am commanding you today is not too hard for you, nor is it too far away. It is not in heaven. . . . Neither is it beyond the sea. . . . No, the word is very near to you; it is in your mouth and in your heart for you to observe. (Deut. 30:11–14)

References: Barth, Karl, *Church Dogmatics* IV/1 *The Doctrine of Reconciliation* (Edinburgh: T. &

T. Clark, 1956), 423–32, 437–445, 453–58, 468–78; Koch, Klaus, "Is There a Doctrine of Retribution in the Old Testament?" in *Theodicy in the Old Testament*, ed. James L. Crenshaw (Philadelphia: Fortress Press, 1983), 57–87; Lindström, Fredrik, *God and the Origin of Evil: A Contextual Analysis of Alleged Monistic Evidence in the Old Testament* (Lund: Almqvist & Wiksell International, 1983); idem, *Suffering and Sin: Interpretations of Illness in the Individual Complaint Psalms* (Lund: Almqvist & Wiksell International, 1994); Miller, Patrick D., Jr., *Sin and Judgment in the Prophets: A Stylistic and Theological Analysis* (Chico, Calif.: Scholars Press, 1982); Stendahl, Krister, "The Apostle Paul and the Introspective Conscience of the West," in *Paul among Jews and Gentiles* (Philadelphia: Fortress Press, 1976), 78–96.

Sojourner The term translated as "sojourner" (*ger*) can also be translated as "resident alien," "refugee," or "immigrant." The problem with the conventional translation of "sojourner" is that it may suggest a condition excessively "pastoral" and verging on the romantic. In fact, the notion of *ger* reflects displaced people who are displaced because of economic, political, or military disruption. They seek life in a new place where they do not belong, because they are no longer welcome or can no longer sustain themselves in their old place. In the new place, such displaced persons may or may not be welcome, but they are clearly outsiders who constitute an otherness in society that is regularly perceived as an unwelcome threat.

The long-term political condition of the biblical environment no doubt had its share of political, economic, and military upheavals that endlessly produced resident aliens, that is, people seeking a new life in a new social context. Of that social condition, which is firmly on the horizon of the Old Testament, the following three dimensions are pertinent:

1. Israel's memory and self-consciousness hold that its own past was that of a sojourner with all the precariousness that such a condition portended. Father Abraham is cast in such a role, seeking food in Egypt (Gen. 12:10–20), and the arrival of Jacob and his family in Egypt indicates an exposed life in an alien environment (Gen. 46:1–47:13). Alongside the Genesis ancestors, the period leading up to and including slavery in Egypt is understood as a sojourn in a strange land where life is endlessly at risk (see Deut. 10:19; 15:15; 23:7). The complicated historical question of being a Hebrew is pertinent to the status of early Israel, for the Hebrews were apparently a group endlessly marginal to an ordered political economy.

2. Israel's recital of faith centers around the conviction that YHWH rescued Israel as a community of at-risk slaves and fugitives, and gave a homeland to people who were otherwise aliens and outsiders in a land not their own. While the reception of the "land of promise" is complex and problematic, in this context YHWH is a God who causes Israel to have a new place of well-being, no longer in the alien or outsider role.

3. Torah commands Israel to welcome the sojourner in a hospitable way and to care for the outsider who has no claim or resources (Deut. 14:29; 16:11, 14; 24:17–21; 26:11–13; 27:19). In these provisions, the sojourner is characteristically linked to widows and orphans, the most vulnerable categories in society. Thus the Torah provides toward sojourners a practice of generosity and hospitality that is rooted in YHWH's own inclination toward needy outsiders.

In its testimony about sojourners, Israel is able to hold together (a) the character of YHWH, (b) its own historical memory, and (c) the ethical practice that the God of all sojourners mandates. Israel's capacity to welcome the "other" has become a distinguishing hallmark of biblical ethics, as well as part of a lively trajectory of interpretation that expands in scope. One example of a developing openness to the other is the way in which Isaiah 56:3–8 seems to overturn in a deliberate way the stricture of Deuteronomy 23:1. The Torah mandate in this regard is an exceedingly pertinent and urgent one in a contemporary biblical ethic, for the church now lives in a global economy that systemically produces displaced persons and is habitually inhospitable to them in their need. The Torah mandate concerning sojourners is a remarkable one in the face of resistance to the other, which is a durable human inclination.

Even though Israel came to be settled in its own land, a strand of piety in ancient Israel continued to recall that even Israelites are welcomed outsiders in YHWH's household:

> The land shall not be sold in perpetuity, for the land is mine; with me you are but *aliens* and tenants. (Lev. 25:23, emphasis added)

> Hear my prayer, O LORD,
>   and give ear to my cry;
>   do not hold your peace at my tears.
> For I am your passing guest,
>   an *alien*, like all my forebears.
>   (Ps. 39:12, emphasis added)

The status of welcomed outsider is not past tense but is very present tense indeed, situating adherents to this text in a context where attentiveness to other outsiders is as urgent as it is inescapable.

References: Miller, Patrick D., "Israel as Host to Strangers," in *Israelite Religion and Biblical Theology: Collected Essays* (JSOTSup 267; Sheffield: Sheffield Academic Press, 2000), 548–71; Spina, Frank Anthony, "Israelites as *gerim*, 'Sojourners,' in Social and Historical Context," in *The Word of the Lord Shall Go Forth: Essays in Honor of David Noel Freedman in Celebration of His Six-* *tieth Birthday,* ed. Carol L. Meyers and Michael O'Connor (Winona Lake, Ind.: Eisenbrauns, 1983), 321–35.

Spirit   The Old Testament, like its cultural environment, assumes that the world is peopled by and busy with many "spirits," forces whose consequences are observable in the world, but who remain prepersonal and inchoate. That is, the world is "enchanted" rather than empty and secular. Our concern, however, is more properly with "spirit" as attribute and agent of YHWH, a way in which YHWH is said and known to be decisively at work in the world as an agent of will and power: "The spirit is yet primarily in the Old Testament the prerogative *kat' exochen* of God and his instrument of revelation and action *par excellence*" (Jacob, 123). (The Greek phrase *kat' exochen* is an equivalent to *par excellence*.)

The Hebrew term rendered "spirit" is *rûaḥ* which can also be rendered "breath" or "wind," all terms that seek to speak theologically about the release into the world of a specific force that is linked to YHWH but which is invisible, inexplicable, and irresistible. Certain texts can be especially identified with each of these translations. In Psalm 104:29–30, for example, the term *rûaḥ* means "breath," even though in verse 30 the NRSV renders "spirit." The verse concerns the capacity to inhale and exhale, the most elemental activity of being alive (see Gen. 6:17; Num. 16:22; Eccl. 12:7). In Exodus 14:21 and 15:8, the term clearly refers to wind, that force known but not seen that can drive back the waters. In 1 Samuel 16:14–16, the word means the impingement of an agency that has theological-psychological specificity.

Nonetheless, although the term can be sorted out in these several ways, for the most part, categorizing such different uses is a mistake, for in the Hebrew, *rûah* regularly connotes any and all of them in a more wholistic sense that refers to an invasive power at work in the world, deeply linked to YHWH's will and purpose, capable of disrupting and transforming earthly reality. Thus the "Godness" of *rûah* is attested in order to assert that God finally orders and wills lived reality, for good or for ill, beyond the ken or control of human capacity.

This enigmatic but undoubted force of God is a decisive agency in creation (Gen. 1:2; Pss. 33:6; 104:29–30). The spirit is the agency that can dispatch human agents in powerful, transformative obedience (see 2 Kgs. 2:9–18). In these verses, although the spirit is termed "the spirit of Elijah" that comes upon Elisha, apparently the reference is, instead, to the spirit of God that rested upon Elijah. In Isaiah 42:1–4 the servant powered by the spirit will bring justice, and in Isaiah 61:1–4, transformed social policy is anticipated because of a spirit-dispatched human agent.

That spirit of God (the irresistible force of God's presence and will in the world) is said to be God's "holy spirit" in Psalm 51:11, where the phrase means life-giving spirit; in Ezekiel 11:14–21 and 36:22–32, the phrase represents God's purified name that is uncontaminated and undistorted by profanation, and thus God's own distinctive capacity for life in the world.

A particularly noteworthy use of the term is in Joel 2:28–29 (see Acts 2:14–21) wherein the spirit will be a gift of imaginative freedom through which all members of the community of faith are capable of futuring beyond the present circumstance of Israel's life. Here the spirit liberates and sets Israel into the world beyond human failure or despair and into God's promised well-being.

"Spirit" is an attempt to speak about Israel's conviction that the world is YHWH's arena of governance beyond human explanation or control. Old Testament formulation about the spirit is dynamic and has nothing of the Spirit as "The Third Person of the Trinity," a Christian formulation arrived at when the faith of the Bible was transposed, in the early church, into the substantial categories of Hellenistic philosophy. In general, Trinitarian Christian theology has not resulted in a well-developed sense of the Spirit, perhaps precisely because the force does not lend itself to such cerebral articulation.

Churches generally characterized as Pentecostal continue to experience the spirit in a direct way as a life-giving force, whereas the more "mainline" churches, in the line of classical Christianity, have articulated the Spirit as "Third Person" in a way other than as an invasive, life-giving force. In any case, the spirit is said in the Old Testament to operate in ways that put the decisive governance of human life well beyond human control or explanation.

References: Jacob, Edmund, *Theology of the Old Testament* (New York: Harper and Brothers, 1958), 121–27; Moltmann, Jürgen, *The Spirit of Life: A Universal Affirmation* (Minneapolis: Fortress Press, 1992).

Suffering Suffering is of course an inescapable lived human reality that is present in the community of ancient Israel as elsewhere. The theological issue regarding suffering turns on the ways in which the raw data of human suffering can be interpreted through and situated within the context of faith.

In the first instance, Israel contains and situates suffering within the limits of the covenant so that human suffering is understood as a consequence of covenantal disobedience. Those who keep Torah are blessed and enjoy a good life that is given by God; those who violate Torah are subject to punishment in the form of a variety of life-diminishing afflictions. This simple, straightforward calculus is especially the claim of the Deuteronomic tradition (see Deut. 30:15–20). The same general assumption, articulated somewhat differently, is expressed in the book of Proverbs: people who choose and act wisely receive life. People who choose and act foolishly receive the negative consequences of their choices and actions (see Prov. 8:35–36).

While this notion of suffering is overly simplistic, it also expresses positive theological convictions, affirming that (a) the world is morally coherent and reliable, and (b) human choices and human conduct are morally significant and contribute decisively to the shape and condition of the future. Such a theological-moral claim is a powerful antidote to the views that human life is meaningless and human conduct is irrelevant to the future, a view that receives proximate articulation in the book of Ecclesiastes (3:16–22; see Job 9:22).

This elemental covenantal claim is immensely important to the practicality of Israel's faith and yields an ethically attentive society. Suffering is thus situated and interpreted through a reliable, public moral calculus.

The lived experience of Israel, however, is honest and forthright about dimensions and degrees of human suffering that cannot be understood sensibly through such a symmetrical explanation. Human suffering is deeper, more painful, and more costly than can possibly be accepted as a consequence of bad human choice and action, and unmerited suffering requires theological candor.

Two important clusters of texts are cru-cial to understand this unmerited, inexplicable suffering: the Psalms and Job. In both books, Israel insists upon theological candor, does not lie or keep silent in order to protect YHWH's reputation as a fair and equitable God, and is willing to both entertain and utter the thought that YHWH's governance is less than reliable and evenhanded.

In the Psalms, Israel's theological, pastoral, liturgical response to unmerited or inexplicable suffering is voiced first in prayers of lament, sadness, complaints about unbearable suffering, and protests of unbearable righteous indignation. In these prayers, Israel expressed in detail the shape of suffering. These portrayals are regularly followed by imperative petitions in which Israel "commands" YHWH to act. In the imperative prayer, Israel assumes that it has claims to make against YHWH and that YHWH has obligations to fulfill to Israel as a covenant partner in need. Alleviation of suffering is considered part of YHWH's covenantal obligation to Israel.

These prayers thus offer to YHWH motivations (reasons) for YHWH to respond to Israel's need, for Israel never doubts that YHWH is able and powerful enough to override the suffering. The only issue is mobilizing God to act in healing, restorative ways. Among the variety of motivations offered to YHWH are:

1. The suffering is a result of Israel's own disobedience, so that the motivation for YHWH is to prompt Israel's repentance and acknowledgment of failure. This motivation is especially apparent in the so-called penitential psalms, of which Psalm 51 is the most prominent. Other psalms sound similar notes:

> While I kept silence, my body wasted away
> through my groaning all day long.

For day and night your hand was heavy
    upon me;
  my strength was dried up as by the
    heat of summer.
Then I acknowledged my sin to you,
  and I did not hide my iniquity;
I said, "I will confess my transgressions to
    the LORD,"
  and you forgave the guilt of my sin.
                              (Ps. 32:3–5)

For I am ready to fall,
  and my pain is ever with me.
I confess my iniquity;
  I am sorry for my sin.
. . . .
Do not forsake me, O LORD;
  O my God, do not be far from me;
make haste to help me,
  O LORD, my salvation.
                        (Ps. 38:17–18, 21–22)

2. The suffering is caused by Israel's enemies, who have oppressively assaulted Israel, perhaps while YHWH was negligent. This petition attempts to secure YHWH's aid and engagement against powerful enemies who remain unnamed, but who are blamed for the suffering:

Rise up, O LORD!
  Deliver me, O my God!
For you strike all my enemies on the
    cheek;
  you break the teeth of the wicked.
                              (Ps. 3:7)

Rise up, O LORD, in your anger;
  lift yourself up against the fury of my
    enemies;
awake, O my God; you have appointed a
    judgment.
. . . .
God is my shield,
  who saves the upright in heart.
God is a righteous judge,
  and a God who has indignation every
    day.
                              (Ps. 7:6, 10–11)

Save me, O God, by your name,
  and vindicate me by your might.
. . . .
For the insolent have risen against me,
  the ruthless seek my life;
  they do not set God before them.
                              (Ps. 54:1, 3)

3. The cause of suffering is YHWH's own abusive silence and disengagement, or even YHWH's active hostility:

You made us turn back from the foe,
  and our enemies have gotten spoil.
You have made us like sheep for slaughter,
  and have scattered us among the
    nations.
You have sold your people for a trifle,
  demanding no high price for them.
                              (Ps. 44:10–12)

You have put me in the depths of the Pit,
  in the regions of dark and deep.
Your wrath lies heavy upon me,
  and you overwhelm me with all your
    waves.
You have caused my companions to shun
    me;
  you have made me a thing of horror to
    them.
                              (Ps. 88:6–9a)

The rhetoric of these various prayers is shaped according to a standard pattern of speech. Within the pattern, however, the rhetoric is bold, candid, and demanding. Indeed, the poetry characteristically moves beyond politeness in ways reflective of unbearable physical or psychic pain, the result of public alienation and shame.

These prayers of lament, complaint, protest, and petition constitute Israel's primary faith strategy for drawing suffering into the orbit of YHWH's concern. With such stylized speech, Israel transposed suffering that is raw, elemental, lived experience into an important, demanding theological datum to which

YHWH must respond. While physical healings and social transformations presumably occurred, the primary reality of such prayer is that suffering becomes a relational matter; the sufferer is not alone but has YHWH as an attentive companion. The relational recharacterization of the raw data of suffering is a primary achievement of this faith. Now Israel in suffering thinks no more of just deserts, which can become mechanical and calculating. Israel thinks rather in terms of fidelity, relationship, and presence—covenantal realities that completely resituate and recharacterize suffering.

A second interpretive text concerning suffering not accounted for by moral calculus is the book of Job. The book of Job is informed by and dependent upon the traditions of lament and complaint, but now the matter is presented in a way that is artistically bolder and theologically more daring. In Job, three friends voice the old Deuteronomic calculus. Job and his friends accept that traditional formulation but insist upon an accounting of the sin that has led to Job's suffering. Job can accept suffering as legitimate punishment if it is covenantally coherent; God's silence, however, makes the suffering incoherent and meaningless. In Job 31, Job states his own covenantal fidelity in a defiant way and finally requires an explanation from God (vv. 35–37). He of course does not receive such a response.

In YHWH's speeches in Job 38–41, God refuses to be drawn into Job's demands. The book of Job offers no explanation of suffering and does not intend to. Rather the text voices a larger theological vision of the power and mystery of God, who will not be caught in the small circle of human suffering. In the refusal to attend to Job at all, the reader is drawn away from suffering to God's large, even overwhelming reality. The effect is to trump suffering with YHWH's reality.

The Old Testament clearly offers no explanation for the inexplicable reality of suffering and no antidote for it. Rather the Scripture offers a recontextualization, whereby suffering is situated in a relationship with YHWH and, in the end, the relationship itself is the be-all and end-all of faith (as in Ps. 73:23–28). The more powerful truth of fidelity reconstitutes suffering as meaningful.

Finally, in a way that is scarcely developed, Isaiah 53:4–5 speaks of substitutionary suffering, whereby one may appropriate the suffering of another and thereby make healing possible. Interpreters do not disagree about the identity of the servant [see SUFFERING SERVANT], and the claim about substituting suffering is unambiguous, regardless of the servant's identity. While remarkable in the Old Testament, this claim is of a piece with the larger process of reconstituting suffering within the context of a defining relationship of fidelity. All around this attempt to connect suffering to the reality of God is the growing affirmation in Israel of the pathos of God: God's capacity to enter into and embrace the suffering of Israel and eventually the suffering of the world. For this motif, the most remarkable texts are Hosea 11:8–9 and Jeremiah 31:20. Israel's staggering affirmation is that YHWH is not an imperial deity of the sort known everywhere in the ancient Near East. Rather this God is so engaged with and committed to the reality of Israel and the world that this God is a party to that suffering, such that Israel and the world are given gifts of newness.

This move to bring suffering into relationship with God is immensely important in a society that has almost completely commodified human life, that believes that mechanical, technological solutions to suffering are available, and that trusts in antidotes in scientific medicine to dull the pain that marks humanness. Such attempts at well-being through techno-logical commoditization often deny the more elemental reality of human solidar-ity that testifies to the solidarity with the God of the covenant as a problem and as the truth of suffering. Such strategies of lament as an antidote to suffering cannot be initiated in an emergency but require long-term communal practice. The char-acteristic antidotes of modern society may deal with the problem of physical pain (no small matter itself), but are unlikely to deal effectively with the more elemental human need of context in a community of fidelity. Israel's practice of pain in candor and fidelity thus has an immediate pertinence to a contemporary world that wants to be remote from such elemental practice.

References: Beker, J. Christiaan, *Suffering and Hope* (Philadelphia: Fortress Press, 1987); Brueggemann, Walter, *Old Testament Theology: Essays on Structure, Theme, and Text* (Minneapolis: Fortress Press, 1992), 1–44; Fretheim, Ter-ence E., *The Suffering of God: An Old Testament Perspective* (OBT; Philadelphia: Fortress Press, 1984); Gerstenberger, E. S., & W. Schrage, *Suf-fering* (Biblical Encounters Series; Nashville: Abingdon Press, 1980); Heschel, Abraham J., *The Prophets* (New York: Harper & Row, 1962); Lindström, Fredrik, *Suffering and Sin: Interpre-tations of Illness in the Individual Complaint Psalms* (Stockholm: Almqvist & Wiksell Inter-national, 1994); Miller, Patrick D., *They Cried to the Lord: The Form and Theology of Biblical Prayer* (Minneapolis: Fortress Press, 1994); Scarry, Elaine, *The Body in Pain: The Making and Unmak-ing of the World* (Oxford: Oxford University Press, 1985); Soelle, Dorothee, *Suffering* (Phila-delphia: Fortress Press, 1975); Westermann, Claus, *The Structure of the Book of Job: A Form-Critical Analysis* (Philadelphia: Fortress Press, 1981).

Suffering Servant   The phrase "suffer-ing servant" has become almost a techni-cal term in the study of the book of Isaiah. In Isaiah 40–55, commonly dated to the sixth-century exile, a reference recurs to a servant of the Lord, who is regularly iden-tified as Israel. Israel itself is unambigu-ously the servant of YHWH who obeys the will of YHWH and who effects YHWH's will for the world (see Isa. 41:8–9; 43:10; 44:1–2, 21, 26; 45:4; 48:20).

A century ago, however, German criti-cal scholarship identified four "servant songs," as they were called: four identifi-able pieces of poetry within the corpus of Isaiah 40–55 that were thought to be dis-crete and distinguished from the other poetry in which they are embedded (Isa. 42:1–4 [5–9]; 49:1–6; 50:4–9; 52:13–53:12). These four poems are peculiarly con-cerned with the role and work of the ser-vant. Because they were singled out on critical grounds and taken to be distinc-tive, "the servant" in these four passages might be considered as one other than "Israel," who is so clearly the servant in the other passages of Isaiah 40–55. As a consequence, a great deal of scholarly energy has been expended on the identity of the servant in these poems. North has usefully summarized the varied and sometimes bizarre scholarly proposals of the identity of the servant in these four poems:

1. The long-standing Jewish interpreta-tion is that the servant in these poems, as in the poetic context around them, is Israel. Israel obeys YHWH's commands and takes on the burden of YHWH's will in the world.

2. Scholars, long mesmerized by histor-ical questions, sought to identify as the servant a historical person in the Old Tes-tament text. Among the numerous candi-dates suggested for the role have been Hezekiah, Uzziah, Jeremiah, Cyrus, and

Jehoiachin—and almost anyone else in Israelite memory who could be called to mind. A subset of such a range of hypotheses is that the servant might be Isaiah of the exile (2 Isaiah) himself, who reflects on his own divine call and anticipates his own death.

3. A messianic interpretation allowed that the servant is an anointed, human agent designated by YHWH who is to be sent into the world and who, by suffering, will heal the world. Given such an anticipation, an easy and obvious move for Christians was to claim that the anticipated servant is indeed Jesus.

These four poems in Isaiah have been subjected to careful analysis and vigorous interpretation over time; at the end of the twentieth century, interpretation had for the most part returned to the Jewish notion that the servant is Israel and not a historical or anticipated individual person. Mettinger has articulated the growing scholarly consensus that the so-called servant songs need to be understood in poetic context and not distinct from it. A consequence of such a critical conclusion is the recognition that the servant in the servant songs is the same servant as in poetic context: Israel.

Clines, however, with some support from Childs, has suggested that the fourth poem (Isa. 52:13–53:12) is deliberately vague and noncommittal about the servant's identity, intentionally using many pronouns with obscure antecedents. Thus, Cline argues, the poem is open to a variety of interpretations but yields no clear answer to the identity of the servant in the text itself.

Isaiah 53:5–6 has received major attention, for these verses, as much as any in the Old Testament, suggest vicarious atonement—that the suffering of one can atone for the guilt of others. To be sure, this breathtaking affirmation is stated in

poetic imagery without the precision that serves theological interpretation, but the phrasing indicates the direction that Judaism took as it dealt with the vexing issues of sin and suffering after the destruction of Jerusalem and subsequent displacement in the world of nations.

Even though the now largely accepted conclusion is that the servant is Israel, the early church clearly found the fourth servant song uncommonly important for interpreting the significance of the life and death of Jesus, for he embodies, according to early Christian confession, the notion of vicarious suffering for others. To be sure, scholars disagree about whether Jesus self-consciously understood himself as "the Suffering Servant" or whether this connection was made in early church interpretation. In either case, reference to Isaiah 52:13–53:12 was crucial in the early church for understanding the life and especially the death of Jesus as an event that healed the sin of the world (see Matt. 12:18–21; 1 Peter 2:22–25; and especially Acts 8:27–39, and less directly Mark 10:45; 14:24, 41; John 1:29; Rom. 5:19).

Having observed the interpretive maneuver in the New Testament to extrapolate the poetry of Isaiah toward Jesus, one must not impose that christological or messianic reading on the Isaiah text itself. Rather, New Testament interpretation means to affirm that Jesus has taken over and reenacted the vocation of Israel in suffering for the sake of others. In the history of interpretation, Christians have more or less competed with Jews to claim the text as their own, seeking to deny any but a christological interpretation. The poetic text itself permits no such settled and closed interpretation, as Clines and Childs have seen. Rather the text permits Jewish and Christian interpretations to stand side by side, for the crucial matter is that one suffers for others, a radical affirmation about a God-given, humanly enacted agency that has room for more than one interpretation.

References: Childs, Brevard S., *Introduction to the Old Testament as Scripture* (Philadelphia: Fortress Press, 1979), 334–36; Clines, David J. A., *I, He, We, and They: A Literary Approach to Isaiah 53* (JSOTSup 1; Sheffield: JSOT Press, 1976); Farmer, William R., and William H. Bellinger, eds., *Jesus and the Suffering Servant: Isaiah 53 and Christian Origins* (Harrisburg, Pa.: Trinity Press, 1998); Mettinger, Tryggve N. D., *A Farewell to the Servant Songs: A Critical Examination of an Exegetical Axiom* (Lund: C. W. K. Gleerup, 1983); Mowinckel, Sigmund, *He That Cometh* (Nashville: Abingdon Press, n.d.), 187–257; North, Christopher R., *The Suffering Servant in Deutero-Isaiah: An Historical and Critical Study*, 2d ed. (Oxford: Oxford University Press, 1956); Orlinsky, Harry M., *The So-Called "Servant of the Lord" and "Suffering Servant" in Second Isaiah* (SVT XIV; Leiden: Brill, 1967).

■ ■ ■

Temple   The temple in Jerusalem occupies a prominent place in the religious imagination of the Old Testament, even though its origin and function are problematic and even though it was subject to the vagaries and violences of public history as well as the harsh theological critique of the prophetic traditions.

The history of the Jerusalem temple consists of three constructions and their subsequent destructions. The first, preeminent, and most dramatic was the temple of Solomon. According to tradition, King David purchased land for the temple (2 Sam. 24:18–25) but was prevented by divine oracle from building the temple (2 Sam. 7:4–7). His son Solomon (962–922) prepared for, financed, built, and properly dedicated the temple that dominated the landscape and religious vision of the Jeru-

salem dynasty for four hundred years (1 Kgs. 5–8), until it was destroyed by the Babylonian army in 587 (2 Kgs. 25:1–22).

After the deportation of the leading citizens of Jerusalem (see Jer. 52:28–30) and the initial return of deportees from Babylon under a Persian permit (see Ezra 1–2), a much more modest temple was built, commonly referred to as the Second Temple. This construction, under the leadership of Zerubbabel, signified the restoration and resumption of official, legitimate ordered life in Jerusalem in the years 520–516. The building project is reflected in the oracles of Haggai and Zechariah 1–8, and was closely linked to the Persian empire, which exercised hegemony in Judea after 537. The visionary oracles of Ezekiel 40–48 anticipate a rebuilt temple, a powerful symbol indicating Jewish recovery of independence and legitimacy. The Second Temple was authorized and permitted by Persian authorities and may have been financed by them as well. The temple functioned, moreover, not only as a center for emerging Jewish faith, but as an instrument of imperial tax collection and as a visible sign of the Jewish leaders' necessary acceptance of Persian political domination in exchange for internal Jewish freedom in the practice of faith and communal life.

The Second Temple endured until 70 C.E., when the Romans destroyed it in a struggle for control of the territory of Jerusalem signified by control of the temple. Even earlier, however, in the first century B.C.E., the struggle for Jewish independence in the face of Roman pressure caused a dispute over the temple. In 37 B.C.E. Herod captured the temple site and undertook substantial enough renovations that Herod's reconstruction is sometimes reckoned as a "Third Temple," though in the function of the temple no disruption from the Second Temple occurred. Herod's project may be reckoned as a third distinctive effort but in fact is only a footnote to the Second Temple. The so-called "Wailing Wall" in Jerusalem today is the still-standing western wall of the Herodian construction and is Israel's most sacred site, a crucial symbol of the religious-political legitimacy in Jerusalem.

Attention to the plan and construction of the Solomonic temple shows that the temple was indeed a new feature in Israel's religious life. From the outset, Israel of course had shrines and sanctuaries where worship of the God of the Mosaic tradition was conducted, but they were likely quite simple in both their construction and function. By contrast, Solomon's temple was quite extravagant in scope. Its materials and craftsmen were appropriated from Hiram, a Phoenician trading partner of Solomon, who was not at all familiar with Israel's covenantal traditions. It is plausible that the tabernacle was a projection backward of the Jerusalem temple; that is, it may not have existed in actual fact but may have been placed retrospectively in the history of the exodus in order to buttress theological claims about the temple by later generations. Cross, however, suggests that the tabernacle and the temple had quite contrasting significance for Israel's religious life.

Two particular elements in the temple's construction are noteworthy. First, the floor plan provided for three distinct chambers: an outer court, a holy place, and a "Holy of Holies." This three-chamber plan was used elsewhere in Canaan and was apparently a conventional design; Solomon's use of a conventional design indicates Israel's ready use of what was available in its cultural environment, without excessive scruples about being "destructive" of Judaism. Most importantly, such a design provides for "gradations of holiness"—so that the closer one moved toward the "Holy of Holies," the more "qualified" one must be, thus indicating distinctions of religious class and assuring an elite embodied in a special priestly order subservient to the monarch. This arrangement was surely contrasted to the democratic communitarian modes of Israel's earlier worship. Second, the materials for the temple were expensive, even exotic—cedar wood and a great deal of gold—signifying the Solomonic dynasty's capacity for opulence, surely a contrast with worship arrangements in an earlier peasant economy.

In terms of both the stratification and the opulence, the temple no doubt reflected the socioeconomic, political innovations under Solomon's royal power. While the temple of course was intended to enhance YHWH over competing deities, the stratification and opulence also celebrated and enhanced Solomon's enormous achievements and successes. Thus the temple that signified Israel's changed economic circumstance also decisively reshaped and redefined Israel's theological identity away from its revolutionary foundations in Moses to an exhibit of royal equilibrium and stability marked by success and prestige. Such a recharacterization of Israel inevitably brought with it a decisive recharacterization of Israel's God as well.

The primary function of the temple is the worship of YHWH, an assured offer of the liturgic presence of YHWH. Every such Yahwistic act was likely and inescapably also an act of legitimacy for the dynasty that presided over the temple. Thus the temple in Jerusalem was likely not first of all a community sanctuary but more a "royal chapel" to serve the governing establishment (see also Amos

7:10–17). Alongside serious theological intentionality, the temple in its function was probably heavily laden with ideological freight serving a socioeconomic, political establishment. The theological and ideological functions, moreover, could hardly be disentangled, as is evident in the endless attentiveness that the kings in Jerusalem gave to the temple (see, for example, 2 Kgs. 12:1–16). Three characteristic activities of the temple served this dual function of theology and ideology:

1. The temple was *a place of sacrifice*, of public acts of submission to the rule of YHWH by material acts freighted with sacramental significance. The catalogue of Leviticus 1–7 suggests a complex system of sacrificial practices closely supervised by legitimated priestly orders, which scholars believe was codified in the exile or later—that is, after the termination of the temple of Solomon. The late codification reflects earlier regularized practices designed to assure the presence and favor of YHWH toward both the regime and the community.

2. The temple was *a place of singing*, of lyrical, poetic enhancement of YHWH as the God of Israel and the creator of heaven and earth. The "Songs of Zion" portrayed in particular the temple and the city of Jerusalem as the mythic center of the universe from which comes the gift of life, the vision of justice, and the guarantee of a viable order for life (see Ps. 46; 48; 84; 87). These psalms feature a large mythic reference that was perhaps already present in pre-YHWH worship in Jerusalem, together with reference to the earlier traditions of Israel.

The actual Songs of Zion are perhaps more specifically located by reference to the orders of "temple singers" and choirs identified in 2 Chronicles as temple functionaries and known in the superscriptions of the Psalms in orders such as "Asaph" and "Korah." To be sure, the data in both Chronicles and the Psalms are commonly taken as later, but that presentation surely reflects earlier practices for a temple that was no doubt refined and "professional" in its conduct of worship.

The Songs of Zion that celebrate the splendor and significance of the temple have as their counterpart the communal lamentations of Psalms 74, 79, and 137 and the book of Lamentations. These songs and poems grieve the destruction and loss of the temple and acknowledge the total nullification of the huge religious claims made for the temple in the Songs of Zion. The affirmative and the negative psalms must thus be taken together to sense the deep passion stirred by the reality and the loss of the temple.

3. The temple was the site of *extravagant liturgical enactments* that on a regular basis had the intent and effect of solidifying the orderliness of creation in the face of every chaotic threat, and derivatively, enhancing the Davidic heirs who sponsored and supervised the temple liturgies. Scholars hypothesize that such a regularized liturgical celebration concerned renewal of covenant, renewal of Zion, or renewal of YHWH's divine kingship. In any case, the great psalms of enthronement of YHWH (93, 96–99) surely reflect a liturgical drama that either effected or anticipated the supreme rule of YHWH, which guaranteed the *shalom* of the realm.

Particular attention should be given to 1 Kings 8 (see also 2 Chr. 6), which provides a complex reflection upon the temple and its large theological claims. The text likely contains actual reminiscences of Solomonic liturgy, but over a long period of development the text also came to reflect later adaptations to lived circumstance:

> The chapter retells the liturgic legitimation of the temple and may pro-

vide a script for periodic reenactment of that great dedicatory festival (1 Kgs. 8:1–13).

The drama includes the transfer of the ark into the temple, thus subordinating the primary totem of early Israel to the larger, more comprehensive symbolic claims of the monarchy (1 Kgs. 8:4). The drama submits tribal memory to royal reality.

The liturgical procession of priests, elders, and Levites reflects a highly stratified religious establishment, congruent with royal differential (1 Kgs. 8:1–4).

The "cloud" of 1 Kings 8:10 signifies the palpable presence of God and stands in close parallel to the "cloud of glory" in the tabernacle (Exod. 40:34–37). This presence, in the singing of 1 Kings 8:12–13, makes YHWH the patron (and perhaps prisoner) of the Solomonic temple. These verses voice the most extreme claim of guaranteed divine presence anywhere in the tradition. The implied reference to the tabernacle tradition, moreover, suggests that the temple pertains not only to the well-being of Israel, but to the ordering of all of creation that the shape of the tabernacle replicates.

The notation of 1 Kings 8:9 and 27 indicates a critical awareness in Israel that such high claims for the palpable presence of YHWH run the risk of foreclosing YHWH's celebrated freedom to act transformatively in the world (on which see 2 Sam. 7:6–7). These verses, alongside 1 Kings 8:12–13, evidence the profound tension about which Israel always knew concerning divine presence and divine freedom.

Solomon's prayer of blessing attests that the temple was known to be a generative instrument for the *shalom* of YHWH in Israel (1 Kgs. 8:56–61).

The long recital of 1 Kings 8:30–53 is surely a subsequent development of the text. By its reference to defeat (vv. 33–34), drought (vv. 35–36), famine and blight (vv. 37–40), and exile (vv. 46–53), the recital appeals to the old stock curse formulation of Israel (see Lev. 26:14–39; Deut. 28:15–68; and Amos 4:6–11). Now, however, that curse formula is in the service of a later exilic community that seeks forgiveness of its every sin against YHWH, in hope of restoration to the land. The temple is now, given the needs and circumstance of the community, not so much about palpable presence as about the attentiveness of God who may forgive people who are remote from the temple (in exile) but who rely completely upon the attentiveness and graciousness of the God known in the temple. The temple becomes, subsequently, a powerful symbol of Israel's hope for reconciliation to YHWH and for restoration to the land.

The temple is intended to enact the splendid transcendence of YHWH by its use of cosmic myth, its lyrical exaggeration of rhetoric, and its gradations of holiness. But because of its intimate connection to dynastic interests, the witness of the temple to the transcendence of God becomes too often in fact the domestication of YHWH in order to serve the interests of the established regime. As a result, that the temple and the domesticated religion it embodies became the object of deep prophetic critique is not surprising. The prophets came to understand the temple, in their most savage rhetoric, as a distortion of YHWH. Best known is the stricture of Jeremiah 7, which anticipates that unless Israel engages in neighborly Torah obedience, the temple in Jerusalem will end up like the massively destroyed northern shrine of Shiloh. This threat is matched by the very different visionary critique of Ezekiel 8–11, which cites the temple as an offensive place of "abomination" from which God's presence will surely depart.

Worthy of note is that Josiah, in his reform, closed down all local places of worship ("high places") and concentrated everything in the temple [see REFORM OF JOSIAH]. While much celebrated in the text of 2 Kings 22–23, this act surely was not innocent. With his consolidation, Josiah strengthened the grip of the monarchy in gaining a monopoly upon Israel's religious imagination, an act in the ancient world not unlike the monopoly of media corporations in the modern world. Thus, the Jerusalem temple, like every such religious symbol, was vulnerable to utilitarian exploitation, all in the name of religious devotion.

In the end, the temple is a deeply ambiguous fixture in Israel's imagination, an assertion of YHWH's cosmic governance and faithful predilection for Israel, while also a distortion of the God said to be present in Israel. Derivative Christian tradition often notes that in the large anticipation of Revelation 21:1–5, concerning new heavens, new earth, and new Jerusalem (see Isa. 65:17–25), no temple is mentioned, perhaps now taken to be superfluous in the newly ordered rule of God (see John 4:21–24). That claim, of course, does not solve the ambiguity

cleanly, for the Christian tradition of necessity promptly founded "places of presence" in order to sustain its faith. None of the formulations of presence, Jewish or Christian, can neatly escape the tension of presence and freedom, though characteristically every attempt falls out on one side or the other: presence with diminished freedom for God or freedom with uncertain presence of God. Given the elusive character of the Lord of the temple, perhaps this situation cannot be otherwise.

References: Ackroyd, Peter R., "The Temple Vessels: A Continuity Theme," *Studies in the Religious Tradition of the Old Testament* (London: SCM Press, 1987), 46–60; Albertz, Rainer, *A History of Israelite Religion in the Old Testament Period,* vol. 1 (Louisville, Ky.: Westminster John Knox Press, 1994), 126–38; Brueggemann, Walter, "The Crisis and Promise of Presence in Israel," *HBT* 1 (1979), 47–86; Cross, Frank Moore, *From Epic to Canon: History and Literature in Ancient Israel* (Baltimore: Johns Hopkins University Press, 1998), 84–95; Haran, Menahem, *Temples and Temple Service in Ancient Israel: An Inquiry into Biblical Cult Phenomena and the Historical Setting of the Priestly School* (Winona Lake, Ind.: Eisenbrauns, 1985); Lundquist, John M., "What Is a Temple? A Preliminary Topology," in *The Quest for the Kingdom of God: Studies in Honor of George E. Mendenhall,* ed. H. B. Huffmon et al. (Winona Lake, Ind.: Eisenbrauns, 1983), 205–19; Meyers, Carol, "David as Temple Builder," in *Ancient Israelite Religion: Essays in Honor of Frank Moore Cross,* ed. Patrick D. Miller et al. (Minneapolis: Fortress Press, 1987), 357–76; Ollenburger, Ben C., *Zion: The City of the Great King: A Theological Symbol of the Jerusalem Cult* (JSOTSup 41; Sheffield: Sheffield Academic Press, 1987); Stevenson, Kalinda Rose, *The Vision of Transformation: The Territorial Rhetoric of Ezekiel 40–48* (SBL Dissertation Series 154; Atlanta: Scholars Press, 1996); Terrien, Samuel, *The Elusive Presence: Toward a New Biblical Theology* (San Francisco: Harper and Row, 1978).

Thanksgiving Israel's songs and prayers are permeated with words and gestures of gratitude to YHWH. In a generic sense, "thanks" may be understood as a synonym for "praise," a general affirmation back to YHWH in response to YHWH's way of goodness. The expression of thanks in Israel's repertoire of song and prayer, however, is quite stylized and much more concrete and specific than is praise [see THE HYMN]. Whereas praise is expansive and general in its exuberance, thanksgiving characteristically is a response to a concrete gift or a concrete transformation wrought by God that can be named and is durably treasured.

Westermann has identified a quite stylized form of thanksgiving, with four components:

1. An introduction that announces an intent to thank (Pss. 30:1; 138:1–3).
2. A review of a crisis that YHWH has resolved, about which earlier prayers of petition were made (Pss. 30:8–11; 116:2–4).
3. An account of a rescue from trouble, which is fully credited to YHWH (Pss. 30:11; 40:2–3; 66:19; 116:8).
4. An invitation that the community join in the thanksgiving that the speaker voices (Pss. 22:22–24; 138:4–6).

This stylized thanksgiving contrasts the prior condition of trouble and the present condition of well-being, and identifies YHWH as the agent who has intervened to make the transformative difference. The speaker tells of a change that has been experienced and thereby attests to the community the concrete, decisive, and powerful way in which YHWH has acted. The very act of narrating the transformation is itself an act of thanks.

We may notice three features of this pattern of speech:

1. A characteristic inventory of real-life troubles, from which YHWH delivers, is identified as the subject of Israel's gratitude. This representative list concerns actual situations in which the Israelite speakers know the speaking selves to be impotent and helpless. Psalm 107 provides a list of such circumstances: hunger and thirst (vv. 4–5), prison and hard labor (vv. 11–12), sickness (vv. 17–18), and storm at sea (vv. 23–27).

2. The glad testimony of thanks is given to the community, and the community is invited to join the speaker in praise (Pss. 30:4; 66:1–4). Gratitude cannot be private, but requires the engagement of the entire community.

3. The utterance of thanks is characteristically matched with a thank offering, the presentation of a material offering to express concrete gratitude for a concrete rescue (Lev. 7:12–15; Pss. 22:23–26; 40:10–11; 66:13–15; 116:12–19).

We must not be so preoccupied with the rhetorical form of the prayer or the mechanics of sacrifice that we neglect the main theological point of thanksgiving. Israel did not doubt that YHWH is the decisive agent who has the will and the capacity to intervene actively and transformatively. That intervention, moreover, was understood as YHWH's response to lament and petition. The thanks Israel speaks is thus a completion of the process that begins in Israel's truth-telling to YHWH about pain, need, and trouble. In the dialogic existence of Israel with YHWH, a central issue concerns human, historical need with which YHWH is intimately engaged. In this truth-telling, Israel cedes its life over in gratitude to YHWH and attests publicly in the world that YHWH is reliable and adequate for every circumstance of life.

From this action we can extrapolate that:

1. Israel's gratitude—in speech and gesture—is not generic, but YHWH-specific. Israel knows the name of the God who matters. Israel's praise may tell the long account of YHWH's goodness, but thanks incorporates this speaker in this moment with this miracle into the ongoing praise of YHWH.

The temptation to thank the wrong agent is reflected in Hosea 2:8, where Israel is condemned for infidelity for receiving gifts from YHWH but lavishing them on Baal in deference and worship. Israel's rhetoric eschews gratitude to any other source, and knows that the God who has "just now" acted is the same God endlessly at work on behalf of Israel. The notion of thanking the wrong god seems remote, until we ponder the fact that almost every television commercial is staged the same way Israel does these prayers, with a precondition of trouble and a postcondition of well-being. In between, as the transformative agent, is "the product." The ads propose that the product is the trustworthy agent who can transform life. In Israel's parlance, trust in any such agent in any serious way is an act of misguided gratitude—that is, idolatry.

2. Gratitude, made specific and quite stylized, is a glad impetus for obedience to YHWH. In the Reformed tradition of Christian faith, gratitude is understood as the primal motivation for a life of faith. Gratitude is rooted in a recognition, which Israel readily embraced, that all of life is a gift of God. Gratitude is the antithesis of self-sufficient self-congratulations, and one may imagine that in a postindustrial economy of ample consumer goods, the capacity to thank grows remote in a society that has too much and in its satiation notices no giver. Gratitude may thus be an elemental protest against self-sufficiency in the contemporary world.

3. In Christian extrapolation, thanks given is quintessentially expressed in "Eucharist," Holy Communion named by the Greek word for "thanks." Imagine having the key sacrament named "thanks"! Guthrie has traced the steady (but not exclusive) development of the ancient thanks of Israel to the Christian life of Eucharist. In every phase of that history of gratitude, "word and gesture"—testimony to YHWH, the giver of newness, and gestures of response—have always entailed a tangible commitment of gratitude.

References: Guthrie, Harvey H., *Theology as Thanksgiving: From Israel's Psalms to the Church's Eucharist* (New York: Seabury Press, 1981); Miller, Patrick D., *They Cried to the Lord: The Form and Theology of Biblical Prayer* (Minneapolis: Fortress Press, 1994), chap. 5; Westermann, Claus, *The Psalms: Structure, Content and Message* (Minneapolis: Augsburg Publishing House, 1980), chap. 4.

Theodicy The term "theodicy"—introduced into the philosophical vocabulary of Europe in the eighteenth century—concerns the question of God's goodness and power in a world that is manifestly marked by disorder and evil. The term *theo-dike* combines the Greek words for "God-justice" and asks about the justice of God in such an unjust world.

The logic of modern philosophy has dominated the discussion of this important theme, producing an unanswerable riddle:

1. That God may be *powerful and good* if there is *no evil*
2. That God may be *good* and there can be *evil* if God is *not powerful*
3. That God may be *powerful* and there can be *evil* if God is *not good*

This riddle was given modern, existentialist expression in MacLeish's *J.B.*, a contemporary presentation of Job:

> If God is God He is not good,
> If God is good He is not God.
>
> (11)

Of the three elements of the question—goodness, power, and evil—any two together can be logically affirmed, but in no logical way can all three elements hold together.

The Old Testament takes up these human issues, which refuse a rational, logical resolution, opting instead for a relational understanding of God, world, and the community of faith. This biblical perspective never permits that lively relationship to be reduced to such cold rationalities as Western theology has preferred.

The Bible proceeds in the conviction of the deep moral cohesion of God's world, expressed variously in the commands of Sinai, articulated in Deuteronomy, voiced by the prophets, and affirmed by the wisdom teachers. That is, the sense of moral cohesion is everywhere present in the faith of ancient Israel. This coherence insists that the obedient receive blessings from God, and the disobedient receive curses. For the most part, the Old Testament is content with such a coherence, nicely summarized in Deuteronomy 30:15–20.

That theodic settlement, however, is placed in jeopardy by the honest recognition that disobedient people receive blessings and obedient people receive curses. The evidence of life is that no trustworthy connection exists between covenant-keeping, commandment-obeying obedience and covenant curses or blessings. The failure of the theodic settlement (that Israel so treasures and affirms) is not diffi-cult to discern in lived life. That failure, moreover, leads to a theodicy crisis, because the Old Testament is fully aware that lived experience cannot be reduced to theological or moral absolutes.

While such experienced and recognized "violations" of covenantal coherence must have always taken place in ancient Israel, many of these dissonances could be contained in a category of guilt, wherein human failure is the cause of trouble, so that neither God's goodness nor God's power is in question. The apparent contradiction of obedience and blessing is due, in such formulation, to unacknowledged failure to obey, which thus maintains an acceptable linkage of disobedience and curse. That explanation may have often been adequate, but not fully so in ancient Israel, however, around the crisis of 587 B.C.E. when Jerusalem was destroyed. While more official interpretations explained the crisis in terms of Israel's guilt (as in 1 and 2 Kings), alternative voices bravely insisted otherwise. These alternative voices include two noteworthy texts:

> Why does the way of the guilty prosper?
> Why do all who are treacherous thrive?
>
> (Jer. 12:1)

> Why do the wicked live on,
> reach old age, and grow mighty in power?
>
> (Job 21:7)

These two outcries protest to God about evident injustice. In neither case does the cry of protest receive an adequate answer from God, who refuses to be drawn into the issue. The book of Job is the fullest struggle in the Old Testament concerning this issue. The protest of Job most probably receives an answer in chapters 38–41. God does not, however, offer an answer to

Job's actual question. Rather the speaker in the whirlwind overrides Job's question by a focus on God's power that simply disregards the question.

The quest for meaning inescapably surfaces the question of theodicy, and is inevitably asked in any religious perspective that insists upon serious moral cohesiveness. The Old Testament, however, never answers the question that is framed in such a logical, rational way. Indeed such texts as Deuteronomy 32:39, 1 Samuel 2:6–7, and Isaiah 45:7 accent the freedom of YHWH, a freedom that resists every explanation and instead requires all the risks of a relationship of freedom and fidelity. The Old Testament is not interested in explanations but only in the deep and dangerous intimacy of communion that makes available God's own engagement in the midst of inexplicable suffering. The chief evidence for this interpersonal response to the theodicy crisis that refuses every rational resolution is in the psalms of lament and protest, which characteristically begin in pain and end in joy, because of God's attending presence. A biblical approach to this demanding question is at bottom pastoral and relational, with a determined refusal to be drawn into logical explanation. Israel's stance in the midst of such inexplicable suffering is to voice anguish and hope, and to insist on the legitimacy of the protest that intends to move God to concern. Characteristically God's response to such protest is an attentiveness that provides care, sustenance, and compassion. God still will not be trapped in any moral calculus, overriding such calculus in presence and solidarity.

In recent time the question of theodicy has emerged most acutely in the suffering of Jews in the Nazi Holocaust, which was indeed an attempted genocide and an evil that defies every rationality, precluding logical justification or explanation. Philosophy is never an adequate response to that evil, for the crisis in the end demands face-to-face access to the raw holiness of God, who is not interested in logic but who is palpably available even in the most unbearable extremes. The practice of faith in all its dangerous commitment provides a way of responding to the inexplicable mystery of evil. In such crisis, faith is the characteristic response provided in the Old Testament. Israel denies nothing of the problem of evil but holds, in any case, to the God found in the midst of suffering.

References: Blumenthal, David R., *Facing the Abusing God: A Theology of Protest* (Louisville, Ky.: Westminster/John Knox Press, 1993); Braiterman, Zachary, *God after Auschwitz: Tradition and Change in Post-Holocaust Jewish Thought* (Princeton: Princeton University Press, 1998); Crenshaw, James L., ed., *Theodicy in the Old Testament* (Philadelphia: Fortress Press, 1983); MacLeish, Archibald, *J.B.: A Play in Verse* (Cambridge, Mass.: Riverside Press, 1956–1958); Tilley, Terence W., *The Evils of Theodicy* (Washington: Georgetown University Press, 1991).

Theophany "Theophany" is the term used in Old Testament studies to refer to direct confrontations that God enacts toward specific historical persons and historical communities. The term is a combination of two Greek words, *theos* (= God) and *phainos* (= appear), and the "appearance of God" is most often related to the awesome or ominous coming of a great light that shatters and disturbs.

The direct experience of theophany that is given to us in the biblical text in a more or less stylized narrative form. The form includes (a) the disruptive enactment of "natural" forces (such as a storm) to indicate the awesome, "unnatural" coming of God; (b) the utterance of God, who is said to be present in the context of disturbing circumstance—utterance that asserts the presence, self-identity, sovereignty, and, most often, the commands of God; (c) the fearful and/or submissive response to God by the one(s) addressed in God's coming; and (d) an indication that the encounter has changed everything.

Theophany is an encounter in the life of a person or community whereby the future is radically and abruptly redefined. The prime example of this dramatic coming of God in intrusive ways is the episode of the burning bush, where God encounters Moses and binds him to a radically new vocation that puts his life at risk in his defiance of Pharaoh (Exod. 3:1–6). The encounter offers, as its only visual, "unnatural" feature, a bush afire but "not consumed." From that flaming bush, God speaks, addressing Moses directly and compellingly; Moses responds, and the exodus encounter with Pharaoh begins. A similar immediacy is evident in God's encounter with Elijah in 1 Kings 19:11–18. While the Elijah narrative characteristically parallels that of Moses, here the theophanic encounter is unlike Moses', for it includes no wind, earthquake, or fire, but only a "sheer silence" (v. 12). The same forceful encounter-issuing-invocation occurs among the prophets in narrative accounts of prophetic calls (see Isa. 6:1–10; Jer. 1:4–10). Of characteristic importance is that while the disruptive performance of "natural" phenomena is a stylized way to narrate the encounter, the narrative most often is not interested in these phenomena, but focuses on the recruitment of the addressee into a new vocation that concerns the future way of God in Israel and in the world.

Theophany can also happen to an entire community, for which the classic case is the encounter of Israel at Mt. Sinai (Exod. 19:16–25; see Deut. 4:9–14). The description of a disturbance of "natural" phenomena is unmistakable; what counts for the narrative, however, is God's utterance, from the midst of the disturbance, of the Ten Commandments, which become a defining aspect of Israel as the people of Torah (Exod. 20:1–17). This same sort of communal experience is either offered or expected in prophetic anticipation for God's public judgment upon, variously, Israel and the nations (see Zeph. 1:14–18). These vivid scenarios accent the coming, irresistible sovereignty of YHWH that is exceedingly disruptive, dangerous, and demanding.

In these stylized characterizations of God's confrontive appearances, biblical rhetoric seeks to bear witness to a transformative intrusion of and encounter with God that resists description and defies categorization. These well-developed modes of narrative reportage and poetic actualization attest to the awesome seriousness of such encounters. They cannot, however, characterize in any rational or explanatory way what occurred, precisely because the situations that they speak of and to which they attest are not to be contained in or domesticated by reportage or description. The literary genre of theophany deals in encounters that are always elusive and always lie beyond any descriptive capacity. Theophanic rhetoric is an inadequate means through which to give voice to such direct confrontation with God, but the inadequacy of means is itself of enormous theological significance. That very inadequacy attests to the claim and conviction that the raw reality of God, when faced directly, defies human categorization, for this realm of transcendence, holiness, and divine glory is beyond human comprehension. The report of such encounter is of course necessary to the larger presentation of faith, for the durable faith of the community rises precisely from such unutterable encounter. The inadequacy of the report that perforce falls short in its task is indeed itself evidence of the inevitable incommensurability between event and report. A crucial point to remember is not to mistake the report for the event, which always eludes our grasp and understanding.

Theophany deals with immediacy of encounter, totally on God's terms. Immediacy is the wonder of God's dread-filled presence in the midst of human reality, but theophany is always a genre of inadequacy. From this primal theological awareness, five derivative points may be suggested:

1. These theophanic narratives are rare indeed and occur only seldom in the long narrative account of Israel's faith. They occur amidst long patches of time when Israel's life of faith is carried on conventionally without such holy intrusion. Also, different elements in the final form of the tradition articulate divine encounters differently. Sometimes the encounters are direct and immediate; sometimes they are mediated by an angel or through a dream. On the grounds of rarity, we may be suspicious of contemporary religious claims of frequent experiences of divine intimacy, for this God is not easily, readily, or frequently accessible or intimate.

2. For the most part, Israel's life with God is enacted in mediated forms (not "immediate," which means "without mediation"). Because God's holiness is beyond reach, the religious traditions of Israel (like every religious practice) devised mediating forms of God's presence—among them Torah, priesthood, wisdom, and kingship. By and large, the community relies upon and is sustained by the practice of mediated forms of presence, which must be practiced with care and attentiveness.

3. Public worship and stylized liturgy are characteristically the primal mediations of God's theophanic presence in Israel. In a variety of ways, liturgy seeks to replicate raw theophany; theophanic narratives like Exodus 19:16–25 are stylized in ways that reflect liturgical shaping. For example, the vocational vision in Isaiah 6 is in the temple, perhaps appealing to both the liturgical forms and the architecture of the temple in a presentation of theophany. Moreover, the temple is where Israel expects to "see God" (as in Pss. 11:7; 17:15). We are not clear what such rhetoric intends, but likely the temple provides a mediated presence that on occasion is experienced and known to be immediate. While of course no guarantee of divine presence, the liturgy does offer forms that generate a certain degree of readiness for direct encounter.

4. The situation is not different in the New Testament. In the categories of later church interpretation, Jesus can indeed be perceived as the definitive "theophany of God":

> In the beginning was the Word, and the Word was with God, and the Word was God. . . . And the Word became flesh and lived among us, and we have seen his glory, the glory as of a father's only son, full of grace and truth. (John 1:1, 14)

> For it is the God who said, "Let light shine out of darkness," who has shone in our hearts to give the light of the knowledge of the glory of God in the face of Jesus Christ. (2 Cor. 4:6)

If, however, we focus on concrete narrative reports of immediate encounter, we may also notice the Bethlehem birth narrative and the appearance of the angels in theophanic splendor (Luke 2:9–14) and the narrative report of Paul's conversion encounter en route to Damascus (Acts 9:3–9). The narrative accounts of immediate encounter in the New Testament are deeply informed by the narrative conventions of the Old Testament theophanic reports.

5. In the modern world, the raw directness of theophany is not easy, given the power of rationality to explain everything without reference to God's holiness, and given the temptation to a religious innocence and intimacy that tends to coziness with God and that eschews such dramatic encounters of the transcendent. Theophany as a statement about the quality and decisiveness of meeting with God that accents divine intrusion, divine sovereignty, and divine transcendence is thus to be understood as an important resource against perennial attempts to reduce the raw reality of God to convenient companionship. The God of theophany is characteristically no easy friend, but a demanding, life-changing authority.

In the modern world, Rudolf Otto, following the clues of Immanuel Kant in his characterization of the Sublime, has famously written of the *Mysterium Tremendum*. Otto uses this terminology to refer to the ominous, awesome quality of God against every rational domestication. He refers to the terrible reality of God that surges in power and in danger beyond every human capacity to contain God's reality. At the beginning of the twentieth century, Karl Barth wrote decisively about God as "Wholly Other" in protest against the temptation of continental theology to accommodate God to the nationalism and naturalism that pervaded that culture. More recently, Arthur Cohen has used similar language to testify to the hidden reality of God in the midst of the Jewish Holocaust, to see that particular episode of barbarism as a theological reality and as a theological problem that defies doctrinal, moral, rational containment of any kind. Taken theologically, the attestation of theophanic reports is the deep conviction that God is indeed God in an irreducible way, the one to whom creation must submit; yet the one who is here and there known as God gives God's own presence in concrete moments. The immediacy of God who is genuinely God is a remarkable experience requiring a genre of attestation that leaves open what is inscrutable, inexplicable, and beyond domestication.

References: Cohen, Arthur A., *The Tremendum: A Theological Interpretation of the Holocaust* (New York: Crossroad, 1981); Kuntz, Kenneth, *The Self-Revelation of God* (Philadelphia: Westminster Press, 1967); Miller, Patrick D., Jr., *The Divine Warrior in Early Israel* (Cambridge: Harvard University Press, 1973); Otto, Rudolf, *The Idea of the Holy* (London: Oxford University Press, 1924); Terrien, Samuel, *The Elusive Presence: Toward a New Biblical Theology* (San Francisco: Harper and Row, 1978).

Torah   This expansive Hebrew term is characteristically rendered in English, in Christian tradition, as "law" and is transposed in the Greek New Testament as *nomos*. Given the strictures against "law" in Augustine and Luther, such a rendering is an unfortunate reduction. The Hebrew noun is from the verb *yarah*, which means to "throw," "cast," or "point." The noun from such a verbal gesture comes to mean "instruction" or "guidance."

We should first understand Torah (guidance, instruction) as any authoritative teaching, such as that of a parent (see Prov. 1:8; 6:20, 23). When drawn into the sphere of faith, such authoritative teaching is understood as the instruction of God and is mediated through the work of priests (Jer. 18:18), or perhaps even more precisely, the Levites (Deut. 33:10–11). These latter teachings likely pertain to quite specific instructions about the management of religious matters such as sacrifice and purity; proper instruction is needed in order to avoid an unnecessary and unintended affront of God.

In the formation of the Old Testament, however, the notion of Torah is transposed from such concreteness to refer to large bodies of instruction that are taken to be generically authoritative for the community. In the Old Testament's final form, all of the commandments given at Sinai, in their rich variation, are taken as a single corpus of obligation for Israel in assenting to be the people of God at Sinai. Thus Torah is a function and subset of covenant, wherein Israel's life in covenantal obedience is fully explicated. This transposition from concrete instruction to an authorized body of teaching happened over a long period of time and through layers and layers of interpretation over many generations. That body of instruction intends that every aspect of Israel's life should come under obedience; perhaps the two largest themes of this programmatic claim concern, in turn, purity and then justice.

In the end we may identify two characteristic and important uses of the term "Torah," both of which bespeak the sovereign will of YHWH, now coded into teaching that is palpably available in scrolls. First, the term is particularly used in the book of Deuteronomy in speaking of "this Torah" (Deut. 1:5; 4:8, 44; 17:18; 27:3, 8, 26; 28:58; 29:20, 27; 30:10; 31:9–12, 24, 26), self-consciously referring to the instructional scroll of Deuteronomy itself together with its tradition. The other important elements in the commandments of Torah include the Covenant Code (Exod. 21–23), and the priestly tradition (Exod. 25:1–Num. 10:10) with the Holiness Codes (Lev. 17–26) as a subset. But Deuteronomy and its derivative traditions occupy the central space and exemplify the dynamic processes of a teaching tradition that keeps developing

through interpretation to meet new circumstances. In one sense, the covenantal tradition of Deuteronomy most fully voices Israel's conviction that Israel must respond in obedience to YHWH in every aspect of its life.

Second, the term "Torah," in the final form of the text, comes to refer to the whole of the Pentateuch: the first five books of the Bible, Genesis through Deuteronomy. This final corpus is the decisively authoritative text for Judaism and, derivatively, for Christianity. In this usage, Torah comprises not only instruction but also narrative. The instructions in the law codes of the Pentateuch include a series of quite distinct formulations of God's will for Israel, all gathered together under the rubric of Sinai. This varied collection represents a long and complicated traditioning process, but that entire process is understood, in the final form, as YHWH's single will for Israel. The narrative parts of this corpus include an account of creation and the ancestors in Genesis, and the exodus and wilderness traditions. Perhaps the narrative provides the frame and context for instruction, or maybe the narrative is, in its final voicing, also instruction. That is, the act of remembering, reciting, and retelling is in effect instruction on "how to be Israel," for the present character of the covenant community is given already in anticipation in the tradition. The final form of the Pentateuch is in sum a statement of what it means to situate community existence in the texted account of YHWH's activity and will. This material as narrative and instruction is not mere reportage, but rather literature that intends and evokes a response of trust and obedience.

This dynamic process of a tradition that keeps forming and re-forming Israel as God's covenant people is visible in four usages of Torah in the ongoing tradition:

1. By the time of Ezra (perhaps 450 B.C.E.), the Pentateuch—the first five books of the Bible—were likely in something like "final form" [see EZRA]. Nehemiah 8 reports on an incident taken commonly as the founding occasion of Judaism: Ezra and the leading elders reading "from the book, from the law of God, with interpretation" (v. 8). This report may attest the completed form of the literature, but more importantly reports a characteristic moment of interpretation in Judaism, because what happens through Ezra's work in this moment is what Judaism regularly does. The community hears again the narrative instruction that forms Israel; the people hear with interpretation that makes the instruction viable in a new circumstance and so is situated, yet again, in this authorized and authorizing text. The text heard and interpreted offers the community a peculiar identity and vocation in the world. Torah is thus community-evoking and community-authorizing.

2. In the final form of the book of Psalms, completed sometime after the Ezra movement, the editing and arrangement of the Psalter was likely done in a commitment to "Torah piety," that is, the piety voiced in the older Torah scrolls. The strategic placement of Torah Psalms 1, 19, and 119 suggests that these Psalms provide a clue to reading and singing the Psalter in an affirmation that glad, obedient embrace of Torah instruction is the way to well-being. Special attention should be given to the long acrostic poem of Psalm 119, which is a summary of Torah piety. The Psalm embodies pedagogical passion, artistic sensitivity, and perhaps liturgic engagement. The outcome of the interface of Torah and Psalter is that the community is not only taught but sings so that this piety feeds and shapes Israel's liturgic imagination.

3. In the period after Ezra, Judaism was largely formed through the leadership of scribes (see Neh. 8:1), learned men who handled the older Torah scrolls wisely and with ongoing authority [see SCRIBES]. These scribes were not voices of "new teaching" but were people who valued, interpreted, and kept alive the old Torah traditions. In this way, emergent Judaism, in years remote from older scrolls, remained committed to the old authorizing materials by continued teaching and interpretation. As a consequence, the piety and imagination of Judaism were shaped in the conviction that obedience to God's disclosed, enscrolled will is the purpose and vocation of Jewish life.

4. In one of the most expansive and likely late poetic visions in all of the Old Testament, the prophetic oracle of Isaiah 2:2–4/Micah 4:1–4 envisions all of the nations coming to Jerusalem for well-being in time to come. That the nations in this vision do not come to Jerusalem in order to submit to royal, political power is crucial; rather they come to receive "instruction" (Torah) that will make disarmament, peace, and well-being possible. These texts suggest an awareness that the Torah is not only defining instruction for Judaism, but is the ultimate instruction for all of the nations (see also Isa. 42:4 where the NRSV renders Torah as "teaching"). This Torah is boldly understood as the tradition of teaching that holds the secret of well-being for the world, a secret that in sum is God's will disclosed at Sinai but offered for the whole of creation.

In the postbiblical development of rabbinic Judaism, the conviction and practice emerged of an "oral Torah," an authorized tradition of venerated teaching that is well known and trusted, even if not enscrolled. Moreover, the Torah is, in important ways, the matrix in which Christianity emerged out of Judaism. In the long tradition of Christian stereotyping, Judaism was unfortunately regarded and represented as "legalistic." Christian interpretation has regularly misunderstood and distorted the positive, generative power of Torah that in Judaism is "reviving the soul" (Ps. 19:7). As Jesus declared that he came to "fulfill" the Torah (Matt. 5:17), we may understand that his work was received as an expression of Torah's life-giving power. As Christian interpreters move beyond the unfortunate stereotypes, we are able to see that in the early church of the New Testament, the Torah continued to be an important and authorizing resource, even when first-century interpretation of the Torah was deeply problematic. Christians in the end are, like Jews, about the business of glad obedience to God's disclosed purposes. The Torah is a primal source of such disclosure upon which the future of faith deeply depends.

References: Crüsemann, Frank, *The Torah: Theology and Social History of Old Testament Law* (Edinburgh: T. & T. Clark, 1996); Miller, Patrick D., "Deuteronomy and Psalms: Evoking a Biblical Conversation," *JBL* 118 (1999): 3–18; Sanders, E. P., *Paul and Palestinian Judaism: A Comparison of Patterns of Religion* (Philadelphia: Fortress Press, 1977); Sanders, James A., "Torah and Christ," *Interpretation* 29 (1975): 372–90.

Tradition   Tradition refers to both (a) the treasured lore of the community, which is stylized, treasured, and transmitted to the next generation, and (b) the process of transmission whereby one generation entrusts this treasure to the next generation.

The substance of tradition in the Old Testament can be understood in two ways. First is the Great Tradition, the narrative story line of faith that eventually became the backbone of canonical Scripture. The Great Story, consensus generally holds, includes, in sequence, creation (Gen. 1–11), the ancestors (Gen. 12–50), the exodus (Exod. 1–15), wilderness sojourn (Exod. 16–18), Sinai (Exod. 19–Num. 10), wilderness sojourn (Num. 11–36), the rearticulation of Sinai (Deuteronomy), and the taking of the land (Josh. 1–12). This tradition-become-canon attests to YHWH's governance as creator of heaven and earth and as the covenant partner of Israel. Israel, moreover, is embedded in this account of reality and is the primal recipient of YHWH's graciousness, so that every Israelite in each new generation appropriates this account as the true account of his or her own life. The Great Tradition may be lived out in more than one way; see, for example, the suggestion of Friedman.

Second, alongside and in the midst of the Great Tradition are many smaller traditions that make much more modest claims and operate in much more modest scope, but which have nonetheless claimed a place in Scripture. Among these, for example, are the narratives concerning Elijah (1 Kgs. 17–21) and Elisha (2 Kgs. 2–9) and many like memories that helped shape the world and situate Israel in it. How the little stories relate to the Great Tradition is not always clear, but the little stories continue to insist upon having their own say and are not fully absorbed into the Great Tradition. The ongoing negotiation between the Great Story and the little stories is of great importance in the Bible's formation and use.

The process of transmitting the traditions (Great Tradition and small stories) is also termed the "traditioning process." This process in ancient Israel, which led to the formation of the scriptural canon, is one of great vitality and imaginative freedom. We do not know the specific processes and contexts of transmission, but they must have included both the family and village (see Judg. 5:10–11) and the formal worship centers (see Exod. 12–13) of Israel and, in the later period, scribal schools. These several centers of transmission, operated by different agents from different perspectives, proceeded in a rich variety of ways.

Much of the earlier transmission appears to have been oral, so that the listening community heard and perhaps memorized what was given of the tradition. The one who remembered and transmitted the tradition—the defining memory—did so in stories and songs that have become part of the canon. Material that was shaped orally came in various times to be written and kept in treasured scrolls. In both oral and written form over time, Israel settled on an ordered account of its past.

Clearly the younger generation was the key target and recipient of the lore that constitutes Israel's identity as YHWH's people. Indications survive of an intentional pedagogy (Exod. 12:26–27; 13:8–10, 14–16; Deut. 6:20–25; 26:5–10; Josh. 4:20–24) [see EDUCATION]. Indeed Exodus 10:1–2 suggests that YHWH's purpose in elongating the process of the plagues against pharaoh is educational, so that grandparents will have a rich supply of triumphant narrative to transmit to their grandchildren about YHWH's mystery and Israel's destiny.

Israel's traditionists, moreover, are quite aware of the life-or-death urgency of transmitting the memory that gives identity and vocation to Israel:

We will not hide them from their children;
  we will tell to the coming generation
the glorious deeds of the LORD, and his
    might,
  and the wonders that he has done.
He established a decree in Jacob,

and appointed a law in Israel,
which he commanded our ancestors
  to teach to their children;
that the next generation might know them,
  the children yet unborn,
and rise up and tell them to their children,
  so that they should set their hope in
    God,
and not forget the works of God,
  but keep his commandments;
and that they should not be like their
    ancestors,
  a stubborn and rebellious generation,
a generation whose heart was not
    steadfast,
  whose spirit was not faithful to God.
                                (Ps. 78:4–8)

The process of traditioning must be done intentionally so that future generations may "set their hope in God." Negatively the failure of the traditioning process will produce a generation of children (or grandchildren) that forgets, and when forgetting disobeys. Disobedience in turn will produce a "stubborn and rebellious generation" unable to be faithful. The traditioning process is thus urgent in a directly pragmatic way, for the absence of tradition will cause a waywardness, a departure from Torah command that will lead to Israel's nullification.

The urgency of tradition is matched, perhaps surprisingly, with the immense imaginative freedom in the transmitting process. The passing along of the defining memory of Israel was not in cold, settled formulations. Rather, the tradition was reformulated in inviting ways in each generation so that the tradition is never past but always present, never "meant" but always "means." Each new generation receives and embraces the memory as its own; each new generation is the one to which the narrative and song refer. This supple capacity for imaginative reformulation is a hallmark of the biblical tradition even in the Bible itself. This capacity has permitted Judaism to find a way between a frozen, flattened fundamentalism and a dismissive indifference to the claims of tradition.

An appreciation of the vitality and freedom in the traditioning process inescapably leads to wonderment about the historical reliability of the narratives and songs. Critical judgments about historical reliability vary from season to season; critical scholarship is presently in a mood to minimize the historical claims of the tradition. Contemporary dispositions ebb or flow as time passes. Clearly, though, the narrating, singing community itself did not ask that kind of historical question, because the tradition is not, to begin with, presented as facticity in any case. The tradition is presented in an environment of wonder, amazement, and gratitude that yields glad obedience. Like the lore that defines any family tradition, principle precludes the question of facticity. To ask such a question is by definition to become an outsider to the tradition's claim and power.

The key insight of Israel in its transmitting process is that intentional transmission is indispensible for the maintenance of a self-conscious community of praise and obedience. Such a community cannot be maintained either by a flattened, authoritarian formulation that lacks contemporaneity or by a skeptical, dismissive questioning of tradition. This vibrant awareness, which evokes Israel's best interpretive imagination, may indeed give pause to people who care about the future of the church as a community of praise and obedience. The church in the West—liberal and conservative—is deeply impinged upon by an Enlightenment consciousness that resolved in an intentional way to overcome faith traditions. In more liberal settings, the propensity is a near dismissal of tradition. In more conservative settings, the temptation is a flattened tradition that is taken as normative but without vitality. Neither approach will work in the long run to sustain a vibrant community of praise and obedience.

The traditioning process requires great intentionality. More than that, the process requires adults who themselves are engaged with and alive to the claims of the tradition that legitimate and authorize a peculiar way in the world. The traditioning partners, both the transmitters and the receivers, stand in the tradition of Moses, that great traditionist, who declared:

Not with our ancestors did the LORD make this covenant, but with us, who are all of us here alive today. (Deut. 5:3)

References: Brueggemann, Walter, *Abiding Astonishment: Psalms, Modernity, and the Making of History* (Louisville, Ky.: Westminster John Knox Press, 1991); idem, *The Creative Word: Canon as a Model for Biblical Education* (Philadelphia: Fortress Press, 1982); Fishbane, Michael, *Biblical Interpretation in Ancient Israel* (Oxford: Clarendon Press, 1985); Friedman, Richard E., *The Hidden Book of the Bible: The Discovery of the First Prose Masterpiece* (San Francisco: Harper, 1998); Niditch, Susan, *Oral World and Written Word: Ancient Israelite Literature* (Louisville, Ky.: Westminster John Knox Press, 1996); Rad, Gerhard von, *Old Testament Theology*, vol. 1 (San Francisco: Harper and Row, 1962); Toulmin, Stephen, *Cosmopolis: The Hidden Agenda of Modernity* (New York: The Free Press, 1990); Yerushalmi, Yosef Hayim, *Zakhor: Jewish History and Jewish Memory* (Seattle: University of Washington Press, 1982).

■ ■ ■

Vengeance Vengeance in the Old Testament may be an act of power to redress an inequity or retaliate for a wrong. In this context, vengeance aims at symmetry between affront and response and takes place in a judicial context where the action exacts the due claim of law. Of course such redress, retaliation, and exaction live at the edge of equity and can easily spill over into brutality. Vengeance thus lives at that fine edge of legitimate response to affront (or felt affront) and pushes characteristically against the restraints of fairness.

In one of the oldest poems in the Old Testament, Lamech pledges vengeance "seventy-sevenfold" (Gen. 4:24, on which see the counterpoint in Matt. 18:22). Lamech's proposed response is well beyond any symmetry. This emotive sense of injustice and unbounded retaliation (perhaps present in every society) constituted an issue for legal authorities in ancient Israel. The legal tradition of Israel thus worked through equitable and symmetrical legal remedies to contain a thirst for justice. The outcome is evident in the dictum of Exodus 21:25:

> If any harm follows, then you shall give life for life, eye for eye, tooth for tooth, hand for hand, foot for foot, burn for burn, wound for wound, stripe for stripe.

The command seeks to establish proportion in retaliation, to assure retaliation but to curb brutality that is endlessly the temptation of a thirst for vengeance.

This "legal" sense of proportion appears theologically in the conviction that YHWH is the sovereign who takes the necessary executive actions to maintain order and security and to punish people who violate that sovereign will for order. The clearest examples of YHWH's sovereignty as legitimate proportion related to affront are the covenant curses in Leviticus 26:14–39 and Deuteronomy 28:15–46 that suggest a match between affront and punishment. In the long negative devel-

opment of Deuteronomy 28:47–68—completely disproportionate to the positive blessings—symmetrical punishment is tilted toward unrestrained brutality for the offender. In a very different matrix, one may also suggest that the plagues of Exodus 7–11 constitute enactments of sovereignty over Pharaoh, a vassal of YHWH who has been disobedient and therefore is subject to severe punishment. The plagues then are measures taken to assure the continuing sovereignty of YHWH over Pharaoh, who has been recalcitrant.

That notion of YHWH's legitimate exercise of sovereignty through judicially modulated means is in deep tension with the thirst for vengeance that seems apparent in the Song of Lamech and is voiced in many prayers of Israel. The cry for vengeance is evident in many psalms; among the more spectacular cases are Psalm 137:7–9 and 109:6–20, in which the speaking community petitions YHWH to make swift and harsh retaliation that is commensurate with the brutality and slander that has been perpetrated upon the speakers. Israel's prayers are honest and unrestrained, for this God is the one "from whom no secret can be hid." The same prayer, surely borrowed from Israel's liturgy, is on the lips of Jeremiah:

> Let my persecutors be shamed,
>   but do not let me be shamed;
> let them be dismayed,
>   but do not let me be dismayed;
> bring on them the day of disaster;
>   destroy them with double destruction!
>   (Jer. 17:18; see 18:21–23)

On other occasions, Israel confronts YHWH, who has meted out to Israel punishment that is disproportionate and undeserved. In such cases Israel contends that YHWH has violated the norm of appropriate administration of retaliation (Ps. 44:9–22 and often in Job).

The issue of vengeance is so acute in the Old Testament because the tension is never fully resolved between unrestrained brutality propelled by humiliation, shame, and rage and limited, proportionate judgment. The closest the text comes to resolving this tension is recognizing that vengeance fully belongs to God and not to human persons (Deut. 32:35). Vengeance belongs to YHWH, who is entitled to enforce sovereignty. Vengeance does not belong to human persons because they are not free to enact their thirst for it. God is thus, at the same time, a legitimate source of vengeance and a restraint on illegitimate human vengeance. As a remarkable result, in the prayers of Israel, as venomous as they are, no suggestion is made of human persons actually taking vengeance; rather the need for vengeance is spoken to God, who is expected to act.

Four observations sum up this review:

1. Humans, as Israel knows, do indeed thirst for vengeance, and that thirst is itself never censured. The theological question is how to manage that thirst. One may act out the thirst, deny it, or cede it to YHWH in prayer. The last option seems to have been Israel's practice at its most intentional.

2. In this rubric, YHWH is known to be able and willing to enact vengeance, even if not according to the petitioner's specific requirements. Positively such a claim implies that YHWH is a responsible governor who can (like a responsible parent) intend and enact appropriate judgments. This highly reassuring theological conclusion, however, is jarred more than a little by Israel's awareness that YHWH's own emotional life sometimes runs beyond judicial restraint, so that the God of the Old Testament sometimes enacts retaliation with emotive power.

3. The practice of vengeance is the attempt to manage a quid-pro-quo world of meaning. But a quid-pro-quo world is itself not always bearable. Israel can entertain the thought that YHWH has the capacity to break the pattern of quid pro quo in an act of generous mercy. Thus:

> He does not deal with us according to our
>   sins,
>   nor repay us according to our
>   iniquities.
>   (Ps. 103:10)

> If you, O LORD, should mark iniquities,
>   Lord, who can stand?
> But there is forgiveness with you,
>   so that you may be revered.
>   (Ps. 130:3–4)

4. When the assurance of valid redress, retaliation, and exaction are in question, vengeance may be undertaken outside the rule of law. Theologically God administers the rule of law to which God's subjects adhere. Where there is doubt—theologically about God's reliability or sociologically about the reliability of justice in society—vengeance may be taken directly and without restraint. The Old Testament knows about the restraint; it also knows about the ominous, endless push beyond restraint. That the procedures of redress are adequate in Israel is never unambiguously clear. The lack of clarity on occasion makes for frantic, insistent petition and for unrestrained brutality.

References: Brueggemann, Walter, "Vengeance—Human and Divine," in *Praying the Psalms* (Winona, Minn.: St. Mary's Press, 1982), 67–80; Jacoby, Susan, *Wild Justice: The Evolution of Revenge* (New York: Harper & Row, 1983); Mendenhall, George E., "The 'Vengeance' of Yahweh," in *The Tenth Generation: The Origins of the Biblical Tradition* (Baltimore: Johns Hopkins University Press, 1973), 69–104; Zenger, Erich,

A God of Vengeance? Understanding the Psalms of Divine Wrath (Louisville, Ky.: Westminster John Knox Press, 1996).

Violence The Old Testament is saturated with violence, knowing very little of civic structure or restraint and nothing of the restraint that belongs to more recent notions of civil rights and human rights. The most important tasks for the Bible reader are to face up to the pervasive tone of violence in the text, and to recognize that this violence constitutes an immense theological problem for faith communities that take the text seriously.

The most obvious place of violence in the text is the conquest tradition of the book of Joshua. Whereas the "land of promise" is elsewhere said to be God's gift to Israel, in this text the is land seized from its previous occupants. Indeed, its previous occupants are to be annihilated and granted no chance for life [see CANAANITES]. The land tradition as a matrix of violence is of primal importance because the land traditions stand at the center of Israel's confession and self-understanding.

Along with narratives that report on violence enacted, attention must be paid to the rhetoric of violence that the prophets employed. What passes theologically for the judgment of God upon disobedient Israel (or the recalcitrant nations or identifiable sinners) is in fact violent, abusive treatment. We have learned from feminist interpreters, moreover, that much of the interpersonal rhetoric of husband-wife or parent-child that functions metaphorically constitutes a rhetoric of violence against women and children, for the perpetrating God is regularly cast in the role of assertive parent or aggressive husband.

The prayers of Israel often constitute a wish for violence against other members of the community, wished-for violence that of course is understood and practiced (as always) as a response to violence, but which nonetheless contributes to the spiral of violence (see Pss. 3:7; 6:10; 7:12–13; 10:15). The one who speaks such a prayer, filled with humiliation and rage, feels such prayer to be legitimate. The speaker, moreover, does not doubt that YHWH is capable of such hoped-for violence and will indeed enact it.

These accent points on conquest, rhetoric, and prayers of violence all lead to the awareness that in the Old Testament text, YHWH is deeply implicated in the practice of violence. God's own life and history are permeated with violence, for this God is at times a crude, ruthless sovereign who will in the most savage ways impose a will upon any who stand in the way of God's sovereignty. God's propensity toward violence, moreover, is intensified by Israel's solidarity in that violence, prayers and actions based on the assumption that "the enemy of my friend is my enemy." As a consequence, the psalmist can pray, with apparent innocence:

> Do I not hate those who hate you, O LORD?
> And do I not loathe those who rise up
>   against you?
> I hate them with perfect hatred;
>   I count them my enemies.
> (Ps. 139:21–22)

That same innocence is characteristically engaged by those who uncritically assume that God fully shares their passions and convictions.

This quality of violence in the portrayal of God and of life with God constitutes an immense problem for theological interpretation. Violence is a problem theologically for Christians and Jews who intend the Bible to be a coherent attestation to justice and mercy. Violence is a problem, derivatively, when the violence attributed to God becomes a warrant for violence on the part of people who adhere to God, and who act on what they perceive to be God's will. A long history of "militant righteousness" is not squeamish about violence on behalf of the violent God. Here one may refer to a long history of "religious wars," including the U.S. practice in Vietnam of destroying villages in order to save them, to more recent bombings of abortion clinics . . . all on behalf of the will of God.

Three strategies are commonly used to overcome this problem in the text:

1. The preferred strategy in faith communities is simply to read past such texts and to pretend they are not there.

2. An available strategy is to understand such presentations of God's will and character as ideological mistakes. That is, the text community has imposed upon God such qualities that do not in fact bespeak God's true character.

3. The preferred critical response is to treat God through a developmental lens, so that a God primitive and violent at the outset becomes over time increasingly merciful and benign as Israel's religious development advances. The most spectacular case of this notion is that of Rene Girard, who claims that the work of the Christian Gospel is to overcome the long-standing problem of violence with reference to God. Such developmentalism has within it unacceptable hints of supersessionism whereby the truth of Christianity is said to prevail over a "less noble" Judaism. (Jack Miles can trace the same "development" but seemingly without a supersessionist inclination.)

Each of these strategies has merit and is, yet, deeply problematic. In the end, the violence of God reflected in the violence of the faith community cannot be readily explained away. If we take the text with theological seriousness, we must entertain the testimony that deep in God's history and deep in God's character are powerful residues of violence that are not readily overcome. Some Christian interpretation suggests that this God-based violence has its ultimate expression in the crucifixion and the violence worked against Jesus on Good Friday. The interface of violence and God is one to ponder by believers in the United States, the most violent society in the contemporary "developed" world. This society is saturated with violence, so much so that we scarcely notice except for the most dramatic occasions. No great imagination is needed, moreover, to suggest that widely practiced, accepted, and sanctioned violence has deep theological warrants behind it.

References: Brueggemann, Walter, "Texts That Linger, Not Yet Overcome," in *Shall Not the Judge of All the Earth Do What Is Right?" Studies on the Nature of God in Tribute to James L. Crenshaw,* ed. David Penshansky and Paul L. Redditt (Winona Lake, Minn.: Eisenbrauns, 2000), 21–41; Dempsey, Carol J., *The Prophets: A Liberation-Critical Reading* (Minneapolis: Fortress Press, 2000); Girard, Rene, *Violence and the Sacred* (Baltimore: Johns Hopkins University Press, 1977); Gunn, David M., "Colonialism and the Vagaries of Scripture: Te Kooti in Canaan (A Story of Bible and Dispossession in Aotearoa/New Zealand)," in *God in the Fray: A Tribute to Walter Brueggemann,* ed. Tod Linafelt and Timothy K. Beal (Minneapolis: Fortress Press, 1998), 127–42; Levenson, Jon D., "Is There a Counterpart in the Hebrew Bible to New Testament Antisemitism?" *Journal of Ecumenical Studies* 22/2 (1985): 242–60; Miles, Jack, *God: A Biography* (New York: Random House, 1997); Schwartz, Regina M., *The Curse of Cain: The Violent Legacy of Monotheism* (Chicago: University of Chicago Press, 1997); Suchocki, Marjorie H., *The Fall to Violence: Original Sin in Relational Theology* (New York:

Continuum, 1995); Weems, Renita J., *Battered Love: Marriage, Sex, and Violence in the Hebrew Prophets* (OBT; Minneapolis: Fortress Press, 1995).

■ ■ ■

War   War is a commonly assumed political strategy that pervades the Old Testament. The act of war may be understood as an arm of policy, but its practice in that ancient world—as in the contemporary world—is saturated with violence and brutality that are regularly excused for reasons of state.

Israel is a sociopolitical community in the Old Testament that had to make its way in the world of *Realpolitik* . . . often at risk and under threat, often surrounded and threatened by political powers stronger than itself. Israel is regularly engaged in forming alliances, building coalitions, and engaging in combat. What strikes a reader most about such reports is how ordinary and unexceptional war is regarded. Among the issues regularly considered in interpreting Israel's wars are these:

1. Are the wars of Israel defensive or offensive? Some scholars have suggested that Israel only defends itself, but the intricacies of diplomacy seek always to establish the other party as the aggressor.

2. Are the wars "holy" or in some sense secular? Israel's rhetoric about and conduct of war are certainly saturated with references to YHWH, as is every other sphere of life. Sometimes Israel's battles are explicitly at the behest of YHWH (2 Sam. 5:19); on other occasions the wars seem more likely to be a part of "rational" policy as society moved in a more "secular" direction (as in 2 Sam. 8:1–12).

3. Are the wars fought by a citizen militia or by a standing army of state? The

hypothesis that the seizure of land in Canaan was a peasant revolt would serve the notion of a summoned militia, but in other cases, the army seems much more regularized.

On all three questions, a variety of answers may be given, for the conduct of war and its interpretive rhetoric vary greatly, depending upon the political and material condition of the community and the mode of its organization. In all aspects of these questions, war in one form or another is clearly a constant, available strategy about which Israel has no special qualms.

For our purposes, the more important issue concerns what is made theologically of the political reality of war. At the core of Israel's theological rhetoric, YHWH is a "warrior" (Exod. 15:3). Without that facet of YHWH, no exodus would have taken place and no ensuing story of Israel's faith. Thus some of Israel's wars are at the behest of YHWH, but in some others, YHWH's own person is said to be at the center of the combat. In such rhetoric Israel participates in a common mythological deposit of its milieu and seeks to adapt it for its peculiar covenantal claims. Thus YHWH is portrayed as a ready, able warrior whose hand is not "shortened" (Isa. 50:2, 59:1), but who has the power to effect change in assertive and violent ways.

The notion of YHWH as a warrior God—expressed most regularly as "Lord of Hosts"—becomes a carrier of important theological claims for Israel:

1. YHWH as warrior is a function of YHWH's sovereignty over the nations. Any sovereign must have the capacity to enforce governance; states regularly seek a "monopoly of violence" that is usually presented as a police force or an army. In Israel's rhetoric, YHWH will not be mocked, nor will YHWH's governance be

mocked (Isa. 36–37). YHWH will instead act against those who belittle or trivialize YHWH's governance (see 1 Sam. 17:16).

2. YHWH as warrior works as the special protector, defender, and liberator of Israel, so that the image of warrior is a function of Israel's chosenness as YHWH's holy people. Thus, in Exodus 14:13–14, YHWH's military intervention against the Egyptian armies is on behalf of Israel:

> "Do not be afraid, stand firm, and see the deliverance that the LORD will accomplish for you today; for the Egyptians whom you see today you will never see again. The LORD will fight for you, and you have only to keep still."

The outcome of the struggle with Pharaoh indicates, according to Israel's testimony, that YHWH is more than capable against every military challenge, and against every rival god who stands with and for Israel's political enemies.

3. YHWH as warrior who protects Israel and who enforces sovereignty also, on occasion, acts as warrior against Israel to inflict injury and punishment upon Israel when recalcitrant:

> I am going to turn back the weapons of war that are in your hands and with which you are fighting against the king of Babylon and against the Chaldeans who are besieging you outside the walls; and I will bring them together into the center of this city. I myself will fight against you with outstretched hand and mighty arm, in anger, in fury, and in great wrath. (Jer. 21:4–5)

Thus the imagery of YHWH as warrior is an immensely supple metaphor that can serve in a variety of ways to make the peculiar theological claims that Israel asserts for its God. For example, in Zechariah 9 the imagery is readily transposed to serve apocalyptic discourse.

The key interpretive problem is to adjudicate between the concrete, practical reality of war and warrior and the metaphorical use made of the imagery that is no longer closely tied to that concreteness. The metaphor takes on a theological life of its own; indeed, subsequent claims in apocalyptic literature and in the New Testament concerning God's defeat of evil (as in Jesus' defeat of demonic powers) requires some such vocabulary. The problem of course is that any use of the imagery in a metaphorical way is never free of the concreteness of violence to which the imagery belongs.

A great yearning is currently in vogue to eradicate such nuance and to transform the God of the Bible into a gentler, more therapeutic agent. As long as biblical faith, however, is understood as salvation faith wherein God delivers, such imagery will remain as crucial as it is problematic. (The problematic aspect is evidenced in the broad attempt to purge Christian hymnals of martial imagery. A parallel practice is evident in many lectionary readings in the *Revised Common Lectionary* that simply skip over the "hard parts." While such efforts acknowledge a real and deep problem, they do not in any noticeable way face the cruciality of the imagery for what the Bible asserts.) Theological interpreters cannot easily escape the rich metaphorical field of war and warrior, even while acknowledging the acute problem in this rhetoric of violence, brutality, and patriarchy.

The violence endemic even in Old Testament visions of peace may be noticed in three familiar texts:

1. In Isaiah 9:6, a text much used in messianic context by Christians in Advent, the wondrous affirmation awaits the coming king:

> For a child has been born for us,
>   a son given to us;

authority rests upon his shoulders;
    and he is named
Wonderful Counselor, Mighty God,
    Everlasting Father, Prince of Peace.

The coming king is "prince of peace." What is not often noticed and sometimes skipped over are the immediately preceding verses:

For the yoke of their burden,
    and the bar across their shoulders,
    the rod of their oppressor,
    you have broken as on the day of
        Midian.
For all the boots of the tramping warriors
    and all the garments rolled in blood
    shall be burned as fuel for the fire.
                                    (Isa. 9: 4–5)

That is, the "peace" the new king will bring is not due to reconciliation but to a complete routing of the enemy.

2. Psalm 46:10 is often taken to be assurance inviting calmness and serenity. The preceding verse, however, affirms that confidence in God expressed in verse 10 is based on a violent seizure of enemy weapons, a seizure and destruction only made possible by immense force:

Come, behold the works of the LORD;
    see what desolations he has brought on
        the earth.
He makes wars cease to the end of the
        earth;
    he breaks the bow, and shatters the
        spear;
    he burns the shields with fire.
                                    (Ps. 46:8–9)

3. Micah 4:3 (see Isa. 2:4) is a vision of disarmament that anticipates a new era of peace:

[T]hey shall beat their swords into
        plowshares,
    and their spears into pruning hooks;
nation shall not lift up sword against
        nation,
    neither shall they learn war any more.

The precise same imagery is used in an antithetical way in Joel 3:9–10:

Proclaim this among the nations;
Prepare war,
    stir up the warriors.
Let all the soldiers draw near,
    let them come up.
Beat your plowshares into swords,
    and your pruning hooks into spears;
    let the weakling say, "I am a warrior."

These texts are not presented here to defend the motif of war with its inescapable violence, nor to defeat the deep hope for coming peace, also clearly voiced in these texts. Rather the purpose for citing these texts is to indicate how complex and difficult the issue is. The text, here as with many other questions, yields no single answer that permits ideological certitude. Rather the complexity of the text invites (and requires) endless interpretive negotiation. YHWH as warrior is of course not the only imagery offered in the text for God; however, the characterization is prominent enough to admit no easy resolution.

References: Cross, Frank Moore, *Canaanite Myth and Hebrew Epic: Essays in the History of the Religion of Israel* (Cambridge: Harvard University Press, 1973); Miller, Patrick D., Jr., *The Divine Warrior in Early Israel* (Cambridge: Harvard University Press, 1973); Moran, William L., "The End of the Unholy War and the Anti-Exodus," *Biblica* 44 (1963): 333–42; Myers, Ched, *Binding the Strong Man: A Political Reading of Mark's Story of Jesus* (Maryknoll, N.Y.: Orbis Books, 1991); Niditch, Susan, *War in the Hebrew Bible: A Study of the Ethics of Violence* (Oxford: Oxford University Press, 1995); Rad, Gerhard von, *Holy War in Ancient Israel,* trans. by Marva J. Dawn, with an introduction by Ben C. Ollenburger (Grand Rapids: Eerdmans, 1991); *The Revised Common Lectionary: The Consultation on Common Texts* (Nashville: Abingdon Press, 1992); Wright, G. Ernest, *The Old Testament and Theology* (New York: Harper & Row, 1969), chap. 5.

Widow One strand of ethics in the Old Testament includes the concern of YHWH, and consequently the concern of Israel, for the weak and vulnerable. Among that class is the widow, most often grouped with orphan and alien as among the most vulnerable in society. In a society organized according to patriarchal power (and a text reflective of that social organization), widows, orphans, and sojourners characteristically have no social entitlements of their own. Women and outsiders are dependent upon male patrons to protect them and to represent their interest in a male-ordered, male-dominated society.

A widow, of course, is one who has lost her husband; without a protector she is exceedingly vulnerable. She is dependent upon support and protection from people who have no legal obligation to support or protect. Israel is characteristically enjoined in the Torah commandment to care for the widow (and orphan and sojourner), to provide protection and maintenance to a member of the community (Exod. 22:22; Deut. 14:29; 16:11, 14; 24:17–21; 26:12; 27:19; see Isa. 1:17, 23; Jer. 7:6). These commands, rooted in the intention of YHWH, anticipate a social practice in which the resources and energies of the strong are committed to the well-being of the weak and exposed, thus a network of welfare maintenance. Behind that recurring ethical provision is the hymnic assertion of Israel that YHWH—as the supreme male protector—is committed to the well-being of the widow:

> Father of orphans and protector of widows
>   is God in his holy habitation.
> God gives the desolate a home to live in.
>   (Ps. 68:5–6)

> The LORD watches over the strangers;
>   he uphold the orphan and the widow,
>   but the way of the wicked he brings to
>   ruin.
>   (Ps. 146:9; see Deut. 10:18)

Thus the social requirement commanded in Israel is linked to and grounded in a theological claim. The practical outcome is that the social community of covenant is reimagined, not as a competitive interaction, but as a neighborly network that sustains people who cannot sustain themselves, thus resulting in a clear restraint against society as a competition among males.

Deuteronomy 25:5–10 includes a practical provision for the protection of a widow by assuring her a safe place in the family of her deceased husband. Even the protection is shaped to conform to the reality of a male-oriented society. (The same provision is plausibly practiced by Boaz in the narrative of Ruth.)

The Old Testament offers a suggestive array of narratives about widows, including those of Tamar (Gen. 38), Ruth (the book of Ruth), the widow of Zarephath (1 Kgs. 17:8–24), and the Shunammite woman (2 Kgs. 8:1–6). In each case, the narrative concerns an act of courage and self-assertion that results in an astonishing turnaround. The movement toward finding voice for self-assertion in these narratives is not unlike the contemporary, much celebrated case of Katherine Graham.

The social reality of widows bereft of patron and protection is transposed into a metaphor to characterize a defeated city. Thus in Lamentations 1:1, the city of Jerusalem is now bereft of protection and is exposed to great danger and humiliation. Conversely Isaiah 47:8 anticipates that Babylon in turn will be in like manner unprotected and vulnerable.

The care and protection of the widow in law, doxology, and in poetic metaphor exhibit the way in which Israel reflects upon the realities of social relationships and transposes those realities into theological cadences that stay clearly connected to social reality. The outcome is an attestation to YHWH as a key player in social relationships who protects the unprotected and who commands that same protection within the community. For the most part, the imaginative construal of the widow in social contexts stays, without objection, within the arena of male domination. YHWH, however, acts differently and emerges as a protector of vulnerable, exposed women.

References: Fensham, Charles F., "Widow, Orphan, and the Poor in Ancient Near Eastern Legal and Wisdom Literature," *Journal of Near Eastern Studies* 21 (1962): 129–39; Hiebert, P. S., "'Whence Shall Help Come to Me?' The Biblical Widow," in *Gender and Difference in Ancient Israel*, ed. Peggy L. Day (Minneapolis: Fortress Press, 1989), 125–41; Jacobs, Mignon R., "Toward an Old Testament Theology of Concern for the Underprivileged," in *Reading the Hebrew Bible for a New Millennium: Form, Concept, and Theological Perspective* (Studies in Antiquity & Christianity I; Harrisburg: Trinity Press International, 2000), 205–29.

Wilderness The wilderness tradition of Exodus 15:22–17:15 and Numbers 10:33–22:1 and 33:1–37 constitutes a major motif in Israel's normative theological memory. Traditionally the period of wilderness wanderings lasted forty years and featured, in narrative form, the waywardness of Israel, the anger of YHWH, and the generosity of YHWH in a contentious pattern of restless interaction.

The historical questions about the wilderness sojourn, as with all of Israel's early traditions, are problematic. Davies has credibly proposed a geographical routing of the sojourn that makes sense with the location of oases. For the most part, however, the reader is left with the theological intentionality of the wilderness tradition. Israel was required to be in a locus of vulnerability after its departure from Egypt in order to come to the

covenant at Mt. Sinai and in order to come to the land of promise. The wilderness is a precondition for both covenant and land. Taken theologically, wilderness bespeaks vulnerability, for without visible life support systems, direct dependence upon YHWH's care is intense, and anxiety is rampant. Thus the wilderness is an arena for "testing," to find out about the seriousness of Israel's faith and about the reliability of YHWH's presence and promise (see Exod. 17:1–7; see Matt. 4:1–11; Luke 4:1–13).

The dominant narrative in the tradition is the story of manna in Exodus 16. All of the components of a stressed relationship are operative in this text:

Israel complains in its anxiety (vv. 2–3).

YHWH responds with sustenance (vv. 13–14).

Israel gathers and is satisfied (vv. 16–18).

Israel hoards and loses what it has gathered (vv. 19–21).

The fact that the narrative culminates in verses 22–30 with reference to the Sabbath suggests a parallel to the culmination of the creation account in Genesis 2:1–4a; the giving of bread signifies that the wilderness is also a place under the generative sovereignty of the creator God.

The wilderness sojourn is much remembered in Israel's liturgical life and the subject of a dynamic traditioning process (see Pss. 78; 105; 106). The fact that the final form of the text on the wilderness contains exilic materials suggests that the "wilderness" became an effective metaphor for "exile"; the exilic community, like the remembered wilderness community, is dependent upon the wondrously given sustenance of YHWH in an environment that is hostile to it and lacking in normal channels of sustenance for YHWH's covenanted people. Filtered through the exile, the wilderness thus became a way of understanding the condition of faith that trusts in YHWH alone because no other adequate source of life exists (see Isa. 55:1–2 in exilic context).

While the wilderness tradition attests to risk, danger, and contentiousness, in Hosea 2:14–20 and Jeremiah 2:21 the tradition is used to articulate an original context of "honeymoon," when no contentiousness was present in the covenantal relationship, but only pure trust and therefore joy.

The metaphor of wilderness, over a long period of interpretation, is remarkably supple. In the extrapolation of the New Testament, the wilderness theme of Israel's faith is likely transposed into the radical context of the cross, when Jesus, son of Israel, is left without resources for life.

References: Coats, George W., *Rebellion in the Wilderness* (Nashville: Abingdon Press, 1968); Davies, Graham I., *The Way of the Wilderness: A Geographical Study of the Wilderness Itineraries in the Old Testament* (Cambridge: Cambridge University Press, 1979); Sakenfeld, Katharine Doob, "The Problem of Divine Forgiveness in Numbers 14," *CBQ* 37 (1975): 317–30.

Wisdom   "Wisdom" in the Old Testament refers to a body of accumulated teaching based on discernment and reflection about the character and mystery of life. The teaching is theological-ethical reflection "from below," grounded in experience that, as such, constitutes a tradition alternative to the better-known traditions of salvation history rooted in God's miracles and expressed as covenant. Wisdom teaching contains almost

nothing of salvation miracles or covenantal commandments, only the slow, steady pondering of the gifts and demands of lived life.

These wisdom materials in Israel closely parallel non-Israelite wisdom teaching and are in part borrowed from elsewhere. Wisdom theology represents a most urbane pursuit of truth that for the most part lacks the primitive particularity of Israelite faith. These teachings are as close as Israel comes to what later became scientific reflection and what came to be called material theology. The wisdom materials are most valuable for culture exchanges concerning science and religion.

This teaching is rooted in common sense and has a high degree of prudential concern. That is, wisdom literature asks about "what works," what risks may be run, what realities can be trusted, and where the practice of human choice, human freedom, and human responsibility can be exercised.

That prudence, however, is not mere pragmatism, for even the most practical teaching is theologically based. The pragmatic approach seeks to come to terms with the nearly-hidden order of God that must be embraced and accepted as the only viable context in which an effective, joyous, and secure life can be lived. This pragmatic-theological perspective that insists on hidden, theologically authorized givens seeks to counter the propensity of "fools" who believe that life is completely open and pliable, available for managing or manipulation according to one's whim. Such fools who carelessly or arrogantly engage in such willful conduct characteristically bring destruction upon themselves and trouble upon the community, because the hidden shape of reality will not yield to such autonomy. Thus the wisdom tradition seeks to conserve the shapes of community for well-being and is immensely germane in a modern cultural context where technology may serve any unchecked whim. Precisely in the face of such human capacity and ingenuity does the wisdom tradition, in understated ways, assert the boundaries of God's given life against excessive self-assertion. The prudence expressed in wisdom teaching is deeply rooted in the reality of God and God's will.

Put more broadly, wisdom teaching is creation theology, a reflection upon lived experience in an attempt to discern the regularities of life that are taken to be the ordering of reality that the creator God decreed and guaranteed. Such regularities are most characteristically expressed as simple proverbial sayings, such as the familiar "pride goeth before a fall" (see Prov. 11:2 KJV). Such a saying that appears simple, however, is in fact a discerning conclusion based on many cases, expressed in an artistic, imaginative way. Such wisdom teaching is not a report on experience, but a shrewd and seasoned reflection that processes and generalizes experience in order that the new generation may benefit from the accumulated insight that arises from reflection upon older experience.

The discernment and articulation of recurring patterns of behavior and outcome permit the wisdom teachers to insist that God's world is reliable, though the claim is rooted in experience rather than in revelation. The regularities to which these teachers attend—concerning givens, limits, the connection of deeds and consequences, and the occasionally noticed breaks of grace in the midst of regularities—make possible a sustainable community, free of self-destructive conduct, a community congruent with the near-hidden purposes of God. The accumulated lore of wisdom teaching thus is an enterprise of socialization and a program of ethical nurture and admonition for the young. Beyond that, wisdom perspectives are also as close as the Old Testament comes to scientific thought, for the wisdom teachers give attention to the natural as well as social environment of human life and ponder the regularities of nature (= creation).

No scholarly consensus exists regarding the "habitat" of such teaching, and very likely it reflects multiple contexts. Among the likely loci of such teaching are (a) the family or clan (prototypically father to son), which is preoccupied with the nurture of the young into the approved ways of the family; (b) the royal court (prototypically king to heir), which reflects about the nature of governance and the possibilities and limits of power; and (c) schools, which nurture the children of the elite in the ways of power. The evidence for any of these contexts is not conclusive, but we may be certain that ancient Israel had more or less formal contexts in which it socialized its young into responsible life for the sake of the community.

In these several possible contexts, different forms of teaching were formulated, all of them characteristically discerning and artistic. Some of the wisdom teaching must have been oral and in short units, while some of it appears "more learned" and was at the outset more extended and likely literary. In any case, over time the various offers of wisdom reflection and instruction grew into larger collections, extended literary bodies, and eventually into "books."

The wisdom books in the Old Testament include Proverbs, Job, and Ecclesiastes and in the larger canon of Roman Catholicism also Sirach and the Wisdom of Solomon. The book of Proverbs (as well as Sirach) is a collection of conventional teachings that is basically conservative relating to the coherence and order of the community that is tried and true. This instruction is particularly alert to the boundaries of human behavior which, when violated, bring trouble and death. The book of Job assumes teaching like that of the book of Proverbs (reflected in Job's "friends"), in which reflection on experience has been hardened into dogmatic conviction that requires experience to conform to preconceived patterns of morality. The book of Job thus is a literature of protest against conclusions like those in the book of Proverbs, which have closed off the chance to learn from new experience. The book of Ecclesiastes is a later wisdom teaching that is cast not in a tone of protest but of resignation. The teaching underlying Ecclesiastes is that reality is ordered, but it is hidden and beyond human comprehension; consequently the best humans can do is to settle for conventional conduct.

The rich diversity of Proverbs, Job, and Ecclesiastes suggests that at its best the wisdom tradition was an ongoing reflective conversation in which different interpreters proposed different instructional judgments. Such judgments were to some extent open, ready to be revised in the face of continuing experience. One can see in some of his dispute with the Pharisees in the New Testament that Jesus continues the dialogical, even disputatious, probing of what an ordered life requires and permits (as in Mark 12:13–37). The paradigmatic form in which Jesus is exhibited as a wisdom teacher in the Gospel narratives is in his parables, which are narrative developments of Hebrew proverbs. That openness to experience inclines to keep wisdom instruction characteristically short of absolute conclusion, but cases can also be cited in which the tradition has become absolute, no longer a discernment about new experience.

Much in wisdom instruction is prudential, but alongside the pragmatic is a directly theological strand that is especially visible in Proverbs 8:22–31. In this poem "wisdom" speaks as a person (a woman!) and is said to be God's primal companion in the process of creation. This remarkable teaching has long been important in theological reflection. In Christian tradition the theme of Proverbs 8 appears to be taken up in John 1:1–18 as the "logos of creation," that is, the hidden but decisive rationality of God's creation that in Christian confession is embodied in Jesus of Nazareth. Thus Jesus is not only a wisdom teacher, but he is the embodiment of the wisdom of God that provides the coherence and visibility of God's creation. Thus, Paul can write of Jesus as "the wisdom of God" in a way that echoes the teaching of Proverbs 8 (1 Cor. 1–2). In subsequent philosophical reflection in the church, moreover, this wisdom-logos theme of God's pervasive presence in the world is articulated as the Second Person of the Trinity, a theological claim larger and deeper than simply the historical Jesus.

More recently, this theological characterization of wisdom in Proverbs 8 as the generative force of God's creation has been especially important in feminist theological reflection, for "wisdom" in Hebrew (hokmah) is a feminine noun, and so some scholars have suggested that the world as God's creation has as its driving impetus a principle of femininity that enacts and articulates the creator God. That wisdom, as a feminine figure in the tradition, provided a resource for the development of the Christian doctrine of the Trinity where the Second Person (the Son) is the logos (= rationality) of creation is entirely plausible.

The wisdom traditions are preoccupied with the mystery of creation. This intellectual, ethical, theological commitment, expressed in a rich literature, is an important resource for theological reflection.

1. The wisdom tradition asserts that the ethical realities of God's world are not as one-dimensional and settled as sometimes thought with reference to the traditional commandments given in revelation. Ethics cannot be so fully settled in a world that refuses to be decoded.

2. In a modern/postmodern world that settles for data and proclaims that knowledge is power by transposing data into technical capacity, the wisdom tradition continues to insist that the demands and the possibilities of human life are richer, more complex, and less directly available than technique may suggest. In part, knowing requires yielding to a nondecoded mystery.

3. The wisdom tradition attests that all of the data is not in, and therefore ethical judgments and conclusions are endlessly provisional and open to reformulation.

The interpretive practice of the wisdom teachers, taken up by the scribes, has given Judaism (and derivatively Christianity) enormous interpretive vitality that knows that the truth of life is hard work that requires ongoing discernment, fresh imaginative articulation, and receptivity to matters that may challenge and veto old settlements. The process of transmitting wisdom to the next generation provides a model for education as monitoring disciples. Education on this horizon is not the importation of data, but socialization into an ethical perspective rooted in the theological reality of God's ordering of creation. The dynamic quality of this interpretive tradition at its best is commensurate with the world as God's creation over which God retains inscrutable but decisive governance.

References: Brown, William P., *Character in Crisis: A Fresh Approach to the Wisdom Literature of the Old Testament* (Grand Rapids: Eerdmans, 1996); idem, *The Ethos of the Cosmos: The Genesis of Moral Imagination in the Bible* (Grand Rapids: Eerdmans, 1999); Crenshaw, James L., *Education in Ancient Israel: Across the Deadening Silence* (New York: Doubleday, 1998); idem, *Old Testament Wisdom: An Introduction* (Louisville, Ky.: Westminster John Knox Press, 1998); idem, *Urgent Advice and Probing Questions: Collected Writings on Old Testament Wisdom* (Macon, Ga.: Mercer University Press, 1995); Gutierrez, Gustavo, *On Job: God-Talk and the Suffering of the Innocent* (Maryknoll, N.Y.: Orbis Books, 1987); Murphy, Roland, *The Tree of Life: An Exploration of Biblical Wisdom Literature* (New York: Doubleday, 1990); Rad, Gerhard von, *Wisdom in Israel* (Nashville: Abingdon Press, 1972); Witherington, Ben, *Jesus the Sage: The Pilgrimage of Wisdom* (Minneapolis: Fortress Press, 1994); Yoder, Christine Roy, *Wisdom as a Woman of Substance: A Socioeconomic Reading of Proverbs 1–9 and 31:10–31* (BZAW 304; Berlin: Walter de Gruyter, 2001).

Worship The community of ancient Israel in the Old Testament, like every historical community rooted in a particular circumstance, lived in a world of recurring human realities: the local, familial realities of birth and death and the public realities of wars and rumors of wars. Israel's lived circumstance that was its context for worship was in no way exceptional. If we are to understand worship in that ordinary context, we may take one of several approaches:

We may consider a *historical* approach, as do Albertz and Miller, and attend to the religious practices of Israel such as festivals, sacrifices, and rules for purity.

We may take a more *theological* approach, as does Kraus, and notice the claims made for YHWH who judges and saves, and who governs Israel, the nations, and the entire creation.

As chosen here, we may consider a *cultural-symbolic anthropological* view of worship as exemplified in the study of Samuel Balentine, an approach that is greatly informed by the anthropological perspectives of Mary Douglas, Clifford Geertz, and Victor Turner. In this approach, worship is clearly the management and enactment of symbols, in order to represent and redescribe the world in new, different, and alternative ways. Such an understanding does not detract from the theological "seriousness" of worship, for obviously people who led and participated in worship took as real and substantive the symbolization enacted. For example, the "God of Exodus" is not a mere symbol, but is understood as the real agent who enacted the real emancipation of Israel from Egyptian bondage. Thus, the redescription of reality that takes place in Israel's worship is to recharacterize the familial world of birth and death and the public world of war and economy with reference to YHWH, who is seen in worship to be the key actor in the world arising in and through such worship. While this worshiping community takes up the data of life common to every human community, the particular rendering of reality through reference to YHWH in all of YHWH's "thickness" means that the result (and consequent assumption) of such worship is a world very different from the world resulting from any other worship or symbolization. In worship, Israel redescribes

The world as the creation of YHWH, over which YHWH presides in effective sovereignty and in generous beneficence.

Human society as a community evoked by YHWH and willed to be a community of compassion, mercy, and justice.

Its own life in the world as a community of obedience, as a community that has received its own life and its world from the abundance of YHWH, and that has sworn in glad loyalty to live its life back to YHWH in joy. For this reason, the extended Sinai traditions stand at the center of the Torah, for the God who meets Israel is the one who commands and who will be obeyed.

Six practices are pivotal in Israel's imaginative engagement with the creator of heaven and earth who sojourns with Israel:

1. Israel's worship consists in exuberant *acts of praise*, as is evidenced in the Psalter (see, for example, Pss. 145–150). Praise is an unrestrained, glad act of ceding life over to YHWH in awe, amazement, and gratitude. Praise aims to enhance the life and aegis of YHWH at the expense of all other gods and of every other loyalty.

2. Israel's worship consists in *lament and complaint*, as is evident in the Psalter (see, for example, Pss. 3–7). Israel has to do with this God "from whom no secret can be hid." For that reason, Israel before YHWH speaks fully and freely about its loss. This accent becomes acute in the worship of Israel in the sixth-century exile, but the theme is pervasive. Such prayers are characteristically acts of hope, for Israel issues urgent petitions to which it fully expects YHWH's active, intervening response.

3. Israel's worship consists in attentiveness to the requirements for *purity and holiness*. The God that Israel worships is holy—beyond every control or comparison, marked by purity and righteousness. Israel in worship seeks to conform itself to that character of YHWH

in order that YHWH can be present in the community.

4. Israel's worship consists in *attentiveness to the neighbor,* an attentiveness that is derivative from and commensurate with singular devotion to YHWH. Thus, Israel's festivals and sacrifices are on occasion provision for the feeding of needy neighbors, from which may be extrapolated a neighborly ethic.

5. Israel's worship consists in *vigorous, disciplined remembering* of YHWH's "mighty deeds," most often a memory of YHWH's goodness (as in Pss. 105, 136), but also a remembrance of Israel's recalcitrance in response to YHWH (as in Neh. 9, Ps. 106). The world is redescribed as an arena for astonishingly transformative wonders.

6. Israel's worship consists in acts of *vigorous imagination about the future,* whereby the world is construed in ways fully congruent with YHWH's purpose and intention.

Through the process of such worship, Israel delineated its own community and the world as fully gifted by and responsive to YHWH. At the same time, YHWH's own character and purpose are more fully and palpably available to Israel through this process. Such resolved, reiterated redescription was decisive for generating a holy people committed to a holy God.

Of course, worship in Israel is immensely varied. The text exhibits many different worship practices from many different literary sources, times, circumstances, and perspectives. Each warrants detailed attention. The main lines of worship show, nonetheless, that insofar as worship is Israel-as-YHWH's-covenant-partner-pondering-YHWH, worship is the formation and practice of a community that is counter to the governing assumptions of its environment. While the historical particularities of practice merit attention, they should be understood as vehicles and instruments for constructing an alternative social world. Worship in Israel was not only reflective of theological conviction about YHWH, but was also generative of that conviction. The embrace of theological conviction, in order to remain vitally linked to lived reality, depends upon sustained liturgical enactment and redescription. Thus worship is that sustained activity that permitted Israel to be the gladly obedient people of YHWH who is known in the Torah.

Protestant Church traditions—both liberal and conservative—seldom recognize that worship is precisely where energy, insight, and resolve are generated for an alternative life in the world. While the profoundly personal element is evident in Israel's worship, that personal articulation is fully lodged in the generative processes of the community. The psalmist can thus express a most personal, intimate yearning for God:

> As a deer longs for flowing streams,
>   so my soul longs for you, O God.
>   (Ps. 42:1)

But the same psalmist knew that participation in the community of worship in the designated place of community worship is the true joy and the quenching of personal thirst:

> O send out your light and your truth;
>   let them lead me;
> let them bring me to your holy hill
>   and to your dwelling.
> Then I will go to the altar of God,
>   to God my exceeding joy;
> and I will praise you with the harp,
>   O God, my God.
>   (Ps. 43:3–4)

References: Albertz, Rainer, *A History of Israelite Religion in the Old Testament Period,* 2 vols.

(OTL; Louisville, Ky.: Westminster John Knox Press, 1994); Anderson, Gary A., *A Time to Mourn, A Time to Dance: The Expression of Grief and Joy in Israelite Religion* (University Park, Pa.: Pennsylvania State University Press, 1991); Balentine, Samuel E., *The Torah's Vision of Worship* (OBT; Minneapolis: Fortress Press, 1999); Brueggemann, Walter, *Israel's Praise: Doxology Against Idolatry and Ideology* (Philadelphia: Fortress Press, 1988); Harrelson, Walter, *From Fertility Cult to Worship: A Reassessment for the Modern Church of the Worship of Ancient Israel* (Garden City, N.Y.: Doubleday, 1969); Kraus, Hans-Joachim, *Worship in Israel* (Richmond, Va.: John Knox Press, 1966); Miller, Patrick D., *The Religion of Ancient Israel* (Library of Ancient Israel; Louisville, Ky.: Westminster John Knox Press, 2000).

■ ■ ■

YHWH These four letters in Hebrew signify the name of the God of the Old Testament; because the name is constituted by four consonants, scholars refer to the term as the "tetragrammaton." They are four consonants in the Hebrew text of the Bible that are left unpronounced; they lack the necessary vowels to permit vocalization. This four-consonant term is the "proper name" of the God of Israel, whereas the other familiar references to the God of Israel—God, Lord, El Shaddai—are either generic names for deity (of which there are many in the world of the Bible) or titles that give respect or identify attributes for this God. In most English translations of the Bible, "God" is a translation of *Elohim*, whereas "Lord" variously translates YHWH or *'Adon*. In either case they are not "proper names." Thus the four-consonant reference is distinctive among all the appellations for God and draws the reader of the Bible closest to the inscrutable reality of the God of Israel.

The pronunciation of the name is an intentional bafflement. The vowels to match the consonants are not given us in the tradition, and therefore the name is likely not intended to be pronounced, thus preserving the mystery of the name and the freedom of the one named. To be sure, in the conventional Hebrew text, through a standard scribal device, vowels appear above and below the consonants. But these vowels (*e, o, a*) do not belong to the consonants; a knowing reader recognizes that these vowels require different consonants that are "understood" by the reader but not printed in the text; thus with "supplied" consonants the vowels yield the term *adonai* = "my Lord." That term results from supplied consonants and is not related to the four consonants in YHWH. Moreover, a traditional mismatch occurs in practice whereby the four consonants are pronounced with the vowels in the text, yielding "Jehovah." That term, however, is a complete misunderstanding, yielding a nonword, bringing together vowels and consonants that cannot possibly belong together. This anomaly likely was a sixteenth-century Christian misconstrual, in ignorance of Hebrew and perpetuated since that time. Moreover, a conjecture and then a convention among Christian scholars is to hypothesize that the appropriate vowels for the four consonants are *a* and *e*, which yields "Yahweh." This reading is found in many books, but is a Christian, scholarly convention that is characteristically affrontive to Orthodox Jews because it assumes an intimacy and familiarity with YHWH that is either impossible or blasphemous. For different reasons then, it is clear that all of these conventions—Adonai, Jehovah, Yahweh—are used for different reasons with different merits, but none of them approach the meaning of the name itself, which remains unpronounced and unpronounceable.

A common proposal among scholars is that the name YHWH derives from the verb *hyh*, "to be." The verb with an initial "y" may make it causative, thus "cause to be," thus "create." Frank Moore Cross, following a line from Paul Haupt, has proposed that YHWH is "the one who creates," thus "YHWH," and completes the verb with a direct object, "hosts," thus "who creates the hosts," thus "YHWH of hosts." (The "hosts" variously refers to heavenly armies or the armies of Israel, for when YHWH is identified as "lord of hosts," reference is to leadership of a military kind.) While having some merit and representing the fullest hypothesis we have, the proposal remains just an explanatory attempt that does not penetrate the mystery of the God named or Israel's intent in the naming.

When taken from the verb "to be," the name can be understood with reference to the "I am" statements that Harner has identified in the book of Isaiah and that have connections to the "I am" statements of Jesus in the Fourth Gospel. The name clearly attests, in Israel's use, to singular sovereignty, a claim that is related in complex ways to the rise of monotheism, to the divine assembly, and to the question of a female consort for this God [see ASHERAH, DIVINE COUNCIL, and MONOTHEISM].

The origin of the name of this God, and so the origin of this God, is as obscure as its pronunciation and meaning. While some people have suggested that this God and this name originate in the desert, no explanation is given in the Old Testament; YHWH as it appears in the text is an already established, fully functioning God about whom no question of origin is asked.

Perhaps the most important text for our topic is Exodus 3:14, in which YHWH enigmatically announces God's own name to Moses. The statement has been variously translated, "I AM WHO I AM," or "I am what I will be(come)," or "I will be what I will be(come)." That formulation, however, only hides what it claims to reveal. That narrative text, moreover, moves immediately to identify this God as (a) the God of the ancestors in Genesis (Exod. 3:15–16) (b) who now promises to deliver Israel from slavery into the new land. (Exodus 6:2 also acknowledges that something new of YHWH becomes known in and through Moses.) That is, the God disclosed to Moses is known by the narratives and songs in which YHWH is embedded that tell of YHWH's intentions, actions, and attributes. This God is known in the doxologies of Israel as the one who dominates creation and appears in storms and fire (see Exod. 19:16–25). At the same time, and integral to the disclosure of the text, this God is known primarily as the God of Israel who is bound in covenant to Israel and who is known in and through the "miracles" enacted in the life and history of Israel. Thus this God is unknown and unavailable except in and through Israel and derivatively in and through this text. All of that theological affirmation of YHWH as creator of heaven and earth and covenant partner and savior of Israel is poured by the interpretive, doxological process into the enigmatic four consonants. The unpronounceable name thus signifies the one richly known in all of this tradition.

As Jews and Christians more seriously engage in conversation, the matter of pronunciation is an acute problem, for the conventional, Christian rendering "Yahweh" is, as mentioned earlier, an affront to Orthodox Jews. Moreover, the conventional Jewish "Adonai" (Lord) is not unproblematic in feminists' sensitivity. We may have recourse to the Jewish mystical practice of *ha-shem* ("the name") that is substituted for the name itself. For now we have no acceptable, adequate way to pronounce the name. The best approach is to write "YHWH" and recognize that whatever oral expression is given is less than adequate, which is the exact intention, for our references are in the presence of the inscrutably holy one of Israel. The written "YHWH" only makes sense to those who bring knowledge of the entire tradition of creation and rescue to the four consonants. But then, only those who know the narrative and song well should attempt YHWH's name. Strangers who draw too close are likely to reduce YHWH to something generic and therefore misunderstand and violate everything that is at stake in a name that remains beyond our ken. The "I am" of the alleged verb opens to the New Testament, but that lies beyond our question.

References: Cross, Frank Moore, *Canaanite Myth and Hebrew Epic: Essays in the History of the Religion of Israel* (Cambridge: Harvard University Press, 1973), chap. 3; Harner, Philip B., *Grace and Law in Second Isaiah: "I Am the Lord"* (Lewiston, N.Y.: Edwin Mellen Press, 1988); McCarthy, Dennis, "Exod. 3:14: History, Philology, and Theology," *CBQ* 40 (1978): 311–21; Mettinger, Tryggve N. D., *In Search of God: The Meaning and Message of the Everlasting Names* (Philadelphia: Fortress Press, 1988), chap. 2; Miller, Patrick D., *The Religion of Ancient Israel* (Louisville, Ky.: Westminster John Knox Press, 2000), chap. 1; Seitz, Christopher, *Word Without End: The Old Testament As Abiding Theological Witness* (Grand Rapids: Eerdmans, 1998), chap. 17.

SCRIPTURE INDEX

Genesis

Reference	Page
1	83
1–2	40, 191
1–11	220
1:1–2	40
1:1–2:4a	40, 151
1:1–2:25	16
1:2	28, 200
1:22	19
1:24	82
1:26	56
1:26–28	105–7
1:28	19, 67
1:31	40
2:1–4a	33, 40, 180, 231
2:3	99
2:4	152
2:4b–25	40–41
2:7	47
2:15	67
2:18	191
2:22	191
2:23	191
2:24–25	191
3	16, 41, 79–80, 197
3–11	2, 157
3:16–19	191
3:22	56
4	41
4:24	223
5:1	105–6, 152
5:3	191
5:24	65
6–9	29, 41, 175
6:6	172
6:9	152
6:17	199
7:1–16	150
8:15–18	169
8:21–22	157
8:22	16, 82
9:6	105–7, 191
9:8–17	29, 37–38, 50, 62, 157, 169
9:12	33
9:16	39
10:1	152
11:1–9	18
11:7	56
11:10	152
11:27	152
11:30	1, 90
11:31	23
12–24	1
12–36	101
12–50	156, 220
12:1	120
12:1–3	101, 62, 157
12:2	2
12:3	19
12:5	23
12:10–20	59, 198
13:12	23
13:18	1
14:19	116
15:6	2, 77, 156
15:7	72
15:7–21	37–38
15:18	2
15:18–21	120
16:3	23
16:7–11	4
17	33, 150
17:2–21	2
17:7–19	39
18:18	2, 19, 157
18:19	61
18:22–32	148
18:25	179
19	192–93
21:15–19	148
21:15–21	4
22	93
22:11–12	4
22:18	2, 19, 157
24–26	1
25 –27	1
25–36	1
25:7–11	47
25:12	152
25:19	152
25:21	1, 90
26:4	2, 19, 157
26:21	187
27	20
28:10–22	1
28:13–15	101, 157
28:14	19
29:31	90
30:1	1
32:9–12	148
35:9–15	150
36:1	152
37:2	152
37–38	1, 59
37–50	1, 59
38	192, 230
38:8	163
46:1–47:13	198
47	60
47:7	20
47:13–26	59

48:8–20	20	16:31	131	32:11–14	141, 148
49:29–33	47	17:1–7	231	32:25–29	155
49:33	47	17:8–16	92	32:32	85
		19–24	22, 35, 50	33:19	63
Exodus		19:6	99, 116	34:6–7	76, 127
1–15	72, 220	19:16–25	50, 215–16, 239	34:7	195
2:23–25	72, 124, 184	20:1–17	22, 38, 50, 66,	34:9	85
3:1–6	215		215	34:13	106
3:2–6	4	20:2	50	34:18–26	84
3:7	120	20:2–3	94, 138	34:19–20	182
3:7–9	140	20:3	12, 135	34:20	164
3:10	140	20:4–5	106	35–40	150
3:14	239	20:5–6	127	40:34–37	29
3:15–16	239	20:6	126	40:34–38	88
4:22	61	20:8–11	50, 180		
4:24–26	33	20:12	50	**Leviticus**	
6:6–7	163	20:17	135, 143, 191	1–7	151, 154, 182, 197, 208
6:12	34	20:18–21	50, 141	4	182
7–11	29, 223	21–23	218	4:20	85
7–12	60, 145	21:1	20	4:26	85
8:10	146	21:1–23:33	20	4:31	85
9:14	146	21:15–17	21	4:35	85
10:1–2	146, 221	21:18–21	21	5	182
10:17	145	21:22–25	21	5:16	85
11–36	220	21:25	223	7:12–15	182, 211
11:7	146	21:26–27	21	7:28–36	182
12–13	84, 221	21:28–36	21	10:10	154
12:26–27	57, 221	22:1–7	21	11–16	152
12:32	19	22:1–15	133	16	13–14, 67, 84, 85, 183
12:38	35	22:10–13	21	16:9	13
13:8–10	57, 221	22:18–20	21	17–26	98, 152, 193, 218
13:13–15	164	22:21–27	21	18	152, 193
13:14–15	57	22:22	230	18:22	98, 193
13:14–16	221	22:23–24	22	19	152
14:4	73, 88	22:27	22	19:2	152, 196
14:13–14	77, 228	22:28–29	182	19:13–18	142
14:17	73, 88	23:6–9	21	19:18	126, 142, 152
14:21	199	23:10–11	21	19:19	98
15	16, 29	23:12–13	21	19:33–34	152
15:1–18	72, 132, 141	23:14–17	21, 84	19:34	126, 143
15:3	227	23:20–23	4	20	152
15:13	163	24:1–28	35	20:10	192
15:18	116	24:3	38	20:13	98, 193
15:20	103	24:7	20, 38	21:9	192
15:20–21	90, 132	24:15–18	88, 151	23	84
15:21	14, 72, 141	25–31	150, 180	23:26–32	84
15:22–17:15	231	25:1– 10:10	218	25	67, 121, 133
16–18	220	25:10–16	9	25:10	86
16–28	141	28:41	127	25:23	199
16:2–3	231	29:7	127	26	38, 48, 145
16:13–14	231	30:30	127	26:3–13	19, 101
16:16–18	231	31	180	26:4	34
16:19–21	231	31:12–17	180	26:14	29
16:22–30	231	32	155–56	26:14–39	175, 223
16:27–30	180	32:11–13	85		

Numbers

1:1–10:10	150
6:22–26	154
6:24–26	19
10–36	141
10:33–22:1	231
10:35–36	9, 88
11:11–15	141
12	132
14:13–19	141, 148
14:13–20	85
14:14	9
16:22	199
21:2–3	91
22:22	188
22:32	188
28–29	84
33:1–37	231

Deuteronomy

1–3	52
1–11	141
1:5	52, 68, 75, 141, 215
2:34	91
3:5–6	91
3:7–11	53
4:8	218
4:44	218
5:1	124
5:3	222
5:6–7	93–94
5:6–21	51, 141
5:10	126
5:12–15	51, 180
5:14	181
5:21	191
5:22–23	141
5:27	124
6:4	124, 139
6:4–7	126
6:4–9	93, 123
6:5	124
6:7	57
6:20–25	57, 221
7:2	91
7:5	16
7:6–8	61
7:7	125
7:8	164
9:1	124
9:4–7	61
9:26	164
10:1–5	9
10:6–16	53
10:8	155
10:14–15	61
10:15	125
10:16	34
10:17–18	179
10:18	126, 134, 230
10:19	143, 198
11:8–32	53
11:17	116
12–25	22, 51–52, 68, 124
12:2–12	94
13:1–5	159
13:4	53
13:5	164
14:2	61
14:21	143
14:22–29	182
14:24–26	182
14:29	198, 230
15:1–8	114, 133
15:1–18	21, 121
15:15	133, 164, 198
15:21	164
16:1–8	165
16:1–17	21, 84
16:11	198, 230
16:14	198, 230
16:18–20	21
16:21	10
16:22	16
17:14–20	54, 117
17:16	60
17:18	218
18:5	62
18:9–14	161
18:15–22	160
18:17	64
19:4–6	163
19:11–13	86
20:14	191
20:14–15	91
20:16–17	91
20:16–18	91
21:18–21	86
22–23	22
22:13–20	191
22:21	192
22:22	86
23:1	143, 199
23:1–8	143
23:7	198
23:19–20	193
23:20	143
24:1–4	194
24:1–5	191
24:9	132
24:16	79
24:17–21	133, 198, 230
25:5–10	163, 230
25:17–19	92
25:28	218
26:5–10	221
26:8–9	120
26:11–13	198
26:12	230
26:16–19	52
27:3	218
27:8	218
27:19	198, 230
27:26	218
28	38, 48, 52, 145
28:1–14	11, 19
28:15–46	223
28:15–68	29, 175
28:68	60
29:20	218
29:27	218
29:30	86
30:1–3	171
30:6	34
30:10	218
30:11–14	197
30:15–20	53, 127, 175, 196, 201, 213
31:9–12	218
31:24	218
31:26	218
32:9–10	61
32:35	224
32:39	116, 173, 187, 214
33:10	155
33:10–11	217
33:38	154

Joshua

1–4	53
1–12	96, 220
1:7–8	168
1:16–17	168
2	192
2:10	92
2:12	127
4:20–24	221
4:21–24	57
4:23–24	72
5:2–9	33
6:7	127
6:17–21	91
10:28–40	92
11:11–21	92
12:7–24	63

21:43–45	101, 157	16:14–16	199	4:20–28	134
24:26	36	16:21	126, 128	5:3	134
		17:16	228	5:13–18	187
Judges		17:26	33	6:20–22	134
3:7–10	184	17:36	33	7:1–8	134
3:9	184	18:21	126	7:8	60
3:31	184	18:22	126	8	28
5:1–31	90	19:20–24	159	8:1–4	209
5:10–11	57, 221	20:14–15	77	8:1–8	9
6:14	184	20:14–17	127	8:1–13	209
6:25–32	15	23:6–12	154	8:4	209
10:1	184	24	92	8:9	9, 29, 131
11:29–40	182	26:19	137	8:10	29
13:2	90	28:3–25	48	8:12–13	18, 209
14:3	33	29:4	187	8:27	209
15:18	33	30:18–20	92	8:30–53	209
19	192	31:4	33	8:31–53	45, 148, 171
				8:33–34	209
1 Samuel		**2 Samuel**		8:33–53	85
1–2	89, 148	5:5	18	8:35–36	209
1:7–8	90	5:6–10	18	8:37–40	209
1:13	90	5:19	227	8:46	209
1:20–28	90	6:1–19	9	8:56–61	209
2	155	7	44, 157	9:17–19	134
2:1–10	90, 104	7:1–6	54	9:24	60
2:6	173	7:1–16	38, 44, 157	9:26–28	134
2:6–7	214	7:1–17	117, 121	10:14–22	134
2:35	155	7:11–16	127	11:1	60
4–5	88	7:18–20	148	11:1–8	36, 53, 112
4:3	9	7:4–7	206	11:1–18	134
4:8	72	7:6–7	209	11:14	187
5	138	8:1–12	227	11:23	187
5–6	146	9–20	43	11:25	187
5:6–7	88	9:1	77, 127	12	121
6:6	72	9:9–10	2	12:1–19	36
6:10–7:2	9	10:1	127	14– 25	117
7–15	117	10:2	77	14:9–14	53
7:9	124	11–12	44	14:23	93
8:5	99, 134	11:14	189	14:25	59
8:7	92	12:1–15	161	15:3	53
8:8	124	12:13	92	15:4–5	117
8:10–17	117	15:29	155	15:5	44
8:20	99, 134	19:21	128	15:11–15	53
8:22	92	19:22	187	15:13–18:19	10
9	92	24:1	188	15:14	93
9:1–10:16	93	24:18–25	206	16:30–31	112
10:9–13	159			16:31–33	112
12:7	179	**1 Kings**		17–21	159, 220
13–15	117	1:7–8	128	17:8–24	230
14:6	33	1:39	155	17:9–16	64
15	92	2:27	155	17:17	173
15:14–15	92	3	192	17:17–24	64
15:24	92	3–11	60	18	15, 64, 80, 112
16:1–13	90, 117	3:2–4	93	18:21	112
16:12–13	128	4:7–10	134	18:26	125

18:26–29	138	19:35–37	12	21:12–15	32
18:37	124	21–25	117	29–31	22, 32
18:40	159	21:3	10	29:1–31:21	164
19:11–18	215	21:13–15	169	29:5–11	166
19:12	215	21:14	170	29:10	165
19:16	127	22	52–53, 169	29:16	165
20:42	92	22–23	165–67, 210	30:1–9	165
21	64, 112, 114–15	22:3–14	54	30:8–9	166
21:8	189	22:8–13	36	30:10–22	166
21:19–26	112	22:14	103	30:18	166
21:20–24	65	22:14–20	102	31:1	93
21:25	112	22:16–17	103	31:20–21	166
22:19–23	3–4, 55	22:16–20	103	32:12	94
22:20	56	23	167	34–35	32, 166
22:43	93	23:4	10	34:22–28	12
22:52	112	23:4–5	15	36:17–21	32
27	115	23:5–9	94	36:22–23	32
		23:21–23	165	36:23	32, 144
		23:25	54		

2 Kings

				Ezra	
2–9	159, 220	23:26	168	1–2	26, 32
2:9–12	65	23:26–27	168	1:2–4	144
2:9–18	200	23:28–29	59	1:2–11	71
3:2	16, 112	23:28–30	167	4	186
3:26–27	182	23:29–30	17	6:3–5	144
4:8–37	131	23:30	128	6:19–22	75
4:31–37	173	24:4	86	7:6	189
4:38–41	131	24:13–17	17	9:1–4	75, 112
4:42–44	131	25	53	9:8–15	170
8:4	131	25:1–22	26	9:15	172
9–10	112	25:7	17		
9:1–6	230	25:27–30	17, 32, 117	**Nehemiah**	
9:30	112			2:9–19	186
9:30–37	65	**1 Chronicles**		4:1–7	186
10	15	1:1	31	6:1–14	186
10:15–17	36	4:9–10	32	6:14	103
10:26–27	106	9:35–44	31	8	54, 144, 155, 189
11:12	128	10	31	8:1	219
11:18	106	10:13–14	31	8:1–8	36
12:1–16	28	11–29	31	8:7	165
15:17–22	12	21:1	187–88	8:7–8	75
16:7	12	28:2	9	9:29–31	172
17	70, 187	29:10–13	31	10–13	75
17:3–4	12	29:14	31, 137	13:23–27	112
17:5–6	12, 186				
17:5–23	12	**2 Chronicles**		**Esther**	
17:13	160	1–9	32	3:7	84, 162
17:14	124	6	28	9:18–28	162
17:24–41	186	7:14	32	9:20–32	84
18–19	164	7:16	62		
18:4	93, 164	10–36	32	**Job**	
18:12	124	13:2–20	32	1–2	56, 187
18:13–17	164	16:1–6	32	9:22	201
18:22	93	18:1–34	32	21:7	213
19:4	124	18:8–27	32	30:20	124
19:32–34	12	21:11	93		

31	175, 177	24:1-2	68	51:4	87		
31:35–37	203	24:3-6	68	51:11	200		
38–41	149, 203, 213	24:7-10	68	51:16-17	183		
		27:1	101, 184	54:1	202		
Psalms		29	41	54:3	202		
1	219	29:1	56	55:2	124		
1:2	172	29:1-2	88	55:15	49		
1:5	178	29:9	88	55:18	164		
1:6	170	30:1	211	56:13	49		
2	44, 117	30:8-11	211	57:3	76		
3-7	236	30:9	48	60:5	124		
3:1-2	148	30:11	174, 211	61:7	76		
3:4	124	31:5	164	66:13-15	211		
3:7	185, 202, 225	32	85, 87, 197	66:19	211		
4:1	124	32:3-4	86	67:3-5	104		
6	85	32:3-5	202	68:5-6	230		
6:4	185	32:5-6	86	69:16	124		
6:10	225	33	41	69:18	163		
7:1	185	33:6	200	71:12	147		
7:6	202	33:19	49	71:13	187		
7:6-8	148	34:4	124	72	44, 117		
7:10-11	202	34:4-5	101	73:17	109		
7:12-13	225	34:6-8	185	73:23-28	203		
8	41	35:17	147	73:24	173		
8:5-8	106	35:22-23	147	74	109, 119		
10:2	135	37	177	74:2	163		
10:3-4	178	38:1-3	211	76	109		
10:8b-11	178	38:17-18	202	77:7-9	147		
11:7	109, 216	38:21	187	77:15	163		
12:5	135	38:21-22	202	78	62, 231		
12:7-8	135	39	119	78:4-7	57		
13:1-3	147	39:12	199	78:4-8	221		
13:1-4	119	40:1-2	149	78:22	184		
13:3	124	40:10	76	78:35	163		
13:5-6	119	40:10-11	211	78:42-53	146		
15	177, 179	42:1	237	78:60	62		
17:15	109, 216	43:3-4	237	78:67-71	62		
18	44	44:9-16	78	78:68-71	108		
18:4-5	49	44:9-22	224	79	109, 119		
18:21	124	44:10-12	202	82	56		
19	136, 219	44:12	164	84	109, 208		
19:1-6	68	44:17-18	78	85:10	76		
19:7	220	44:26	78, 164	87	109, 208		
19:7-10	68	45	44	87:4	60		
20	44	46	109, 208	88	119, 149		
20:1	124	46:1	109	88:6-9a	202		
21	44	46:4-5	109	88:10-12	48		
22:1-21a	119	46:7	109	89	44, 117, 157		
22:3	116	48	109, 208	89:1-17	38		
22:3-5	148	49:12	136	89:14	76		
22:21	124, 185	49:14	49	89:38-51	117		
22:21b-31	119	49:16	173	89:46-49	149		
22:22-24	211	49:20	136	89:49	77		
22:23-26	211	50:2	87	90:10	47		
24	177	51	44, 85, 147, 197, 201	93	58, 101, 109, 208		

93:1 116
96 41
96-99 58, 101, 109, 208
96:4 88
96:10 116
96:11-13 101
97:1 116
97:6-7 88
98:6 116
99:1 116
99:4 116, 126
101 44
102 85
103:1-2 47
103:4 76, 163
103:8 76, 104
103:8-14 179
103:10 224
103:11 76
103:14 196
103:17 76
103:21 56
104 41
104:27-28 16, 82
104:29-30 199–200
104:30 199
104:34 67
105 184, 231, 237
105:26 62
105:27-36 146
106 184, 231, 237
106:10 163
107 184
107:2 163
107:4-5 211
107:6 149
107:8 131
107:11-12 211
107:13 149
107:13-16 185
107:15 131
107:17-18 211
107:19 149
107:19-22 185
107:21 131
107:23-27 211
107:28 149
107:31 131
109:4 187
109:6-20 223
109:20 187
109:29 187
110 44, 117
110:2-3 211
112:4-9 177

115:1 76
115:4-8 138
115:6 125
116:1-2 149
116:2-4 211
116:8 211
116:12-19 211
117:1 104
119 219
122:1 109
124 179
130 85
130:3-4 86, 179, 197, 224
131 148
132 44, 117, 157
132:11-12 38
135:15-18 138
135:17 125
136 237
137 70, 109
137:1 109
137:7-9 223
138:2 76
138:4-6 211
139:8 47
139:21-22 225
140:6 124
143 85
143:7 124
144 44
145-150 104, 236
145:4-7 130
145:8-9 104
145:15-16 82
145:20 67
146:7-10 116
146:7c-9 104
146:9 163, 230

Proverbs
1:8 217
2:16 192
5:3 192
5:20 192
6:20 217
6:23 217
6:24 192
7:5 192
8 234
8:22–31 234
8:35–36 21, 49
10:2 177
10:4 136
10:7 177
10:11 177

10:15 136
10:21 196
11:2 232
11:5 177
11:8 177
11:10 177
11:18 136
11:28 136
12:15–16 196
12:24 136
13:19–20 196
14:31 136
16:1–2 176
16:9 176
17:5 136, 196
19:14 176
19:21 176
20:24 176
21:30–31 176
22:17–23:12 60
30:7–9 136

Ecclessiastes
3:8 86
3:16–22 201
6:1–6 136
12:1–8 49
12:7 199

Isaiah
1:9–10 193
1:17 135, 230
1:23 230
1:25–26 170
2:2–4 101, 110, 158, 219
2:12 45
4:2–4 170
5:1–7 161
5:7 178
5:26–29 29
6:1–7 4
6:1–8 3–4, 99, 159
6:1–10 215
6:3 99
6:8 56
6:9–10 124
6:24 82
7:9 13, 77
7:10–17 128
8:17–22 48
9:2–7 118, 128, 157
9:4 46
9:6 228
9:7 178
10:5 13

11:1–9	101, 118, 128, 157	45:21	184	65:24–25	110
11:10	46	46:1–2	138	66:13	126
13–14	18	46:1–7	88		

Jeremiah

17:4–6	169	47:6	17		
19	60	47:6–7	18	1:4–10	159, 215
19:23–25	13, 46, 60, 63	47:8	163, 230	1:5	62
24–27	5	48:11	88, 91	2:2	194
24:21	46	48:12	137	2:4	124
25:6	48	48:12–19	42	2:21	232
25:6–10	174	48:20	204	3–4	171
25:6–10a	173	49:1–6	204	3:1–4:4	194
25:7–8	173	49:5	62	3:12	171
26:19	48, 173	49:6	63	3:14	171
30:7	60	49:19–20	122	3:15–18	10
30:30–33	182	49:25	184	3:22	171
32:17	135	49:26	184	4–6	29
36–37	164, 228	50:1–2	227	4:1–2	171
36:17	70	50:2	164	4:2	178
37:16–20	148	50:4–9	204	4:4	34
37:22–29	13	51:2	2	4:23–26	29
37:22–38	109	51:7	178	5:8	192
38:16–19	48	51:9–10	29	5:21	124
40:1–2	85–86	51:11	164	5:26–29	135
40:9–11	185	52:7	184	5:27–28	178
40:12–31	42	52:7–8	185	5:31–34	32
40–55	41–42, 70, 122, 163, 204	52:10	184	6:10	34
41:8	2	52:13–53:12	204–5	7	29
41:8–9	204	53:4–5	203	7:6	230
41:8–10	62	53:5–6	205	7:9	51, 192
41:14	163	53:6–7	143	7:13	124
41:17–20	42	54:4–6	194	7:16	124
42:1–4	200, 204, 219	54:7–8	39	8:23	169
42:5–9	204	54:9	29, 169	9:25–26	34
42:6–7	63	55:1–2	232	10:5	138
42:8	88	55:3	39	10:5–7	138
43:1	62, 163	55:6–7	172	10:10	138
43:3	184	55:7	85–86	11:2	124
43:3–4	164	55:10	82	11:4	37
43:10	204	55:12	16	11:6	124
43:10–13	138	56:3–7	170, 180	12:1	213
43:11	137, 184	56:3–8	199	12:1–4	179
43:12	185	56:8	71	13:10	124
43:14	163	57:3	194	13:11	124
43:16–21	70, 72	58:6	86	14:12	124
44:1–2	62, 204	58:8–9	158	15:1	85, 90, 141
44:6	163	58:11–12	158	15:2	145
44:21	24	59:1	227	17:18	223
44:22–24	163	60:17	178	18:8	172
44:26	24	61:1	127	18:18	217
44:28	144	61:1–4	115, 129, 200	18:21–23	223
45:1	144	61:8	39, 116, 126	19:5	182
45:6	204	61:10–11	178	21:4–5	228
45:7	116, 187, 214	62:4	16	21:5	72
45:15	184	63:9	184	23:5	178
45:18–19	42	65:17–25	42, 110, 210	23:5–6	118, 128, 157

23:9–22	159	3:40–57	176
23:14	193	3:42	86
23:15–22	56	5:22	86, 157
24	76		
24:5–7	171	**Ezekiel**	
24:7	37	1–3	159
24:10	145	9–10	153
25:8–29	7	10:18–19	88
25:9	17	11:14–21	200
26:24	54	11:20	37, 76
27:9	17	13:1–19	159
28:1–17	159	14:11	37, 76
29–33	157	15:1–8	169
29:23	192	16:32	192
30–31	70, 122	16:40–43	126
30–33	101	16:41–42	138
30:22	37	16:46–56	193
31:4–14	110	18:1–4	79
31:12–14	122	18:32	172
31:20	126, 203	20:5	62
31:29–30	79	22:26	98, 153–54
31:31–34	39, 70	23:27	192, 194
31:33	37, 86	28:10	34
31:34	86, 197	29–30	60
31:38–40	122	29:3	60
32:2	145	30–32	60
32:6–15	163	31:18	34
32:12–16	189	32	60
32:38	37	32:19–32	34
33:14–16	118, 157	32:31	60
33:15	178	33–48	70, 101, 122, 157
33:17–18	128	34	117
33:19–22	128	34:23–24	118, 128
35:1–11	36	36:22–32	153, 200
36	54, 169	36:22–33	86
36:4–32	189	37:1–14	48, 71, 174
36:10–12	54	37:13–14	122
39:14	54	37:26	39
40:5–11	54	38:19–20	29
41:2	54	40–48	153, 206
43–44	60	43–44	110
43:6	54	43:1–5	88
45	54	44:10	156
45:1–2	189	44:15	156
46	60	47:13–14	122
46:10	46	48:35	110
50–51	18		
51:2–3	122	**Daniel**	
51:59–64	7, 154	2–3	106
51:64	18	2–4	18
52:28–30	17, 70, 206	4:13–26	4
		4:34–37	18
Lamentations		7:10	4
1:1	230	7:13–14	157
3:22–23	78	10:7–10	4

10:20	4		
12:1	4		
12:2	48, 173		
Hosea			
2	85		
2:2–13	82		
2:4	194		
2:8	212		
2:14–20	232		
2:14–23	16, 82		
2:16–17	82		
2:19–20	126, 194		
2:21–23	82		
3:1	192		
3:8	194		
4:1–2	83		
4:1–3	83		
4:2	51		
4:3	83		
4:13–14	192		
6:1–3	173–74		
6:6	77		
10:12	178		
11:1	72		
11:8–9	126, 203		
11:9	99		
13:4	184		
13:14	49, 174		
Joel			
2:1–21	45		
2:28–29	200		
Amos			
1–2	68		
3:2	62		
3:7	56		
3:14–15	175		
4:4–8	135		
4:6–11	145, 209		
5:18–20	45		
5:7	178		
5:24	178		
6:12	178		
7:10–17	13, 27		
8:4–6	180		
9:7	63, 72, 74		
9:11	128		
9:11–12	118		
9:11–15	46		
Jonah			
3:10	172		
4:1–2	179		

Micah

2:1–3	175
2:1–4	45
4:1–4	101, 110, 158, 219
5:1–2	128
6:4	132
6:5	179
6:6–8	182–83
6:8	77

Habakkuk

2:4	77
3:17–18	45

Zephaniah

1:14–16	46
1:14–18	215

Haggai

1–3	122
1:12–14	170
2:2	170
2:6–7	157
2:10–14	153
2:21–22	157

Zechariah

1–8	26, 110, 122, 144
1:1–17	4
1:14	109
3:1–2	187–88
3:8	157
4:14	157
6:1–8	4
6:10–13	157
7:9–10	133
8:2–8	109
8:6–12	170
9:9–10	44, 128
9–14	5
14:12–14	46

Malachi

4:5–6	32, 65

Sirach

39:1–4	190
39:7–9	190

2 Esdras

4:12	80
4:38–39	80
7:48–50	80
7:54	80

1 Maccabees

1:15	34

2 Maccabees

2:4–8	10
7:28	28, 40

Matthew

1:6	44
2:15	72
2:19–23	61
2:26–29	39
4:1–11	231
5:17	220
5:20	190
5:21	142
5:21–37	51
5:27	142
5:31	142
5:33	142
5:38	142
5:43	142
6:10	45, 118, 122
6:12	86
6:25	20
10:5	187
10:15	47
11:14	65
12:18–21	205
13:14–15	124
13:52	190
16:14	65
17:3	65
17:11–12	65
18:22	223
19:16–30	51
23:2	141
23:13	190
23:15	190
23:23	190
23:25	190
23:27	190
23:29	190
24–25	5
27:47–49	65

Mark

1:15	47, 172
4:12	124
8:28	65
8:30	129
9:4–5	65
9:11–13	65
10:45	205
12:13–27	234

12:18–27	174
12:28–31	196
12:29	139
12:31	152
13	5, 7
14:24	205
14:41	205
15:35–36	65

Luke

1:17	65
1:46–55	90
1:55	3
2:9–14	216
2:14	89
3:23–38	31
4:18–19	86, 115, 129
4:25–26	65
7:19	157
7:19–20	128
7:20	118
7:22	128
8:10	124
9:8	65
9:19	65
9:30–33	65
9:31	72
9:51–52	187
10:25–27	187
10:29	126
10:29–37	143
13:16	3
17:11–19	187
18:14	179
19:19	3

John

1:1	216
1:1–18	234
1:14	76, 89, 214
1:21–25	65
1:29	205
4:9	187
4:21–24	210
4:39–42	187
8:48	187
12:37–43	124
14:9	107
20:1–10	132

Acts
2:14–21	200
8:25	187
8:27–39	205
9:3–9	216
28:26–27	124

Romans
2:5	47
2:25–29	34
3:24	179
3:25	183
4:1–25	3
5:12–21	79
5:19	205
8:15–17	122
8:29	107
9–11	63
11:2–4	65
11:33	15
12:1–2	183
14:7–8	49

1 Corinthians
1–2	234
1:8	47
5:7	73
7:19	34
11:7	107
11:25	39
15:21–22	79
15:42–49	48
15:45–49	79
15:49	107
15:54–55	49, 174

2 Corinthians
4:4	107
4:6	216

Galatians
3:6	179
3:6–18	3
3:8	2
4:21–5:1	3
4:1–7	122
5:3	34
5:6	34
6:15	34

Ephesians
4:22–24	107
5:25	125

Philippians
1:10	47

Colossians
1:15	107
3:9–10	107

Titus
3:7	179

Hebrews
6:17	122

7–10	153
8:8–13	39
9:23–10:18	183
10:10	104
11:8–12	3
11:17–22	3
11:39–40	158

James
5:17	65

1 Peter
2:22–25	25

1 John
4:17	47

Revelation
1:9–11	5
4:11	105
5:9–14	105
6:17	47
9:18	145
11:15	7
17–18	7
21:1–5	210
21:2–3	111
22:20	7

2 Baruch
6	10

NAME INDEX

Abraham, William J., 27
Ackroyd, Peter, 71, 210
Ahlstrom, Gosta W., 24
Albertz, Rainer, 5, 11, 16, 23, 37, 84, 94, 166, 210, 235–54
Albright, William F., 104
Alt, Albrecht, 158
Alter, Robert, 27
Anderson, Bernhard W., 43, 74, 102, 180
Anderson, Gary A., 120, 184, 238
Angel, Leonard, 133
Anselm, Saint, 183–84
Ash, Paul S., 61
Augustine, Saint, 191

Bailey, Lloyd R., Sr., 50
Balentine, Samuel, 149, 238
Balthasar, Hans Urs von, 89
Banks, Robert, 140
Barr, James, 80, 83, 107, 174
Barrick, W. Boyd, 94
Barth, Karl, 16, 29, 80–81, 94, 97, 191, 197, 217
Barton, John, 27, 68–69, 161
Bayer, Charles, 71
Beal, Timothy, 149, 162, 226
Beker, J. Christiaan, 204
Bellis, Alice Ogden, 18, 64
Belo, Fernando, 100
Beron, A., 45
Berry, Wendell, 123
Birch, Bruce C., 69, 149
Bird, Phyllis, 107, 192, 195
Blenkinsopp, Joseph, 59, 76, 153, 161
Bloom, Harold, 27
Blum, Erhard, 143
Blumenthal, David R., 214
Boff, Leonardo, 56

Borowitz, Eugene B., 137
Braiterman, Zachary, 214
Braulik, Georg, 142
Braun, R. I., 33
Brenner, Athalaya, 91, 133
Brettler, Marc Zvi, 33
Brimley, Robert W., 76
Brodie, Thomas L., 114
Brown, William P., 59, 188, 235
Brueggemann, Walter, 10, 27, 43, 45, 51, 55, 61, 64, 66, 71, 74, 76, 83, 89, 91, 105, 111, 120, 123, 139–40, 142, 146, 156, 158, 169, 177, 181, 185, 204, 210, 222, 224, 226, 238
Buber, Martin, 74, 97, 129–30, 142, 147
Budde, Michael L., 76
Buechner, Frederick, 3
Burns, Rita, 133

Camp, Claudia V., 114
Campbell, Anthony F., 55, 169
Campbell, J. C., 170
Cazelles, Henri, 169
Cerny, Ladislav, 47
Charlesworth, James H., 8, 129
Childs, Brevard, 26, 27, 29, 45, 51, 69, 205–6
Claburn, W. Eugene, 168–69
Clements, R. E., 13, 149
Clesin, J. E., 91
Clines, David J., 3, 50–51, 56, 205–6
Coats, George W., 23, 142, 232
Cobb, John B., 116
Cohen, Arthur, 217
Collins, John J., 5, 8, 174
Coote, Robert B., 114
Crenshaw, James, 59, 69, 177, 198, 235
Croft, Steven J. L., 185
Cross, Frank Moore, 16, 76, 104–5, 156, 210, 229, 240

Crüsemann, Frank, 23, 51, 69, 142, 153, 220
Culley, Robert C., 66, 133

Dahood, Mitchell, 173–74
Daly, Herman E., 116
David, Ellen, 61
Davies, Graham I., 231–32
Davies, Philip R., 97, 190
Davies, W. D., 123
Dawn, Marva J., 182, 229
Day, John, 11
Day, Peggy L., 188, 231
De Vries, Simon, 30, 33
Deane, S.W., 184
Dearman, J. Andrew, 190
Dempsey, Carol, 194–95, 226
Dever, William G., 97
Donfried, Karl P., 80
Douglas, Mary, 100, 142, 154, 236
Durham, John I., 190

Edelman, D. V., 140
Eilberg-Schwartz, Howard, 35
Emerton, John A., 94

Farmer, William, 206
Fensham, Charles F., 231
Fisch, Harold, 120
Fishbane, Michael, 29, 59, 125, 190, 222
Fohrer, Georg, 69
Ford, David F., 105
Freedman, David Noel, 24, 104–5
Fretheim, Terence E., 61, 74, 146, 173, 204
Frick, Frank, 118
Friedman, Richard E., 61, 222
Fukuyama, Francis, 73–74

Gadamer, Hans-Georg, 85
Gammie, John, 59, 100
Geertz, Clifford, 236
Gerstenberger, Erhard S., 142, 204
Gilkey, Langdon, 43
Gilson, Anne, 87
Girard, Rene, 226
Glatzer, N. N., 97
Gottwald, Norman K., 24, 37
Gowan, Donald E., 74, 102, 135, 137, 158
Grabbe, Lester L., 76
Graf, David Frank, 24
Gray, John, 118
Green, Garrett, 27
Greenberg, Moshe, 149
Green-McCreigh, Kathryn, 61
Gunn, David M., 45, 93, 226
Guthrie, Harvey H., 212

Habel, Norman C., 16, 83, 123
Hadley, Judith, 11
Halpern, Baruch, 45, 98, 118
Handel, G. F., 163
Hanson, Paul D., 8, 37
Haran, Menahem, 154, 156, 210
Hardy, Daniel W., 105
Harner, Philip B., 240
Harrelson, Walter, 51, 74, 83, 238
Harris, Maria, 116
Hasel, George, 170
Haughey, John C., 137
Hays, Richard B., 35
Heschel, Abraham J., 47, 79, 127, 161, 182, 204
Hess, Richard, 111
Heyward, Carter, 87
Hiebert, P. S., 231
Hiebert, Theodore, 43
Hill, John, 18
Hillers, Delbert R., 39
Holladay, William L., 173
Hoppe, Leslie J., 111
Hort, Greta, 145–46
Houston, Walter, 100
Huffmon, H. B., 210
Huner, A. Vanlier, 173

Iersel, Bas von, 74

Jacob, Edmund, 5, 199–200
Jacobs, Mignon R., 231
Jacobson, Rolf, 105
Jacoby, Susan, 224
Japhet, Sara, 33
Jenson, Philip Peter, 100
Jobling, David, 35, 45
Johnson, Aubrey R., 50
Johnson, William Stacy, 140
Jones, Gregory L., 87
Jones, Gwilym H., 33

Kaufman, Stephen, 142
Kearney, Peter J., 154
Kinsler, Gloria, 116
Kinsler, Ross, 116
Klausner, James, 129
Klein, L. R., 91
Klein, Ralph W., 71, 76
Knierim, Rolf P., 180
Knight, Douglas A., 23, 108
Knohl, Israel, 15, 100, 154
Koch, Klaus, 8, 162, 175, 177, 198
Kovacs, Brian W., 169
Kraftchick, Steven J., 64, 111
Kraus, Hans-Joachim, 45, 235, 238

Kuntz, Kenneth, 217
Kuschke, Arnulf, 111

Lang, Bernhard, 137
Leiman, S., 27
Lemaire, Andre, 59
Lemche, Niels Peter, 24, 98
Levenson, Jon D., 24, 29, 61, 64, 74, 164,
    184, 226
Levine, Baruch, 184
Levinson, Bernard, 142
Linafelt, Tod, 149, 226
Lindblad, Ulrika, 142
Lindström, Fredrik, 50, 79, 196, 198, 204
Lohfink, Norbert, 39, 154, 169
Long, Burke O., 23
Lowery, Richard H., 116, 182
Lundquist, John M., 210
Luther, Martin, 18, 26

MacLeish, Archibald, 213–14
Malamat, Abraham, 142
Marin-Archard, Robert, 50
Marshall, J. W., 23
Martin-Archard, R., 174
Marx, Karl, 134
Matthews, V. H., 91
McBride, S. Dean, 125
McCarthy, Dennis J., 40, 55, 146, 240
McFague, Sallie, 139–40
McKenzie, Steven L., 45
McLellan, David, 137
McNutt, Paula, 45
Meeks, M. Douglas, 116
Mendenhall, George E., 224
Mettinger, T. N. D., 129, 206, 240
Meyers, Carol, 91, 199, 210
Miles, Jack, 140, 226
Milgrom, Jacob, 15, 154, 184
Miller, J. Maxwell, 107
Miller, Patrick D., 10–11, 15, 23, 51, 56, 64, 87,
    91, 94, 100, 105, 108, 118, 120, 125, 149, 156,
    177, 182, 198–99, 204, 210, 212, 217, 220, 229,
    235, 238, 240
Mitchell, C. W., 20
Moberly, R. W. L., 3
Mollenkott, Virginia, 142
Moltmann, Jürgen, 56, 200
Moran, William, 126–27, 229
Moriarty, F. L, 166
Mowinckel, Sigmund, 129, 158, 206
Muilenberg, James, 69, 190
Murphy, Roland, 235
Myers, Ched, 229
Myers, Jacob M., 166

Nakanose, Shigeyuki, 168–69
Napier, B. Davie , 66
Naven, J., 45
Neal, Marie Augusta, 116
Nelson, Richard D., 156
Neusner, Jacob, 35, 37, 71, 83, 85, 129
Newman, Judith, 149
Newsom, Carol A., 114, 164
Newsome, James D., 33
Nicholson, E. W., 40, 55, 169
Nickelsburg, George, 8
Niditch, Susan, 222
Nielsen, Eduard, 51
North, Christopher, 206
Noth, Martin, 132–33
Nullen, E. Theodore, 56

O'Brien, Conor Cruise, 123
O'Brien, Mark A., 55, 169
O'Connor, Michael, 199
O'Day, Gail, 91
Ollenburger, Ben C., 111, 210, 229
Olson, Dennis T., 51, 55, 142
Olyan, Saul, 133
Oppenheim, A. L., 13
Orlinsky, Harry M., 206
Otto, Rudolf, 217
Overholt, Thomas, 162

Patrick, Dale, 23
Pedersen, Johannes, 50
Peli, Pinchas H., 182
Penchansky, David, 226
Perdue, Leo, 59, 69, 164, 169
Petersen, David L., 69, 188
Phillips, Anthony, 52
Pixley, Jorge, 74
Plastaras, George W., 74
Plaut, W. Gunther, 182
Pleins, J. David, 52, 69
Polkinghorne, John, 43
Polzin, Robert, 45, 55
Porteous, Norman W., 111
Porter, J. R., 190
Pressler, Carolyn, 191, 195

Rad, Gerhard von, 10, 33, 47, 55, 69, 79, 81, 83, 87, 89,
    102, 111, 142, 154, 158, 162, 166, 176–77, 180, 185,
    222, 229, 235
Raitt, Thomas M., 173
Raschke, Carl A., 108
Raschke, Susan D., 108
Redditt, Paul, 226
Redford, Donald B., 61
Reif, Stefan, 149

Rendtorff, Rolf, 40
Renteria, Tamis Hoover, 114
Ricouer, Paul, 80, 188
Ringe, Sharon, 87, 114, 116
Ringgren, Helmer, 129
Roberts, J. J. M., 10, 118
Rosenbaum, J., 166
Rouner, Leroy, 108
Rowley, H. H., 64
Rubenstein, Richard, 176–77

Saebo, Magne, 28
Saggs, H. W. F., 13, 18
Sakenfeld, Katherine Doob, 79, 87, 127, 232
Sanders, E. P., 220
Sanders, James A., 28, 37, 140, 220
Scanzoni, Letha, 143
Scarry, Elaine, 204
Schmid, H. H., 178, 180
Schmidt, Werner, 174
Schrage, W., 204
Schwartz, Regina, 93, 140, 226
Scott, James M., 71
Seitz, Christopher, 13, 61, 240
Seow, Choon-Leong, 10
Shank, Duane, 18
Silberman, Neil Asher, 98
Simpson, Timothy F., 45
Smith, Daniel L., 18, 72
Smith, Mark S., 16, 140
Snaith, Norman H., 79, 127
Soelle, Dorothee, 204
Spina, Frank Anthony, 199
Sprinkle, J. M., 23
Steck, Odil Hannes, 162
Stendahl, Krister, 80, 198
Stern, Philip, 93
Steussy, Marti J., 45
Stevenson, Kalinda Rose, 123, 210
Stone, M. E., 8
Stroup, George W., 64, 74
Stuhlmacher, Peter, 180
Stuhlmueller, Carroll, 43, 164
Stulman, Louis, 55
Suchocki, Marjorie, 226

Terrien, Samuel, 89, 125, 210
Thompson, Thomas L., 3, 24, 98
Throntveit, M. A., 33

Tilley, Terence W., 214
Toorn, Karel van der, 114
Toulmin, Stephen, 222
Trible, Phyllis, 108, 113–14, 133, 191, 195
Tsevat, Matitiahu, 181–82
Tucker, Gene M., 108
Turner, Victor, 236

Unterman, Jeremiah, 173

Vajta, Vilmos, 83
Van Buren, Paul, 64
Van Seters, John, 3, 98
VanderKam, James C., 8
Vaughn, Andrew, 166
Vaux, Roland de, 10, 85, 156
Vermes, Geza, 8

Walzer, Michael, 75
Washington, Harold, 191, 195
Weems, Renita, 194–95, 227
Weibberg, Joel, 37
Weiler, Alton, 75
Weinfeld, Moshe, 3, 54, 116, 127
Weisberg, Joel, 37
Wells, Jo Bailey, 100
Wenham, Gordon, 111
Westermann, Claus, 3, 20, 83, 102, 120, 158, 186, 212
Wheaton, Philip, 18
Whitelam, Keith W., 24, 98, 118
Whybray, R. Norman, 135–36
Wiesel, Elie, 129
Williamson, Hugh G., 33
Willis, John T., 91, 91
Wilson, Robert R., 37, 103, 162
Wise, Michael, 130
Witherington, Ben, 235
Wolff, Hans Walter, 55, 102, 158
Wright, Christopher J. H., 116
Wright, G. Ernest, 83, 229
Wybrow, Cameron, 43

Yerushalmi, Yosef Hayim, 98, 222
Yoder, Christine Roy, 192, 195, 235
Yoder, John Howard, 116

Zenger, Erich, 225
Zimmerli, Walther, 102